Organizing Inclusion

Organizing Inclusion brings communication experts together to examine issues of inclusion and exclusion, which have emerged as a major challenge as both society and the workforce become more diverse.

Connecting communication theories to diversity and inclusion, and clarifying that inclusion is about the communication processes of organizations, institutions, and communities, this book explores how communication as an organizing phenomenon underlies systemic and institutionalized biases and generates practices that privilege certain groups while excluding or marginalizing others. Bringing a global perspective that transcends particular problems faced by Western cultures, the contributors address issues across sub-disciplines of communication studies, ranging from social and environmental activism to problems of race, gender, sexual orientation, age, and ability. With these various perspectives, the chapters go beyond demographic diversity by addressing interaction and structural processes that can be used to promote inclusion. Using these multiple theoretical frameworks, *Organizing Inclusion* is an intellectual resource for improving theoretical understanding and practical applications that come with ever more diverse people working, coordinating, and engaging with one another.

This book will be of great relevance to organizational stakeholders, human resource personnel, and policymakers, as well as to scholars and students working in the fields of communication, management, and organization studies.

Marya L. Doerfel (Professor of Communication and Director of the Network Science Lab, School of Communication and Information, Rutgers University) examines social networks, community building, and organizational and community transformation. She has been funded by the National Science Foundation with recent peer-reviewed articles, including "Engaging Partnerships," "The Story of Collective Action, (Un)Obtrusive Control in Emergent Networks," and "Digitizing the Strength of Weak Ties."

Jennifer L. Gibbs (Professor of Communication, Editor of *Communication Research*) investigates collaboration in global teams and other distributed work arrangements, as well as the social and organizational impacts of new technologies. She has published over 50 peer-reviewed journal articles and book chapters, as well as a recent book titled *Distracted: Staying Connected without Losing Focus.*

Routledge Studies in Communication, Organization, and Organizing

Series Editor: François Cooren

The goal of this series is to publish original research in the field of organizational communication, with a particular—but not exclusive—focus on the constitutive or performative aspects of communication. In doing so, this series aims to be an outlet for cutting-edge research monographs, edited books, and handbooks that will redefine, refresh and redirect scholarship in this field.

The volumes published in this series address topics as varied as branding, spiritual organizing, collaboration, employee communication, corporate authority, organizational timing and spacing, organizational change, organizational sense making, organization membership, and disorganization. What unifies this diversity of themes is the authors' focus on communication, especially in its constitutive and performative dimensions. In other words, authors are encouraged to highlight the key role communication plays in all these processes.

Methodological and Ontological Principles of Observation and Analysis
Following and Analyzing Things and Beings in Our Everyday World
Edited by François Cooren and Fabienne Malbois

Dis/Organization as Communication
Exploring the Disordering, Disruptive and Chaotic Properties of Communication
Edited by Consuelo Vásquez and Tim Kuhn

Authority and Power in Social Interaction
Methods and Analysis
Edited by Nicolas Bencherki, Frédérik Matte and François Cooren

Organizing Inclusion
Moving Diversity from Demographics to Communication Processes
Edited by Marya L. Doerfel and Jennifer L. Gibbs

Organizing Inclusion

Moving Diversity from Demographics to
Communication Processes

**Edited by
Marya L. Doerfel and
Jennifer L. Gibbs**

Routledge
Taylor & Francis Group

NEW YORK AND LONDON

First published 2020
by Routledge
605 Third Avenue, New York, NY 10017

and by Routledge
2 Park Square, Milton Park, Abingdon, Oxon, OX14 4RN

First issued in paperback 2022

Routledge is an imprint of the Taylor & Francis Group, an informa business

Library of Congress Cataloging-in-Publication Data
A catalog record for this title has been requested

ISBN: 978-1-03-240008-2 (pbk)
ISBN: 978-1-138-32527-2 (hbk)
ISBN: 978-0-429-45049-5 (ebk)

DOI: 10.4324/9780429450495

Typeset in Baskerville
by codeMantra

Contents

Figures and Images

Tables

Contributors

Walid A. Afifi (PhD, University of Arizona, 1995) is a Professor in the Department of Communication at the University of California-Santa Barbara. He has published over 75 journal articles, chapters, and books, the majority of which focus on understanding individuals' management of their uncertainties within interpersonal contexts.

Ana M. Aguilar is a PhD candidate in Organizational Communication and Technology at The University of Texas at Austin. Her research focuses on resilience across varying levels of social analysis (micro to macro) using a temporal perspective.

Dawna I. Ballard (PhD, University of California at Santa Barbara) is an associate professor of communication studies at the University of Texas at Austin. Her research centers on what drives our pace of life and its impact on the communication practices and long-term vitality of organizations, communities, and individuals.

Joshua B. Barbour (Associate Professor of Communication and Director of the Automation Policy and Research Organizing Network, University of Texas at Austin) studies how organizations design and discipline communication to solve problems. His work emphasizes the macro-morphic character of communication, and his current research focuses on the datafication and automation of work.

Patrice M. Buzzanell is Chair and Professor of the University of South Florida's Department of Communication and Endowed Visiting Professor for Shanghai Jiaotong University's School of Media and Design. Her research, teaching, engagement, and grants coalesce around career, work-life policy, resilience, gender, and engineering design.

Stacey L. Connaughton is an Associate Professor in the Brian Lamb School of Communication at Purdue University. Her research examines leadership and identification in geographically distributed contexts. She is the Director of the Purdue Policy Research Institute and is the Director of the Purdue Peace Project. She is the recipient of Purdue's Faculty Engaged Scholar Award and Purdue's Trailblazer Award.

Monica Cornejo, Doctoral student in the Department of Communication at the University of California Santa Barbara, conducts research among underrepresented communities. Particularly, she focuses on stress, coping, resilience, and identity of immigrant communities. Her goal is to identify communicative-action oriented strategies that can empower immigrant communities to effectively manage immigration-related stressors.

Shardé M. Davis (PhD, University of Iowa) is an Assistant Professor in the Department of Communication at the University of Connecticut. Her primary area of specialization is interpersonal communication, with emphases in racial and gender identity, intra/intergroup dynamics, and supportive communication, as well as resistance, counter hegemony, and resilience.

Jean Dennison (Osage Nation) is an Associate Professor of American Indian Studies and the Co-Director for the Center for American Indian and Indigenous Studies at the University of Washington. Through her ongoing research with the Osage Nation, she is examining the effects of colonial distrust on Native nation governing institutions.

Marya L. Doerfel (Professor of Communication and Director of the Network Science Lab, School of Communication and Information, Rutgers, The State University of New Jersey). Her research has been funded by the National Science Foundation and focuses on community resilience with a particular interest in disruptions that impact inter-organizational relationships and their broader community networks.

Bernadette M. Gailliard (PhD, UC Santa Barbara) studies the experiences of underrepresented groups in organizations focusing on identity and membership negotiation. She applies her work as a career coach, consultant, and director of faculty development programs. Her research has been published in *Management Communication Quarterly, Communication Yearbook,* and *Human Relations.*

Jennifer L. Gibbs (Professor of Communication, Co-Editor of *Communication Research*) investigates collaboration in global teams and other distributed work arrangements, as well as the social and organizational impacts of new technologies. She has published over 50 peer-reviewed journal articles and book chapters, as well as a recent book titled *Distracted: Staying Connected without Losing Focus.*

Amy L. Gonzales is an Assistant Professor in the Department of Communication at the University of California, Santa Barbara. Her work examines the psychological and health benefits of interpersonal connection via social media, and the consequences of having access to that technology disrupted. She is especially interested in these phenomena for people from disadvantaged communities (e.g., racial/ethnic minorities, low-income populations, LGBTQ individuals, etc.).

Katrina N. Hanna (Kat) is an assistant professor of rhetoric at California State University, Long Beach. She is generally interested in social justice inquiries specific to race and additional intersectional identities. She generally uses rhetorical field methods within the context of educational policy and spaces.

Dorothy Holland was the Boshamer Distinguished Professor of Anthropology, Emeritus, at the University of North Carolina at Chapel Hill. She was co-founder and founding director of the Graduate Certificate in Participatory Research, former Chair of the of the Department of Anthropology at UNC-CH, and past President of the Society for Psychological Anthropology. She died in April 2019 after a three-year battle with cancer.

Darvelle Hutchins is an Organizational Communication doctoral candidate in the Department of Communication at the University of Missouri. Darvelle's research focuses on diversity, power, and stigmatized identities in organizational contexts.

Melvin Jackson is a principal partner with The PRIME Collective, LLC, a group of community experts who consults and partners with investigators on how to incorporate principles of community engagement into all phases of research. He is the founding community Co-Director of the Graduate Certificate in Participatory Research.

Jared T. Jensen (Assistant Instructor of Communication and Research Assistant for the Automation Policy and Research Organizing Network, University of Texas at Austin) examines the intersections of power dynamics, temporal dilemmas, and technology in organizing.

Michael L. Kent is a Professor of Public Relations and Advertising at the University of New South Wales (UNSW) in Sydney Australia. Kent conducts research on Dialogue, Engagement, New Technology, Mediated Communication, Social Media, International Communication, and Web Communication. Kent consults on research methods, message design, mediated communication, journalism, and public relations. In 2006, Kent spent the fall semester in Riga, Latvia on a Fulbright Scholarship.

Nneka Logan is an Associate Professor in the Department of Communication at Virginia Tech. Her research and teaching interests include public relations, organizational communication, race, diversity and rhetorical studies. Prior to receiving her doctorate, she worked in corporate communication management for nine years.

Rebecca J. Meisenbach is an Associate Professor in the Department of Communication at the University of Missouri. She is also currently the editor of *Management Communication Quarterly*. Her research addresses issues of identity and ethics in organizational life.

Rahul Mitra (PhD, Purdue University) is an Associate Professor at Wayne State University in Detroit MI. His scholarship focuses on environmental organizing, sustainability, and corporate social responsibility (CSR), and meaningful work discourses. His work has appeared in outlets such as *Environmental Communication, Management Communication Quarterly, Human Relations*, and *Public Relations Review*.

Patricia S. Parker is Chair of the Department of Communication at the University of North Carolina at Chapel Hill, and Director of the Graduate Certificate in Participatory Research. Her research advances a community-based leadership praxis grounded in womanist, anti-racist, and decolonizing organizing traditions. She is co-editor of the University of California book series on Communication and Social Justice Activism.

Jennifer K. Ptacek is an Assistant Professor in the Department of Communication at University of Dayton. Her research examines intersections of health and organizational communication. She is a former research assistant for the Purdue Peace Project, which is a political violence prevention initiative.

Robert J. Razzante (PhD, Arizona State University) is a visiting assistant professor of communication in the Department of Communication at the College of Wooster. His engaged scholarship seeks to strengthen communities and organizations through collaborative learning and transformative conflict.

Shelbey L. Rolison (Assistant Instructor of Communication and Research Assistant for the Automation Policy and Research Organizing Network, University of Texas at Austin) examines inter-professional collaboration and the negotiation of new technologies in existing workflows and through professional identification.

Sara H. Smith is Associate Professor of Geography at the University of North Carolina, Chapel Hill. She is a feminist political geographer studying how territory is constituted through intimate acts of love, friendship, and birth. Her research engages with these questions in Ladakh, India, and in the US and global context.

Sarah J. Tracy (PhD, University of Colorado) is Professor and Director of The Transformation Project in The Hugh Downs School of Human Communication at Arizona State University, Tempe. Her use-inspired research focuses on compassion, organizational wellbeing, qualitative methods, leadership, conversation, and transformational scholarship.

Odile Vallée is an Associate Professor in the Communication and Culture Department at Audencia Business School in Nantes, France. She examines how texts, narratives, and visual forms include or marginalize voices, particularly in contexts like Microfinance, Social Entrepreneurship, and

Humanitarian Communication. She investigates the subsequent ethics of representation built and circulated in the public sphere.

Harry Yaojun Yan is a third-year PhD student at Indiana University-Bloomington, dual majoring in Media Arts and Sciences, at the Media School & Complex Networks and Systems, at Luddy School of Informatics, Computer, and Engineering. His research applies the Complex System Theory and computational methods to investigate various topics including media effects on attitudes change toward minorities, digital inequality, audience networks, human-bots interaction, online misinformation spreading, etc.

Preface

While there are entire careers built on understanding issues of diversity and inclusion, this book brings a particular lens—that of organizational communication—to examine inclusion/exclusion processes that support and undermine diversity. The contributing authors originally convened during a full-day preconference held in 2017 at the National Communication Association. As a result of that day, *Organizing Inclusion* was born.

That preconference assembled many of the contributors to this book and the unanswered questions from that day led us to invite additional voices as authors. Some of our contributors have built their careers on addressing diversity, minoritized groups, inequalities, racism, sexism, colonialism, homophobia, and other institutionalized biases that are pervasive in groups, businesses and organizations, and society as a whole. Other contributors care about these issues deeply, though their careers have been driven by other human communication phenomena. Both types of scholars were excited about taking the time to think more deeply about the challenge we used to organize the preconference. We asked our contributors to consider:

How does [your area of expertise] contribute to organizational practices of exclusion versus inclusion?

We invited our pre-conference panelists to consider the following options as possible ways to answer this overarching question:

- Report on the state of the literature / state of affairs on this topic
- Identify the salient organizational stakeholders and what their social profile is (e.g., policymakers, employers, educators)
- Overview the types of data that shed light on inclusion/exclusion with respect to their particular theoretical framework (e.g., drawn from empirical studies, population statistics, case studies, etc.)
- Critically evaluate inclusion using familiar research or critically evaluate research you are familiar with using an inclusion/diversity lens.

This book is thus a compilation of voices and perspectives on inclusion. The voices, themselves, represent a cross-section of scholars, ranging in rank, ethnicity, global location, and area within the discipline of communication. The chapters offer ways to think about inclusion as something that is active and structuring. The chapters help us see that inclusion and diversity are the two sides of the same coin. While inclusion encompasses human communication activities that invite or marginalize, diversity is a way to assess the impacts of such actions through counting representation of groups and beliefs.

The many ways inclusion is discussed by us and our contributors show that inclusion is not easy. Intellectually and in our daily routines, we struggle with these issues personally, professionally, as a field, and in society. The challenges around issues of inclusion and diversity are complex and nuanced and addressing them is not always straightforward or clear cut. Well-intentioned individuals often get it wrong.

Reflections on Events at the 2019 NCA Organizational Communication Division Top Paper Panel

Just before this book went to press, Marya got it wrong in a very public way, relative to the organization we are a part of—the Organizational Communication Division of the National Communication Association (NCA). The following are three first-person perspectives (from Marya, Jennifer, and Patricia Parker, one of the chapter co-authors) on what happened and how those events became a catalyst for thinking about "inclusion" in more transformative ways, including in this volume.

Marya's Response:

At the OCD top paper panel at NCA in 2019, I gave a speech that revealed my own part in reproducing racism. I am a full professor at an elite research-1 (R1) university, a white woman in the middle class, and a leader in the organizational communication division (OCD). I realize now that my positionality in systems where institutional racism persists comes with a responsibility to educate myself about race and racism. My remarks hurt members of my organization plus many who heard about the contents of my top paper response speech second-hand. The "OCD top paper response" was part of my job as division leader (I held an elected position in the organizational communication division from 2016 until shortly after that speech in 2019). Top paper responses generally involve reading the division's highest ranked papers (in 2019, four papers) that were presented by their authors at the OCD Top Paper Panel and responding to them in a public forum with about 150–200 people in attendance. In this particular year, a theme that clearly crossed three of the papers was inclusion—something I have been thinking a lot about, given this book was about to go to press.

My speech ended up revealing my own biases, leading to several audience members walking out (according to some, 15–20 people left the room in unison, including three of the top paper authors). After careful reflection, I have come to realize that my response functioned to reproduce racism at the institutional level. I did so through enacting a "tradition" in responses. In the process of trying to address certain institutional norms for the top paper response (e.g., injecting humor, thinking outside of the box, offering sage counsel), my performance of these norms ended up working at odds with sensitivity to diversity concerns. That tradition was enacted when I asked one of the authors to more clearly define a key term in her paper: white supremacy. While defining key concepts is an expected scholarly norm, this comment also served as a speech act that did two things. First, it offended members in the audience who have devoted entire careers to the term and who, like many people in and out of academia commonly use this term today and throughout history. Indeed, such scholars have demonstrated and have been working hard to undo the fact that we are taught to associate white supremacy with violent groups (Gray, 2019). Those beliefs all too often cause harm to others in emotional and physical, life-threatening ways. Through the extensive reading and conversations I have done and had since my top paper response, I now recognize that I associated white supremacy only with extreme acts of violence and hate (which are easy to exclude ourselves from). After deeper research and reflection, I recognize that white supremacy actually refers to a much broader and institutionalized system that we all participate in that works to privilege white people in many ways while working against those who are not white or members of the dominant group (c.f. Rodriguez, Dutta, & Desnoyers-Colas, 2019 and their entire special issue). In this way, we are all complicit in either perpetuating or challenging these norms and practices. This leads to a second way my comments harmed others.

Second, my explanation of why the term needed clarity revealed my own discomfort with the term. I narrowed its usage, effectively redefining the author's use in her paper by stating that many people hear 'white supremacy' and equate that with neo-Nazis. Yet, the author was using the term as its historical roots and above explanation suggests – white supremacy just is. It is seen in discursive practices; it operates across levels and imbeds itself through perpetuating a system of beliefs and practices that supports the legitimacy and dominance of white values, norms, culture, and ways of talking. While this normative system may fuel groups like neo-Nazis, it is also what drives evaluation systems in organizations and society that implicitly treat and privilege whiteness as the norm (Frankenberg, 1993). The author's use of the term white supremacy "outed" my own discomforts, or as Robin Diangelo (2018) has called *white fragility*. The use of white supremacy was particularly disruptive to my "comfort zone" because the author's arguments demonstrated how academic institutions and our discourses, specifically in organizational communication, has white supremacy baked into the structures that shape the field (Harris, 2019).

My response reflects what Diangelo (2018) criticized as a binary treatment of racism: racists are bad versus progressive allies are good. That binary "frees ourselves" (white progressive allies) from *not* developing skills to think critically about racism, let alone use our positions of power to challenge and be transformative in problems of inequality. In that speech, I also argued that we needed a way to re-frame the ideas so that we can have a dialogic conversation about difference. In other words, I revealed how the use of the term white supremacy makes some people [read: white people] uncomfortable and wish to avoid having an awkward conversation, if any. In my speech, I expressed concern with how we might have a "more dialogic" conversation about these issues; concerned that use of words like white supremacy are problematic. That "concern" became an act of tone policing, where white people ask people of color to moderate their tone (Nuru & Arendt, 2019). In that point, I discursively performed an example of what Ahmed (2012) has shown as a way to shift the focus of the conversation away from what is uncomfortable and toward figuring out how to make (white) people comfortable. By protecting the comfort of those in positions of power, we do not change those powerful positions. As an R1 full professor and as the chair of the division, I hold a very powerful position. I gave a speech that shifted the conversation away from how white supremacy was evident in our division to making myself and possibly others (white people uncomfortable with a term) more comfortable.

The above comments were only one part of my speech, but that speech and how I framed my ideas unintentionally worked to perpetuate racism in the OCD as an institution. In preparing for and giving the speech, I ended up performing the very ways in which white supremacy is institutionalized, including participating in some of the very practices the papers were critiquing. But the challenge that these very events posed for the people who were directly harmed by my words was not yet over because I had yet to grasp what had happened that led to a walkout.

A group walkout is a highly unusual event in the history of the division. Afterwards, I talked to the authors and many other respected colleagues— including scholars of color and those with expertise in diversity, equity, and inclusion (DEI)—to try to understand what I said and what my speech "did" as walk-out worthy. [Truth telling: I realize now that relying on others to educate me about these issues can cause further harm to those who live and experience those everyday realities. Some of the people I spoke with were harmed by my words and then had to tell me why. They therefore had to relive the very pain I caused.] Those people were gracious and pointed me to many resources, some of which I was already familiar with and others that were new to me; all of which I read or reread far more personally than I had or would have before my speech. The materials I read (see, for example, the references at the end of this preface) deepened and opened up my understanding about inclusion and diversity in general and specifically on race, racism, and institutionalized racism. The reading I did showed specifically how white supremacy causes real harm to people's emotional, material, and physical well-being as well as to people's personal safety. The reading was not easy, because I came to understand that I was complicit in reproducing racism in multiple levels of the organization (e.g., as a member of organizational communication as a discipline; in conversations where I asked people to educate me about this issue; as a leader of the organizational communication division which is part of a professional association, NCA). In my position of power, I shut down the conversation about racism and protected the historically white institution from having an opportunity to change. Had it not been for the group walk-out, my act would have furthered the resilience of the division. And although resilience has been recently viewed as an asset for organizations, resilience can also be anathema to change.

Bonanno (2004) and others (for a full review, see Williams, Gruber, Sut-cliffe, Shepherd, & Zhao, 2017) argue that the dark side of resilience is that resilient individuals may be impervious to negative impressions—they may endure social numbing, which can be seen as a "liability as opposed to an asset for individuals, teams, and organizations" (Williams et al., 2017, p. 257). Williams et al. ask "what are the costs and benefits of having resilient leaders in organizations? Does a leader's emotional disassociation generate organi-zational resilience but at the cost of personal and/or organizational member functioning?" (p. 257). Emotional adversities are opportunities and disrup-tions to normal functioning that can advance learning and transformative change for both individuals and institutions. Normalized practices along with organizational structures that group people into divisions and professional as-sociations perpetuate road blocks (or in Ahmed's words, brick walls) for people and organizations to be transformative. Simply put, such people and human systems block inclusion because of their resilient features.

Although the resilient side of me wanted to move on and many reminded me that the personal public embarrassment would pass (I heard the adage, "this too shall pass" from many), I knew that resilience is not always the solu-tion. As many of our contributors show in their chapters, change requires vul-nerability and openness. One way the top paper response has helped me work on my own role is that it has helped me change my perspective from simply seeing others as racist to asking myself, how might I be? I can approach rac-ism from being a part of it rather than looking at it as if I'm an outsider. With that shift in perspective, I have come to better understand my own role in the perpetuation of white supremacy. This part is the most personally difficult and still very much feels like a work in progress. But recognizing that diversity and inclusion work—and anti-racism in particular—is ongoing, frees us from the binary. This perspective shift helps us be supportive of change rather than block the very change we (white progressive people) claim to want to make.

Even though "pre NCA" I *thought* I understood the idea that "anyone can perpetuate racism," I did not actually **practice** the kind of critical intentionality that would help me see racialized systems. I looked "at" racism as an outsider as something applying to others, only. In doing so, it was really easy to see how others were racist or how institutions held people down and undermined equality. In looking "at" racism, I "freed" myself from being implicated. As the division leader, by looking "at" racism, I also protected the division from being implicated. As a respondent, I asked "if" I or the division was racist rather than following the lead of the authors and the scholarship of many to ask "how" we are racist. By recognizing our own role in racism, we shift our perspective. I can challenge myself. As a division, we can and should challenge ourselves in direct, self-reflexive, and therefore transformative ways.

Jennifer's Response

I was not at NCA, but I heard about Marya's top paper response directly from her as well as others after the event, and I read about it in detail on social media. Knowing Marya as a dear friend and colleague for many years, it was difficult for me to square the accounts of her response with what I knew of her as a person. The initial preconference that gave birth to this book was her idea, and much of the labor that has gone into editing the book has been hers. She has been a vocal ally and advocate for issues of diversity, equity, and inclusion throughout her career. In her role as NCA OCD Chair, she made significant efforts to promote diversity through spearheading a climate survey of members. Hearing about what happened made me question my own beliefs and commitments, as I could imagine myself being in her position. This spurred an intense process of critical reflection and sensemaking, in which I talked with a variety of respected colleagues, read to educate myself further, and spent time thinking about these issues in a much deeper and more personal way than I ever had before. This was no longer an academic topic, but a real one that implicated me and people I respect directly.

In the process, I have come to understand much more poignantly the ways in which white supremacy perpetuates itself, including my own role and complicity in such processes as an educated white woman. While the many additional hours I spent wrestling with this were challenging, I am very grateful for the resulting personal growth. The NCA incident has made the focus of this book much more personal to me. It helped me recall an encounter I had many years ago with an African-American colleague who let me know that words that I said in a meeting were perpetuating a stereotype about Black women. At the time, I could not see how what I perceived as an innocuous phrase could be taken as a micro-aggression. I had not intended it that way. I have thought about it over the years, but in the time I have taken to further educate myself, I now see that it was. This is but one example of how the complexity of race shapes our discourse. It illustrates how racism and white supremacy are not so much about intentions as about behaviors and outcomes. This explains how well-intentioned people often (whether intentionally or unintentionally) take part in practices that work to perpetuate systems of inequality. Thus it is not simply a matter of not being racist, but of being actively anti-racist to change and transform the systems and structures through which inequalities are perpetuated. I am sure I will continue to have blind spots around my own privilege, but I will keep working to illuminate those blind spots and to use my own position of privilege (as a full professor, division chair, and journal editor) to make our academic structures more inclusive and equitable.

Pat's Response

I arrived at the OCD top paper panel shortly after the walk-out, unaware of what had just happened. About a dozen or so people were standing outside the entrance to the meeting room. Some of them appeared to be so visibly shaken I wondered if a medical emergency was in progress. A colleague gave me the highlights of Marya's remarks and the strong reaction to them. To be honest, my initial reaction was a sense of relief that colleagues (mostly white) had taken a stand (with scholars of color) against what seemed to be blatant racism and a stunning example of protecting institutionalized racism as the status quo. I am a Black woman who has advanced through several historically white academic institutions—from entering a desegregated elementary school in the US South, to completing doctoral studies at a leading Research 1 University, to chairing a large communication department at another leading Research 1 University. In my experience, institutional racism is rarely disrupted unless there is a direct intervention of anti-racist collective activism. As I spoke with people who walked out that day or had heard about the speech, I listened to their hurt, anger, and frustration and shared some of my own. In some cases, the conversation turned to the question of how this critical incident could lead to something transformative. I mentioned the book Marya was co-editing and how that would have to be a starting place for me since I had a co-authored chapter scheduled for publication in the volume.

A few days later, my coauthors and I (along with all of the contributors of this book) heard from Marya and Jennifer. They were writing for our assistance in heading off backlash in response to the publication of this volume that might surely come given the events surrounding Marya's remarks at NCA. They mentioned the book was already past-due but asked the authors to take a few days to review our chapters for any blind spots and to be sure we were citing people of color.

At this point, my coauthors, who are all outside the communication discipline, knew nothing about the events leading up to Marya's and Jennifer's email. I convened a conference call to discuss the matter. Based on that conversation, I responded to Marya, Jennifer, and the other chapter authors to express our concerns. We were concerned that the initial response Marya and Jennifer presented, especially with concerns about the pressing deadline, was a surface-level proposition that was reactive. It would further perpetuate the kind of discursive work that situates the chapter authors—including those of us who are people of color—as defenders of whitewashing practices. Organizing structures like the pressing deadline they had as editors prevent more contemplative work. In this case, deeper revisions and a full engagement with this important moment would be a transformative way to address racism rather than a quick fix or surface-level proposition such as 'making sure people of color are cited.'

But my coauthors and I also expressed our hope that this volume could clearly challenge, rather than obscure, white supremacy and institutional racism. We proposed a potentially transformative—rather than a reactive—response to the current context. Such a moment has the potential to be truly transformative. Transformation comes through critical reflexivity, reflection, dialogue, and action. Writing on behalf of myself and my coauthors, I reminded Marya and Jennifer of our commitment to interrogating inclusion from the very outset. As our chapter states:

> In this chapter, inclusion is interrogated at the level of knowledge production in academic research. In our many years working in universities we have seen that efforts focused broadly on "diversity" and "inclusion" have failed to shift the academy in significant ways. Rather, as Ahmed (2012) has argued, the language of inclusion and diversity has been deployed as *nonperformative* terms, that is, terms that are used and promoted in order to avoid doing the work of transformative justice that the university requires. It is not enough to get different people into the room and to give everyone equal space, when academic disciplines are so clearly premised on and geared toward majority interests. We must, as Megan Ybarra argues, "be the killjoy who argues not only for admission into graduate school (i.e., inclusion), but also argues that classes, classrooms and reading lists should change with their arrival (i.e., transformation)" (2019, p. 8, following Ahmed, 2010). Academic spaces, even when diverse and inclusive, too often continue to be driven by majority values and commitments that make marginalized students feel unsafe, unwelcome, or at best, uninterested in the academy.

As communication scholars working within and across disciplines, we have the tools to dismantle institutional racism and other structures of oppressive power to create more equitable systems. I think each of us is called to find a route toward the collective work of transformative justice.

Marya and Jennifer's Comments about this Book

We acknowledge that, as white women scholars, our viewpoint may contain blind spots that reflect our own privilege. In the aftermath of Marya's comments at NCA, Marya and Jenn sought advice from the contributors of this book (as well as others) about what to do, given that the book was complete and ready to be printed. The result was humbling but transformative. Patricia Parker's leadership about how we might improve this book was vital. In the email she describes above, she made recommendations that we and several of the contributing authors drew on to revise our chapters. Her recommendations included the following steps:

1   Delay publication and use this forum to devise a plan for how this edited volume can make an intervention, given the events that have transpired. Give each author the time to really reflect on the critiques offered in the

OCD's top paper panel and elsewhere, and to think deeply about our citation practices, building them into our chapters.

2　Rewrite the preface and the introduction as a critical reflection on the events, and the opportunity they present for social justice transformation.

3　Challenge the very notion of "inclusion" at the outset. As a condition of offering our chapter for publication, my coauthors and I made it clear that we would be challenging these notions. (Email from Patricia Parker, dated December 1, 2019).

Pat's leadership was foundational to the revisions of this preface and our introduction chapter. Despite her busy schedule and her own book deadline happening at the exact same time as this one, she willingly came on as an author on this preface and consulted with us on the introduction. It is thus with humility that we thank her for her leadership and intellectual contributions to this work.

As emphasized in Parker et al.'s chapter as well as in other parts of this book, Marya and Jennifer recognize that our emphasis on the term inclusion may reflect a limited understanding of the issues, and that it is important to go beyond inclusion of minoritized groups into existing structures (which serves to reinforce white supremacy) and to transform such structures to ensure equity, equality, and social justice for all. We believe the chapters in this volume speak to issues of structural change. We also acknowledge that, as organizational communication scholars, we take a perspective that is more reformist than radical. While we agree that structural change is necessary, our commitments steer us more toward constructive dialogue and re-building of structures rather than burning structures and institutions down altogether. We value those—including the scholars who walked out of Marya's top paper response—who take a more radical (status-quo challenging) approach and hope to bring reformist and radical voices together into a generative dialogue given that we are all members of a shared disciplinary community. As such, we hope that this collection of articles will help to advance the conversation, and that it will generate new conversations, institutional structures, and communicative practices.

Marya L. Doerfel, Jennifer L. Gibbs, and Patricia Parker

References

Ahmed, S. (2010). *The promise of happiness*. Durham, NC: Duke University Press.

Ahmed, S. (2012). *On being included: Racism and diversity in institutional life*. Durham, NC Duke University Press.

Bonanno, G. A. (2004). Loss, trauma, and human resilience: Have we underestimated the human capacity to thrive after extremely aversive events? *American Psychologist, 59*(1), 20–28. doi:10.1037/0003-066X.59.1.20

Diangelo, R. (2018). *White fragility: Why it's so hard for white people to talk about racism*. Boston, MA: Beacon Press.

Frankenberg, R. (1993). *White women, race matters: The social construction of whiteness*. Minneapolis: University of Minnesota Press.

Gray, A. (2019, June). *The bias of "professionalism" standards*. Stanford Social Innovation Review. Retrieved from https://ssir.org/articles/entry/the_bias_of_professionalism_standards

Harris, K. L. (2019, November). *Unlearning border defense, undermining white supremacist violence: Renewing the case for interdisicplinary inquiry in organizational communication*. Top paper presented at the top paper panel of the Organizational Communication Division of the National Communication Association. Baltimore, MD.

Nuru, A. K., & Arendt, C. E. (2019). Not so safe a space: Women Activists of Color's responses to racial microaggressions by White Women allies. *Southern Communication Journal, 84*(2), 85–98. doi:10.1080/1041794X.2018.1505940

Rodriguez, A., Dutta, M., & Desnoyers-Colas, E. (2019). Introduction to special issue on merit, whiteness, and privilege. *Departures in Critical Qualitative Research, 8*(4), 3–9. doi:10.1525/dcqr.2019.8.4.3

Williams, T. A., Gruber, D. A., Sutcliffe, K. M., Shepherd, D. A., & Zhao, E. Y. (2017). Organizational response to adversity: Fusing crisis management and resilience research streams. *Academy of Management Annals, 11*(2), 733–769. doi:10.5465/annals.2015.0134

Ybarra, M. (2019, January 23). *On becoming a LatinX geographies killjoy*. Society and Space. https://www.societyandspace.org/articles/on-becoming-a-latinx-geographies-killjoy

Acknowledgements

We thank the contributors who give this book depth and rigor, thoughtfulness, and expansive examples of inclusion and exclusion. We especially thank each author for their continued support of this project; even when the events surrounding Marya's remarks at NCA became known, they saw the value in the project and trusted that we would integrate this important issue. We thank François Cooren and the anonymous reviewers who saw that the ideas captured in these pages were worth publishing. We are particularly grateful to our editor Suzanne Richardson at Taylor & Francis, who trusted us when we asked for the extra time our revisions needed and supported us with patience, understanding, and additional resources despite the additional cost and work it required for her and her staff. Most importantly, we recognize that we are not the first to write about inclusion, diversity, and race. This book would not exist without the great thinkers and activists who have helped all of us recognize the importance of creating communicative structures and interactions that are inclusive for all groups. We hope that it will spark energy and conversation around these issues, that will then be continued by others.

Marya L. Doerfel and Jennifer L. Gibbs

1 Organizing Inclusion

Top-Down and Bottom-Up Approaches

Marya L. Doerfel and Jennifer L. Gibbs

In her memoire *Becoming*, former United States first lady Michelle Obama (2018) wrote about her time at Princeton, recalling her experiences engaging ethnically blended groups. Despite great strides in the civil rights movement in the United States (US) and even with legal changes to the US constitution, she still felt like an outsider and recognized the challenge that she had experienced. She explained, "(b)ut even today, with white students continuing to outnumber students of color on college campuses, the burden of assimilation is put largely on the shoulders of minority students. In my experience, it's a lot to ask" (p. 74). Obama's view underscores the complexity that comes with modernity—a world where society's understanding of equality coevolves with issues of inclusion and exclusion.

Inclusion, as in Obama's experience, is communicative and is also a function of perspective. From Princeton's point of view, these new policies designed to open up access and increase diversity were progressive. But underlying such inclusion policy is that those being brought in are expected to blend in (Ahmed, 2012). Obama's perspective illuminated the tendency for those in positions of power to invite and enable assimilation (blending in) into existing institutional structures. To blend into the dominant group, however, is not enough, nor does it substantially alter how organizing processes generate lenses defined by elites and outsiders. That is not the intent of our use of inclusion. Rather, our intent is to show how communicating can be structured for unique voices to be heard. What structures support polivocal organizations? How do individual-level interactions transform organizations?

People have a tendency to trust and, therefore, build relationships with people like themselves (McPherson, Smith-Lovin, & Cook, 2001). This tendency reveals how everyday events define deeper-rooted hegemonies. True inclusion involves changing such tendencies and transforming existing institutional norms and structures to listen to "others" rather than expecting "others" to conform and blend in. Obama's experience at Princeton is an example of organizational initiatives falling short by emphasizing diversity over inclusion (see Gailliard, Davis, Gibbs, & Doerfel's chapter). Inclusion under such circumstances reproduces whiteness (Ahmed, 2012). When diverse people communicate, white people may feel uncomfortable (as Doerfel described in the preface). Candor and disagreement are difficult and can shift the focus from being about the issue to making the uncomfortable people feel better about themselves (Diangelo, 2018). Mutual trust, then, is necessary so that differences are opportunistic rather than casting blame on those who bring up those differences to begin with.

Both Obama's experience and the case of the organizational communication division's (OCD) top paper response illustrate that issues of inclusion are obvious to the excluded, yet can be unapparent as marginalizing acts to those in positions of power and privilege. Exclusion is not just the result of overt forms of racism and sexism. Though overt forms of exclusion still exist, inclusion, and its counterpart exclusion, can be difficult to identify when people become part of or are excluded from a dominant, insider, or powerful group. That dominant group can be defined by a variety of demographics but can also be socially constructed through expertise and knowledge (see Barbour, Rolison, & Jensen's along with Gailliard et al.'s chapters in this volume), access to resources (as in Gonzales & Yan's chapter), a stigmatized trait or behavior (see Meisenbach & Hutchins' chapter), or in the ways in which white supremacy becomes an underlying organizing mechanism because white people are over-represented due to their roles in society (see Afifi & Cornejo's and Parker et al.'s chapters). Even those who claim to support diversity may inadvertently take part in systems of exclusion, as both the top paper response (see the case detailed in our preface and Gailliard et al.'s chapter) and a recent debate about how distinguished scholars are selected by the National Communication Association (NCA) vividly illustrates (see Gailliard et al.'s chapter). In this way, academic institutions (e.g., universities, professional associations) are designed around a certain set of values constructed by homogeneous groups (i.e., white men) that serve to keep these groups in power and reproduce these systems in their own image (Ahmed, 2012; Allen, 2011). As the NCA controversy demonstrates, a false dichotomy is often drawn between "diversity" and "merit" that reveals that the criteria used to define merit have white supremacy inherently baked into them. Similarly, treating racism as a dichotomy (either racist or not) can lead to the fragility white people feel when they are challenged to consider how their own actions may perpetuate racism (Diangelo, 2018). The top paper response described in our preface illustrated the quandary white progressives make for themselves when they frame racists as bad; non-racists as good. In doing so, we perpetuate institutionalized racism. Doing so frees the progressive from recognizing her own role. To truly be progressive and therefore contribute to organizational transformation, it is important to be reflective about our own identities and the experiences that go with those identities (Allen, 2011). To that point, Diangelo (2018) implores that people ask themselves to consider the experiences that come with their identities and ask "how did [one's particular identity] shape me as a result of being that identity?" (p. 12). Today, as Gailliard et al. explain, universities' track records show that tweaking a system is not enough.

Inclusion and exclusion can be obvious, especially when public discourse, debates, and positioning overtly identify groups as desirable or not. But more often than not, roadblocks are subtle and difficult to recognize. For example, Ahmed's (2012) study of diversity officers employed at universities around Australia and Europe showed how diversity initiatives at universities can be superficial:

> Diversity provides a positive, shiny image of the organization that allows inequalities to be concealed and thus reproduced… Diversity is a way of not addressing institutional cultures, or perhaps addressing them only 'slightly,' which implies that a slight address can be a way not to address.
>
> (p. 72)

Issues of inclusion and exclusion have emerged as a major challenge facing organizations and institutions as both society and the workforce become more diverse. Yet white supremacist ideologies persist which in turn cause emotional, material, and physical harm to people of color.[1] An obvious case of this can be seen in a central argument US President Donald Trump made in his years leading up to and has made since his 2016 election. Through speeches, social media commentary, and policy, he persists in vilifying Mexican immigrants, referring to them as "drug dealers, criminals, and rapists" (BBC. com, 2016). A recent attack came in an ad leading up to the 2018 midterm elections, which CNN analyst Stephen Collinson (2018) argued was "the latest example of the President's willingness to lie and fear-monger in order to tear at racial and societal divides" (¶3). At the same time and in the years since, some aspects of the national discourse have been driven to counter both overt and subtle forms of divisive mistreatment of people based on their identities.

Such counterattacks are driven by goals of inclusion, but they are also geared to reverse societal exclusion and unfair treatment of people who are not in positions of power. Counter movements include organized actions and communication campaigns like the now viral #metoo and #takeaknee movements, the #CommunicationSoWhite movement in academia, countless news articles about diversity and inclusion, as well as the statements some organizations and businesses across the spectrum are now providing about their diversity and inclusion efforts. Divisive public discourse and political rhetoric further divide implicitly, as well. Because such discourse may be obviously racist to progressives, the obvious events like these further perpetuate treating racism as a binary, as discussed above. The public racism becomes a red herring that then distracts people in their everyday lives from awareness of the problems that exist in their own institutions. The top paper response illustrates this all too well. As Doerfel explains in her own words:

> Lately, hate groups have been in the news so much and their public disdain for people of color seems even more vocal than ever. It is easy to see their racism and their belief in white supremacy. But I allowed their

obvious-ness to narrow my own use of the concept of white supremacy. As a result, my underlying thinking was binary in terms of evil/good: 'They're white supremacists; I'm/we're not.' As such, I became defensive about its use against the organization in which I was a leader. I treated it as a binary rather than recognizing how we are all capable of reproducing white supremacy.

While some strides have been made in valuing diversity and providing more equal opportunities to workers of different race, ethnicity, gender, age, ability, and sexual orientation, policies and practices designed to promote inclusion are contested, imperfect, and ignored. As discussed above, policy can also be window dressing. "But in being spoken, and repeated in different contexts, a world takes shape around diversity. To speak the language of diversity is to participate in the creation of a world" (Ahmed, 2012, p. 81).

While speaking the language of diversity is vital, Ahmed warns that inclusive policies and practices can put the onus on those whom such policies attempt to help (as in Obama's experience at Princeton; as in the scholars who walked out of the OCD top paper panel). Such policies and concomitant practices are only progressive when everyone engages in them. Unfortunately, what happens too often is that only a few speak up. Those few who speak up get framed by those who don't as "difficult." To frame their actions as 'disrupting peace' undermines progress toward social justice. A possible solution is to reframe policies as prototype (see Buzzanell's chapter in this volume). Viewing diversity policies as prototypes offers a way to reorient social systems and the people who design them. Some prototypes can be tweaked and incrementally coevolve with changes that happen in those systems' environments, while other changes (corrections to the prototypes) may be substantial. Change can be consequential and imperfect. Recognizing systemic corrections as prototypes is a more realistic way to think about the complexities that come when people aim to coordinate and control their environments.

Framing progress through a series of prototypes offers a challenge to improve circumstances without suffering the consequences of not getting solutions right in the short run. Diversity management programs were a first step toward providing opportunities for women and minorities in institutions. Using the language of diversity, however, was critiqued for driving quotas rather than being transformative (see Gailliard et al.'s chapter). Inclusion reorients institutions through identifying ways to give voice to previously silenced groups (see Tracy, Razzante, & Hanna's chapter). Through this inclusive orientation, problem-solving and the discussions that support problem-solving do not just facilitate improved outcomes but also improve the experience for the people involved. Kent and Logan's chapter in this volume elaborates on the ethical consequences that come with a sense of connection and engagement when people are included.

There are also many systemic and institutionalized ways in which implicit biases work against inclusion. Fundamental assumptions prioritize rationality over emotionality and efficiencies and profits over people (see Mitra's chapter). Some organizational practices privilege certain groups while excluding or marginalizing others. Exclusion and marginalization are especially felt by people whose identities are intersectional such that an individual may be (for example) both a woman and a person of color and thus doubly stigmatized due to their membership in multiple disenfranchised groups (Crenshaw, 1989). Universities are no different (see Gailliard et al.'s chapter). For individuals, professors whose identities intersect across categories experience challenges on multiple levels of their institutions in every day life (Cruz, McDonald, Broadfoot, Chuang, & Ganesh, 2018). Institutional practices contribute to exclusion through hiring practices that inadvertently preference applicants within managers' close social networks, micro-aggressions at work that insult or invalidate certain groups (see Tracy et al.'s contributions), global work practices that create status differences among employees at headquarters versus remote subsidiaries (see below), and professional domains that require defining expertise to certify belonging (see Barbour et al.'s chapter).

Exclusionary practices can also be observed at community levels, where change may impact a variety of stakeholders. Progress and solutions do not always specify clear goals nor assign fixed responsibility (see Mitra's chapter). How various stakeholders orient themselves toward their own local issues can be overshadowed even by the most well-intentioned outsiders aiming to help (see Connaughton & Ptacek's chapter as well as Mitra's). Over time, new voices may enter the conversation. As the conversation evolves, solutions may reveal unexpected goals. Those goals and solutions may run counter to initial presumptions. To wit, Connaughton and Ptacek report on the value of inclusion when it comes to defining the very essence of peace, not as a Western construct but as a way of life that is meaningful for the local community the Purdue Peace Project aims to help. This point is underscored by Tracy et al.'s chapter in that inclusion can be beneficial in terms of both process and outcomes. Inclusion, Tracy et al. argue, "feels good."

At the same time, organizations are trying to downsize, streamline, offshore, and operate on razor-thin margins to maximize profits. These efforts to increase efficiency while cutting overhead have resulted in a rupture in the traditional psychological contract between employers and employees (De Cuyper, Notelaers, & De Witte, 2009). This has led to the rise of nontraditional work arrangements (e.g., part-time, temporary or contingent work, global outsourcing and offshoring, virtual teams) that are often driven by pressures to cut costs and reduce investment into employee training and welfare. Such work models complicate what constitutes employment. Organizational boundaries get blurred. Organizations are tasked with dividing attention between internal constituents and a broader system of external stakeholder networks. We thus see a shift in who is viewed as legitimate and worthy of inclusion, a problem we discuss in this chapter in the context of globalization. Legitimacy and inclusion are also deconstructed in Barbour et al.'s chapter on professions. Often lost in these discussions are the various ways in which new work arrangements contribute to inclusion and exclusion of workers, an issue we address in many chapters in this book.

Modern organizational pressures to be more efficient to maximize profits underscore tensions between designers and implementers of inclusion. While academics and policymakers think about inclusion and equal opportunity, some employers claim to be "colorblind" and motivated to have equity and diversity. But because policy can systematically exclude and generate different forms of exclusion (Stevens, Plaut, & Sanchez-Burks, 2008), employers' claims or attempts to be color-blind are actually myopic. Treating everyone the same quashes any chance for organizations to be diverse (Ahmed, 2012; Diangelo, 2018). Change involves more than invoking policy, but recognizing who has a stake and ensuring they have a voice in how change facilitates progress (Ahmed, 2012; Lewis, 2019; Lewis, Hamel, & Richardson, 2001).

Some advances in policy, like cradle-to-career initiatives (Reilly, 2018), and Parker, Holland, Dennison, Smith, and Jackson's chapter that describes a participatory certificate program at the University of North Carolina, attempt to address these tensions. Yet pervasive in American discourses, politicians and pundits challenge the validity of claims about inclusion, pay equity, systemic "isms" like white supremacy, and work processes that reveal privileged access to resources and job growth opportunities. These skeptics do not see that the very ways work processes are designed, or even timed in terms of how quickly work is expected to be done, are inherently exclusion-driving mechanisms (see Ballard & Aguilar's chapter in this volume). Even location matters. The literatures on global organizations and social networks (see below sections in this chapter) point to systematic ways employees at headquarters enjoy higher status over their offshore counterparts. Communication scholars are particularly suited to examine such complexities through multiple theoretical frameworks, at varying levels of analysis, and with mixed methods. The result is a robust set of intellectual resources that can be brought together and leveraged to improve both understanding of and practices associated with communicative processes that organize inclusion and exclusion.

This chapter thus overviews formal versus informal organizational communication as well as macro and micro organizing as phenomena that construct opportunities and constraints. These phenomena can be seen through both top-down and bottom-up types of organizing and have grown more complex as globalization has transformed work and working arrangements. Figure 1.1 depicts the cycle of organizing in terms of formal/informal and macro/micro organizing.

Formal and informal communication differentiates rules, policies, and standard operating procedures (SOPs) from the implicit norms, social influence, and forms of control that happen in everyday interactions. Michelle Obama's understanding of such formal policies not aligning with everyday interactions at Princeton revealed the formal versus informal organizing quandary: "I imagine that the administrators at Princeton didn't love the fact that students of color largely stuck together" (p. 74). Likewise, as Doerfel described

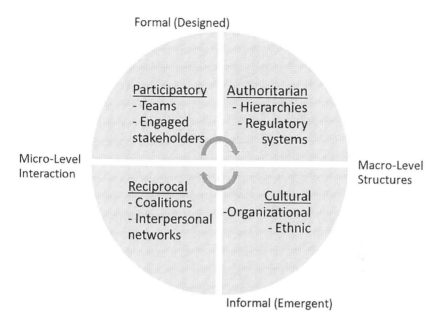

Formal (Designed)

Participatory
- Teams
- Engaged
stakeholders

Authoritarian
- Hierarchies
- Regulatory
  systems

Micro-Level
Interaction

Macro-Level
Structures

Reciprocal
- Coalitions
- Interpersonal
networks

Cultural
-Organizational
- Ethnic

Informal (Emergent)

Figure 1.1 Inclusion and exclusion involve micro- and macro-level communication processes that influence each other through both formal and informal organizing.

in the preface, the OCD top paper panel illustrated implicit biases baked into the division's norms and traditions. In the top paper case, even though the topic was on inclusion, the response aimed to discuss inclusion ended up making some members of that audience to feel excluded. In both cases, the ideal (formal structures aimed to change practice) and the actual observed practices at the micro level of interaction were divergent.

Macro and micro approaches capture different levels of organizing as systemic "macro" structures shape local action, while micro approaches help articulate the ways in which everyday interpersonal and team-level interactions come to shape, reify, or transform social structures. Figure 1.1 describes the circumstances when organizing tends to be more or less formal/informal and macro/micro. Given that interorganizational relationships are themselves a form of organization (Koschmann, Kuhn, & Pfarrer, 2012), this figure illustrates examples in each quadrant when it comes to organizing inside organizations or among them. For example, inside organizations, authoritarian structures can be seen in the hierarchy, such that hierarchies depict clear reporting and accountability structures. Externally, organizations are accountable to regulatory bodies for reporting and compliance. These formal, macro structures aim to control who gets work done and how that work is designed and implemented. Informal macro structures can be seen in cultures.

They also block change when the existence of structures such as diversity programs becomes the story of the organization, despite what goes on inside (Ahmed, 2012). Cultural norms, rites, and rituals that define a culture become powerful sources of influence when it comes to people's behavior.

In the rest of this chapter, we use research to show how inclusion and exclusion are constituted by these organizational communication processes. We elaborate on how they manifest in the context of globalization. We also use this framework to organize the chapters, recognizing that inclusion and exclusion coevolve through formal and informal as well as macro- and micro-level organizational communication. In this way, we hope this collection clarifies for our readers how communication provides opportunities for inclusive organizing while also constructing exclusion.

Organizing Inclusion through Formal and Informal Communication

Formal communication refers to those rules and policies, hierarchical power, training manuals and videos, and SOPs that are explicitly designed to clarify how to get work done. These are formally designed ways to communicate who does what, how, when, and where and with what consequences when such rules are broken. These rules exist within organizational boundaries and are also generated in response to policy dictated by governmental laws and mandates. In the US, for example, the implementation of the Equal Employment Opportunity Commission (EEOC) required that all private employers and government contractors report their employment records as a way of tracking the inclusion of female and minority members of the workforce since 1966 (US EEOC). Over some five decades, the numbers remain dismal, and even where some progress has been made, the way the commission assesses equality is based on nine general categories that contain some 818 different job titles. In addition to the "Executive/senior level officials and managers" category, the nine EEOC categories are:

1. First/mid-level officials and managers
2. Professionals
3. Technicians
4. Sales workers
5. Administrative support workers
6. Craft workers
7. Operatives
8. Laborers and helpers
9. Service workers

There are 33 different types of "first/mid-level officials and managers" that include a range of descriptions, such as Advertising and Promotions Managers; Architectural and Engineering Managers; Compensation and Benefits

Managers; Computer and Information Systems Managers; Construction Managers; Education Administrators, All Other; Emergency Management Directors; Farmers, Ranchers, and Other Agricultural Managers; to Financial Managers and Food Service Managers. Not surprisingly, these categories lump a wide range of managerial levels into one category that implies women and minorities are gaining equal ground. Lumping together such a wide range of job types, however, has been criticized since "women and African Americans are crowded in the lowest ranks of management" (Kalev, Dobbin, & Kelly, 2006, p. 590).

In their interviews of some 700 businesses, Kalev et al. found that formal organizational structures such as diversity committees and diversity staff positions facilitated the efficacy of training, mentoring, network programs, and so forth. Such programs have shown strong promise in equalizing voice in universities, as described in chapters in this volume by Parker et al. and Gailliard et al. It is important to clarify, however, that work described by Parker et al. and Gailliard et al. is ongoing and transformative such that the diversity work happens across the universities; not just isolated in one office. Such evidence suggests that organizations should have formal structures in place that clarify expectations at work. Such expectations need to be folded into all aspects of the organization and not 'merely' operate at a policy level. If diversity is only policy, then it operates as red tape; as mere paperwork (Ahmed, 2012). Diversity becomes a superficial checklist rather than an ongoing process. As such, formal structures need to be institutionalized and part of the culture of daily work (Dobbin, Sutton, Meyer, & Scott, 1993; Parker, Holland, Dennison, Smith, & Jackson, 2018; Weinberg & Lankau, 2011). Indeed, Dobbin et al.'s (1993) study of 279 organizations suggests that the equal employment opportunity law (title VII of the 1964 Civil Rights Act) was the catalyst to organizations formalizing promotion mechanisms since 1964. They found that the treatment of workers shifted to presuming all classes of workers are ambitious. Dobbin et al. argued:

> In short, public policy helped to create broad models of organizing that were embraced as just and rational by all sorts of organizations; it did not force a narrow range of targeted organizations to adopt specified practices in order to avoid sanctions.
>
> (p. 422)

Interestingly, while social networks in organizations have historically been seen as the way people work around formal structures, it is the implementation of formal structures (policy; mentoring programs) that appears to facilitate working around emergent social structures.

Despite the influence policy brings to bear on improving inclusive practices, the emergent and informal structures that social networks generate are an important factor to consider when thinking about inclusion. This can be seen in Gonzales and Yan's chapter on technology reuse, where collaborations are emerging between interorganizational networks among nonprofits that refurbish and redistribute and corporations that replace technology routinely. Such cross-sector alliances reduce the digital divide for low-income individuals. Social networks represent a persistent fact in organizations: regardless of formal rules, structures, and other institutionalized practices that are designed to coordinate and control work, people do not always follow those rules. Hierarchies prescribe reporting structures while social networks reflect the emergent social structures as a result of informal interactions among workers. Moreover, the quality of relationships facilitates the ability for networks to grow and persist (Taylor & Doerfel, 2003). Indeed, the quality of informal relationships involves dialogue and engagement, as described in Kent and Logan's chapter in this volume. Such networks offer a meaningful framework for prioritizing inclusion over exclusion. As such, social networks can be mutually beneficial for both employees and the organization. But social networks can be subversive, too. At work, for example, people may share information with peers rather than their direct supervisors out of resistance or frustration (e.g., Gossett & Kilker, 2006). Regardless of the intent, when solving problems, workers often turn to others in their networks (an informal resource) rather than to manuals (a formal resource) for advice. People tend to turn to others who they perceive as similar to themselves when communicating. In this way, organizational social networks perpetuate systems of exclusion. Executives seek support from other executives; organizations become homogeneous in terms of values through hiring and socialization processes (Giberson, Resick, & Dickson, 2005; Ibarra, 1993). As discussed above, women and minorities in the US have historically been at the lowest ranks of leadership positions. In this way, social networks perpetuate access for those people who are similar to managers and others who hold positions of power. Often this tendency to seek advice from such homophilous networks can undermine organizations' productivity and performance. And that is not recognized by those seeking advice who are in positions of power. For example, when asked whom they turn to for advice about investment decisions, corporate executives revealed that they turned to their close-tie networks (McDonald & Westphal, 2003). McDonald and Westphal linked relatively poor performance to homophilous advice-seeking networks. The flipside is that organizations benefit when people network with diverse rather than similar others (Gargiulo & Benassi, 2000).

So, while networks may provide access, they can also create echo chambers and in-group/out-group divides. Such networks may help some people but can also ultimately undermine firm-level outcomes. Because people tend to turn to people more similar to themselves for friendship and social support (McPherson et al., 2001), what seems natural—to seek advice from one's friends—is an act that further perpetuates privilege and access for the dominant group while further marginalizing those outside of it (Ibarra, 1993). What's more, dominant group norms do not translate for others. For example, leadership qualities tend to favor white men because the same qualities (e.g., assertiveness; confidence) do not translate to women, minorities, minority men, and people whose identities intersect across those groups (Gist, 2017; Parker, 2001, 2005). It stands to reason, then, that how one interacts in their networks, even if those networks are diverse, can still perpetuate white status quo. For example, Logan (2011) demonstrated such racial imbalance that biases white leaders in public relations. The fact that white males still dominate the highest ranks of organizations in most sectors is not due to conscious choices to hire the best talent so much as implicit preferences that perpetuate their own identities and values.

Work gets accomplished with shortcuts and workarounds, decisions are made without consulting the SOPs, and the rationality of structures is less salient than the stories of how work gets done (Dailey & Browning, 2014; Kirby & Krone, 2002). When making decisions at work, people rely on their gut instincts, advice from others, emotions, and memories of how past similar problems were managed (March & Simon, 1993; Mumby & Putnam, 1992; Weick, 1993). Moreover, social pressures like keeping up with peer productivity (i.e., concertive control; cf. Barker, 1993) can undermine even national and organizational policies that attempt to regulate work-life quality (Ter Hoeven, Miller, Peper, & den Dulk, 2017). In other words, organizations' everyday decisions and routines are embedded in social structures formed through relationships. Indeed, informal structures evolve as the gap widens between how work is supposed to be accomplished relative to how work actually gets done (Meyer & Rowan, 1977). These informal approaches and the relationships that support them rest on the ability for communication to flow in and around the system (Doerfel, 2016; Doerfel, Lai, & Chewning, 2010). Social networks embody intangible resources workers come to rely on to find out what is necessary and important. Workers turn to each other to figure out how to get work done and they access information as they come to understand who knows who knows what at work (Contractor et al., 1998; Monge & Contractor, 2003; Shumate & Contractor, 2014).

Formal and informal structures can be considered together to understand the opportunities and constraints that arise for people accessing information and power (Doerfel, 2016). Formal structures such as diversity initiatives may be helpful in recruiting more women and minorities into lower level managerial ranks. Formal mentoring programs are meant to help break challenges of retention and promotion (Phillips, Dennison, & Davenport, 2016). But social networks are the underground informal social economy that creates both opportunities and constraints when it comes to inclusion. Or, as Krackhardt and Hanson (1993) asserted, social networks, relative to the hierarchy, are the "company behind the chart" (p. 104).

Networks represent opportunities and constraints in and among organizations. How people are connected and the overall social structure has implications for power and influence of individuals as well as group norms and in/out group identification (Borgatti, 2005; Brass, Galaskiewicz, Greve, & Tsai, 2004; Monge & Eisenberg, 1987; Shumate & Contractor, 2014). Such patterns have been observed at the interorganizational and global levels, too.

For example, in their examination of global trends in the diffusion of technology, Nam and Barnett (2011) identified a core-periphery network structure in the flows of technology and capital between core countries (Japan, the US, Germany, South Korea, and France) and peripheral ones. The asymmetrical flows indicate that the core countries are relatively self-sufficient and therefore do not need to forge ties with those in the periphery. Their flows reflect exclusivity, which creates barriers for less developed countries to make strides in the technology sector. Nam and Barnett argue:

> While neoliberalization supports the practice of using multilateral rules and policies, like exclusive IPRs [International Property Rights as part of the 1995 World Trade Organization (WTO) agreement], as instruments to facilitate the transfer of technology and a cornucopia of commodities, empirical findings indicate that regimes have only partial autonomy from the core countries that create them to reflect the interests of dominant states.
>
> (p. 1481)

In this case, the WTO has formal power and authority over global trade rules while the collaborations, organizations, and businesses have with each other are emergent and generate social networks.

Regardless of work being among individuals or organizations, the formality that is observed in hierarchies, policies, and laws communicates responsibility and accountability. In networks, positions of power are seen in various forms relative to who controls information flows (Astley & Sachdeva, 1984). Power in networks comes from having a lot of connections relative to others, being brokers who facilitate information flows because brokers connect various different groups that would otherwise not be connected to each other, and/or from having connections to others who are well connected themselves (Borgatti, 2005; Smith et al., 2014). Various overall network structures also have implications with respect to information flows, such as when cliques form and over time the members of the clique come to identify strongly with each other. As a result, the overall network forms a core-periphery structure where the core members are the elite while the periphery are excluded and lack connections to generate their own organized system (Borgatti & Everett, 2000). Such strong relationships in the core of a network can result in strong, trusting relationships (as discussed above) but can also become insular with clear boundaries that distinguish members and non-members. More decentralized networks, on the other hand, may facilitate more rapid information flows and also ward off threats if any one part of the network disbands (Castells, 2011, 2013). These structural features all have implications for the opportunities and constraints social networks generate when it comes to inclusion.

Even with access to those at the top and in power through mentoring programs, women and minorities have to double down. To rise through the ranks, they need mentors to introduce them to the executive networks while women and minority's social support and mentors come from people more like themselves. The women and/or minorities' mentors may be powerful but when those mentors are only white men, the social support connections are typically not in positions of power (Ibarra, 1993; Ibarra, Kilduff, & Tsai, 2005). To add to the complexities created by innate tendencies to network with homophilous others, organizational structures are shifting in modern work to be global in scope. The following section draws on theory and research on globalization and work arrangements in a global context. The globalization literature complements this section on social networks by unpacking differences that are location-based, cultural, ideological, and linguistic, at both macro and micro levels of organizing.

Organizing Inclusion at Macro and Micro Levels

Contemporary organizing is increasingly occurring through global work structures, due to the existence of new communication technologies that allow for working across time, space, and other boundaries. Global work often takes place through micro-level team structures that reflect more macro-level networked forms of organizing, in that they are set up to encourage information sharing and input across geographical locations. At both micro and macro levels of organizing, global work often ends up inadvertently privileging certain perspectives while devaluing or discounting others. Thus, global work practices often end up organizing exclusion rather than inclusion of certain types of workers, based on their nationality, ethnicity, language, location, job function, gender, and other characteristics. Like the similarity principle of social networks, similarity breeds inclusion while differences drive exclusion.

While individual micro-level demographic characteristics are often highlighted as the source of social inequalities, in global work there are macro-level systemic organizational and institutional practices that create other types of inequalities as well. Broader globalization processes are imbued with power dynamics on a macro, geo-political scale, as they create and reinforce status hierarchies that separate developed and developing countries. There are ways to mitigate such differences in partnership across economic, ideological, and educational boundaries (see Connaughton & Ptacek's chapter in this volume). In global organizations, core-periphery dynamics are likely to arise that mirror those of the world system, in which the world is divided into core countries that control the means of capitalist production and periphery countries whose labor and resources are exploited (Nam & Barnett, 2011; Wallerstein, 1974). This has been seen in communication as a discipline (Chakravartty, Kuo, Grubbs, & McIlwain, 2018) and felt first hand by non-US professors in US-based institutions (Cruz et al., 2018; Kapoor, 2019; Rodriguez, Dutta, & Colas, 2019). Likewise, in global or multinational corporations, similar status inequalities are likely to arise between the headquarters site (which is often located in a Western or core country) and remote or subsidiary locations. They may also play out in relationships among organizations or institutions from different sectors. For instance, one study of transnational corporate power studied the discourse of the Transatlantic Business Dialogue (TABD), a formal agreement between businesses and governments of the European Union and the US, and found that the discourse of dialogue worked to legitimate corporate hegemony and empower free markets in global trade (Zoller, 2004). Such discourses are also seen in institutional documents and the "semantic reservoirs" they produce, as Vallée's chapter in this volume examines. Macro-level organizational and cultural discourses may act as competing influences on the negotiation of work-life balance at the micro level by shaping the meanings of work and corresponding expectations and norms (Wieland, 2011). Like Nam and Barnett's (2011) findings about the diffusion of technology patents around the world, discourse on a global scale differentiates groups, and meaning of work becomes defined by the ideals of dominant cultures.

Scholarship at the micro level advocates that individual managers take a global mindset, defined as a cosmopolitan orientation that goes beyond the assumptions of a single country, culture, or context and the cognitive complexity to synthesize across diverse perspectives (Boyagiciller, Beechler, Taylor, & Levy, 2004; Gupta & Govindarajan, 2002) and at the macro level that multinational firms take a geocentric orientation, defined as a world-oriented view that involves a collaborative approach between headquarters and subsidiaries and aims to develop the best people for key positions around the world regardless of nationality (Perlmutter, 1969). As Perlmutter acknowledges, despite the desirability of taking a geocentric orientation, few firms actually do so due to obstacles such as nationalism and distrust between home and host countries, language and cultural barriers, and the tendency to centralize decision-making at the headquarters site. These trends echo the proclivity to build social networks with similar others, generating barriers to inclusion.

Micro-level research on global work has found that members of the global headquarters location often take on higher status than those from remote locations, and that these status differences tend to be reinforced through their interactions (Kim, 2018; Leonardi & Rodriguez-Lluesma, 2013; Levina & Vaast, 2008). For example, an ethnographic study of a global automotive manufacturer revealed that employees from lower status locations such as Mexico often misrepresented their work in an effort to conform to their perceived occupational stereotypes of the ideal US engineer in order to boost their perceived status in the eyes of higher status locations such as the US headquarters but that their reliance on faulty stereotypes ended up confirming perceptions that they were less competent and committed and reinforced their position of lower status (Leonardi & Rodriguez-Lluesma, 2013). Another study of a global high-tech organization found that although workers from remote locations attempted to use enterprise social media in strategic ways to gain more communication visibility with the corporate headquarters, this communication ended up highlighting knowledge disparities among remote and headquarters workers and thus reinforcing the lower status associated with the remote location (Kim, 2018).

Disparities between headquarters and remote locations are perhaps most pronounced in global outsourcing arrangements, as multiple national and organizational boundaries overlap to produce an imbalance of resources between onshore and offshore participants that creates status differences and inhibits collaboration (Levina & Vaast, 2008). Bringing offshore workers onsite on short-term assignments to work on development projects is one strategy for improving collaboration by bringing workers into physical proximity, but it also activates status differences between temporary contractors from offshore centers and their permanent counterparts at the client site (Gibbs, 2009).

Global teams are an important boundary-spanning coordination mechanism for multinational corporations and other types of global organizations. They are often set up to enable knowledge sharing and coordination of work across geographical and cultural boundaries (Cramton & Hinds, 2014), and their geographical distribution and dynamic structure provides access to distributed expertise and creative, flexible response designed to increase innovation (Gibson & Gibbs, 2006). However, global teams are often fractured by geographical and cultural fault lines (Cramton & Hinds, 2005; O'Leary & Mortensen, 2010) as well as by status differences that arise on the basis of language, job function or expertise, location, and other characteristics. These status differences work to exclude certain members by discounting their knowledge and perspectives, limiting their input and participation. In other words, although the teams may be formally structured to collaborate, the informal social networks that emerge among people who work in those teams do not span physical and social distances. For example, an ethnographic study of a global software team that was distributed between the US and India found that the Indian software developers took on lower status than the US developers due to their remote location, which resulted in their work being discounted. Further, the US developers engaged in informal status closure strategies that reinforced and deepened perceived status differences (Metiu, 2006). Likewise, even when macro-level structures of interaction aim to facilitate information sharing among people, micro-level active talk may generate barriers, echoing Ahmed's (2012) study of diversity workers discussed in above sections. This issue was observed in an analysis of participation in conference calls of nine global teams in a global minerals and mining corporation. The attendees were diverse, with all global team members present, but the actual communication revealed exclusion. The communication patterns demonstrated that the calls were dominated by leaders and members at the Australian site, who made up about two-thirds of the turns at talk. Interviews with global team members revealed that this inequality was due to a mixture of language and cultural factors as well as organizational power dynamics among the team locations (Gibbs, Grushina, Gibson, Dunlop, & Cordery, 2013). Communication as a mechanism of inclusion and exclusion can also be seen in other studies that have identified language proficiency as associated with status differences within global teams (Hinds, Neeley, & Cramton, 2014). Research has found that enforcing English as the lingua franca in global organizations results in a loss of status for non-native English speakers (Neeley, 2013) as well as in unearned status gain for native English speakers (Neeley & Dumas, 2016), regardless of their actual level of fluency. Thus, global work structures tend to promote practices of organizing at both macro and micro levels that inadvertently exclude certain groups on the basis of geographical location, organizational status, language, and other factors.

Conclusion: Top-Down and Bottom-Up Approaches to Organizing Inclusion

As our chapter has shown, even when formal structures aim to be inclusive, exclusion persists. Formal structures may be observed in macro-level organizational arrangements such as when SOPs reflect policy and laws like equal opportunity. Formal structures can persist at the more micro level, too, such as when all members of a global team are included in meetings. But organizing practices and the ways organizational members communicate often inadvertently exclude rather than include other organizational members from minority or low-status groups or put undue pressure on those minority groups to be included. Formal diversity initiatives, however well intentioned, are limited as they focus on representation rather than inclusion (Ahmed, 2012; see also Gailliard et al.'s chapter). Inclusion goes well beyond ensuring a certain quota or percentage of employees of underrepresented groups in the workforce. It must be embedded in organizational structures, including formal ones along with informal social networks, teams, and work arrangements at micro and macro levels. Norms must be open to not just visible difference, but intellectual and decision-making differences, too. As Diangelo (2018) argues, being nice, or as Ahmed (2012) showed, being agreeable (not upsetting the status quo), further impedes real inclusion. While many companies take a top-down approach by focusing on the creation of anti-discrimination policies, these policies are not always effective and may conflict with informal work practices and norms (e.g., Kirby & Krone, 2002). Moreover, social networks can generate powerful core-periphery structures that make moving around and up an organization even more challenging. How can heterogeneous others break through social barriers generated by and reified through social similarity and associated camaraderie? How can heterogeneous others have their voices heard? Implicit bias is evident in hiring and promotion practices that privilege managers' as well as academics' own homophilous social networks, and in global team structures that serve as microcosms for geo-political inequalities that create status differences among team members based on their country location. For this reason, both top-down and bottom-up approaches are needed for organizing inclusion.

Informal communication practices should actively promote inclusion and equality of participation. The chapters in this book attempt to expand on understanding challenges of inclusion while also addressing specific policy, training, and interventions from all directions—top-down, bottom-up, and lateral shifts in peer-to-peer organizational communication. We used the framework depicted in Figure 1.1 to organize this book. Our contributors bring their unique voices to challenge scholars, leaders, and the general workforce to consider what are the deeply rooted assumptions, everyday practices, retold stories and myths, relationships, norms, policies, and rules that perpetuate boundaries that prevent inclusion and perpetuate exclusion. The contributors' chapters stitch together the coevolving and dynamic processes that are inherently communicative and shape opportunities and constraints as organizing mechanisms of inclusion. Likewise, this volume challenges the reader to consider: What are the organizing and communication processes that facilitate adaptation to inclusive communicative practices and mitigate exclusion? How do we restructure organizing to allow for peripheries to organize and be elite in their own right? Can new formal and informal forms of organizing shift thinking from dominance to shared, inclusive, and participatory organizing?

Note

1 We recognize that using the concept "people of color" inherently centers white people as the "norm" against which others are identified, compared, separated, etc.

References

Ahmed, S. (2012). *On being included: Racism and diversity in institutional life*. Durham, NC: Duke University Press.

Allen, B. J. (2011) *Difference matters: Communicating social identity* (2nd Ed.). Long Grove, IL: Waveland Press.

Astley, W. G., & Sachdeva, P. S. (1984). Structural sources of interorganizational power: A theoretical synthesis. *Academy of Management Review, 9*, 104–113.

Barker, J. R. (1993). Tightening the iron cage: Concertive control in self-managing teams. *Administrative Science Quarterly, 38*(3), 408–437. doi:10.2307/2393374

BBC.com. (2016, August 31). "Drug dealers, criminals, rapists": What Trump thinks of Mexicans. Retrieved from https://www.bbc.com/news/video_and_audio/headlines/37230916/drug-dealers-criminals-rapists-what-trump-thinks-of-mexicans

Borgatti, S. P. (2005). Centrality and network flow. *Social Networks, 21*, 55–71. doi:10.1016/j.socnet.2004.11.008.

Borgatti, S. P., & Everett, M. G. (2000). Models of core/periphery structures. *Social Networks, 21*, 375–395. doi:10.1016/S0378-8733(99)00019-2

Boyagiciller, N., Beechler, S., Taylor, S., & Levy, O. (2004). The crucial yet elusive global mindset. In H. W. Lane, M. L. Maznevski, M. E. Mendenhall, & J. McNett (Eds.), *Handbook of global management* (pp. 81–93). Malden, MA: Blackwell.

Brass, D. J., Galaskiewicz, J., Greve, H. R., & Tsai, W. (2004). Taking stock of networks and organizations: A multilevel perspective. *Academy of Management Journal, 47*, 795–817. doi:10.2307/20159624

Castells, M. (2011). A network theory of power. *International Journal of Communication, 5*, 773–787.

Castells, M. (2013). *Communication power.* Oxford: Oxford University Press.

Chakravartty, P., Kuo, R., Grubbs, V., & McIlwain, C. (2018). #CommunicationSoWhite. *Journal of Communication, 68*(2), 254–266. doi:10.1093/joc/jqy003

Collinson, S. (2018, November 1). Trump shocks with racist new ad days before midterms. CNN Politics. Retrieved from https://www.cnn.com/2018/10/31/politics/donald-trump-immigration-paul-ryan-midterms/index.html

Contractor, N. S., Zink, D., & Chan, M. (1998). IKNOW: A tool to assist and study the creation, maintenance, and dissolution of knowledge networks. In T. Ishida (Ed.), *Community computing and support systems: Social interaction in networked communities* (Vol. 1519, pp. 201–217). Berlin: Springer Berlin Heidelberg.

Cramton, C. D., & Hinds, P. J. (2005). Subgroup dynamics in internationally distributed teams: Ethno-centrism or cross-national learning? *Research in Organizational Behavior, 26*, 231–263.

Cramton, C. D., & Hinds, P. J. (2014). An embedded model of cultural adaptation in global teams. *Organization Science, 25*, 1056–1081.

Crenshaw, K. (1989). Demarginalizing the intersection of race and sex: A black feminist critique of antidiscrimination doctrine, feminist theory, and anti-racist politics. University of Chicago Legal Forum, 139–167. Retrieved from https://chicagounbound.uchicago.edu/cgi/viewcontent.cgi?article=1052&context=uclf

Cruz, J., McDonald, J., Broadfoot, K., Chuang, A. K. C., & Ganesh, S. (2018). "Aliens" in the United States: A collaborative autoethnography of foreign-born faculty. *Journal of Management Inquiry.* doi:10.1177/1056492618796561

Dailey, S., & Browning, L. (2014). Retelling stories in organizations: Understanding the functions of narrative repetition. *Academy of Management Review, 39*(1), 22–43. doi:10.5465/amr.2011.0329

De Cuyper, N., Notelaers, G., & De Witte, H. (2009). Job insecurity and employability in fixed-term contractors, agency workers, and permanent workers: Associations with job satisfaction and affective organizational commitment. *Journal of Occupational Health Psychology, 14*, 193–205. doi:10.1037/a0014603

Diangelo, R. (2018). *White fragility: Why it's so hard for white people to talk about racism.* Boston, MA: Beacon Press.

Dobbin, F., Sutton, J. R., Meyer, J. W., & Scott, R. (1993). Equal opportunity law and the construction of internal labor markets. *American Journal of Sociology, 99*, 396–427. doi:10.1086/230269

Doerfel, M. L. (2016). Networked forms of organizing, disaster-related disruptions, and public health. In T. R. Harrison & E. A. Williams (Eds.), *Organizations, communication, and health* (pp. 365–383). New York: Routledge.

Doerfel, M. L., Lai, C. H., & Chewning, L. V. (2010). The evolutionary role of inter-organizational communication: Modeling social capital in disaster contexts. *Human Communication Research, 36*, 125–162. doi:10.1111/j.1468-2958.2010.01371.x

Gargiulo, M., & Benassi, M. (2000). Trapped in your own net? Network cohesion, structural holes, and the adaptation of social capital. *Organization Science, 11*(2), 183–196.

Gibbs, J. L. (2009). Dialectics in a global software team: Negotiating tensions across time, space, and culture. *Human Relations, 62*, 905–935.

Gibbs, J. L., Grushina, S. V., Gibson, C. B., Dunlop, P., & Cordery, J. (2013). Encouraging participation in global teams: Unpacking the role of language, culture, and communication practices. In T. Lee, K. Trees, & R. Desai (Eds.),

Refereed Proceedings of the Australian and New Zealand Communication Association conference: Global Networks-Global Divides: Bridging New and Traditional Communication Challenges. ISSN 1448-4331. Retrieved from www.anzca.net/conferences/past-conferences/161.html

Giberson, T. R., Resick, C. J., & Dickson, M. W. (2005). Embedding leader characteristics: An examination of homogeneity of personality and values in organizations. *Journal of Applied Psychology, 90*(5), 1002–1010. doi:10.1037/0021-9010.90.5.1002

Gibson, C. B., & Gibbs, J. L. (2006). Unpacking the concept of virtuality: The effects of geographic dispersion, electronic dependence, dynamic structure, and national diversity on team innovation. *Administrative Science Quarterly, 51,* 451–495.

Gist, A. N. (2017), "I knew America was not ready for a woman to be president:" Commentary on the dominant structural intersections organized around the presidency and voting rights. *Women's Studies in Communication, 40* (2), 150–154. doi:10.1080/07491409.2017.1302261

Gossett, L. M., & Kilker, J. (2006). My job sucks: Examining counterinstitutional web sites as locations for organizational member voice, dissent, and resistance. *Management Communication Quarterly, 20,* 63–90. doi:10.1177/0893318906291729

Gupta, A. K., & Govindarajan, V. (2002). Cultivating a global mindset. *The Academy of Management Executive, 16,* 116–126.

Hinds, P., Neeley, T., & Cramton, C. (2014). Language as a lightning rod: Power contests, emotion regulation, and subgroup dynamics in global teams. *Journal of International Business Studies, 45,* 536–561.

Ibarra, H. (1993). Personal networks of women and minorities in management: A conceptual framework. *Academy of Management Review, 18,* 56–87.

Ibarra, H., Kilduff, M., & Tsai, W. (2005). Zooming in and out: Connecting individuals and collectivities at the frontiers of organizational network research. *Organization Science, 16,* 359–371. doi:10.1287/orsc.1050.0129

Kalev, A., Dobbin, F., & Kelly, E. (2006). Best practices or best guesses? Assessing the efficacy of corporate affirmative action and diversity policies. *American Sociological Review, 71,* 589–617. doi:10.1177/000312240607100404

Kapoor, P. Provincializing whiteness: *We are all Calibans. Departures in Critical Qualitative Research, 8* (4), 16–22. DOI: https://doi.org/10.1525/dcqr.2019.8.4.16

Kim, H. (2018). The mutual constitution of social media use and status hierarchies in global organizing. *Management Communication Quarterly, 32,* 471–503. doi:10.1177/0893318918779135

Kirby, E., & Krone, K. (2002). "The policy exists but you can't really use it": Communication and the structuration of work-family policies. *Journal of Applied Communication Research, 30,* 50–77. doi:10.1080/00909880216577

Koschmann, M. A., Kuhn, T. R., & Pfarrer, M. D. (2012). A communicative framework of value in cross-sector partnerships. *Academy of Management Review, 37,* 332–354.

Krackhardt, D., & Hanson, J. (1993). Informal networks—The company behind the chart. *Harvard Business Review, 71*(4), 104–111.

Leonardi, P. M., & Rodriguez-Lluesma, C. (2013). Occupational stereotypes, perceived status differences, and intercultural communication in global organizations. *Communication Monographs, 80,* 478–502.

Levina, N., & Vaast, E. (2008). Innovating or doing as told? Status differences and overlapping boundaries in offshore collaboration. *MIS Quarterly, 32*, 307–332.

Lewis, L. K. (2019). *Organizational change: Creating change through strategic communication*. Hoboken, NJ: John Wiley & Sons.

Lewis, L. K., Hamel, S. A., & Richardson, B. K. (2001). Communicating change to nonprofit stakeholders: Models and predictors of implementers' approaches. *Management Communication Quarterly, 15*(5), 5–41. doi:10.1177/0893318901151001

Logan, N. (2011). The white leader prototype: A critical analysis of race in public relations. *Journal of Public Relations Research, 23*, 442–457. doi:10.1080/1062726X.2011.605974

March, J. G., & Simon, H. A. (1993). *Organizations* (2nd Ed.). Cambridge, MA: Blackwell.

McDonald, M. L., & Westphal, J. D. (2003). Getting by with the advice of their friends: CEO's advice networks and firms' strategic responses to poor performance. *Administrative Science Quarterly, 48*, 1–32. doi:10.2307/3556617

McPherson, M., Smith-Lovin, L., & Cook, J. M. (2001). Birds of a feather: Homophily in social networks. *Annual Review of Sociology, 27*, 415–444. doi:10.1146/annurev.soc.27.1.415

Metiu, A. (2006). Owning the code: Status closure in distributed groups. *Organization Science, 17*, 418–435.

Meyer, J. W., & Rowan, B. (1977). Institutionalized organizations: Formal structure as myth and ceremony. *Journal of Sociology, 83*, 340–363.

Monge, P. R., & Contractor, N. S. (2003). *Theories of communication networks*. New York: Oxford University Press.

Monge, P. R., & Eisenberg, E. M. (1987). Emergent communication networks. In F. M. Jablin, L. L. Putnam, K. H. Roberts, & L. W. Porter (Eds.), *Handbook of organizational communication: An interdisciplinary perspective* (pp. 304–342). Newbury Park, CA: Sage.

Mumby, D. K., & Putnam, L. L. (1992). The politics of emotion: A feminist reading of bounded rationality. *The Academy of Management Review, 17*, 465–486. doi:10.2307/258719

Nam, Y., & Barnett, G. A. (2011). Globalization of technology: Network analysis of global patents and trademarks. *Technological Forecasting & Social Change, 78*, 1471–1485. doi:10.1016/j.techfore.2011.06.005

Neeley, T. B. (2013). Language matters: Status loss and achieved status distinctions in global organizations. *Organization Science, 24*, 476–497.

Neeley, T. B., & Dumas, T. L. (2016). Unearned status gain: Evidence from a global language mandate. *Academy of Management Journal, 59*, 14–43.

Obama, M. (2018). *Becoming*. New York: Crown Publishing Group.

O'Leary, M. B., & Mortensen, M. (2010). Go (con)figure: Subgroups, imbalance, and isolates in geographically dispersed teams. *Organization Science, 21*, 115–131. doi:10.1287/orsc.1090.0434

Parker, P. S. (2001). African American women executives' leadership communication within dominant-culture organizations: (Re)conceptualizing notions of collaboration and instrumentality. *Management Communication Quarterly, 15*, 42–82. doi:10.1177/0893318901151002

Parker, P. S. (2005). *Race, gender, and leadership: Re-envisioning organizational leadership from the perspectives of African American women executives*. Mahwah, NJ: Lawrence Erlbaum Associates.

Parker, P. S., Holland, D., Dennison, J., Smith, S. H., & Jackson, M. (2018). Decolonizing the academy: Lessons from the Graduate Certificate in Participatory Research at The University of North Carolina at Chapel Hill. *Qualitative Inquiry, 24,* 464–477. doi:10.1177/1077800417729846

Perlmutter, H. V. (1969). The tortuous evolution of the multinational corporation. *Columbia Journal of World Business, 4,* 9–18.

Phillips, S. L., Dennison, S. T., & Davenport, M. A. (2016). High retention of minority and international faculty through a formal mentoring program. *To Improve the Academy, 35*(1), 153–179. doi:10.1002/tia2.20034

Reilly, C. (2018). The bigger picture: Behind millions in grants to drive policy and systems change on education. *Inside Philanthropy.* Retrieved from https://www.insidephilanthropy.com/home/2018/9/4/the-bigger-picture-behind-millions-in-grants-to-drive-policy-and-systems-change-on-education

Rodriguez, A., Dutta, M. J., & Desnoyers-Colas, E. F. (2019). *Departures in Critical Qualitative Research, 8* (4), 3–9. DOI: https://doi.org/10.1525/dcqr.2019.8.4.3

Shumate, M., & Contractor, N. S. (2014). Emergence of multidimensional social networks. In L. L. Putnam & D. K. Mumby (Eds.), *The SAGE handbook of organizational communication: Advances in theory, research, and methods* (3rd Ed., pp. 449–474). Thousand Oaks, CA: Sage.

Smith, J., Halgin, D., Kidwell, V., Labianca, G., Brass, D. J., & Borgatti, S. P. (2014). Power in politically charged networks. *Social Networks, 36,* 162–176. doi:10.1016/j.socnet.2013.04.007

Stevens, F. G., Plaut, V. C., & Sanchez-Burks, J. (2008). Unlocking the benefits of diversity: All-inclusive multiculturalism and positive organizational change. *The Journal of Applied Behavioral Science, 44*(1), 116–133. doi:10.1177/0021886308314460

Taylor, M., & Doerfel, M. L. (2003). Building inter organizational relationships that build nations. *Human Communication Research, 29,* 153–181. doi:10.1111/j.1468-2958.2003.tb00835.x

Ter Hoeven, C. L., Miller, V. D., Peper, B., & den Dulk, L. (2017). "The work must go on": The role of employee and managerial communication in the use of work–life policies. *Management Communication Quarterly, 31,* 194–229. doi:10.1177/0893318916684980

United States Equal Employment Opportunity Commission. Retrieved May 15, 2019, from https://www.eeoc.gov/

Wallerstein, I. (1974). *The modern world system.* New York: Academic Press.

Weick, K. E. (1993). The collapse of sensemaking in organizations: The Mann Gulch disaster. *Administrative Science Quarterly, 38,* 628–652.

Weinberg, F. J., & Lankau, M. J. (2011). Formal mentoring programs: A mentor-centric and longitudinal analysis. *Journal of Management, 37,* 1527–1557. doi:10.1177/0149206309349310

Wieland, S. M. B. (2011). Struggling to manage work as a part of everyday life: Complicating control, rethinking resistance, and contextualizing work/life studies. *Communication Monographs, 78,* 162–184.

Zoller, H. M. (2004). Dialogue as global issue management: Legitimizing corporate influence in the Transatlantic Business Dialogue. *Management Communication Quarterly, 18,* 204–240.

Part I
Bottom-Up Approaches

2 Stigma Communication and Power

Managing Inclusion and Exclusion in the Workplace

Rebecca J. Meisenbach and Darvelle Hutchins

Stigmatization is a key communicative process in the construction and under-mining of inclusion in organizing. Stigma itself originally denoted a physical mark (stigmata) on a person that clearly identified their status as the bearer of an undesirable characteristic. In contemporary scholarship, stigma no longer means a visible mark is always present, but it still represents an undesirable characteristic that has negative consequences for the bearer, including exclusion from aspects of organizational life. Stigma can be defined as an "attribute that is deeply discrediting and that reduces the bearer from a whole and usual person to a tainted, discounted one" (Goffman, 1963, p. 3). This reduction of a person's humanity runs counter to the goals of belonging, connection, and community that are desired outcomes of organizational life. At the same time, most understandings of organizations involve creating boundaries be-tween what is and is not an organization. In other words, organizational life typically creates both inclusion and exclusion. When exclusionary processes involve not only marking groups and their members as different from one another but also involve suggesting that any of those differences constitute an undesirable state that discounts members, stigma is at work.

Our focus in this chapter is on how stigma functions as a power-laden or-ganizing practice that contributes to processes of inclusion and exclusion in the workplace. We first introduce recent theorizing of and research on stigma, highlighting the presence of and opportunities for recognizing the role of com-munication and power in stigma's facilitation of inclusion and exclusion. Next, we discuss a range of stakeholders whose power-laden interests and experi-ences drive the construction, experience, and management of stigma. Finally, we discuss how a focus on power relations among these stakeholders points to research and practice to (re)organize stigmas and exclusion in the workplace.

Theorizing Stigma

At its core, the concept of stigma is concerned with the inclusion and exclusion of societal members. Scholars study the process by which dominant members of society build and maintain their dominance while members associated with stigmatized identities struggle to gain full societal acceptance (e.g., Benoit, Jansson, Smith, & Flagg, 2018; Brewis, SturtzSreetharan, & Wutich, 2018;

Corrigan, Druss, & Perlick, 2014; Hing, Russell, & Gainsbury, 2016). Alongside this broader work, some scholars highlight stigma as a communication process and outcome (e.g., Chang & Bazarova, 2016; Meisenbach, 2010; Smith, 2007; Zhu & Smith, 2016). Further, an extensive body of literature has focused on stigma strategies in the workplace (e.g., Adams, 2012; Ashforth & Kreiner, 1999; Ashforth, Kreiner, Clark, & Fugate, 2017).

Understanding how stigmatizing messages work throughout society is necessary to deconstruct powerful organizing patterns that inhibit the inclusion of marginalized and stigmatized individuals. Yet, very little stigma research has highlighted the power dynamics at play in stigmatization. Therefore, in this section, we discuss how existing research suggests that stigma is constructed, experienced, and managed, with an eye toward the role of power in how individuals are included and excluded in organizing.

When considering contemporary research on stigma, almost every scholar cites Goffman's (1963) work. He conceptualized stigma as a deeply discrediting mark that reduces the sense of the person from a holistic individual to one who is primarily defined by the stigmatizing characteristic. Furthermore, he stressed that "a language of relationships, not attributes, is really needed" (p. 3) to discuss stigmas. He was highlighting the contextual and communicative nature of the concept, laying groundwork for communication scholars who research stigma.

Goffman focused primarily on understanding how individuals cope with and manage experiences of being stigmatized as they interact with dominant members of society, labeled as "normals." He suggested that individuals experiencing stigma are denied full acceptance into society because they are associated with at least one of three types of attributes that society views as deeply discrediting. These three types of stigma attributes include physical stigma (deformities of the body), moral stigma (blemishes of individual character), and group or tribal stigma (undesirable race, nation, and religion group memberships). These stigma attributes serve as markers that create social disruption, redirecting a person's attention toward the discrediting mark, which, in turn, interferes in the communication between stigmatized and non-stigmatized individuals.

Considerations of privilege and power are mostly implied in Goffman's work rather than being explicitly tackled. However, he did explain that non-stigmatized individuals hold a higher degree of social privilege in comparison to people who have to navigate society as marked. Thus, unmarked individuals operate in a privileged position where they get to decide whether or not to discriminate against and/or alienate those who embody a stigma. He argued that given the power of dominant members of society who are able to create "us" versus "them" societal viewpoints, scholars who study stigma should study both the groups that stigmatize and those who feel stigmatized.

The second best known definition of stigma among communication researchers comes from Link and Phelan (2001) who suggested that stigma involves the co-occurrence of five elements: labeling, stereotyping, separation, status loss, and discrimination by individuals or groups who occupy a position of power. This framework has been used to guide a large body of empirical research on stigma and its relationships to other variables (e.g., Benoit et al., 2018; Rogers, Schneider, Gai, Gorday, & Joiner, 2018; Wagner, Kunkel, Asbury, & Soto, 2016). Link and Phelan and their colleagues have used the framework themselves to investigate health communication issues such as parent-child talk about mental health and stigma (Villatoro, DuPont-Reyes, Phelan, Painter, & Link, 2018) and whether presentations of online information about mental health and mental illness would reduce stigma toward individuals with schizophrenia or depression (Schomerus et al., 2016).

Key to our discussion is how Link and Phelan argued for understanding power as fluid and always at play throughout the stigmatization process. Specifically, because stigmas are formed by and survive through powerful societal groups, they argued that a discrediting mark is something that should be viewed as affixed upon an individual (through power-laden social interaction and perceptions) rather than as a marker a person comes into the world with or permanently acquires throughout life. For example, though a person is born with a particular skin tone that may designate one's race or ethnicity, any sense that race is stigmatizing is determined through power-laden communication and other material practices. They later developed a focus on stigma power to "refer to instances in which stigma processes achieve the aims of stigmatizers with respect to the exploitation, control or exclusion of others" (Link & Phelan, 2014, p. 24). Overall though, relatively few studies that have used Goffman's and Link and Phelan's frameworks address power in the stigmatization process. Thus, in the discussion that follows, we will discuss new potentials for considering the role of power as we analyze what current scholarship has offered about how stigmas are constructed, experienced, and managed in relation to organizational life.

How Stigma Is Constructed

First, many scholars have studied the construction of stigma. The best known communication work in this area is by Rachel Smith (e.g., 2007, 2012; Smith, Zhu, & Fink, 2017). In her Stigma Communication Theory (SCT) Smith (2007) defined stigma as a normalized and publicly shared image of the disgrace of certain people. Her model of stigma communication suggests stigma messages contain four specific types of content: *marks, labels, responsibility,* and *peril.* She first explained that a stigmatizing message may contain a *mark* or cue that categorizes an individual into a discredited group. Second, a message's content may include a *label* that is affixed on an individual and/or group in a way that brings attention to one's stigma. Third, a message may pinpoint the person(s) *responsible* for someone's placement in a stigmatized group. Finally, the content of a message may illustrate the *peril* or dangers associated with the stigma.

Smith (2007) also theorized how Goffman's normals will respond to a stigma message in ways that typically further promote and (re)create the stigma. She explained that stigma messages produce affective responses such as feelings of fear, anger, and disgust in ways that create a separation between members of a group who view themselves as normal and others who are marked through stigmatizing messages. For example, in a study on perceptions of infectious disease messages, Smith (2012) found that uninfected publics began to isolate themselves from individuals who were infected by a disease due to fear of negative outcomes. More recently, pulling from existing research on rumor transmission, Zhu and Smith (2016) have explored how and why individuals construct stigmas by sharing stigmatizing messages.

Building on Smith's conceptualization of the construction of stigma, Meisenbach (2010) argued that stigma messages depend on the contextual perceptions of both the message senders and receivers. She also sought to bring attention to the shifting nature of stigma construction based on social and material realities. The influence of these realities in her theorizing hints at but does not directly address the role of power in stigma construction.

Schneider and Remillard (2013) more directly considered the role of power in stigma construction. They analyzed how social inequality and exclusion are imbued in statements that can be characterized as caring statements about individuals experiencing homelessness, such that even these positive-seeming messages maintain and perpetuate stigmatizing conceptions of homelessness. They highlight the role of power, saying:

> stigma is both perpetuated by single individuals within lived contexts and enmeshed in the fabric of social relationships. Social interaction takes place in specific contexts of power and inequality, and it is through social interaction that power, inequality, and stigma are produced and reproduced.
>
> (p. 96)

In thinking about the construction of workplace stigma in particular, some of the most interesting research focuses attention on prostitution or sex work as a profession (e.g., Benoit et al., 2018; Blithe, Wolfe, & Mohr, 2019). Benoit et al. (2018) offered examples of how prostitution stigmas are constructed and maintained via macro, meso, and micro levels of discourse. For example, they suggested that laws against the practice of prostitution represent a stigmatizing macro-level societal discourse, while the everyday practices and policies of the U.S. justice system represent meso-level discourses of stigmatization. They concluded that stigma is the outcome of power struggles or group competition where one group seeks to have dominance over another group. Meanwhile, in their book about the experiences of sex workers in Nevada's legal brothels, Blithe et al. (2019) explored how sex work stigmas are still constructed even when the work itself is legal. Overall, much more research is needed on how workplace stigmas are constructed on multiple levels.

How People Experience Stigma

A second key area of stigma research in organizations addresses the experience of the stigmatized persons. Much of the research here focuses on health care organizations and health-related stigmas. For example, Kosenko, Rintamaki, Raney, and Maness (2013) offered a qualitative analysis of how transgender individuals report experiencing stigma as part of their interactions with health care professionals. They described experiences of mistreatment that coalesced around six themes: gender insensitivity, displays of discomfort, denied services, substandard care, verbal abuse, and forced care. Other work has centered on HIV/AIDS health care workers' experience of courtesy stigma (stigma experienced by an otherwise "normal" individual due to their work with and/or for stigmatized individuals) (Bachleda & El Menzhi, 2018).

Other research has focused specifically on stigmas experienced in particular jobs. Ashforth and Kreiner (1999) theorized about occupation-specific stigmas that they call dirty work. Dirty work encompasses physical, social, or moral taint in occupational roles that society views negatively because of their contaminating nature, whether directly related to one's tasks (e.g., garbage worker who handle trash) or indirectly related because of the people they interact with (e.g., the courtesy stigma of AIDS service workers who deal with stigmatized populations). Dirty work is a robust sub-area of research that has assessed how various populations experience and manage some form of occupational stigma (e.g., Ashforth & Kreiner, 2014a, 2014b; Baran, Rogelberg, & Clausen, 2016; Dick, 2005; Drew, Mills, & Gassaway, 2007; Tracy & Scott, 2006). More recently, Rivera (2015) has expanded dirty work literature by theorizing the distinct existence of emotional taint (undesirable emotional aspects/qualities associated with work). She analyzed how U.S. Border Patrol agents experience and make sense of work-related stigma, and she argued that they used their emotions to manage their occupational stigma and the experience of emotional taint.

One of the promising directions for work-related stigma research is on how people experience multiple intersecting stigmas. Remedios and Snyder (2015) argued that current stigma theories do not account for the experiences of people who are experiencing multiple forms of stigma and prejudice. Indeed, operationalizing and measuring intersecting stigmas is a difficult endeavor. Dougherty, Rick, and Moore (2017) qualitatively studied experiencing intersecting stigmas of unemployment and social class. In particular, they found that the upper class unemployed person was viewed as being so voluntarily, leading to a negative perception of them as enjoying unearned privilege, whereas the lower class unemployed person was seen as having lazily made bad choices. However, the upper class person experienced a minimized form of unemployment stigma that was countered by their social economic status, while their lower class counterpart experienced an amplified stigma.

Such findings about the role of social class connect to earlier research that highlighted the power-laden role of prestige in the management of occupational stigma. Tracy and Scott (2006) found that firefighters and correction officers experience stigmatization differently because firefighters enjoy a greater public perception of prestige than correction officers do. Similarly,

Ashforth et al. (2007) offered a low-prestige/high-prestige framework for understanding the degree to which occupations are considered dirty in relation to how prestigious publics perceive them to be. As an example, sex workers' stigma-related need to limit their public visibility also limits their abilities to advertise any transferable skills in pursuit of different work (Blithe et al., 2019). Thus, sex work stigma can disempower the women in terms of pursuing mobility and career changes.

Given that research on intersectionality originated with a focus on the experiences of Black women, it is particularly surprising that research on intersecting stigmas in organizational settings has barely addressed racial stigmas. Yet, individuals who often experience a stigmatized racial identity (e.g., Blacks/African Americans) are very likely to face intersecting stigmas because their racial identity is always visible and cannot be concealed. Thus, as we touch on different types of stigma in this chapter, we must consider the unique challenges of intersectional stigmas such as being Black and homeless, a Black prostitute, Black and disabled, etc. Furthermore, we call for research on intersectional stigma that addresses racial stigmas in the workplace and other organizations.

How People Manage Stigma

Perhaps the most robust area of workplace stigma research is on the management of stigma. Returning to the dirty work literature, Ashforth and Kreiner (1999) presented a two-process model to explain how people deal with occupational stigmas. In the first process, they explained that people deal with occupational stigma by reframing, recalibrating, and refocusing. *Reframing* involves a process of shifting one's perspective to recognize the positive aspects of the stigmatized part of their work; *recalibrating* is when a person adjusts the standards in how they evaluate their work; and finally, *refocusing* is done by focusing on non-stigmatized aspects of one's work. The second process addresses power dynamics more, if implicitly. Here, social weighting described a process whereby those who are stigmatized evaluate the societal members who are doing the stigmatizing. For instance, individuals who experience stigma may choose to condemn those who condemn them, support those who support them, distance themselves, and/or compare themselves in context to a more highly stigmatized group. These options are tied to perceptions of social status of the stigmatizer and stigmatized in a given interaction. In other words, whether a stigmatized person might choose to condemn their condemner or distance themselves from them is likely related to evaluations of each person's social power. In 2007, an updated typology emerged, stemming from a greater focus on individual level tactics including those available to upper level managers. This analysis of managers' talk about dirty work generated additional stigma management tactics, including confrontational and defensive tactics (Ashforth, Kreiner, Clark, & Fugate, 2007).

Building off of the dirty work literature and SCT (Smith, 2007), Meisenbach (2010) developed her Stigma Management Communication (SMC) model and theory, generating a comprehensive explanation and range of stigma management strategies individuals may employ when receiving a stigma message. She suggested that the attitudes a person takes on after receiving a stigmatizing message will determine which management strategy they employ. The categories of SMC strategies include accepting (e.g., passively accepting, apologizing, isolating oneself), avoiding (e.g., hiding/denying mark, distancing oneself from the stigma), evading responsibility (e.g., claiming provocation or defeasibility), reducing offensiveness (e.g., bolstering, refocusing, reframing), denying (e.g., providing evidence), and ignoring the stigma message/openly displaying the stigma as a form of challenge to the stigma message. Her model has been used to help understand stigmas related to both organizational and personal life, including those associated with burn survivors (Noltensmeyer & Meisenbach, 2016), family abuse (Brule & Eckstein, 2016), and security contractors (Brewis & Godfrey, 2018).

Other scholars have explored the power dynamics at play in managing organization-related stigma. For example, Jensen (2018) analyzed how individuals at a homeless shelter were using undignified humor to construct an empowering sense of dignity for residents. Perhaps the most in-depth discussion of power in organization-related stigma management stems from an analysis of interviews with 44 prisoners in Helsinki Prison in Finland (Toyoki & Brown, 2014). Their analysis discussed how prisoners' stigma management talk was both an effect of disciplinary power and an empowering enactment of personal agency. The authors concluded, "stigmatized identities are not appropriately regarded as passive, neutral, disinterested or impartial, or rendered in simplistic terms as 'functional/dysfunctional' or 'positive/negative', but are, rather, embedded in relations of, and suffused with, power." (p. 729). The sometimes deeply embedded relations of power also can be seen in a recent study of breastfeeding stigma in the workplace that noted the difficulties of resisting stigmas that are not verbally expressed (Zhuang et al., 2018). Additional research is needed on how the subtlety of unexpressed, yet present stigma limits a stigmatized individual's management options.

Moving forward, a useful framework for understanding the role and experience of power in relation to stigma and exclusion is Dougherty's (2011) notion of a web of power. When theorizing social class she offered: "Imagine social class as a web in which different strands represent different types and processes of power" (p. 82). We encourage scholars and practitioners to consider stigma in a similar way, such that stigma can be understood as a web, consisting of strands representing various power processes. This metaphor highlights the interconnected nature of multiple forms of power and stigma. An individual might be able to resist one strand of power (e.g., reporting a peer who is engaging in bullying behavior), but they may simultaneously or consequently find themselves "re-stuck" in a disempowering reputation as a tattletale and whistleblower. These strands of power are constantly being woven, destroyed, and rewoven by and around various organizational members and levels.

Stigma as a Web of Power Involving Many Stakeholders

Our analysis of stigma research has highlighted its connections and relevance for organizing, as well as whether and how scholars address the functioning of power around inclusion and exclusion. In this section, we take a closer and more practical look at how stigma functions in organizational settings. Specifically, we unpack the presence and implications of power in how key stakeholders engage in stigma management in ways that create both inclusion and exclusion in the workplace.

Employees as Stigma Stakeholders

Employees are clear stakeholders in stigma. Organizational workers are frequently marked by stigmatization processes, and they also help construct stigmas on an interpersonal level; that is, in Goffman's (1963) terms, sometimes employees are the stigmatized and sometimes they are the normals.

First, as individuals who are sometimes stigmatized in their organizational lives, employees have a strong interest in the construction and management of stigmas. Certainly, they are key participants in the management of stigma discussed earlier in this chapter, yet, employee voice is often not the most powerful in a stigmatizing interaction. Employees' various social category identities (e.g., race, class, gender, occupation) combined with their non-managerial status in the workplace weave a web of power that inhibits their abilities to conceal and manage stigmas.

However, sometimes employees enact some control over their stigmatization through the choice of whether, when, and where to disclose their association with a stigmatizing characteristic. Communication Privacy Management (CPM) theory offers a helpful framework for understanding how people with concealable stigmas negotiate disclosure decisions (Petronio, 2002). The theory offers five criteria regarding decision making about private information that center on ownership, privacy rules, and boundary turbulence. Individuals who have stigmas they view as private information must negotiate whether to reveal their deeply discrediting attribute. Recent research has applied CPM to organizational life and stigma, finding that stigma perceptions directly impacted individuals' willingness to disclose health information at work (Westerman, Currie-Mueller, Motto, & Curti, 2017).

Such findings are understandable given that consequences of disclosing or hiding a stigma are powerful. For example, employees may fear that any attempt to garner support or accommodation in the workplace through stigma disclosure may result in mistreatment (McCarthy, Haji, & Mackie, 1995).

Individuals conceal chronic illnesses in the workplace because they fear the stigma outcomes such as job loss they may experience if they disclose their potentially stigmatizing status (Butler & Modaff, 2016). Thus, it is not uncommon for these individuals to hide the stigmatizing characteristic in a variety of ways (Spradlin, 1998). However, the decision to not disclose does more than reduce the risk of stigmatization. It may also mean missing the opportunity to receive accommodations needed to help them perform their roles effectively (Clair, Beatty, & MacLean, 2005).

Thus far we have discussed how employees have a stake in stigma as an individual or member of a group being stigmatized; however, employees may also take on the role (intentionally or not) of being the stigmatizer. Building on the ideas covered in the section on constructing stigma, employees may promote stigmas and exclusionary practices in organizational settings through bullying. A central element of bullying is one person's intent to exert power and control over another person (Astrauskaite, Kern, & Notelaers, 2014; Lutgen-Sandvik & Tracy, 2012). Stigmatized individuals, who are often in vulnerable positions, become a target for name-calling and stigmatizing messages that result in feelings of helplessness and reduced productivity (Lutgen-Sandvik & Tracy, 2012). Thus, workplace bullying is concerned with systems of meaning and power differentials. From this perspective, new research highlighting the discursive web of power can clarify how organizational members can and do foster inclusion and avoid bullying related to the experience of stigma.

Managers as Stigma Stakeholders

Moving to a second set of key stakeholders in stigmatization, we now discuss how organizational leaders and managers embody powerful positions in organizational stigma processes. Though they may be individuals who experience and create stigma as individuals (as discussed above), they do so as someone with a higher level of organizational prestige and traditional authority attached to their position in the organizational hierarchy. Interestingly, some of the research on dirty work has focused on how the higher level managers manage the stigma rather than on how the individuals actually doing the stigmatized dirty work are managing it (e.g., Ashforth et al., 2007, 2017). We posit that this focus may be because managers have greater power than lower level employees, both to counter occupational stigmas and to speak with researchers and fill out surveys during their workday. In addition, managers are more directly held responsible for organizational productivity and effectiveness than lower level employees. This positionality and responsibility warrant distinct consideration of their role as stakeholders in stigma, inclusion, and exclusion in organizational settings.

One of the stigma management factors for organizational leaders is passivity. Passivity regarding stigma manifests in a lack of motivation to advocate for change in the status quo and its attendant, often hidden, exclusionary practices woven into an organization's web of power. In practice, managerial passivity about exclusionary practices often looks like business running as usual and well. Thus, organizational leaders will often perceive no need to change current practices. Unfortunately, managerial passivity is problematic in relation to issues of marginalization and stigma in an organization. Overlooking and/or choosing not to participate in enhancing inclusivity can reinforce existing values that permit or promote exclusion and stigma. The discussion (or lack thereof) of organizational values impacts how stigma is enacted in organizational settings (Bisel, 2017). Research has found that when leaders are willing to openly discuss ethical issues and decision making, employees are more likely to follow suit (Zanin, Bisel, & Adame, 2016). Conversely, when managers do not explicitly speak about moral issues, employees are likely to do the same, constituting a hierarchical moral mum effect (Bisel, Messersmith, & Kelley, 2012). This moral mum effect can maintain and reinforce the marginalization and exclusion of certain populations in organizations.

The underlying point is that through both their action and inaction, managers are powerful organizational members, setting standards of behavior and values that are central to exclusionary practices and beliefs. Those standards include how stigmas are (de)constructed through both their everyday communication behaviors and through the policies they have helped establish.

Human Relations Departments/the Organization as Stigma Stakeholders

The third key set of stakeholders in workplace stigma is the human resources (HR) department or organization itself. This stakeholder group represents a traditional seat of organizational authority and is typically responsible for managing personnel hires and policies. HR departments work to implement fair and legal policies and treatment of workers. They also want employees to feel a strong sense of identification and inclusion with the organization in contrast to other "lesser" organizations they wish to exclude from the field as competitors (e.g., Coke vs. Pepsi). Thus, their role is generally designed to avoid and eliminate exclusion inside the organization even as they may encourage employees to exclude those who work at other organizations. To the extent that an organization uses a negative form of what Burke (1969) called identification by antithesis (fostering identification among a group by focusing attention on a common enemy), the organization may be creating stigmas. Thus, the work of organizational leaders and HR departments may unintentionally foster some stigmas even as they seek to ameliorate other stigmas.

Another way that HR departments impact stigmas is through their interaction with ideal worker discourses that set powerful and exclusionary high expectations for what is normal in an organization (e.g., Meisenbach & Feldner, 2019). Organizational HR policies often assume that employees affected by organizational policies are the ideal worker, that is, a mentally and physically able-bodied, breadwinning, white, heterosexual male with a female wife and children. Mescher, Benschop, and Doorewaard (2010) suggested that ideal workers have "full-time availability, mobility, high qualifications, a strong work orientation and no responsibilities in life other than the ones required by the organization" (p. 24). Policies and standard practices often assume workers all fit this ideal such that those who violate the norm in any way will frequently find themselves in violation of company policies and expectations, potentially creating stigmatization. For example, organizations that set policies regulating bathroom breaks may stigmatize individuals with urinary and digestive issues and diseases. Breastfeeding mothers can face exclusion and stigma in their organizations as well (Turner & Norwood, 2013). Thus, a growing body of research analyzes how the powerful meso- and macro-level communication stemming from organizational policies and societal norms impacts the experience of inclusion and exclusion in the workplace. Overall, the organization and its policies should be viewed as powerful stakeholders in the construction and management of workplace stigmas.

(Re)organizing Power-laden Stigmas and Exclusion in the Workplace

In this chapter, we have explored how stigma and stigmatization are being researched as a power-laden communicative outcome and process. Much has been learned about how stigmas are constructed, experienced, and managed in ways that often foster negative outcomes for those affected. The webs of power that constitute stigma make eliminating stigmas challenging and connected to fleeting moments of success rather than the eradication of stigma. Widespread and more permanent alteration of a stigma perception involves a weaving together of power-laden communication from interpersonal, organizational, and societal stakeholders. In this section, we discuss some of the emerging avenues for weaving such webs.

Ally Communication

Returning again to Goffman's terminology, individuals may be either the stigmatized or the normal. Yet, Goffman (1963) also mentioned a third category of person, called "the wise." These "normal" individuals are accepted by the stigmatized persons as understanding of their experience. Goffman's wise persons can be usefully subdivided into active and passive supporters (Smith, 2012) and are worthy of consideration as allies whose communication helps manage stigmas. As an active supporter, an ally is understood as someone who has social power or privilege that they use to "stand against injustice directed at people who lack such privilege" (DeTurk, 2011, p. 570).

Stigmas and organizational exclusion will usually be perceived as an injustice and as such are ripe for consideration as a site of what Anderson (2019) and DeTurk (2011) are calling ally communication. DeTurk discussed how ally communication can take distinct forms at interpersonal, organizational, and societal levels. Organizations that seek to lessen exclusion and stigma in the workplace may wish to turn attention to fostering allyship among their membership at all three levels. For example, being confronted by a role model who can acknowledge someone's humanity while confronting them with their prejudice is one of several paths that DeTurk (2002) found led to someone adopting an identity as an ally. That ally in turn will be likely to engage in ally communication when they encounter stigmatizing messages directed toward the group or persons they feel allied with. The allies leverage their power and privilege on behalf of and in situations where another person with less relevant power and privilege is being stigmatized. Thus, we encourage more research and potential organizational trainings on ally communication.

Employee Resource Groups

Another current path for supporting those who are experiencing negative impacts from various stigmatizing identities is found in Employee Resource Groups (ERGs). Organizational leaders and HR departments have increasingly been supporting the development of ERGs to challenge organizational bias toward exclusionary ideal worker norms. Indeed, nearly 90% of Fortune 500 companies have ERGs (Employer Assistance and Research Network, n.d.). The origin of the ERG concept is attributed to organization affinity groups formed in the 1960s in response to increasing racial tensions in the United States (Douglas, 2008). Today ERGs focus on various social identities (e.g., gender, sexuality, and race/ethnicity), offering regular meetings and social events. The groups are officially acknowledged and sponsored by the organizations that host them, but they are typically self-run by employees who voluntarily choose to join the group.

The specific goals and outcomes of such groups are varied, but they are believed to provide benefits for both organizational members and the organization as a whole. Researchers have suggested that these groups are essential in creating inclusive workplace cultures and offer individuals important professional development opportunities (Kaplan, Sabin, Smaller-Swift, 2009). ERGs create these benefits by providing support for group members, generating new ideas, and advocating for group interests to the larger organization. However as Welbourne, Rolf, and Schlachter (2017) pointed out, very little research has empirically tested these suggested outcomes. We encourage scholars interested in pursuing such research to read their detailed set of propositions in need of additional or initial testing.

One of the interesting negative side effects of these groups, however, is that they too can create exclusion even as they seek to create space for inclusion of diverse interests and needs. Leaders should consider the potential for questions such as "why isn't there a group for X?" or "why can't I participate in this event?" from majority group members in their organizations. Some organizations have sought to quell this outcome by requiring that ERGs welcome any employee who wants to join (Kaplan et al., 2009). Thus, on at least one level, the choice surrounding inclusion and exclusion resides at the individual level. But that choice to join may harm the sense of community created by an ERG. Such dilemmas exemplify the web of power that constitutes stigma in organizations.

There are also issues of addressing an ERG's concerns throughout the organization, not just inside the groups' meetings. For example, one organization that the second author worked at offered a formal support group for alcoholics. However, the group existed within an organization that still served liquor at almost every organizing function. Every function generated struggles and the need to navigate the stigmas associated with both choosing and not choosing to drink in front of their colleagues. In summary, considering how the needs and interests of ERGs are met across the organization is a key to allowing such groups to ameliorate rather than exacerbate issues of exclusion.

Ethical Considerations

Throughout this chapter we have focused on exclusion via stigma as an undesirable situation in organizational life. However, some scholars (see Eckstein & Allen's, 2014, introduction to a special issue on stigma in *Communication Studies*) have questioned whether there are times when stigmatization is a good or desirable process and outcome. For example, drunk drivers and Nazis represent undesirable characteristics that cause harm in society. However, stigmatization, as defined in this chapter, involves the reduction of a full human being down to that undesirable and harmful characteristic. The few examples of research that suggest stigma may be beneficial tend to redefine stigma as not requiring the dehumanizing element that is central to Goffman's (1963) definition (e.g., Striley, 2014). Smith and Hughes (2014), in considering the issue of whether stigmas can ever be good, considered the case of infectious disease stigmas. They noted evidence that at an earlier point in human history, stigmatizing those with an infectious disease helped prevent the spread of infection. However, they argued that in modern society, stigmatization does not stop disease spread, has no other positive impacts, and in fact may lead to failures in public health and illness prevention.

A goal of organizational life can be understood as the reduction of harm, sometimes by eliminating harmful behaviors, such as bullying, but we join Smith and Hughes in advocating for doing so without reducing the humanity of the person engaging in the undesirable behavior. In other words, yes we believe that humans stigmatize other humans at times for behaviors that create measurable harm in the world, but there appear to be unintended negative consequences to stigmatizing these individuals that may outweigh any benefits. Additional research should investigate the relationships between stigmas and various social, organizational, and health outcomes concerning stigma conditions that are viewed as harmful to society. Whether stigmatizing a sexual harasser or terrorist organization member has more positive outcomes than negative ones is a question worth considering. These questions are fraught with ethical dilemmas and choices about the use of power. As scholars and humans in this modern society, we remain hopeful that there are ways to reduce and eliminate harm that do not require the reduction of anyone's humanity.

Conclusion

In this chapter we have offered an overview of the research on stigma as relevant to processes of inclusivity in the workplace. Within that framework we focused on how power can and should be more carefully considered in our stigma research and practices. In addition, we explored how three key stakeholders participate in these stigmatizing processes and practices. This chapter suggests new ways to study and transform how stigmatization is enacted by and impacts the organizational pursuit and realization of organizational inclusivity. Additional research is needed on the role of exclusionary stigmas in hiring and promotion procedures. We hope researchers will consider questions such as what are the consequences of a state or organization's policy regarding felony disclosures on applications? We also urge scholars to consider how Link and Phelan (2001) pointed out that writers who publish work on stigma are usually people who cannot recall an experience of being stigmatized (Link & Phelan, 2001). What are the consequences of workplace stigma research being conducted by the normals and the wise, versus the stigmatized persons themselves?

Overall, organizational inclusivity requires a conscious and ongoing effort from organizational stakeholders (employees, managers, and HR alike), at every level of the organizing process. Stigma is a power-laden phenomenon inherently connected to these processes, suggesting that theorizing on stigma and organizational exclusion/inclusion can mutually inform one another. Individuals at all levels of an organization and organizational policies discursively shift, convey, and are implicated in power dynamics that encourage and discourage exclusion of certain identity groups via stigmatization. We have argued that individuals, policies, and their organizations create and are created by a web of power that weaves and unweaves stigma. Greater understanding and investigation of the role of stigma in organizational life can transform and develop the inclusivity of organizational lives.

References

Adams, J. (2012). Cleaning up the dirty work: Professionalization and the management of stigma in the cosmetic surgery and tattoo industries. *Deviant Behavior, 33,* 149–167. doi:10.1080/01639625.2010.548297

Anderson, J. (2019). *Ally communication: Standing in discursive solidarity with people experiencing injustice.* Unpublished manuscript.

Ashforth, B. E., & Kreiner, G. E. (1999). "How can you do it?": Dirty work and the challenge of constructing a positive identity. *Academy of management Review, 24,* 413–434. doi:10.5465/amr.1999.2202129

Ashforth, B. E., & Kreiner, G. E. (2014a). Contextualizing dirty work: The neglected role of cultural, historical, and demographic context. *Journal of Management & Organization, 20*, 423–440. doi:10.1017/jmo.2014.38

Ashforth, B. E., & Kreiner, G. E. (2014b). Dirty work and dirtier work: Differences in countering physical, social, and moral stigma. *Management and Organization Review, 10*, 81–108. doi:10.1111/more.12044

Ashforth, B. E., Kreiner, G. E., Clark, M. A., & Fugate, M. (2007). Normalizing dirty work: Managerial tactics for countering occupational taint. *Academy of Management Journal, 50*, 149–174. doi:10.5465/AMJ.2007.24162092

Ashforth, B. E., Kreiner, G. E., Clark, M. A., & Fugate, M. (2017). Congruence work in stigmatized occupations: A managerial lens on employee fit with dirty work. *Journal of Organizational Behavior, 38*, 1260–1279. doi:10.1002/job.2201

Astrauskaite, M., Kern, R. M., & Notelaers, G. (2014). An individual psychology approach to underlying factors of workplace bullying. *The Journal of Individual Psychology, 70*(3), 220–244. doi:10.1353/jip.2014.0020

Bachleda, C. L., & El Menzhi, L. (2018). Reducing susceptibility to courtesy stigma. *Health Communication, 33*, 771781. doi:10.1080/10410236.2017.1312203

Baran, B. E., Rogelberg, S. G., & Clausen, T. (2016). Routinized killing of animals: Going beyond dirty work and prestige to understand the well-being of slaughterhouse workers. *Organization, 23*, 351–369. doi:10.1177/1350508416629456

Benoit, C., Jansson, S. M., Smith, M., & Flagg, J. (2018). Prostitution stigma and its effect on the working conditions, personal lives, and health of sex workers. *The Journal of Sex Research, 55*(4–5), 457–471. doi:10.1080/00224499.2017.1393652

Bisel, R. S. (2017). *Organizational moral learning: A communication approach.* New York, NY: Routledge.

Bisel, R. S., Messersmith, A. S., & Kelley, K. M. (2012). Supervisor-subordinate communication: Hierarchical mum effect meets organizational learning. *The Journal of Business Communication, 49*, 128–147. doi:10.1177/0021943612436972

Blithe, S. J., Wolfe, A. W., & Mohr, B. (2019). *Sex and stigma: Stories of everyday life in Nevada's legal brothels.* New York, NY: New York University Press.

Brewis, A., SturtzSreetharan, C., & Wutich, A. (2018). Obesity stigma as a globalizing health challenge. *Globalization and Health, 14*(1), 1–6. doi:10.1186/s12992-018-0337-x

Brewis, J., & Godfrey, R. (2018). 'Never call me a mercenary': Identity work, stigma management and the private security contractor. *Organization, 25*, 335–353. doi:10.1177/1350508417710830

Brule, N. J., & Eckstein, J. J. (2016). "Am I really a bad parent?": Adolescent-to-parent abuse (AtPA) identity and the stigma management communication (SMC) model. *Journal of Family Communication, 16*(3), 198–215. doi:10.1080/15267431.2016.1160908

Burke, K. (1969). *A rhetoric of motives.* Berkeley: University of California Press.

Butler, J. A., & Modaff, D. P. (2016). Motivations to disclose chronic illness in the workplace. *Qualitative Research Reports in Communication, 17*(1), 77–84. doi:10.1080/17459435.2016.1143387

Chang, P. F., & Bazarova, N. N. (2016). Managing stigma: Disclosure response communication patterns in pro-anorexic websites. *Health Communication, 31*(2), 217–229. doi:10.1080/10410236.2014.946218

Clair, J. A., Beatty, J. E., & MacLean, T. L. (2005). Out of sight but not out of mind: Managing invisible social identities in the workplace. *Academy of Management Review, 30*(1), 78–95. doi:10.2307/20159096

Corrigan, P. W., Druss, B. G., & Perlick, D. A. (2014). The impact of mental illness stigma on seeking and participating in mental health care. *Psychological Science in the Public Interest, 15*(2), 37–70. doi:10.1177/1529100614531398

DeTurk, S. (2002, February). *Openmindedness, ethnorelativism, and the decentering experience: A phenomenological investigation.* Paper presented at the Western States Communication Association, Long Beach, CA.

DeTurk, S. (2011). Allies in action: The communicative experiences of people who challenge social injustice on behalf of others. *Communication Quarterly, 59,* 569–590. doi:10.1080/01463373.2011.614209

Dick, P. (2005). Dirty work designations: How police officers account for their use of coercive force. *Human Relations, 58,* 1363–1390. doi:10.1177/0018726705060242

Dougherty, D. S. (2011). *The Reluctant Farmer: An exploration of work, social class and the production of food.* Leicester, UK: Troubadour Publishing.

Dougherty, D. S., Rick, J. M., & Moore, P. (2017). Unemployment and social class stigmas. *Journal of Applied Communication Research, 45,* 495–516. doi:10.1080/009 09882.2017.1382708

Douglas, P. H. (2008). Affinity groups: Catalyst for inclusive organizations. *Employment Relations Today, 34*(4), 11–18. doi:10.1002/ert.20171

Drew, S. K., Mills, M. B., & Gassaway, B. M. (2007). *Dirty work: The social construction of taint.* Waco, TX: Baylor University Press.

Eckstein, J., & Allen, M. (2014). Reclaiming stigma: Alternative explorations of the construct. *Communication Studies, 65,* 129–131. doi: 10.1080/10510974. 2014.893708

Employer Assistance and Resource Network (EARN). (n.d.) *A Toolkit for Establishing and Maintaining Successful Employee Resource Groups.* AskEarn.org. Retrieved from www.askearn.org/wp-content/uploads/docs/erg_toolkit.pdf.

Goffman, E. (1963). *Stigma: Notes on the management of spoiled identity.* Englewood Cliffs, NJ: Prentice Hall.

Hing, N., Russell, A. M., & Gainsbury, S. M. (2016). Unpacking the public stigma of problem gambling: The process of stigma creation and predictors of social distancing. *Journal of Behavioral Addictions, 5,* 448–456. doi:10.1556/2006.5.2016.057

Jensen, P. R. (2018). Undignified dignity: Using humor to manage the stigma of mental illness and homelessness. *Communication Quarterly, 66,* 20–37. doi:10.1080/ 01463373.2017.1325384

Kaplan, M. M., Sabin, E., & Smaller-Swift, S. (2009). *The Catalyst guide to employee resource groups. Volume 1: Introduction to ERGS.* Retrieved from https://www.catalyst. org/knowledge/catalyst-guide-employee-resource-groups-1-introduction-ergs

Kosenko, K., Rintamaki, L., Raney, S., & Maness, K. (2013). Transgender patient perceptions of stigma in health care contexts. *Medical Care, 51,* 819–822. doi:10.1097/MLR.0b013e31829fa90d

Link, B. G., & Phelan, J. C. (2001). Conceptualizing stigma. *Annual Review of Sociology, 27,* 363–385. doi:10.1146/annurev.soc.27.1.363

Link, B. G., & Phelan, J. (2014). Stigma power. *Social Science & Medicine, 103,* 24–32. doi:10.1016/j.socscimed.2013.07.035

Lutgen-Sandvik, P., & Tracy, S. J. (2012). Answering five key questions about workplace bullying: How communication scholarship provides thought leadership for transforming abuse at work. *Management Communication Quarterly, 26*(1), 3–47. doi:10.1177/0893318911414400

McCarthy, G. M., Haji, F. S., & Mackie, I. D. (1995). HIV-infected patients and dental care: Nondisclosure of HIV status and rejection for treatment. *Oral Surgery, Oral Medicine, Oral Pathology, Oral Radiology, and Endodontology, 80*(6), 655–659. doi:10.1016/S1079–2104(05)80246-X

Meisenbach, R. J. (2010). Stigma management communication: A theory and agenda for applied research on how individuals manage moments of stigmatized identity. *Journal of Applied Communication Research, 38*, 268–292. doi:10.1080/00909882.2010.490841

Meisenbach, R. J., & Feldner, S. B. (2019). Constructing the ideal worker identity: The rhetorical construction of discursive resources in *Undercover Boss*. *Western Journal of Communication*. Advance online publication. doi: 10.1080/10570314.2019.1566564

Mescher, S., Benschop, Y., & Doorewaard, H. (2010). Representations of work—life balance support. *Human Relations, 63*, 21–39. doi: 10.1177/0018726709349197

Noltensmeyer, C., & Meisenbach, R. J. (2016). Emerging patterns of stigma management communication strategies among burn survivors and their partners. *American Behavioral Scientist, 60*, 1378–1397. doi:10.1177/0002764216657384

Petronio, S. (2002). *Boundaries of privacy: Dialectics of disclosure*. Albany, NY: State University of New York Press.

Remedios, J. D., & Snyder, S. H. (2015). How women of color detect and respond to multiple forms of prejudice. *Sex Roles, 73*, 371–383. doi:10.1007/s11199-015-0453-5

Rivera, K. D. (2015). Emotional taint: Making sense of emotional dirty work at the U.S. border patrol. *Management Communication Quarterly, 29*, 198–228. doi:10.1177/0893318914554090

Rogers, M. L., Schneider, M. E., Gai, A. R., Gorday, J. Y., & Joiner, T. E. (2018). Evaluation of two web-based interventions in reducing the stigma of suicide. *Behaviour Research and Therapy, 109*, 49–55. doi:10.1016/j.brat.2018.08.001

Schneider, B., & Remillard, C. (2013). Caring about homelessness: How identity work maintains the stigma of homelessness. *Text & Talk, 33*, 95–112. doi:10.1515/text-2013-0005

Schomerus, G., Angermeyer, M. C., Baumeister, S. E., Stolzenburg, S., Link, B. G., & Phelan, J. C. (2016). An online intervention using information on the mental health-mental illness continuum to reduce stigma. *European Psychiatry, 32*, 21–27. doi:10.1016/j.eurpsy.2015.11.006

Smith, R. A. (2007). Language of the lost: An explication of stigma communication. *Communication Theory, 17*, 462–485. doi:10.1111/j.1468–2885.2007.00307.x

Smith, R. A. (2012). An experimental test of stigma communication content with a hypothetical infectious disease alert. *Communication Monographs, 79*, 522–538. doi:10.1080/03637751.2012.723811.

Smith, R. A. & Hughes, D. (2014). Infectious disease stigmas: Maladaptive in modern society, *Communication Studies, 65*, 132–138. doi: 10.1080/10510974.2013.851096

Smith, R. A., Zhu, X., & Fink, E. L. (2017). Understanding the effects of stigma messages: Danger appraisal and message judgments. *Health Communication*. Advance online publication. doi:10.1080/10410236.2017.1405487

Spradlin, A. (1998). The price of "passing": A lesbian perspective on authenticity in organizations. *Management Communication Quarterly, 11*, 598–605. doi:10.1177/0893318998114006

Striley, K. M. (2014). The stigma of excellence and the dialectic of (perceived) superiority and inferiority: Exploring intellectually gifted adolescents' experiences of stigma. *Communication Studies, 65*, 139–153. doi: 10.1080/10510974.2013.851726

Toyoki S., & Brown A. (2014). Stigma, identity and power: Managing stigmatized identities through discourse, *Human Relations, 67*, 715–37. doi:10.1177/0018726713503024

Tracy, S. J., & Scott, C. (2006). Sexuality, masculinity, and taint management among firefighters and correctional officers: Getting down and dirty with "America's heroes" and the "scum of law enforcement." *Management Communication Quarterly, 20*, 6–38. doi:10.1177/0893318906287898

Turner, P. K., & Norwood, K. (2013). Unbounded motherhood: Embodying a good working mother identity. *Management Communication Quarterly, 27*, 396–424. doi:10.1177/0893318913491461

Villatoro, A. P., DuPont-Reyes, M. J., Phelan, J. C., Painter, K., & Link, B. G. (2018). Parental recognition of preadolescent mental health problems: Does stigma matter? *Social Science & Medicine, 216*, 88–96. doi:10.1016/j.socscimed.2018.09.040

Wagner, P. E., Kunkel, A., Asbury, M. B., & Soto, F. (2016). Health (trans)gressions: Identity and stigma management in trans* healthcare support seeking. *Women & Language, 39*, 49–74.

Welbourne, T. M., Rolf, S., & Schlachter, S. (2017). The case for employee resource groups: A review and social identity theory-based research agenda, *Personnel Review, 46*, 1816–1834. doi:10.1108/PR-01-2016-0004

Westerman, C. Y. K., Currie-Mueller, J. L., Motto, J. S., & Curti, L. C. (2017). How supervisor relationships and protection rules affect employees' attempts to manage health information at work, *Health Communication, 32*, 1520–1528. doi: 10.1080/10410236.2016.1234538

Zanin, A. C., Bisel, R. S., & Adame, E. A. (2016). Supervisor moral talk contagion and trust in-supervisor: Mitigating the workplace moral mum effect. *Management Communication Quarterly, 30*, 147–163. doi:10.1177/0893318915619755

Zhu, X., & Smith, R. (2016). Advancing research on the spread of stigmatizing beliefs with insights from rumor transmission. *American Behavioral Scientist, 60*, 1342–1361. doi:10.1177/0002764216657382

Zhuang, J., Bresnahan, M., Zhu,Y., Yan, X., Bogdan-Lovis, E., Goldbort, J., & Haider, S. (2018). The impact of coworker support and stigma on breastfeeding after returning to work. *Journal of Applied Communication Research, 46*, 491–508. doi:10.1080/00909882.2018.1498981

3 Doing Engaged Scholarship

Inclusion Theory Meets Practice in the Context of a Peacebuilding Initiative in West Africa

Stacey L. Connaughton and Jennifer K. Ptacek

The Purdue Peace Project (PPP) is an engaged scholarship initiative. Engaged scholarship can be defined as "a collaborative form of inquiry in which academics and practitioners leverage their different perspectives and competencies to coproduce knowledge about a complex problem or phenomenon that exists under conditions of uncertainty found in the world" (Van de Ven & Johnson, 2006, p. 803). Since our beginning in 2012, we have benefitted greatly from the wisdom of engaged scholars before us who have pointed to the need to include collaborators, whether they be practitioners or—in our case—everyday citizens in conflict-prone regions of the world, in meaningful ways in peacebuilding efforts (Dempsey & Barge, 2014; Simpson & Seibold, 2008). The mission of the PPP is to convene a diverse group of local citizens from multiple sectors, creating a space in which they may come together to discuss issues that threaten to lead to political violence and develop and implement strategies to prevent such violence. Our collaborations with local citizens take place at the local, community level.

In all of our work to date, we seek to test our theory of change that if we bring together a group of *inclusive*, representative citizens from various stakeholder groups affected by, and affecting, a (potential) conflict they will develop, lead, and implement effective strategies to prevent political violence in their communities. Herein lie both opportunities and challenges. On the one hand, we have an opportunity to embrace inclusion, which we conceptualize and operationalize in multiple ways in our engaged scholarship, and to incorporate inclusion into peacebuilding practice (as others have also done; see Ellerby, 2013; Hudson, 2009; Parker, 2012). On the other hand, we are challenged in negotiating the political, cultural, and institutional constraints to practicing inclusivity. We suggest that these opportunities and challenges provide the foundation upon which we can think about, theorize about, and enhance our practices around inclusion.

PPP is a political violence prevention initiative that is locally driven (Connaughton & Berns, 2019; Connaughton, Kuang, & Yakova, 2017; *Locally Driven Peacebuilding*, 2015). For us, that means that we, as Western engaged scholars based at a large public university in the United States, spend a great deal of time in the local community learning about the context and relating with local citizens, help ready individuals/groups to want to partici-pate in dialogic sessions, help convene these individuals and define the prob-lem space they want to collaborate on to address, support the local peace committee that emerges, and collect data over time to help determine what is working and what is not working and why. Importantly, we do *not* impose a way of doing violence prevention or thinking about it onto local citizens. Local citizens in the local peace committees we help to convene willingly volunteer their time and expertise. They drive the peacebuilding efforts. We, as en-gaged scholars, journey with them. In so doing, we are attentive to cultivating relationships among diverse groups that are sustainable and productive while bringing communication theories and empirical work to bear when appro-priate. This is all part of what we have termed the Relationally Attentive Approach (RAA) to conducting engaged communication scholarship (Con-naughton et al., 2017).

As will be explained in greater detail below, this approach is not without challenges. One of these challenges relates to inclusion—which as noted above is a central component of our theory of change and our approach to peace-building. Yet we have learned through our engaged scholarship that inclusion is a term, and a set of practices, which is also often contested. Despite its con-testation and its challenges in practice, inclusion remains a central aspect of PPP's mission and our vision for the future. The purpose of this chapter is to (a) explain the ways in which inclusion is central to our theoretical motivation, and how we think about and do engaged communication scholarship (RAA, Connaughton, et al., 2017); (b) interrogate the challenges associated with do-ing inclusion in our peacebuilding practice; and (c) imagine a future in which inclusion genuinely is stitched through our patterns of peacebuilding practice and theorizing.

Inclusion: A Theoretical Motivation and How We Do Engaged Scholarship

Our Theoretical Motivation

The PPP believes the communicative is central to peacebuilding practice (Ellis, 2006; Norander & Harter, 2012). Whether we consider divisive dis-course between nation-states (Weidmann, 2015), media discourse that por-trays various groups in negative ways (Saeed, 2007; Van Dijk, 2015), or everyday talk that is inflammatory toward others often from groups other than one's own (Sue, 2010), communication plays a central role. In addition, when we consider that attempts to rectify tense relationships can be through public diplomacy (Cowan & Arsenault, 2008), social media campaigns (Shirky, 2011), and/or dialogue sessions (Kolb & Putnam, 2000), we also see the important role of the communicative in preventing and reducing violent conflict. Moreover, when measuring outcomes and impacts of peacebuilding efforts, we can look to the frequency of positive interactions among members of groups that once were at odds (Pavri, 2009), the renewed ways in which people talk about "others" who they once fought with (Broome & Collier, 2012), and the signing of peace accords that seek to end violent conflict (i.e., Colombia; Casey, 2016), the communicative is front and center. Indeed, as Don Ellis (2006) reminds us, the communicative is tied to transformations in conflict settings.

It is therefore understandable that when we, as the PPP, sought to build notions of inclusion into our peacebuilding approach that we would consider the relationship between the communicative, organizing, and inclusion. Here, we are not alone. Both those who have studied and done peacebuilding and those who have studied other social practices have written about the relationship between the communicative, organizing, and inclusion.

Inclusion is viewed from various contextual lenses, being studied in the workplace (e.g., Major, Terraschke, Major, & Setijadi, 2014), in interpersonal relationships (e.g., Aron, Aron, & Smollan, 1992), and in achieving social change (e.g., Sison, 2017). The definition of inclusion is also ranging. Inclusion can be defined as "an active process of change or integration, as well as an outcome, such as a feeling of belonging" and includes perceptions of fairness and respect as well as value and belonging (Deloitte, 2013, p. 12). Sison (2017) adds that social inclusion "aims to empower poor and marginalized people to take advantage of burgeoning global opportunities" and "ensures that people have a voice in decisions which affect their lives and that they enjoy equal access to markets, services and political, social and physical spaces" (p. 131). In organizational research, the concept of Inclusive Leadership seeks to achieve a mutually beneficial relationship by "doing things with people, rather than to people" through emphasizing respect, recognition, responsiveness, and responsibility for all members (Hollander, 2009, p. 3). This type of leadership not only includes followers' input and participation but encourages them to take part in the leadership process. Despite various definitions of inclusion, common components include fairness, participation, recognition, and being part of decision-making (Sison, 2017).

Prior literature has also focused on some issues in the practice of inclusion. A common consideration with inclusion is the differing needs of collaborators. For example, in engaged scholarship academics and practitioners may have different ideas and boundaries regarding who should or should not be included in the research (Simpson & Seibold, 2008). Additionally, in considering the voices of underrepresented groups, Deetz (2003) warns that we cannot assume one voice in a group represents the entire group, and that "[c]ertain lost 'voices' get expressed at the expense of others" (p. 426). Indeed, well-intentioned attempts at speaking for others in order to include them carry serious problems. This often happens when members of dominant groups communicate with one another about "others," resulting in silencing the un-included others (Buzzanell, 1994; Mohanty, 2003).

To avoid unintentionally silencing others, Alcoff (1991) suggests acknowledging our inability to transcend our own location or perspective when speaking for others, and that speaking on behalf of others may further exclude that person or group. Hence, true inclusion must be physical inclusion rather than merely representation by others. Academics and practitioners can address issues of inclusion throughout the research process by continuously visiting and discussing them (Simpson & Seibold, 2008). Further, Sison (2017) recommends self-reflexivity as a way to effectively practice cross-cultural communication, which "starts from a position of learning and cultural curiosity that acknowledges our limited knowledge rather than our assumptions of expertise" (p. 132). The PPP engages in these practices through our locally driven approach and by incorporating our own self-reflexive interviews and journaling both during and after conducting fieldwork. This also allows us to not only build upon existing literature but to acknowledge ways in which we have found some practices to be either useful or ineffective in our work, which we will discuss later.

For the PPP, the relationship between the communicative, organizing, and inclusion is borne out conceptually and operationally in four areas: (a) inclusion and leadership, (b) inclusion and dialogue, (c) inclusion and knowledge, and (d) inclusion and social change. The paragraphs that follow expand on each area in turn.

Inclusion and Leadership

The PPP is grounded in notions of leadership that see leadership as communicative (Fairhurst & Connaughton, 2014), emergent (Yoo & Alavi, 2004), and democratic (Hackman & Johnson, 2013). We go into our collaborations under the assumption that leaders are not exclusively those with official titles or positions of influence or power (i.e., government officials, heads of corporations). Perhaps they are. But perhaps not. Instead, we go into our collaborations anticipating that if given the space and sometimes the encouragement to do so, anyone regardless of their "station in life" can lead. This assumption is supported by notions of distributed leadership (Bennett, Harvey, Wise, & Woods, 2003; Spillane, Halverson, & Diamond, 2001) put into practice by the United States military among other organizing entities. If an individual believes in a mission or a cause and feels capable of contributing to it, he/she has the potential to emerge in certain situations as a leader and exhibit leadership. This leadership can take many forms depending on the individual's idea of leadership and what they feel comfortable doing. For example, someone may serve as the head of their small group even if they have never led before, or they may lead by example by showing other citizens how to live a peaceful life and work to resolve situations of conflict. As U.S.-based PPP members, we intentionally avoid assuming any leadership roles in our collaborations and instead encourage local citizens in the regions in which we work to select individuals from within the group and take on various leadership roles themselves.

This theoretical motivation is tied to our peacebuilding practice when we first consider a peacebuilding initiative and when we engage in ongoing relationships with collaborators to do it. For instance, when we are considering whether to begin a project, we seek out everyday citizens to express their views on what is causing violence and conflict in their community. We also include voices of local government officials in our information gathering efforts. But we seek purposely to include everyday citizens—men and women, young and mature. Their views are woven into other data points to help us understand what is happening on the ground. Then, after a project begins, rather than us, the engaged Western scholars, designating someone from the community as the leader of the local peace committee, we give the group space to determine who their group leader will be. Sometimes that leader shifts depending on the nature of a particular peacebuilding strategy. The local peace committee decides who leads; not the U.S.-based engaged researchers. Drawing from the academic literature on leadership that we do inspires us to see leadership in others, to try to create the conditions under which such leadership potential can be articulated and followed, and to celebrate everyday acts of leadership.

Inclusion and Dialogue

Another key feature of our peacebuilding work, and one which is of course also fundamentally communicative, is dialogue. Dialogue itself is communicative and is supported by other communicative orientations. Listening is one such orientation. As Kahane (2004) reminds us, when one really engages in dialogue, one privileges listening over speaking. One privileges relating to others over one's self. One seeks understanding as opposed to immediately persuading. We are aligned with and inspired by work that sees dialogue as tension-filled (Bakhtin, 1981, 2010; Deetz & Simpson, 2004), and transformative in its potential (Deetz, 1995).

The PPP convenes individuals from diverse stakeholder groups—many of whom have never spoken with each other before (either at an interpersonal level or group level) yet who have held long-standing opinions of "the other." We convene these individuals and create a space for dialogue to occur. Sometimes it does; sometimes despite our best attempts to ready individuals for these dialogic opportunities, it does not. We have found that dialogue is necessarily accompanied by difference. Those engaging in dialogue seek to embrace difference, not in a naïve way, but in a way that is productive in inspiring lasting change (i.e., enhanced relations among groups; the creation of a path forward). Dialogue is productive when multiple voices are heard and integrated. Yet dialogue is not easy. We provide examples and further detail below.

Inclusion and Knowledge

The PPP is inspired by postcolonial views on knowledge that disrupt dominant notions of how knowledge is produced and by whom (see Dutta, 2007; Parker, 2001). Like our postcolonial and subaltern colleagues we believe that those affected by, and affecting, violence have knowledge that can be brought to bear on finding sustainable solutions to said violence. We seek to include their knowledge in meaningful ways in our peacebuilding collaborations. That is, we do not seek to coopt it for our own personal use. Rather, we seek to elevate it, to make it visible to those who may render it invisible. Through our work, we take on the question: Whose knowledge gets to count in peacebuilding collaborations?

Although we as engaged scholars cannot escape our theoretical knowledge base that has accumulated over time in the academy, nor do we wish to escape it, we find ourselves not beginning interactions with local citizens with us summarizing our theoretical knowledge. We acknowledge that our identities as academics must be contemplated, as the communities we enter may view us as holding some power. Instead, our interactions with local citizens tend to begin by seeking out what they have found to be drivers of conflict, attempted solutions, etc. We certainly do not proceed naively; we triangulate and further research what individuals tell us. But we are willing to accept that we do not have the answers. Ours aims to be an inclusive approach to knowledge production.

Inclusion and Social Change

We are motivated by prior work in the Communication Activism (Frey, 1998; Frey & Palmer, 2017) and Communication for Social Change (Dutta, 2012; Papa, Singhal, & Papa, 2006) traditions that show us that everyday citizens can affect change. We adopt that principle wholeheartedly in our work, and through our work, we seek to proclaim it from the rooftops. Everyday citizens can affect social change.

To date, we have journeyed with everyday citizens as they have advocated for the speeding up of a judicial decision on a decades-long chieftaincy dispute in Ghana, helped to prevent violence associated with the Ebola virus and later presidential elections in Liberia, and helped prevent violence related to land disputes in Nigeria. We have witnessed their determination and resilience. We have seen and heard the positive impacts of their work, both on their local communities and on themselves.

That storyline seems straightforward. Yet how do these notions of inclusion get borne out in practice? Not so simply. Still, inclusion is an ideal we strive for in our peacebuilding practices.

Our Attempts at Inclusionary Practices

Inclusion is intimately tied to how we think about and do our engaged communication scholarship. The RAA (Connaughton et al., 2017) to doing engaged scholarship aims to foster a mindset of inclusion among all collaborators. We strive to include all affected groups within the areas in which we work. In doing so, we must constantly be aware of differing interests and positionalities between groups and members within groups and create space for all voices to be heard. This mindset is meant to be transformed into behavior that embraces and works within differences among local peace committee members and the U.S.-based team. An advantage of this mindset is that the local citizens are able to define the problems in their communities and find the best solutions themselves rather than having outsiders prescribe a solution to them. Yet we have found that political, cultural, and institutional constraints can challenge our best laid attempts at inclusionary practices. There are indeed consequences for leadership and collaborative decision-making when groups ascribe their own meaning to organizing principles, such as an occasional change in group leadership or even group conflicts, but also the benefit of each group finding their own unique solutions. We have found these challenges often strengthen the group and allow them to learn firsthand how to resolve issues. In the paragraphs that follow, we explain some of the strategies we use to practice inclusion. We also detail how we have found our local collaborators to respond to our attempts at inclusion, providing examples from our work to illustrate both the inclusionary strategies themselves and the challenges.

Our Strategies to Try to Be Inclusionary in Our Practice

In our efforts to practice inclusion within our work on the PPP, we employ four major strategies. These include (1) convening an inclusive group of stakeholders to engage in dialogue; (2) including local citizens in peacebuilding processes; (3) supporting local citizens' agency in defining peace and the priorities of our work; and (4) convincing them of our presence even from afar. These strategies have been built from existing research as well as our experiences and efforts to extend and develop the most effective ways of being inclusive in the contexts in which we work.

1   We try to convene an inclusive group of stakeholders to engage in dialogue.

Stakeholders include all affected members of the communities in which we work. For example, in our attempts to bridge conflicts between the pen-pen motorcycle taxi drivers and police officers in Liberia, we convened not only members from both of these groups but also local citizens such as youth, market people, and government workers because they too are affected by the conflict between pen-pen riders and police. This can be a challenge for many reasons. Citizens are often concerned about the ramifications for participating in this work. They may be afraid to be in the same room with certain people with whom they have had violent experiences previously or are in fear of being retaliated against. One way in which we combat these fears is through stressing an open and welcoming environment where citizens do not feel pressured to speak if they do not feel comfortable, or we can speak with them individually rather than in a

large group. Our local facilitators incorporate icebreakers, group activities, and entertainment such as music or sports to help them to feel more
relaxed and we have found that citizens open up and participate more
after engaging in these events. Some citizens are afraid to speak because
of gender or cultural constraints. One way that we overcame this issue
in Ghana was by separating stakeholders into separate focus groups of
people belonging to their own group. For instance, the market women felt
more comfortable speaking about their concerns of violence when they
were surrounded by only other market women. Sometimes citizens are
not convinced dialogue will do anything to change their lived reality. We
have encountered pushback because of this in many of our projects, and
although there are some who remain unwilling to participate because of
this, now that we have worked in some communities for several years we
have built a reputation of successfully resolving conflicts in these areas.
For example, a recent incident in Liberia where a police officer shot and
killed a pen-pen rider (in an incident unrelated to our work in Liberia)
was contained without resulting in violence from pen-pen riders because
the PPP-supported local peace committee at their own will stepped in
and reminded the pen-pen riders of the benefits of remaining peaceful.
Another common response when we try to convene stakeholders is that
they feel they should get paid to attend the meetings. However, certain
constraints do not always allow for monetary compensation. We overcome this constraint by planning enjoyable and meaningful experiences
for those who participate, in ways such as playing music and having dance
competitions, having peaceful marches through town, holding football
tournaments, and providing opportunities for them to share their stories
and experiences with us and each other. Citizens tell us they enjoy these
activities because they are able to make friends, take part in a fun event,
and feel respected and listened to.

2   We try to include local citizens in peacebuilding processes.

This principle and action is at the core of our efforts in achieving inclusion. It is important to listen to the needs and concerns of all people who
are affected. We believe that local citizens know more than we do about
the problems that affect their communities as well as how these issues may
best be resolved, so we approach them by listening instead of prescribing.
Citizens are often stunned that anyone would ask them to take part, so
this is commonly welcomed with a willingness to participate. A frequent
response that we get during interviews is that they appreciate us coming
to hear their stories. They tell us that it is not only therapeutic to be able
to share their experiences with others, but they are able to listen to others'
perspectives, which builds understanding between conflicting groups.
Further, groups are often able to brainstorm and arrive at solutions that
help them to change their behaviors and build peace among one another.
Sometimes, citizens' willingness to offer solutions takes time because they
are used to being told what to do by outsiders like us. They often expect

us to give direction, so we must continuously encourage them to speak up and share their experiences and ideas as well as create action plans on how to move forward. Another issue in bringing together local citizens is that they have difficulty logistically getting to a meeting, as many of them have jobs such as farming that they cannot leave during the day or they cannot find transportation to the meeting nor do they want to leave their livelihoods. We try to overcome this challenge by visiting during different days of the week and year on subsequent visits, and we travel to as many communities as possible so transportation will be easier for them. All meetings and activities are held deep within the communities themselves, ranging from busy marketplaces to police stations, community centers, and even citizens' yards.

3   We try to support local citizens' agency in defining peace and the priorities of our work.

It is important not to impose our own definitions of peace and ideas onto local citizens in order to avoid the problem of "speaking for others." For these communities to achieve peace we must understand how they conceptualize it. We do this by beginning many of our conversations with local citizens by asking them what peace means to them. For some, this means being able to find a job and earn a paycheck to support their family. For others, it means being able to go and vote without being threatened or harmed. Other citizens say peace means feeling that their children will be safe at home and they can sleep through the night without worrying about violence. We listen to the priorities of local citizens so that we may best support their needs for peace. However, sometimes there are challenges with them wanting to do things that we find ethically challenging, such as paying lawyers during a chieftaincy dispute in Ghana (see Connaughton et al., 2017). Although we value their ideas and needs, we also remain committed to the mission of the PPP and the institutions for which we work. Through open and respectful dialogue, we have been able to overcome these challenges by negotiating for solutions that are mutually acceptable. Similarly, sometimes the local citizens and peace committees want resources that we are not able to obtain or provide to them, such as office space, vehicles, or large equipment. Some solutions that we have found to be acceptable are finding community spaces to conduct activities, holding events close to where citizens live, and offering training to local peace committee members on how to do monitoring and evaluation. We also set a clear timeline of data collection and activities to avoid major problems that would prevent them from carrying out their peacebuilding work.

4   We try to convince them that we are "there" with them when we are in West Lafayette, Indiana, USA.

We have not forgotten them. We still feel part of the process. We try to ascertain whether inclusion is being practiced when we are not physically there with them. We do this by keeping in frequent contact, not only with our individual country directors through weekly Skype meetings, but with members of the local peace committees. One way we do this is by keeping in touch through social media. We also try to make sure that people are not being excluded that we do not know about. Therefore, we will talk to multiple different parties, such as market people, youth, and police officers. We check media and news stories in each of the countries weekly. When we do visit the local community, we travel into different parts of the communities and speak with various local citizens within each of the affected groups, and speak with them both individually and as a group. If we are not able to attend a particular event or activity, we make sure to ask for photos and videos of everything that happens.

Our Open Questions about Inclusion: Theoretically and Practically

As members of PPP, we are committed to continuing to think about, and practice, inclusion. We see it as a core value. We also have come to realize that inclusion is nestled within a socioeconomic, political, historically motivated reality that can constrain it. Thus, sometimes our value of inclusion can be only an ideal for us to aim for rather than something we can actually attain. Yet we continue to ponder theories of and empirical work on inclusion, communication, and organizing, and reflect on how it may inform our practice. We also listen to those with whom we work for insights into how to do so. As our theories and our practices talk with each other, they prompt several open questions about inclusion. These questions are:

1   *How can we generate the conditions for inclusive participation?* This is a question that researchers in the Communication discipline and beyond have wrestled with for years in political contexts (Albrecht, 2006; Cornwall & Coelho, 2007), small group contexts (Burkhalter, Gastil, & Kelshaw, 2002; Gastil, 1993), and beyond. In our work, the question becomes how can we create a communication climate where individuals feel as though they can be included and participate to the extent to which they desire? Here, we might integrate work on Psychologically Safe Communication Climate (PSCC; Gibson & Gibbs, 2006) from the organizational literature into work on dialogue among divergent groups. Like this research, we believe that something communicatively happens to foster or not foster the conditions for inclusive participation. At the same time, we note that researchers should consider the historical, material, and other kinds of salient factors that are likely influencing individuals' perceptions of whether or not conditions are ripe for inclusive participation.

2   *How do we determine who is still being silenced? Is it our place to intervene to try to ensure inclusion? Do we let cultural norms (gender, age) play out knowing that some voices may be silenced?* These questions are on our minds quite often. To be sure, the PPP approach locates agency primarily within the minds, talk,

and behaviors of locals who are affected by, and are affecting, violent conflict. Yet we are also journeying with and collaborating with them. If our approach centralizes inclusion, then one could argue we should care about voices that are silenced and try to act to un-silence them. Or do we? Is it our role to "ensure inclusion"? Are we being imperialistic to dictate inclusionary norms as we see them (as Western engaged scholars)? Moreover, Clair (1997) warns us about acting as a voice for marginalized people and encourages us to think about the media we use to represent marginalized individuals. Our goal is that through including the voices of all groups affected (at least attempting to), encouraging them to define what peace means to them, and by finding solutions themselves, we create the space in which local citizens can find and hear their own voice.

3   *How do our identities as Western engaged researchers influence inclusionary and exclusionary practices in our work?* We often reflect on how our various identities, specifically as Western engaged researchers, influence our perceptions of our work with collaborators and how we practice inclusion. We make it a point to frequently check our privileges and cultural differences while we are working in the field and interacting with others as well as when interpreting the responses of others. We acknowledge we can never fully understand their experiences and our attempts to describe and interpret their experiences will still be with the words and meanings established by our own culture (Winch, 1977). It is a constant learning process that teaches us cultural humility (Ross, 2010) as well as how to do better moving forward. We hope that by encouraging local citizens to use their own definitions of peace and their own solutions toward building peace, we are being as inclusive as possible.

4   *How can we be more inclusive in other aspects of our engaged scholarship?* In our authoring? Who should be speaking in our writings about PPP? How can we be more inclusive in our evaluations of our work? Some of the ways in which we have aimed to be more inclusive in this area are to bring in our country directors in the areas where we work to serve as co-authors, invite them to present work in certain arenas (i.e., the U.S. Institute of Peace), and to serve as reviewers of our writing. We still question how we can be more inclusive of others in these respects, as we acknowledge the importance of exploring the various meanings in communication when working in another culture (Philipsen, 2010).

Our Hope Moving Forward

To date, we have learned that inclusion is about (a) being physically present with others, (b) creating the space for diverse voices to be heard and for diverse peoples to act, and (c) doing alongside/with difference. In this regard, inclusion is epistemological and ontological. In other words, inclusion involves both the sharing of knowledge, beliefs, and methods for achieving peace as well as disrupting dominant forms of knowledge and knowledge production.

To be inclusive, we argue, necessitates that one must be willing to acknowledge and embrace (the production of) knowledge that is locally constituted and situated. Inclusion also suggests doing alongside/with different others and ways of doing and being. It involves being present with diverse human experiences and learning from/with one another, creating what is, and what is to be, together.

As we move forward with our engaged scholarship in peacebuilding, we seek to approach inclusion in another way—by including varied meta-theoretical and disciplinary commitments and voices and creating the space in which these diverse researchers work together. We believe that doing so will advance what is known about, and how to effectively do, peacebuilding. Imagine the following:

- Interpretivists and post-positivists working together to build a predictive model of the likelihood of violence before, during, and after a (PPP) intervention.
- Post-positivists and critical scholars working together on research that leads to meaningful change related to political violence prevention.
- Colleagues in STEM disciplines and Communication working together to help us think about peacebuilding as human-centered design.

These are not pipe dreams. They are examples of research already underway to help address the pressing social problem of political violence.

As Communication scholars, our responsibility in all of that is to take communication seriously (Burleson, 1992). This means putting the communicative front and center in our research and engaged practice, in our conversations with academics and practitioners, and using our communicative sensibilities to work together to prevent violence and better the human condition.

References

Albrecht, S. (2006). Whose voice is heard in online deliberation?: A study of participation and representation in political debates on the internet. *Information, Community and Society, 9*(1), 62–82.

Alcoff, L. (1991). The problem of speaking for others. *Cultural Critique, 20*, 5–32.

Aron, A., Aron, E. N., & Smollan, D. (1992). Inclusion of the other in the self scale and the structure of interpersonal closeness. *Journal of Personality and Social Psychology, 63*, 596–612. doi:10.1037==0022-3514.63.4.596

Bakhtin, M.M. (1981). *The dialogical imagination.* Edited by M. Holquist, trans. by C. Emerson and M. Holquist. Austin, TX: University of Texas Press.

Bakhtin, M. M. (2010). *The dialogic imagination: Four essays* (Vol. 1). Austin, TX: University of Texas Press.

Bennett, N., Harvey, J. A., Wise, C., & Woods, P. A. (2003). *Desk study review of distributed leadership.* Nottingham: National College for School Leadership.

Broome, B. J., & Collier, M. J. (2012). Culture, communication, and peacebuilding: A reflexive multi-dimensional contextual framework. *Journal of International and Intercultural Communication, 5,* 245–269. doi:10.1080/17513057.2012.716858

Burkhalter, S., Gastil, J., & Kelshaw, T. (2002). A conceptual definition and theoretical model of public deliberation in small face-to-face groups. *Communication Theory, 12*(4), 398–422.

Burleson, B. R. (1992). Taking communication seriously. *Communication Monographs, 59*(1), 79–86.

Buzzanell, P. M. (1994). Gaining a voice: Feminist organizational communication theorizing. *Management Communication Quarterly, 7,* 339–383.

Casey, N. (2016). Colombia signs peace agreement with FARC after 5 decades of war. *The New York Times.* Retrieved from https://www.nytimes.com/2016/09/27/world/americas/colombia-farc-peace-agreement.html

Clair, R. P. (1997). Organizing silence: Silence as voice and voice as silence in the narrative exploration of the Treaty of New Echota. *Western Journal of Communication, 61*(3), 315–337.

Connaughton, S. L., & Berns, J. (Eds., 2019). *Locally led peacebuilding: A closer look.* Lanham, MD: Rowman & Littlefield.

Connaughton, S. L., Kuang, K., & Yakova, L. (2017). Liberia's pen-pen riders: A case study of a locally-driven, dialogic approach to transformation, peacebuilding and social change. In T. G. Matyok and P. M. Kellett (Eds.), *Communication and conflict transformation: Local to global engagements* (pp. 71–91). Lanham, MD: Lexington Books.

Connaughton, S. L., Linabary, J. R., Krishna, A., Kuang, K., Anaele, A., Vibber, K. S., Yakova, L. & Jones, C. (2017). Explicating the relationally attentive approach to conducting engaged communication scholarship. *Journal of Applied Communication Research, 45*(5), 517–536. doi: 10.1080/00909882.2017.1382707

Cornwall, A., & Coelho, V. S. (Eds.). (2007). *Spaces for change?: The politics of citizen participation in new democratic arenas* (Vol. 4). London: Zed Books.

Cowan, G., & Arsenault, A. (2008). Moving from monologue to dialogue to collaboration: The three layers of public diplomacy. *The Annals of the American Academy of Political and Social Science, 616*(1), 10–30.

Deetz, S. (1995) *Transforming communication, transforming business: Building responsive and responsible workplaces.* Cresskill, NJ: Hampton Press.

Deetz, S. (2003). Reclaiming the legacy of the linguistic turn. *Organization, 10*(3), 421–429.

Deetz, S., & Simpson, J. (2004). Critical organizational dialogue. In R. Anderson, L. A. Baxter, & K. N. Cissna (Eds.), *Dialogue: Theorizing difference in communication studies* (pp. 141–158). London: Sage.

Deloitte. (2013). *Waiter, is that inclusion in my soup? A new recipe to improve business performance.* Retrieved from Sydney http://www2.deloitte.com/content/dam/Deloitte/au/Documents/human-capital/deloitte-au-hc-diversity-inclusion-soup-0513.pdf

Dempsey, S. E., & Barge, J. K. (2014). Engaged scholarship and democracy. In L. L. Putnam & D. K. Mumby (Eds.), *Handbook of organizational communication: Advances in theory, research, and methods* (pp. 665–688). Thousand Oaks, CA: Sage.

Dutta, M. J. (2007). Communicating about culture and health: Theorizing culture-centered and cultural sensitivity approaches. *Communication Theory, 17*(3), 304–328.

Dutta, M. J. (2012). *Voices of resistance: Communication and social change.* West Lafayette, IN: Purdue University Press.

Ellerby, K. (2013). (En)gendered security? The complexities of women's inclusion in peace processes. *International Interactions, 39*(4), 435–460. doi: 10.1080/03050629.2013.805130

Ellis, D. G. (2006). *Transforming conflict: Communication and ethnopolitical conflict.* Lanham, MD: Rowman & Littlefield Publishers.

Fairhurst, G. T., & Connaughton, S. L. (2014). Leadership: A communicative perspective. *Leadership, 10*(1), 7–35. doi: 10.1177/1742715013509396

Frey, L. R. (1998). Communication and social justice research: Truth, justice, and the applied communication way. *Journal of Applied Communication Research, 26,* 155–164. doi:10.1080/00909889809365499

Frey, L. R., & Palmer, D. L. (2017). Turning communication activism pedagogy teaching into communication activism pedagogy research. *Communication Education, 66*(3), 380–382.

Gastil, J. (1993). *Democracy in small groups: Participation, decision making, and communication.* Philadelphia, PA: New Society Publishers.

Gibson, C. B., & Gibbs, J. L. (2006). Unpacking the concept of virtuality: The effects of geographic dispersion, electronic dependence, dynamic structure, and national diversity on team innovation. *Administrative Science Quarterly, 51,* 451–495.

Hackman, M. Z., & Johnson, C. E. (2013). *Leadership: A communication perspective.* Long Grove, IL: Waveland Press.

Hollander, E. (2009). *Inclusive leadership: The essential leader-follower relationship.* New York: Routledge.

Hudson, H. (2009). Peacebuilding through a gender lens and the challenges of implementation in Rwanda and Côte d'Ivoire. *Security Studies, 18*(2), 287–318.

Kahane, A. (2004). *Solving tough problems: An open way of talking, listening, and creating new realities.* San Francisco, CA: Berrett-Koehler Publishers.

Kolb, D. M., & Putnam, L. L. (2000). Rethinking negotiation: Feminist views of communication and exchange. In P. M. Buzzanell (Ed.), *Rethinking organizational & managerial communication from feminist perspectives* (pp. 76–104). Thousand Oaks, CA: Sage.

Locally Driven Peacebuilding. (2015). A report prepared by the Purdue Peace Project, Catalyst for Peace, Concordis International, American Friends Services Committee, Peace Direct, Peace Initiative Network, Gesr Center for Development, and independent consultants. Retrieved from https://www.cla.purdue.edu/ppp/documents/LDPB%20Report%20Final.pdf

Major, G., Terraschke, A., Major, E., & Setijadi, C. (2014). Working it out: Migrants' perspectives of social inclusion in the workplace. *Australian Review of Applied Linguistics, 37*(3), 249–261.

Mohanty, C. T. (2003). *Feminism without borders: Decolonizing theory, practicing solidarity.* Durham, NC: Duke University Press.

Norander, S., & Harter, L. M. (2012). Reflexivity in practice: Challenges and potentials of transnational organizing. *Management Communication Quarterly, 26,* 74–105.

Papa, M.J., Singhal, A., & Papa, W. H. (2006). *Organizing for social change: A dialectic journey of theory and praxis*. London: Sage.

Parker, C. A. (2012). *Inclusion in peacebuilding education: Discussion of diversity and conflict as learning opportunities for immigrant students* (Doctoral dissertation, University of Toronto, Toronto, Ontario, Canada).

Parker, P. S. (2001). African American women executives' leadership communication within dominant-culture organizations: (Re) conceptualizing notions of collaboration and instrumentality. *Management Communication Quarterly, 15*, 42–82.

Pavri, T. (2009). Shall we talk? Communications during crises in the India-Pakistan conflict. *Round Table, 98*, 473–481. doi:1080/00358530903018079

Philipsen, G. (2010). Researching culture in contexts of social interaction: An ethnographic approach, a network of scholars, illustrative moves. In D. Carbaugh & P. M. Buzzanell (Eds.), *Distinctive qualities in communication research* (pp. 87–105). New York, NY: Routledge.

Ross, L. (2010). Notes from the field: Learning cultural humility through critical incidents and central challenges in community-based participatory research. *Journal of Community Practice, 18*, 315–335. doi:10.1080/10705422.2010.490161

Saeed, A. (2007). Media, racism and Islamophobia: The representation of Islam and Muslims in the media. *Sociology Compass, 1*, 443–462.

Shirky, C. (2011). The political power of social media: Technology, the public sphere, and political change. *Foreign Affairs, 90*, 28–41.

Simpson, J. L., & Seibold, D. R. (2008). Practical engagements and co-created research. *Journal of Applied Communication Research, 36*, 266–280. doi:10.1080/00909880802172285

Sison, M. D. (2017). Communicating across, within and between, cultures: Toward inclusion and social change. *Public Relations Review, 43*, 130–132. doi:10.1016/j.pubrev.2016.10.015

Spillane, J. P., Halverson, R., & Diamond, J. B. (2001). Investigating school leadership practice: A distributed perspective. *Educational Researcher, 30*(3), 23–28.

Sue, D. W. (2010). *Microaggressions in everyday life: Race, gender, and sexual orientation*. Hoboken, NJ: John Wiley & Sons.

Van de Ven, A. H., & Johnson, P. E. (2006). Knowledge for theory and practice. *Academy of Management Review, 31*, 802–821.

Van Dijk, T. A. (2015). *Racism and the press*. London: Routledge.

Weidmann, N. B. (2015). Communication networks and the transnational spread of ethnic conflict. *Journal of Peace Research, 52*, 285–296. doi:10.1177/0022343314554670

Winch, P. (1977). Understanding a primitive society. In F. R. Dallmayr & T. A. McCarthy (Eds.), *Understanding and social inquiry* (pp. 159–188). Notre Dame, IN: University of Notre Dame Press.

Yoo, Y., & Alavi, M. (2004). Emergent leadership in virtual teams: What do emergent leaders do? *Information and Organization, 14*, 27–58.

4 Rhizomatous Dialogue, Organizational Engagement, and Inclusion

Michael L. Kent and Nneka Logan

Rhizomes are one of the most virulent plants in existence. Some rhizomes can regenerate a new plant from shards as small as a thumbnail. Rhizomes that exist are more than 50,000 years old and cover more than a hundred acres of land. As a metaphor, a "rhizomatous dialogue" describes long-lived relationships of productivity and expansiveness. The rhizome, however, is not like the showy, arboreal, tree, that we often see talked about as representing "knowledge" or "stability"; rhizomes are subtler, with the most important action occurring below ground.

In many ways, the rhizome is a perfect metaphor for inclusion and exclusion in organizational communication. Most everyday organizational communication does not take place in the public view but in those private and group interactions that establish organizational culture, relationships, and ties and are the places where engagement takes place and where inclusion and exclusion are enacted. Additionally, in many organizations and countries, "public dialogue" is a mandated activity, with communicative interactions often treated as encounters with oppositional publics (Lane, 2014; Mahin, 2017), rather than as opportunities to build relationships. Mandated interactions are not about inclusion and are not rhizomatous.

We see inclusion and exclusion practiced in organizations every day, evidenced through the various contradictions and paradoxes of organizational life. On the one hand, organizational members are asked to work hard and give their all, while on the other hand, employees are told to keep their mouths shut and conform (cf. Steele and Redding, 1962; Stohl & Cheney, 2001; Watzlawick, Beavin, Jackson, 1967). As Stohl and Cheney suggest, "In the context of workplace democracy and employee participation ... certain efforts to promote democratic participation will tend toward undermining their desired outcomes." Thus, stakeholder and employee *inclusion* is what is called for, but *exclusion* is often what is enacted.

In order to unpack the issue of inclusion and exclusion more fully, this chapter will use the metaphor of the rhizome, and the concept of rhizomatous dialogue. This chapter is divided into four sections. The first section features a review of the literature and key concepts of rhizomatous dialogue. The second section focuses on organizational engagement. The third section describes how groupthink and other variables affect decision-making in ways that exclude more than include. The fourth section focuses on using a dialogical engagement-oriented communication approach in organizations to build stronger networks and encourage inclusion over exclusion. We conclude by reinforcing the usefulness of a rhizomatous, dialogic, engaged, communication approach to organizational communication. We first begin with an overview of rhizomatous dialogue.

Rhizomatous Dialogue in Organizational Settings

The concept of rhizomatous dialogue is integral to our argument about inclusion and exclusion. By its very nature, dialogue is an inclusive conversational ideal. As suggested above, the metaphor of the rhizome is a way for thinking about or understanding organizational relationship building in general. Metaphors influence how every person thinks and makes sense of the world: as safe, dangerous, a struggle, a duty, a gift, etc. As Kent and Lane (2017) explain:

> The rhizome metaphor for dialogic communication is apt because it accounts for the fact that the bulk of the theory is the hidden, un-public part: the hard work, risk, self-disclosure, and time, that go into relationships. Metaphors provide analogies to help us understand more-complicated issues.
>
> (p. 573)

Seeing dialogue as a conversational ideal is not new, but many, perhaps most organizations do not embrace the idea, instead treating dialogue as a technique or one-off strategy for obtaining information rather than building genuine relationships (cf. Lane, 2014; Mahin, 2017).

The concept of the rhizome as a metaphor comes from a quarter-century-old book by Deleuze and Guattari (1993), while the concept of the rhizomatous dialogue metaphor comes from a more recent article by Kent and Lane (2017). In both cases, the metaphor of the rhizome is intended as a way to think about language, communication, long-term relationships, interconnectedness, and the web of relationships.

In their chapter, Deleuze and Guattari contrast the rhizome with the arboreal tree metaphor. As Deleuze and Guattari explain, "Principles of connection and heterogeneity: any point of a rhizome can be connected to anything other, and must be. This is very different from the tree or root, which plots a point, fixes an order" (p. 7). Indeed, from an organizational communication standpoint, the tree represents a common, preexisting, hierarchical organizational structure. Trees are hierarchical, as the vertical physical structure implies. Leaves respond to the sun, roots respond to the need for water, etc. We enter into every preexisting organizational system already part of a hierarchy. "The arborescent system preexists the individual, who is integrated into it [or 'planted'] at an allotted place" (p. 16). A rhizomatous dialogue seeks to challenge that hierarchy and points to the value of understanding dialogue, engagement, and decision-making, more fully. Each concept is briefly reviewed next.

Dialogic Theory and Practice

The practice of dialogue as a strategy for decision-making, learning, research, and understanding goes back thousands of years to ancient Greece. The earliest treatments of dialogue can be attributed to philosophers like Socrates, Plato (1999a, 1999b), and Aristotle (cf. Plato's *Phaedrus* and *Gorgias* dialogues for example) who saw dialogue as part of a philosophical practice or method for discovering Truth. The modern revival of dialogue might be attributed to Martin Buber's (1923) influential text *I and Thou*, as well as a number of other dialogic scholars interested in activism (Freire, 1970), community engagement (Habermas, 1984), feminism (Noddings, 1984), identity (Laing, 1961), language (Bakhtin, 1975; Gadamer, 1975), therapy (Rogers, 1956), and many other areas (Anderson, Cissna, & Arnett, 1994). Buber, nominated for the Nobel Peace Prize in 1959, and recipient of numerous other awards, was one of the most influential philosophers of the 20th century, writing more than 50 books and articles over an almost 60-year-career as a political activist and philosopher (cf. Toledano, 2018; www.iep.utm.edu/buber/#H6).

In everyday practice, there are at least three distinct approaches to the study and practice of dialogue, and not everyone who studies or employs dialogue means the same thing. Among politicians, community groups, and various activist, non-profit, and for-profit, organizations, there is a sense of dialogue as tool for public debate (Habermas, 1984), community engagement (Lane, 2014; Mahin, 2017), and opinion sharing. Politicians speak of having a dialogue with the voters, and by this, they mean simply to talk about issues at town hall meetings or public venues. Rarely do they have their minds changed.

Conversely, literary approaches to dialogue treat texts hermeneutically, and assume that people can have "conversations" and create meaning through the authors or voices from the past (Bakhtin, 1975; Gadamer, 1975). As Capizzo (2018) explains, Bakhtin's "work positions dialogue as an ongoing part of human existence—as a way to understand our relationship to meaning, society, and ourselves" (p. 525).

Finally, in a third approach to dialogue, and the one of interest here, scholars and practitioners of dialogue take a Buberian approach, treating dialogue as a way to co-create meaning (Botan & Taylor, 2004), learn about and understand others, and create what Heath (2006) has called a "fully functioning society." Fully Functioning Society Theory (FFST) maintains that organizations can play a meaningful role in society by empowering stakeholders, publics, and others through ethical communication processes and practices that foster shared culture and meaning co-creation (cf. Heath, 2006; Kent & Taylor 1998, 2002; Lane & Kent, 2018; Pearson, 1989; Theunissen & Wan Noordin, 2012); FFST is about the *inclusion* of employees, relevant parties, and other groups, rather than the tacit exclusion or deception that many organizations practice (Lane, 2014; Mahin, 2017). Ultimately, the commitment to a dialogic approach to organizational communication rests with the organization and its communication professionals.

Dialogue is a relational orientation. A commitment. Dialogue is an approach to organizational communication that is focused on long-term relationships and building connections with members of the organization that are enduring rather than facile. Dialogue, however, is not some new aged relational approach that asks everyone to become "BFFs" or sing *Kumbaya*. Dialogic interactions are serious and structured; rule guided but not rule bound; and based on genuine interpersonal interactions involving self-disclosure, risk, trust, empathy, and open and ethical communication. Dialogue embraces the challenges and the opportunities of inclusion.

A Rhizomatous Dialogue

As mentioned previously, a rhizome metaphor represents what might be thought of as a flat hierarchy. The rhizome does not privilege power, or organizational tenure, or perceived expertise, etc., just patience, having a long-term outlook, perseverance, and taking advantage of opportunities when they arise. The everyday mundane organizational activities, and the activities that build relationships rather than reputations, are the things that rhizomatous dialogue is based on. According to Kent and Lane (2017):

> Ontologically, dialogue is a world of lived experience and relational trust, informed by the actions of others, and past interactions and experiences. Although dialogue is never easy, understanding dialogue as process of relational interaction rather than a problem solving or strategic tool leads to an understanding and treatment of dialogue as an ethically positive activity.
>
> (p. 574)

The idea of the rhizomatous dialogue, then, is that communication professionals will recognize that the capacity for organizations to grow and thrive is contingent on a continuous flow of new and novel information, as well as the ability to take advantage of the relational possibilities afforded through technological advancements. A rhizomatous dialogic approach also helps communication professionals to realize that the well-being of their organization is enhanced by its ability to undertake the hard work, risk and vulnerability that goes into building those authentic, long-lived relationships of productivity and expansiveness that dialogic communication calls for. The next concept, one that has also been tied closely to dialogue and inclusion, is the concept of engagement.

Engagement in Organizational Settings

The importance of the concept of engagement in communication at this time can be seen in the newly published *Handbook of Engagement* by Johnston and Taylor (2018). Like dialogue, engagement is rooted in inclusion.

Engagement initially appeared in the management literature as a way to account for behavior in the workplace. Employees were characterized as engaged when they were able to incorporate and express their personal selves "physically, cognitively, and emotionally" (Kahn, 1990, p. 694) in the workplace and disengaged when they were withdrawn or defensive while performing their roles. Engagement later appeared in the public relations literature as a form of cognitive involvement with campaigns (Johnston, 2014). The rise of engagement as a subject of interest to communication scholars in the latter part of the 20th century coincided with a shift away from conceptualizing communication as information transmission and a move toward more collaborative, deliberative, democratic, and participatory communication processes concerned about community agency as well as organizational effectiveness (Heath, 2018). Despite wide popularity, little consistent agreement exists about what engagement really is or means (Taylor & Kent, 2014). Apart from an implied sense of inclusion, our sense of engagement varies widely.

For example, a brief etymological summary from Theunissen (2018) explained how the term "engage" was associated with challenge and battle during medieval times and has since evolved to more mundane connotations. Heath (2018) emphasized the potential for engagement to positively impact individuals, organizations, and society, asserting that engagement can contribute to a fully functioning society. Focusing on its psychological dimensions, Johnston (2018) defined engagement as, "a dynamic multidimensional relational concept featuring psychological and behavioral attributes of connection, interaction, participation, and involvement, designed to achieve or elicit an outcome at individual, organization or social levels" (p. 19). Finally, Doerfel (2018), taking an interorganizational network approach, described engagement as involving "simultaneous networks of diverse relationships that are not necessarily centralized around one focal organization" (p. 235).

Engagement is characterized here as linkages between interdependent partners who recognize their relationships are embedded within larger networks of individuals, groups, or organizations in society that may be involved in various states of cooperation or competition. Engagement implies inclusion. One cannot engage with individuals or groups that have been excluded. In our postmodern, increasingly fragmented world, a focus on engagement seems to indicate a desire to bring people together in meaningful, ethical, discursive interactions. A shift toward engagement also seems to recognize "several minds are intellectually and ethically better than one" (Heath, 2018, p. 40) and that shared meanings should not be unduly influenced by unequal power dynamics. However, engagement is also often rooted in power relations.

The power that organizations, particularly corporations and governments, have amassed over the course of the 20th and 21st centuries has shaped the study of engagement. Thus, engagement has typically been conceptualized from the point of the organization and too often valued merely as a tool to accomplish organizational goals (Lane & Kent, 2018). As Lane and Kent (2018) have explained, organizational aims are often prioritized over the interests of others within engagement contexts. Engagement then becomes something done to another, rather than an act of inclusion. Yet engagement requires inclusion in the same way "unconditional positive regard for the other" is a requirement of dialogue. Lane and Kent explain:

> Traditionally organizations have been positioned as taking an instrumental or functionalist perspective on their stakeholders. Stakeholders are regarded as a resource to be managed and utilized to help organizations achieve their predetermined aims—aims that have been created by organizations to benefit organizations.
>
> (p. 67)

However, the prevalence of organizational primacy in the engagement literature should not suggest that achieving organizational goals is the only significant priority. Indeed, a key feature of engagement is recognizing the interdependencies between individuals, organizations, and society so that engagement can foster mutual benefit.

Nevertheless, an awareness of the organizational bias traditionally prevalent in engagement literature highlights the need for the kind of more nuanced approach offered by Lane and Kent (2018). They maintain that although accomplishing organizational goals is important, it should not be done at the expense of stakeholders, by instrumentalizing people and situating them as mere means to organizational ends.

Just as many scholars of engagement find at least tentative agreement that organization–public power dynamics require monitoring and management to ensure fairness in interactions is a goal if not a reality, there is also a sense that meaningful engagement requires meaningful communication—and a particular kind of communication at that. Dialogue is recognized as an indispensable aspect of engagement for many reasons (Taylor & Kent, 2014), including how it treats the issue of power. In fact, "Dialogue is considered one of the most ethical forms of communication because it serves to mitigate power relationships, values individual dignity and self-worth, and tries to involve participants in conversation and decision-making" (p. 388).

Dialogic Engagement

In the 1990s, the organizational literature recognized a relationship between dialogue and engagement (Lane & Kent, 2018). The concept of engagement emerged from Kent and Taylor's (2002) principle of propinquity. Propinquity refers to when organizations involve publics about matters that influence those publics and in turn, the publics are willing to articulate their needs to the organizations. Out of this principle, engagement is "an acknowledgement that interactants are willing to give their whole selves to encounters. Engagement assumes accessibility, presentness, and a willingness to interact" (Taylor & Kent, 2014, p. 387).

Dialogue and engagement both direct attention to the role communication can play in enhancing relationships. They focus on authenticity in interactions so that trust can be created and sustained. Dialogue and engagement both emphasize a commitment to the communicative exchange, demonstrate a dedication to inclusivity, and uphold the importance of arriving at shared or negotiated goals. Dialogic interaction when filtered through the lens of engagement theory culminates in an overlapping space where organizations, managers, employees, stakeholders, and publics participate in dialogue grounded in the principles of engagement.

As Lane and Kent (2018) summarized,

> Dialogue within engagement requires turn-taking, or multiple iterations of two-way communication between relationally linked participants: in other words, both the organization and stakeholders send, receive, *and respond* to communication. This iterative, responsive, two-way communication takes place within preexisting relationships, or when participants are working to build relationships.
>
> (p. 66)

Dialogic engagement encourages the thoughts and voices of multiple individuals and groups to join the table of collaborative decision-making and it emphasizes mutual benefits. In doing so, dialogic engagement, grounded in the principles of the rhizome facilitates respectful, principled, contestation and deliberation. Dialogic engagement counters the comfort of arriving at easy, expedient conclusions backed by likeminded others that characterize a lot of organizational decision-making. Unengaged and exclusionary decision-making is captured by the concept of groupthink and is exhibited in how organizations choose to deal with diversity, equality, and inclusion/exclusion, discussed next.

Groupthink, Organizational Relationships, and Decision-Making

Groupthink is an important concept given the emphasis on exclusion and inclusion inherent in its practice. Groupthink stands in stark contrast to the concepts of rhizomatous dialogue and engagement. The concept of groupthink comes from the work of Irving Janis (1982), a Yale University psychology professor, who described groupthink as "a mode of thinking that people engage in when they are deeply involved in a cohesive in-group, [and] when the members' strivings for unanimity override their motivation to realistically appraise alternative courses of action" (p. 9). Groupthink, then, is essentially the opposite of rhizomatous dialogue (see Table 4.1 below).

Table 4.1 Groupthink vs. Rhizomatous Dialogue

Concept	Groupthink	Rhizomatous Dialogue
Inclusion	We know what is best and do not need the help or advice of outsiders.	Bigger networks and broader coalitions are better. Bring in everyone who matters.
Exclusion	Outsiders are not to be trusted. Insiders should not question the will of the group.	No one is excluded, except those who choose to be. Trust is the default response rather than fear.
Trust	Trust no one who is not a member.	Dialogue requires trust, and risk, but trust is earned not assumed, and understanding is ultimately more important.

Lack of trust and suspicion is the default position for many organizational members. Groupthink hinders critical thinking and effective decision-making because remaining loyal to the group by avoiding controversial or alternative perspectives, refusing to question dubious choices, and protecting group decisions—regardless of potential negative outcomes—is prioritized above making the best decision and serving the interests of all relevant organizational members and publics. Indeed, in groupthink, the "best decision" is essentially defined as whatever the group has decided.

One important consideration is that groupthink is not an intentional endeavor. Rather it arises out of positive relationships between people with strong ties, and great respect for, one another. This sense of solidarity forms a veil through which decisions are filtered in ways that reinforce the solidarity of the group instead of strengthening the effectiveness of its decision-making. In many ways, dialogue is similar. In dialogue, strong relationships may be formed and increased trust and respect inevitably develops. By contrast, however, dialogue is also about safeguarding the integrity of the communication process, rather than allowing our relationships to cloud the process.

Groupthink is among the most well-known theories in the behavioral sciences (Turner & Pratkanis, 1998), and yet organizations and individuals continue to fall victim to it because they do not want to be questioned or asked to consider possibilities that are outside of their own personal belief system, or not personally desirable. As Hill (2018), writing in the *Financial Times*, explained,

Groupthink still cripples corporate boards, leads politicians into military misadventures, and threatens economic stability. It has been blamed for the ill-judged invasion and occupation of Iraq, the Volkswagen emissions scandal (among many other corporate calamities), failures to forecast the financial crisis and even the fragile governance of Elon Musk's carmaker Telsa.

(¶3)

Groupthink is especially problematic because of its capacity to foster unwarranted inclusion and exclusion of both people and ideas. As suggested above in Table 4.1, and as Janis (1982) describes the consequences, groupthink involves

> The tendency of groups to develop stereotyped images that dehumanize out-groups against whom they are engaged in competitive struggles and the tendency for the collective judgements arising out of group discussions to become polarized ...
>
> (p. 5)

In organizational contexts, groupthink has often led to exclusion along race and gender lines. Edwards (2015), focusing on race and ethnicity in her exhaustive study of the UK public relations industry, used Bourdieu (1991, 2000) to describe how white public relations practitioners are inculcated into hiring and promoting people who look, sound, and behave as they do, reproducing a habitus of whiteness. Similarly, Nkomo (1992) described how race was excluded from the field of organizational studies, which led it to develop with a presumption of race neutrality, which ultimately had the effect of reinforcing traditional racial hierarchies.

Exclusion in gender contexts is also clear. For example, there were only 24 women CEOs of Fortune 500 companies in 2018 and this represents a 25% decline from the previous year (Zarya, 2018). At the same time while "women comprise nearly 75% of the jobs in the public relations industry, women still only occupy approximately 20% of the senior leadership positions" (Place and Vardeman-Winter, 2018, p. 175). A cursory look at everyday organizational life reveals how inclusion exists alongside exclusion with no shortage of women in service and support roles, but a dearth of women in top management and leadership roles.

As Ashcraft (2004), surmised in her study of the relationship between gender, discourse and organizations, "Organization appears as a key site where differences become manifest and consequential" (p. 277). From a broader perspective, Allen (2011) described how a variety of social identity factors such as gender, race, class, sexuality, ability, and age played out in organizational contexts in ways that reinforced the power of historically dominant groups, and resulting in the subordination and exclusion of traditionally marginalized groups.

Too often, though, organizations attempt to remedy exclusion through tokenism, or merely symbolic efforts, that appear to improve diversity and inclusion without achieving any meaningful change. This leaves underrepresented groups as well as their majority counterparts frustrated and confused about the organization's intentions. This exclusionary deficiency could be remedied by a rhizomatous dialogic engagement approach because it focuses on building long-term relationships with underrepresented groups, valuing their dignity, supporting their self-worth, engaging them in conversations, and welcoming them as equals to the decision-making table. A rhizomatous dialogic engagement approach to inclusion stands in stark opposition to the photo-op tokenism that has become the "diversity" norm in some organizations.

In addition to social identity factors, processes of inclusion and exclusion also occur along departmental lines in organizational contexts. For example, deep divisions can exist among communication, marketing, sales, human re- sources, legal, and operations departments among staff who all compete for limited resources, such as budgets, office space, employees, and face-time with leadership. Organizational divisions may prevent coworkers from sharing key information that affects themselves, other stakeholders, and the organization. Significant gaps exist between members of the "C-suite" and rank and file staff employees that need to be bridged. Additionally, divisions between or- ganizations and their various external stakeholder groups such as the media, government, and communities exist—all of which can contribute to an unpro- ductive "us versus them" mentality in organizations.

This identification by antithesis as Burke called it (1969)—or groupthink to use Janis' (1982) formulation—where members of an organization see out- siders as threats and where members of an organization see themselves as the one pure people is a kind of bifurcation fallacy. A delusion shared by people on both sides of an issue. As Freire (1970) argues:

> [D]ialogue cannot exist without humility ... Dialogue, as the encoun- ter of [wo]men addressed to the common task of learning and acting, is broken if the parties (or one of them) lack humility. How can I dialogue if I always project ignorance onto others and never perceive my own? ... How can I dialogue if I consider myself a member of the in-group of "pure" [wo]men, the owners of truth and knowledge ...?
>
> (p. 71)

The issue of dialogic exclusion, then, is central to our understanding of how dialogue can be used for organizationally inclusive purposes. Organizational communicators need to genuinely engage organizational members and key stakeholders in decisions affecting the organization and the community (to avoid groupthink and other errors), and to genuinely understand the beliefs and values of others (co-creation and building a "Fully Functioning Society").

As Burke (1969) suggests of identification, identification implies both in- clusion and exclusion. Exclusion and inclusion are subtle concepts. On the one hand, the inclusion of a person or group signals the necessary exclusion of other persons and groups. Communicators can play an important role by leading their organizations to navigate these complex processes of inclusion and exclusion in ways that contribute to a more fully functioning society.

Processes of inclusion and exclusion that reinforce unequal relations of power serve as obstacles to developing a diversity of people, ideas, and inno- vations within our organizations, and they hinder relations with our external constituents. Unethical processes of inclusion and exclusion create conditions where only the in-group is invited to the decision-making table, and others who might have something meaningful to contribute are excluded—not on the substance of their thoughts but on the basis of their difference. Thus, exclusion and groupthink runs contrary to the principles of rhizomatous dialogic engagement, which situates difference (culturally, intellectually, socially, biologically) as a welcome part of meaningful communication.

Enacting Rhizomatous Dialogic Engagement Effectively

Almost a century ago, Ivy Ledbetter Lee (Hiebert, 1966), one of the early public communication professionals set forth a declaration of principles that focused on the ethical practices to be followed by organizations when communicating with the media: honesty, transparency, truth. Lee is also remembered for a number of organization friendly communication practices that included:

1   Acknowledging that business and industry should align themselves with the public interest and not vice versa—mutuality/propinquity.
2   Arguing that no program should be undertaken by an organization unless it has active support and personal participation of management—positive regard, trust.
3   Claiming that professional communicators should maintain open and honest communication with the media—risk, honesty, transparency.
4   Trying to humanize business, by using public relations to link the community, customers, and neighbors—mutuality, propinquity, positive regard, trust.

Lee's contributions provide an excellent, practical path toward the type of organizational dialogic engagement that should become more prevalent today (cf. Hallahan, 2002; Hiebert, 1966;).

The first and perhaps most important principle of organizational dialogue might be tied to Lee's first and second contributions: alignment with the public interest and managerial support. Most organizations are inherently hierarchical rather than rhizomatous. The reasons that dialogue is not a more common practice organizationally is because (a) dialogue is hard and most people have not been trained to use it effectively; and (b) the predominant mindset of most organizations is probably a "homo-economicus" (Kent & Taylor, 2016) mindset that places organizational good above the good for customers, employees, managers, and others. "The Homo Economicus framework is the metaphor that drives organizations to treat people instrumentally, and make decisions based on short-term, profit driven motives, and the bottom line, rather than long-term, relational, social capital based reasons" (p. 62).

On the first point about understanding and training, we need to realize that dialogue is both a mindset and a practice. Being open to dialogue (cf. Cypher & Kent, 2018; Kent & Taylor, 1998, 2002; Lane & Kent, 2018) is being open to the potential of a dialogic encounter—something that happens infrequently in the everyday world—and accepting that people should be treated

as ends and not means to ends. As Cypher and Kent (2018) argue, being prepared for a dialogic encounter requires a degree of psychological readiness:

> First ... the interlocutors have to be open to a dialogic exchange, and some
> level of trust must exist...Where there is no trust there is no dialogue ...
> Second, the orientation of individuals coming to a dialogue must be one of
> openness: openness to new information, openness to the dialogic process,
> and openness to persuasion (cf., Theunissen, 2015). Third ... Genuine di-
> alogue is a process that evolves over time. Although there are spontaneous
> dialogues that happen unexpectedly and involve fleeting exchanges, dia-
> logue is also a long-term process that unfolds over many encounters.
>
> (pp. 11–12)

A dialogic orientation, then, involves both psychological readiness as well as
dialogic training and understanding of how to enact a dialogic environment
(Lane & Kent, 2018; Taylor & Kent, 2014). The basis of a dialogic organization is engagement.

Engaged organizations are well positioned to use rhizomatous dialogue in an
ethical manner which involves an other-focused orientation, developing rules/
guidelines for interaction that are focused on ceding power and control to others, including and encouraging others to participate, and trying to find the
truth or best answer in situations, rather than using communication as a per-
suasive tool to serve the organization's self-interests over the public's interests.

Ceding power does not mean giving away privileged information or revealing organizational secrets. Ceding power means sharing power with
stakeholders in collaborative decision-making processes to nurture mutually
beneficial relationships. Engagement and dialogue of course have risks. Nevertheless, today's professionals need bigger networks and stronger connections
(Doerfel, 2018; Granovetter, 1973), which means they will have access to better information and more resources. They can also leverage these advantages
to reduce practices of exclusion and isolation by situating relationship building and strengthening connections with stakeholders as primary organizational goals (Kent, Sommerfeldt, & Saffer, 2016).

Conclusion

Successful, powerful, organizations often just assume that they will always be
in that position, in spite of the fact that according to Bloomberg Businessweek
the average life expectancy of a multinational corporation—Fortune 500 or
its equivalent—"is between 40 and 50 years ... 40 percent of all newly created companies last less than 10 years ... And the average life expectancy of
all firms, regardless of size ... is only 12.5 years" (www.businessweek.com/
chapter/degeus.htm). The job of organizational communicators, then, is to
counter these taken-for-granted, unproductive assumptions of perpetual organizational power by doing the "heavy lifting" that rhizomatous dialogic

engagement requires. This can be difficult because the long-term, purposeful commitment that rhizomatous dialogue brings runs counter to the kind of short-term orientation that characterizes most organizational decision-making in the US and many other countries, but it is precisely what organizations need to survive and thrive.

Although rhizomatous dialogic engagement may be a cure for the cancer of groupthink, it also competes with the destructive behaviors of groupthink that serve primarily or exclusively organizational interests and often seem effective until a catastrophic failure ensues. Building meaningful relationships and networks of professionals and colleagues takes time but offers benefits that are not immediately tangible. The payoff of dialogic engagement is not an adrenaline rush today, but deep satisfaction arriving weeks, months, or years later as members of the organization actually enjoy coming to work and making the world a better place.

In the battle between the inclusiveness of a dialogic orientation and the exclusiveness of groupthink, there is a clear winner. Rhizomatous relationships are durable and have a nearly indefinite lifespan. The showy, arboreal, short-term focused relationships will inevitably succumb to rot, insects, and fires that manifest in organizational contexts as greed, corruption, and mayhem brought on by the self-interested pursuit of short-term goals.

Bibliography

Allen, B. J. (2011). *Difference matters: Communicating social identity*. Long Grove, IL: Waveland Press, Inc.

Anderson, R., Cissna, K. N., & Arnett, R. C. (Eds.). (1994). *The reach of dialogue: Confirmation, voice, and community*. Cresskill, NJ: Hampton Press.

Ashcraft, K. L. (2004). Gender, discourse and organization: Framing a shifting relationship. In D. Grant, C. Hardy, C. Oswick, & L. Putnam (Eds.), *The SAGE handbook of organizational discourse* (pp. 275–298). London: SAGE Publications.

Bakhtin, M. M. (1975/1991). *The dialogic imagination: Four essays*. Austin, TX: University of Austin Press.

Botan, C. H., & Taylor, M. (2004). Public relations: The state of the field. *Journal of Communication, 54*(4), 645–661.

Bourdieu, P. (1991). *Language and symbolic power*. Cambridge, UK: Polity Press.

Bourdieu, P. (2000). *Pascalian meditations*. Stanford, CA: Stanford University Press/Polity Press.

Buber, M. (1923/1970). *I and thou*. (W. Kaufmann, Trans). New York, NY: Charles Scribner's Sons.

Burke, K. (1969). *A rhetoric of motives*. Berkeley: University of California Press.

Capizzo, L. (2018). Reimagining dialogue in public relations: Bakhtin and open dialogue in the public sphere. *Public Relations Review, 44*(4), 523–532.

Cypher, J. M., & Kent, M. L. (2018, April). *Authenticity in the dialogic encounter*. Competitive panel delivered to the Central States Communication Association (CSCA), Milwaukee, Wisconsin.

Deleuze, G., & Guattari, F. (1993). *A thousand plateaus: Capitalism and schizophrenia*. New York, NY: Continuum Publishing Company.

Doerfel. M. L. (2018). Engaging partnerships: A network-based typology of inter-organizational relationships and their communities. In K. Johnston, & M. Taylor (Eds.), *Handbook of engagement* (pp. 233–252). Hoboken, NJ: Wiley-Blackwell.

Edwards, L. (2015). *Power, diversity and public relations.* New York, NY: Routledge.

Freire, P. (1970). *Pedagogy of the oppressed.* (M. B. Ramos, Trans.). New York, NY: Continuum Publishing Company.

Gadamer, H. G. (1975/2004). *Truth and method* (2nd revised ed.). New York, NY: Continuum.

Granovetter, M. S. (1973). The strength of weak ties. *American Journal of Sociology, 78*(6), 1360–1380.

Habermas, J. (1984). *The theory of communicative action (vol. 1). Reason and the rationalization of society.* Boston, MA: Beacon Press.

Hallahan, K. (2002). Ivy Lee and the rockefellers' response to the 1913–1914 Colorado coal strike. *Journal of Public Relations Research, 14*(4), 265–315.

Heath, R. L. (2006). Onward into more fog: Thoughts on public relations' research directions. *Journal of Public Relations Research, 18,* 93–114.

Heath, R. L. (2018). Chapter 3: How fully functioning is communication engagement if society does not benefit? In K. Johnston, & M. Taylor (Eds.), *Handbook of engagement* (pp. 33–47). Hoboken, NJ: Wiley-Blackwell.

Hiebert, R. E. (1966). *Courtier to the crowd: The story of Ivy Lee and the development of public relations.* Ames, IA: Iowa State University Press.

Hill, A. (2018, May 7). Why groupthink never went away. *Financial Times.* Retrieved from https://www.ft.com/content/297ffe7c-4ee4-11e8-9471-a083af05aea7

Janis, I. L. (1972/1982). *Groupthink: Psychological studies of policy decisions and fiascoes* (2nd ed.). Boston, MA: Houghton Mifflin.

Johnston, K. A. (2014). Public relations and engagement: Theoretical imperatives of a multidimensional concept. *Journal of Public Relations Research, 26*(5), 381–383.

Johnston, K. A. (2018). Chapter 2: Toward a theory of social engagement. In K. Johnston, & M. Taylor (Eds.), *Handbook of engagement* (pp. 19–32). Hoboken, NJ: Wiley-Blackwell.

Johnston, K. A., & Taylor, M. (Eds.). (2018). *Handbook of engagement.* Hoboken, NJ: Wiley-Blackwell.

Kahn, W. A. (1990). Psychological conditions of personal engagement and disengagement at Work. *Academy of Management Journal, 33*(4), 692–724.

Kent, M. L., & Lane, A. (2017, September). A rhizomatous metaphor for dialogic theory. *Public Relations Review, 43*(3), 568–578.

Kent, M. L., Sommerfeldt, E. J., & Saffer, A. J. (2016, March). Social networks, power, and public relations: Tertius Iungens as a cocreational approach to studying relationship networks. *Public Relation Review, 42*(1), 91–100.

Kent, M. L., & Taylor, M. (1998). Building dialogic relationships through the World Wide Web. *Public Relations Review, 24*(3), 321–334.

Kent, M. L., & Taylor, M. (2002). Toward a dialogic theory of public relations. *Public Relations Review, 28*(1), 21–37.

Kent, M. L., & Taylor, M. (2016, March). From *homo economicus* to *homo dialogicus*: Rethinking social media use in CSR communication. *Public Relation Review, 42*(1), 60–67.

Laing, R. D. (1961/1990). *Self and others.* New York, NY: Penguin Books.

Lane, A. B. (2014). *Pragmatic two-way communication: A practitioner perspective on dialogue in public relations.* Unpublished doctoral thesis, Queensland University of Technology, Brisbane, Queensland, Australia.

Lane, A., & Kent, M. L. (2018). Engagement as dialogue, dialogue as engagement. In K. Johnston, & M. Taylor (Eds.), *Handbook of engagement* (pp. 61–72). Hoboken, NJ: Wiley-Blackwell.

Mahin, S. (2017). *Public relations practitioner assessments of the role engagement plays in organization to public relationships.* Unpublished doctoral dissertation, University of North Carolina Chapel Hill.

Nkomo, S. M. (1992). The emperor has no clothes: Rewriting "race in organizations." *The Academy of Management Review, 17*(3), 487–513.

Noddings, N. (1984). *Caring: A feminine approach to ethics and moral education.* Berkeley: University of California Press.

Pearson, R. (1989). Business ethics as communication ethics: Public relations practice and the idea of dialogue. In C. H. Botan, & V. Hazelton (Eds.), *Public relations theory* (pp. 111–131). Hillsdale, NJ: Lawrence Erlbaum Associates.

Place, K. R., & Vardeman-Winter, J. (2018). Where are the women? An examination of research on women and leadership in public relations. *Public Relations Review, 44*, 165–173.

Plato. (1999a). *Phaedrus.* Project Guttenberg E-Text. Retrieved from www.gutenberg.net, EBook #1636.

Plato (Benjamin Jowett, Trans.) (1999b) *Gorgias.* Project Guttenberg. Etext #1672. Retrieved from www.gutenberg.org/files/1636/1636-h/1636-h.htm

Rogers, C. (1956/1992). The necessary and sufficient conditions of therapeutic personality change. *Journal of Consulting and Clinical Psychology, 60*(6), 827–839.

Steele, E. D., & Redding, W. C. (1962). The American value system: Premises for persuasion. *Western Speech, 26*, 83–91.

Stohl, C., & Cheney, G. (2001). Participatory processes/paradoxical practices. *Management Communication Quarterly, 14*(3), 349–407.

Taylor, M., & Kent, M. L. (2014). Dialogic engagement: Clarifying foundational concepts. *Journal of Public Relations Research, 26*(5), 384–398.

Theunissen, P. (2015). The quantum entanglement of dialogue and persuasion in social media: Introducing the Per–Di Principle. *Atlantic Journal of Communication, 23*, 5–18. doi:10.1080/15456870.2015.972405

Theunissen, P. (2018). Chapter 4: Philosophy and ethics of engagement. In K. Johnston, & M. Taylor (Eds.), *Handbook of engagement* (pp. 49–60). Hoboken, NJ: Wiley-Blackwell.

Theunissen, P., & Wan Noordin, W. N. (2012). Revisiting the concept "dialogue" in public relations. *Public Relations Review, 38*, 5–13.

Toledano, M. (2018). Dialogue, strategic communication, and ethical public relations: Lessons from Martin Buber's political activism. *Public Relations Review, 44*(1), 131–141.

Turner, M. E., & Pratkanis, A. R. (1998). Theoretical perspectives on groupthink: A twenty-fifth anniversary appraisal. *Organizational Behavior and Human Decision Processes, 73*(2/3), 105–110.

Watzlawick, P., Beavin, J. H., & Jackson, D. D. (1967). *Pragmatics of human communication: A study of interactional patterns, pathologies, and paradoxes.* New York, NY: W.W. Norton.

Zarya, V. (2018, May 21). The share of female CEOs' in the Fortune 500 dropped by 25% in 2018. Retrieved from http://fortune.com/2018/05/21/women-fortune-500-2018

5 Non-Profit Reuse as a Solution to Reducing Digital Divides and Technology Maintenance Inequalities

Amy L. Gonzales and Harry Yaojun Yan

Disparities in access to and use of information and communication technologies (ICTs) have historically emphasized inequalities based on demographic markers (i.e. age, geographic, ableism, etc.) that are different than those foregrounded in recent academic conversations (i.e. race, religion, gender, etc.). As a turn from all of these, this chapter sets out to primarily examine income-based disparities in *stable* access to digital technologies. However, we undertake this examination with the knowledge that research on income-inequality engages other forms of marginalization due to the confounding of race, education, income and wealth in the U.S and elsewhere. In this particular case, we are interested in how non-profit digital refurbishing organizations may provide a stop-gap for those struggling to stay connected to digital resources. We come to these questions with our own perspectives as authors that have been sometimes marginalized and in other ways have received many socio-cultural privileges.

It goes without saying that information and communication technologies (ICTs) have radically transformed the way people communicate, work, and play at the turn of the 21st century. Cell phone and internet technology have proliferated at a fantastic rate in the last few decades: 47.6% of households in the world own a computer; 1.04 cell phones are owned per capita; and 48.0% of the world's population subscribes to internet services as of 2017 (International Telecommunication Union, 2017). These rates are even higher in wealthy countries, where 82.4% households have a computer, 1.27 cell phones are owned per capita, and 81.0% of the population gets online (ITU, 2017). These data certainly demonstrate widespread ICT adoption; however, they may also obscure inequalities in the stability of that access.

As initial access to ICTs saturates we consider how people work to maintain that access, how that differs by socio-economic status, and how organizations support or hinder the process. To explore this, we use a lens of *technology maintenance*. Technology maintenance points to the continued effort needed to ensure stable digital access for all people, but especially those with fewer resources (Gonzales, 2014). This construct has been examined at the individual level, but may work across levels or even at a macro level. That is, institutions and organizations that facilitate maintenance play a role in helping individuals achieve and maintain access to digital devices. As a result, reuse non-profits may be key in ensuring that low-income individuals are included in the 21st-century global economy. Moreover, when institutions promote refurbishing and repair, two types of ICT *reuse*, they are enabling technology maintenance on a global scale.

In this chapter, we analyze interviews with representatives from two leading non-profit organizations to understand how non-profits, private corporations, and the government all interact to address individual-level and societal-level digital inequalities with digital reuse. Through this analysis we broaden the technology maintenance construct beyond the individual-scale to understand how non-profit organizations dedicated to reuse are reducing inequalities. At the same time, we explore new solutions to previously identified technology maintenance problems. This enlarges the scope of the construct and also may provide mechanisms for real-world intervention. It also speaks to how organizations can support the individual-level digital infrastructure needed to ensure equity and inclusion in all aspects of contemporary life.

Our hope is that by finding solutions to technology maintenance problems we can help alleviate future socio-economic inequalities of a variety of sorts by providing all people—especially those at the socio-economic margins—the resources they need to maximize resources and quality of life (e.g. Mesch, 2012; Gonzales, 2017).

Technology Maintenance

There are many types of digital divides. Scholars have long identified the need to look beyond basic ICT ownership and use to understand the nuances behind digital inequalities. For example, many have pointed out that digital literacy matters, with demographic factors such as age, education, and income predicting the ability to effectively navigate new technologies even after ownership and use occur. This *second-level* digital divide has been widely explored (Hargittai, 2002; Ragnedda & Muschert, 2013), and more recently scholars have conceptualized a *third-level* digital divide in the degree to which people benefit from ICT use (van Deursen & Helsper, 2015). However, technology maintenance differs from these in that it returns to a *first-level* divide, or, what van Dijk (2006) refers to as *material access.*

Technology maintenance refers to the ongoing work required to maintain digital access even when computers, cell phones, and internet are initially in the home or accessed through shared means (e.g., family, libraries, etc.). The ability to maintain technology—paying bills; replacing devices; managing time with shared devices—is an imperative for every technology user but varies by socio-economic status: low-income and less educated individuals often struggle to stay connected (Gonzales, 2014). Extant interview data with low-income individuals suggests that disruptions in digital access affect healthcare, employment, and interpersonal social support (Gonzales, 2014; Gonzales, Ems, & Suri, 2016). And according to convenience samples, digital disruptions are associated with greater stress, worse quality of life, and even worse grades

(Gonzales, Calarco, & Lynch, 2018; Gonzales, Yan, Read, & Brown, in press). These costs may further reinforce existing social disparities as access to technology is increasingly essential for work, school, and other means of building social capital (Norris, 2001; van Dijk, 2005; Viswanath & Kreuter, 2007).

Few studies have explored solutions to intermittent digital disruptions from a digital divide perspective. An exception to this, Robinson and colleagues have looked at socio-economic differences in the management of *net time*, intra-familial bargaining over time online (Robinson & Schulz, 2013), or the status of students as *endowed, entrepreneurial,* or *empowered strivers* (Robinson, 2014). In this latter piece, Robinson explores how socio-economic differences enable different coping responses: whereas endowed strivers have in-home digital resources; entrepreneurial strivers turn to shared personal devices and public libraries to compensate for unstable personal access; and empowered strivers particularly benefit from digital resources at school. These studies provide descriptive assessments of maintenance coping at the individual level. A primary aim of this chapter, in contrast, is to identify organizational-level solutions to maintenance problems, especially as they may become more important over time.

Reuse as a Reaction to Technology Maintenance Inequalities

Theoretical Framing

To better understand reuse as a solution, we start by addressing the theoretical and conceptual underpinnings of technology maintenance practices. In addition to the sociological and communication scholarship above, the construct leans heavily on socio-cultural theorizing on breakdown and repair.[1] Although the organizations we review below use reuse and repair to reduce digital divides, much of the research on repair has not focused on economic inequality in wealthy contexts, like the US. Most centrally, Graham and Thrift (2007) explore breakdown and repair as a means of understanding how a system functions. They use Heidegger's work on breakdown to underscore the value of studying breakdown and repair in order to truly understand the meaning of an object. Jackson and colleagues have also done a great deal of work to think through the aesthetics of repair (Jackson, 2014; Jackson, Ahmed, & Rifat, 2014; Jackson & Kang, 2014). In a seminal chapter Jackson (2014) talks about "a deep wonder" for "the subtle arts of repair by which rich and robust lives are sustained against the weight of centrifugal odds, and how sociotechnical forms and infrastructures, large and small, get not only broken but *restored* (p. 222)." Houston and colleagues describe the valuation of repair as impermanent and context-dependent, referencing fixer collectives in the US and for-profit mobile repair shops in Kampala and Dhaka (Houston et al., 2016). Similarly, Rosner and Ames (2014) propose the concept of *negotiated endurance* for thinking about repair in both middle-class and low-income contexts. These different cultural vantage points highlight how repair can be either an act of reverence or an act of necessity, or often both, reflecting the *situated* nature of digital infrastructures brought to the fore during the repair process (Velkova, 2018). Interestingly, according to our observation, most of this research tends to think of technological reuse as choice in wealthy regions (e.g., Europe, US) or as necessity in poorer regions (e.g., Latin America, Africa). Part of our contribution is to investigate reuse as a necessity in the wealthy context of the US for those people who cannot afford to get or stay connected.

Much of the research on reuse in wealthy countries reflects an activist-like ethos on the ability or "right to repair," often with an environmental focus. Activism on reuse is galvanized by the fact that new technology, and even appliances that were once repairable, is being designed today in ways that makes them difficult, impossible, or sometimes illegal to repair without manufacturers' intervention (Beres & Campbell, 2016; Kastrenakes, 2018). In response to these constraints, consumers—sometimes as individuals, other times as communities and collectives—seek ways to subvert or hack technologies that are increasingly complicated and often nearly impenetrable (Graziano & Trogal, 2017; Mitchell, 2018). Fixit and repair collectives have begun to emerge worldwide, often with a commitment to sustainability and a desire to build communities of people invested in protecting and sharing knowledge about repair (Charter & Keiller, 2016; Houston et al., 2016; Rosner & Ames, 2014). This trend is consistent with the idea of repair as *care* for individual goods and craftsmanship as well as the environment (Houston & Jackson, 2017). Our hope is to use this work on repair as an environmental or political act as scaffolding in exploring organizational-led reuse as an act of socio-economic justice.

The Logistics of Reuse

Before analyzing the workings of two reuse non-profits, we look broadly at the logistics of electrical and electronic equipment (EEE) reuse. Reuse is considered preferable to landfill disposal, or even recycling, which can both result in toxic chemicals being released into the environment (Bhuie, Ogunseitan, Saphores, & Shapiro 2004; Cumps, 2015; Murugesan, 2008; Williams et al., 2008). Burning of copper-bearing wires to remove insulation or improper disposal of lead-based cathode-ray tube (CRT) screens, for example, can contaminate air, soil, and water. Mobile and cell phones contain several toxic and hazardous materials such as arsenic, lead, and mercury among many others (Bhuie et al., 2004; Manivannan, 2016). Given all of this, disposal of EEE must follow very specific protocol in order to reduce the harmful environmental effects of these products. In many places, especially countries with limited resources, these protocols are often ignored (Kiddee, Naidu, & Wong, 2013; Williams et al., 2008; Yu et al., 2006).

To better avoid these costs, a great deal of work has investigated the economic, environmental, and social benefits of efficient reuse to promote a *circular economy* (Ellen MacArthur Foundation, 2018; Ghisellini, Cialani, & Ulgiati, 2016). As a prime example, Kissling and colleagues (2012) identify four reuse operating models for EEE. The first two are for-profit models. First, the

Networking Equipment Recovery Model involves the cleaning and recycling of very old networking equipment (e.g., servicers, routers). These systems are typically retired after many years (e.g., 15 years) and either redistributed internally to corporate operations that can tolerate out-of-date systems or are disassembled and sold for parts. Second, the *IT Asset Management Model* is similar, but it instead specializes in for-profit refurbishing and remarketing of computers and laptops, rather than networking equipment. Both of these models profit mainly from reselling products and sorted materials for recycling and by offering services needed to accomplish reuse, including collection, transportation, and certified data cleaning (Kissling et al., 2012).

In the case of non-profit reuse models, the *Close the Digital Divide Model* and the *Social Enterprise Model* function much like the IT Asset Management Model. The former focuses on redistribution of devices to eligible recipients in bulk, primarily by shipping devices from wealthy countries to countries that have high IT needs and fewer resources. The social enterprise model also focuses on refurbishing and remarketing of computers and laptops but typically redistributes domestically with a focus on training for individuals from marginalized groups on how to do the refurbishing. This model helps to keep refurbishing costs low and serves a two-fold social good of providing IT training and fostering device dissemination to needy recipients. We explore a combination of these two non-profit models in our analysis below.

Barriers to Reuse

Despite its benefits, EEE reuse is not without barriers. At the individual level, the high cost of replacement parts and the complicated repair process are the two main reasons consumers are dissuaded from pursuing device repair (Sabbaghi, Cade, Behdad & Bisantz, 2017; Sabbaghi, Esmaeilian, Cade, Wiens, & Behdad, 2016). At the organizational level, a summary of 28 case studies of organizations focused on EEE reuse found that the top two problems with successful reuse are a lack of legislation to incentivize reuse and insufficient supply of used equipment circulating through the second-hand market (Kissling et al., 2013, p. 24). Interestingly, organizations from different regions reported different success factors and obstacles in operations. While the global south (i.e., mostly less wealthy countries) reported the need for a sustainable supply chain and affordable qualified technicians, the global north (i.e., mostly wealthy countries) put more weight on the quality of products for reuse and the complications in helping customers avoid bad reuse practices (Kissling et al., 2013). Differing government policies on reuse were also a factor. On the one hand, organizations in the EU were sometimes frustrated when navigating complex law and regulation; on the other hand, the North American market sees the lack of legislation setting financial incentives as a barrier (Kissling et al., 2013). Overall, the comparison suggested that two main factors determine the success of a reuse organization: (1) an affordable and reliable supply chain and (2) supportive regulation and policy. These recommendations are echoed in our findings below.

Finally, although our analyses focus on desktop and laptop refurbishing, it is also important to mention cell phone reuse as well. One reason that cell phones and other mobile devices are rarely the focus of reuse programs is because the recycling of cell phones for parts is usually difficult or dangerous and thus not cost effective (Geyer & Blass, 2010; Robinson, 2009; Williams et al., 2008). Second-hand use of cell phones is a more economically feasible way to sustain the life of a given cell phone, but the biggest limitation to cell phone reuse is (as many readers may be able to attest to) "the hibernation period of end-of-use handsets in the bottom drawer of their owners" (Geyer & Blass, 2010, p. 518). Mobile phone consortiums and individual companies such as Vodafone and Nokia continue to explore sustainable cell phone innovations (e.g., biodegradable plastics) and support campaigns that encourage consumer recycling or take-backs (Manivannan, 2016). These initiatives show promise, but non-profit refurbishers in the US tend to focus on computers and laptops rather than cell phones in aiming to reduce disparities because of their higher entry-level price point, utility for education and employment, and more accessible design.

Reuse through Inter-Sector Collaboration

Rethinking Motives for Reuse

Much of the research on EEE reuse is motivated by concerns of environmental impact. There is good reason for this, given the rapid rate of ICT production over the last two decades (Spiezia, 2013), consumers' demands for upgrades (Cooper, 2004, 2005), and the toxicity of many of the device components (Bhuie et al., 2004; Williams et al., 2008). However, one of the aims of this chapter is to foreground reuse in response to socio-economic inequality, particularly as organizations play a lead role in fostering reuse as a means of promoting a circular economy. Previous scholars have certainly noted the socio-economic benefit of reuse (e.g., James, 2001; Kissling et al., 2012; Rosner & Ames, 2014; Williams et al. 2008), but that scholarship tends to focus on digital inequalities outside of wealthy countries.

In this chapter we investigate refurbishment non-profits that circulate computers within the US as a means of reducing digital inequalities that persist even in wealthy countries. In doing so we expand upon the *technology maintenance* construct, which had previously only been considered at the individual level. We instead consider solutions to those problems, and how they may be enabled at an organizational level. That is, we explore how non-profit organizations collaborate with corporations and policy makers to facilitate technology maintenance, primarily by refurbishing and repairing second-hand computers for low-income recipients.

Collaborations on the Horizon

According to a recent survey of 1,372 organizations representing a variety of sizes and industries across North America and Europe, over 99% of organizations use desktops and laptops as their primary computing devices (Spicework.com, 2018). The survey also showed that over 50% of the organizations update their devices less than every 3–4 years. Research has showed that the three- to four-year upgrade cycle is mostly a result of pursuing the maximum productivity rather than devices reaching their life limits, and there is even argument for shortening the update cycle to every two years (Ribeiro, 2016). In other words, while some products may need to be recycled due to age, a good portion can and should be cycled back into secondary reuse markets.

Informed by stakeholder theory (Freeman, 1984) and the corporate social responsibility (CSR) framework, we contend that collaborating with nongovernmental organizations (NGOs) that specialize in ICT reuse is not only a practical solution but also a socially conscious practice. In the view of stakeholder theory, corporations are not merely profit-driven entities that function independent from other social actors but constantly react to and are shaped by value creation from stakeholders (Aakhus & Bzdak, 2015). Within this framework, CSR has been greatly emphasized and become an essential element in management (Grayson & Jane, 2017). Moreover, shifting from a reactive charity-driven model, we have witnessed that corporations are taking more proactive roles in building an inter-sector prosocial value-creation network (e.g., Cooper & Shumate 2012; Doerfel & Taylor, 2017; Koschmann, Kuhn, & Pfarrer, 2012; Vogel, 2007).

Collaboration with non-profits specializing in ICT reuse thus can and should be a natural outlet for enacting corporate responsibility. Doing so serves dual social goods: it not only improves environment protection but also alleviates social inequality by reducing digital divides and technology maintenance inequality. Given the value of end-of-use ICTs in most workplaces, we contend that NGOs that are specialized in ICT reuse should be included as a *stable* actor in the inter-sector value-creation network. Following Bryson, Crosby, and Stone's (2006) framework for successfully forming inter-sector collaboration, in the next section, our conversation with NGOs leaders sheds light on how those collaborations can take place.

Analysis: Non-Profits in the US

To explore the themes above, we interviewed the founder and CEO from two non-profits in different parts of the US that promote reuse. In doing so we gain a better understanding of how they make efforts to build legitimacy and trust; craft expertise by streamlining the refurbishing process; and, most importantly, how they produce translational outcomes in addressing digital divides.

The first author met both men for the first time at Net Inclusion 2018, a conference hosted by the National Digital Inclusion Alliance (NDIA), which brings practitioners, corporate representatives, researchers, and policy makers together to discuss policy, programs, and best practices. Subsequent in-depth interviews took place separately to explore the daily workings, strengths, and hardships faced by each organization. These interviews explored the organizational practices of these specific non-profits as well as non-profit refurbishing broadly as a resource for reducing digital inequalities.

Background

Pat Millen is the founder of E2D, which stands for "eliminate the digital divide." This non-profit is made up of a coalition of municipal leaders, corporate supporters, community educators, college students, and civic volunteers in the Charlotte Region who are all focused on reducing digital exclusion. They have devices in over 8,000 homes in the region, serving an estimated 25,600 low-income individuals. Similarly, Casey Sorensen is the CEO from PCs for People, a non-profit organization with an aim to provide "the opportunity for all low-income individuals and nonprofits to benefit from the life changing impact of computers and mobile internet." In 2018 alone, PCs for People distributed over 14,000 computers, assisting over 46,000 low-income individuals in getting access to technology.

Both organizations primarily focus their time and resources on collecting, refurbishing, and disseminating computers to people that qualify. In the case of E2D this is low-income students at eligible schools. In the case of PCs for People it is anyone within 200% of the federal poverty level. Middle- and high-income families are not eligible to receive these subsidized computing devices. E2D only refurbishes laptops, because they are easier to transport and store than desktop computers and are often more desirable to their adolescent recipients. PCs for People refurbishes both laptops and desktops. They also both train individuals from marginalized communities—in the case of E2D it is low-income youth and at PCs for People it is individuals with cognitive disabilities—to conduct the cleaning and refurbishing process, as well as assist in the repair process of broken computers, in this way reflecting the *Social Enterprise Model* described above (Kissling et al., 2012). Finally, PCs for People also provides internet service that costs only $10 dollars a month through collaborations with two other non-profit partners and a nationwide LTW network. Through training, subsidies, and repair both organizations target low-income populations to help meet digital needs.

History and Operations

Computer refurbishment and dissemination is the primary focus of both of these organizations. The origins of E2D stem from a conversation between Pat Millen and his 12-year-old daughter. According to Millen, in 2013 his daughter came home from school one day and shared her observations with her family:

> every assignment we get in our middle school presumes there's a computer at home to do it. But I know there are kids in our school that come from, you know, poor background, that likely *don't* have computers, or I *know* they don't have computers. Therefore, they can't do the work, and the result is that they fall behind. That's not fair and what are we gonna do about it?

Millen and his family realized that retired computers from local businesses could fill this need. But instead of soliciting donations to cover the costs of a handful of computers for his daughter's classroom, they decided to explore methods that would allow them to scale this solution. Eventually, what started as a family's attempt to help provide computer access to families at a single elementary school became E2D, and a non-profit led conversation with principals, superintendents, and eventually state legislators about the digital divide in the region.

Similarly, Casey Sorensen was inspired to invest in digital equity work after hearing about a social worker that changed the life of a troubled youth by providing that youth with technology access. A self-taught programmer, the student had hacked into the school software to change his grades and was then expelled. Fortunately, instead of focusing on punitive responses, a social worker involved with the student had the insight to give him a computer. Inspired by this, Sorensen contacted the social worker and soon after quit his job as a technology consultant to work full time at non-profits designed to reduce digital inequalities. Once in that position, Sorensen started looking beyond individual computer donations for a more sustainable source of devices to disseminate to low-income individuals in his community. Now, two decades later, PCs for People is working with over 700 corporations across several states to provide refurbishing and redistribution of end-of-life electronics to those in need, as well as low-cost internet access.

Millen and Sorensen, and other organizations like theirs, fill the gap in computer access by orchestrating computer donations from companies and government offices that schedule regular computer replacements. Each year thousands of functional computers nationwide are thrown away or sold to secondary markets. For both Millen and Sorensen, a primary goal has been to convince these organizations to donate computers to refurbishers instead. In the case of E2D, for example, the Lowe's headquarters is located in Mooresville, North Carolina, and has become a primary source of donated computers. PCs for People has also relied on corporate partnerships, as well as donations from government offices and individual donations. To encourage donations, they provide pickup and storage services for any donation that has more than 15 computers in the State of Minnesota and in the Denver region of Colorado.

The non-profit refurbishing model helps to fill an important gap between corporate digital excess and low-income digital needs. However, the model is not without limitations. Consistent with the literature (Kissling et al., 2013), both men noted that a key barrier to its success is the ability to convince corporations, government agencies, and other large institutions to donate their computers. Both men mentioned that the age of devices is key, with an ideal age being 3–4 years old, but many being 7–8 years, making them less viable. Part of the problem is simply limited visibility. Millen noted that he spends much of his time lobbying his cause to corporations, policy makers and other stakeholders who might not be aware of organizations like his and would otherwise throw out or sell back old devices. In addition to a lack of visibility, many corporations are also concerned with the risks associated with donating devices that contain proprietary information. The cost of wiping devices clean is not negligible ($99.99 per computer at the local Best Buy) and corporations cannot afford to take risks with their data. As a result, even when financial incentives are not cost prohibitive, corporations may often choose to use leasing companies to exchange devices or dispose of them entirely rather than risk compromising data through donation.

Streamlining Maintenance

In recognition of this problem, Sorensen has used his background in technology consultancy to design a novel system that automates the refurbishing process in 12 steps, which include detecting hardware malfunction, data wiping, and re-licensing with Windows. By moving the wiping process in-house rather than having the corporations contract through a third party (which is what Millen and many other refurbishers have to do), Sorensen has been able to reduce costs to corporate donors and, as a result, convince many more corporate sponsors to donate to PCs for People. As a consequence, PCs for People has been able to increase the number of computers that they deliver to clients. Moreover, Sorensen has shared his software to other refurbishing non-profits so that they could also provide the same in-house computer refurbishing as a way of incentivizing donations and streamlining the refurbishing process. This helps to maximize the number of computers donated and disseminated by refurbishing organizations throughout the country. It also points to an interesting benefit of operating as a non-profit—there is little-to-no competition between organizations. On the contrary, effective internal operating procedures are being shared as best practices in the hope of elevating the visibility of non-profit refurbishing nationwide.

Ensuring that the refurbishing process is relatively simple also allows for workforce training, an important secondary role of both E2D and PCs for People, and another way in which they reflect the *Social Enterprise Model* of digital reuse. Indeed, because Sorensen's automation of refurbishing is very simple, he is able to partner with organizations that fill workforce needs for those with cognitive disabilities. Likewise, although E2D does not have an in-house wiping process, the installation and basic repair at each site is overseen by two full-time adult staff and supported by a team of trained youth from low-income schools. The training program is highly competitive, in part because E2D doubles the minimum wage and provides skills that are transferable to a technology-driven marketplace. Through training people to repair, individual trainees may increase their access to social capital, in the form of jobs, contacts, etc., which also reduces inequality at the individual level. Thus, Millen and Sorensen, and other organizations like theirs, not only reduce social inequalities by channeling refurbished devices to people in need but also by supporting a community of people that value and have expertise in repair. Training-led refurbishment and repair reflects a necessary shift in values that prioritizes repair as a cultural good at a societal level, and one that is likely to continue growing as device ownership continues to rise.

The End Result: Client Benefits

Although each of these organizations engages in little to no advertising, word of mouth generates a steady stream of people interested in receiving subsidized computers. At E2D, each eligible family spends $60 to get a laptop with a brand-new operating system and Windows software with six months warranty. At PCs for People, eligible individuals can choose to get a computer for free, $30, $50, or $100 dollars depending on the quality and age of the device. When asked about the computers people typically choose, Sorensen said that they often "... start with that free one, but come back one year later and get that fifty-dollar one ... They might say 'I want this. I want to learn this. Once I'm more comfortable with it, I will come back.'" Sorensen also mentioned that people often come in to receive a new computer because they have a computer at home that isn't working. However, when clients realize that PCs for People will repair computers for very low costs ($25–$40 dollars depending on the condition, and if the computer was distributed by PCs for People), they often bring in old computers to repair as well, enabling them to have more than one computer in the household.

Repair of privately owned computers is another major component of each of these organizations. Individuals bring in computers to these organizations to be repaired for a variety of reasons (e.g., screen repair, viruses, battery life, etc.). The ability to fix the computers depends largely on the age of the computer and the availability of quality parts. Because both organizations contract large donations from various organizations, they often have replacement parts on hand. But in cases when the computer is more than 12 years or is impossible or too expensive to repair, it makes more sense for the client to receive a newly refurbished computer.

The Future of Reuse in the US

Most non-profit refurbishing organizations in the US are quite small, which limits the nationwide influence they can have on digital breakdown and the digital divide. However, these are just two of at least 90 organizations nationwide that target subsidized computer refurbishing and repair as a way to reduce digital divides by helping people get and maintain access to computers and other technology.[2] They are both affiliated with the Alliance for Technology Refurbishing & Reuse (ATRR), which "seeks to establish a common national voice for ... an increase in the volume and availability of low cost and no cost computers for their respective populations." In addition to trying to create a nationwide network of non-profit refurbishers, ATRR has worked in collaboration with Michael Abensour, who is currently the executive director of the Kramden Institute, to lobby for the Computers for Veterans and Students Act. This act is an update to the Computer for Learning Act that was introduced during the Clinton administration. The passage of this updated act would streamline the process of getting government computers systematically cycled into the refurbishing pipeline. According to Sorensen, the main reason the early act fell short was because schools were asked to bear the cost of storage and transportation, something they are not equipped to do. The current version is improved by "direct[ing] federal agencies to offer the transfer of any surplus computer or technology equipment to a certified non-profit computer refurbisher before they get offered to Computers for Learning." In this way, non-profit organizations such as E2D or PCs for People that are equipped to efficiently process bulk refurbishing can ensure that government surplus reaches people in need and reduces waste. Despite the small size of most refurbishing organizations, this is one example of how their collective efforts may be able to help drive policy in a manner that shifts refurbish and repair norms nationwide.

But policy is not the only way that government institutions may shape the culture of refurbishing and repair in the US. When asked about the role of government in supporting the scalability of refurbishing efforts, Sorensen estimated that the government is one of the biggest annual consumers of technology. He noted that

> something that will take no money and could be done with only a stroke of a pen would be [that] all [retired] government computers go to programs like this. And … that would be a bipartisan [endeavor, which] I would think would meet little resistance [and] doesn't cost any money, as long as the network of non-profits like us can deliver the service.

Systematically channeling government computers through non-profit reuse organizations would be another simple but important means of sourcing donations, a key barrier to refurbishing success.

Finally, both Millen and Sorensen speculated about the future of repair as it is shaped by evolving innovation. Millen hypothesizes that in the coming decades computer ownership needs will be addressed directly by corporations. He presumes that commerce will so entirely rely on computing that corporations from nearly all industries (e.g., household goods, medical care, apparel, food, etc.) will subsidize the cost of computing to ensure widespread basic digital access in order to participate in the corporate marketplace. When Sorensen was asked to predict what their programs would look like in the next two decades, he noted that organizations like PCs for People will have to keep scaling up and out, collaborating with each other and with corporations and government more closely. To this end, PCs for People in 2016 launched its own e-commerce website to be able to deliver its services over all 50 states plus Puerto Rico. They have also started looking into tablet repair and refurbishing. In sum, despite inevitable changes to the ICT market that will change the refurbishing market, both Millen and Sorensen believe that non-profits such as theirs will continue to be relevant for the foreseeable future.

Conclusion, Limitations, and Future Directions

Organizations such as E2D and PCs for People, and others like them, reflect a new take on technology maintenance and its utility for organizational communication scholars interested in equity and inclusion. They extend the technology maintenance construct to examine solutions, not just problems. Moreover, the very existence of these organizations, and their activism at the federal level, demonstrates that technology maintenance is also happening at an organizational level and that cross-sector communications may be key in their success. We argue that reuse non-profits should become *stable actors* in inter-sector value-creation networks, which include corporate, non-profit, and government stakeholders. These collaborations are already taking place. With greater corporate awareness, and policies that can nudge government support, these organizations will likely become even more visible in addressing environmental concerns about digital waste and reducing socio-economic divides caused by lack of digital access.

Until recently there was limited work on the pernicious effect of digital disruption as a form of social exclusion. It is from this perspective that *technology maintenance* originated. Technology maintenance was developed in response to the realization that low-income individuals in wealthy contexts spend a lot of time and relative income in order to stay digitally connected and that that work often goes unnoticed by policy makers, the press, and even researchers (Gonzales, 2014, 2016; Gonzales et al., 2016). Without representative data on the topic, however, there is limited research and even fewer proposed solutions to these problems being discussed in the public sphere. Scholars in this area must continue to press for measurement of digital disruption in order to design effective interventions and optimize inclusion and digital participation for low-income individuals and the organizations that serve them. Involvement of organizational scholars could result in a reconceptualization of the role of organizations in reducing inequality, enhancing digital inclusion, and addressing environmental waste. As Sorensen and Millen make clear, a system for collecting, refurbishing, and disseminating donated devices is already in place. The biggest hurdle to broadening its reach is increasing visibility and reliable corporate buy-in. Organizational scholars can play a major role in addressing these issues.

We close by acknowledging that building a system by which dated devices are consistently passed along to lower-income families could run the risk of reinforcing inequalities. However, both Millen and Sorensen rejected this notion due to their commitment to quality donations. In future projects, we continue to investigate how state and organizational policies interact with the individual experience of digital use and ownership in both expected and unexpected ways. Again, our intention is to learn how to build better digital infrastructures capable of filling the cracks in current systems of technology ownership and access. We do not expect refurbishing and repair to "solve" access inequalities, but we hope this chapter fosters greater conversation among scholars about the need to explore this type of solution over the next two decades. We fear that without investment into maintenance solutions, saturation of ownership and use will obscure persistent inequalities that may never be addressed. Instead of assuming that a minimum standard of access is deserved by everyone, much like electricity, ICTs may come to be absorbed into society much like transportation—a good that varies enormously from person to person and with great consequence. Programs like these may help mitigate the costs of subpar access. Hopefully, this chapter will help to raise awareness about the importance of such programs, and the potential of their role in society over the coming decades in optimizing digital inclusion.

Notes

1 Research within science and technology studies, which is discussed in this paragraph, primarily uses the concept of "repair" whereas research in management and engineering uses the concept of "reuse." For our purposes, we use the concept of "reuse" as a higher-order concept, and then discuss "refurbishing" and "repair" as specific types of reuse, where refurbishing primarily refers to removing and reinstalling software for secondary ownership and repair refers to acts of upkeep by the same owner.

2 We do not conduct any novel research into refurbishing organizations outside of the US, though there is a visible repair movement in the UK, and research on refurbishing and repair has been conducted in the global south, including Bangladesh, Kenya, and Uganda.

References

Aakhus, M., & Bzdak, M. (2015). Stakeholder engagement as communication design practice. *Journal of Public Affairs, 15*(2), 188–200.

Beres, D., & Campbell, A. (2016, June 9). Apple is fighting a secret war to keep you from repairing your phone. *Huffington Post*. Retrieved from https://www.huffingtonpost.com/entry/apple-right-to-repair_us_5755a6b4e4b0ed593f14fdea

Bhuie, A. K., Ogunseitan, O. A., Saphores, J. D., & Shapiro, A. A. (2004). Environmental and economic trade-offs in consumer electronic products recycling: A case study of cell phones and computers. In *Electronics and the Environment 2004 Conference Record. IEEE International Symposium* (pp. 74–79). IEEE.

Bryson, J. M., Crosby, B. C., & Stone, M. M. (2006). The design and implementation of cross-sector collaborations: Propositions from the literature. *Public Administration Review, 66*, 44–55.

Charter, M., & Keiller, S. (2016). *The second global survey of repair cafés: A summary of findings*. Farnham: The Centre for Sustainable Design, University for the Creative Arts. Retrieved from http://cfsd.org.uk/sitepdfs/The%20Second%20

Global%20Survey%20of%20Repair%20Cafes%20-%20A%20Summary%20 of%20Findings.pdf

Cooper, K. R., & Shumate, M. (2012). Interorganizational collaboration explored through the bona fide network perspective. *Management Communication Quarterly*, *26*(4), 623–654.

Cooper, T. (2004). Inadequate life? Evidence of consumer attitudes to product obsolescence. *Journal of Consumer Policy*, *27*(4), 421–449.

Cooper, T. (2005). Slower consumption reflections on product life spans and the "throwaway society." *Journal of Industrial Ecology*, *9*(1–2), 51–67.

Cumps, B. (2015). Extending an ICT4D computer re-use model with e-waste handling activities: A case study. *Information Technology for Development*, *21*(4), 677–693.

Doerfel, M. L., & Taylor, M. (2017). The story of collective action: The emergence of ideological leaders, collective action network leaders, and cross-sector network partners in civil society. *Journal of Communication*, *67*(6), 920–943.

Ellen MacArthur Foundation (2018, July). What is circular economy? Retrieved July 27, 2018 from https://www.ellenmacarthurfoundation.org/ circular-economy

Freeman, R. E. (1984). *Strategic management: A stakeholder approach.* Boston, MA: Pitman.

Geyer, R., & Blass, V. D. (2010). The economics of cell phone reuse and recycling. *The International Journal of Advanced Manufacturing Technology*, *47*(5–8), 515–525.

Ghisellini, P., Cialani, C., & Ulgiati, S. (2016). A review on circular economy: The expected transition to a balanced interplay of environmental and economic systems. *Journal of Cleaner Production*, *114*, 11–32.

Gonzales, A. L. (2014). Health benefits and barriers to cell phone use in low-income urban US neighborhoods: Indications of technology maintenance. *Mobile Media & Communication*, *2*(3), 233–248.

Gonzales, A. L. (2016). The contemporary US digital divide: From initial access to technology maintenance. *Information, Communication & Society*, *19*(2), 234–248.

Gonzales, A.L. (2017). Disadvantaged minorities' use of the Internet to expand their social networks. *Communication Research*, 44, 467–486. https://doi. org/10.1177/0093650214565925

Gonzales, A. L., Calarco, J., & Lynch, T. (2018, online). Technology problems and student achievement gaps: A validation and extension of the technology maintenance construct. *Communication Research*. doi: 0093650218796366.

Gonzales, A. L., Ems, L., & Suri, V. R. (2016). Cell phone disconnection disrupts access to healthcare and health resources: A technology maintenance perspective. *New Media & Society*, *18*(8), 1422–1438.

Gonzales, A., Yan, H. Y., Read, G., & Brown, A. (in press). What is missing? How technology maintenance is overlooked in representative surveys of digital inequalities. In E. Hargittai. (Ed.) *The handbook of digital inequality*.

Graham, S., & Thrift, N. (2007). Out of order: Understanding repair and maintenance. *Theory, Culture & Society*, *24*(3), 1–25.

Grayson, D., & Jane, N. (2017). *Corporate responsibility coalitions: The past, present, and future of alliances for sustainable capitalism.* London: Routledge.

Graziano, V., & Trogal, K. (2017). The politics of collective repair: Examining object-relations in a postwork society. *Cultural Studies*, *31*(5), 634–658.

Hargittai, E. (2002). Second-level digital divide: Differences in people's online skills. *First Monday*, 7. Retrieved from http://firstmonday.org/ojs/index.php/fm/article/viewArticle/942

Houston, L., & Jackson, S. J. (2017). ICTD 2016| Caring for the "next billion" mobile handsets: Proprietary closures and the work of repair. *Information Technologies & International Development*, *13*, 15.

Houston, L., Jackson, S. J., Rosner, D. K., Ahmed, S. I., Young, M., & Kang, L. (2016). Values in repair. In *Proceedings of the 2016 CHI Conference on Human Factors in Computing Systems* (pp. 1403–1414). ACM.

International Telecommunication Union. (2017). *Global and regional ICT data*. Retrieved from https://www.itu.int/en/ITU-D/Statistics/Documents/statistics/2017/ITU_Key_2005-2017_ICT_data.xls

Jackson, S. J. (2014). 11 rethinking repair. In T. Gillespie, P. J. Boczkowski, & K. A. Foot (Eds.), *Media technologies: Essays on communication, materiality, and society* (pp. 221–240). Boston, MA: MIT Press.

Jackson, S. J., Ahmed, S. I., & Rifat, M. R. (2014). Learning, innovation, and sustainability among mobile phone repairers in Dhaka, Bangladesh. In *Proceedings of the 2014 Conference on Designing Interactive Systems* (pp. 905–914). ACM.

Jackson, S. J., & Kang, L. (2014). Breakdown, obsolescence and reuse: HCI and the art of repair. In *Proceedings of the SIGCHI Conference on Human Factors in Computing Systems* (pp. 449–458). ACM.

James, J. (2001). Low-cost computing and related ways of overcoming the global digital divide. *Journal of Information Science*, *27*(6), 385–392.

Kastrenakes, J. (2018, May 1st). Microsoft, Nintendo, and Sony warned by FTC about potentially illegal product warranties. *The Verge*. Retrieved from https://www.theverge.com/2018/5/1/17308042/ftc-illegal-warranty-letters-warning-microsoft-sony-nintendo-asus-htc-hyundai

Kiddee, P., Naidu, R., & Wong, M. H. (2013). Electronic waste management approaches: An overview. *Waste Management*, *33*(5), 1237–1250.

Kissling, R., Coughlan, D., Fitzpatrick, C., Boeni, H., Luepschen, C., Andrew, S., & Dickenson, J. (2013). Success factors and barriers in re-use of electrical and electronic equipment. *Resources, Conservation and Recycling*, *80*, 21–31.

Kissling, R., Fitzpatrick, C., Boeni, H., Luepschen, C., Andrew, S., & Dickenson, J. (2012). Definition of generic re-use operating models for electrical and electronic equipment. *Resources, Conservation and Recycling*, *65*, 85–99.

Koschmann, M. A., Kuhn, T. R., & Pfarrer, M. D. (2012). A communicative framework of value in cross-sector partnerships. *Academy of Management Review*, *37*(3), 332–354.

Manivannan, S. V. (2016). Environmental and health aspects of mobile phone production and use: Suggestions for innovation and policy. *Environmental Innovation and Societal Transitions*, *21*, 69–79.

Mesch, G. S. (2012). Minority status and the use of computer-mediated communication: A test of the social diversification hypothesis. *Communication Research*, *39*(3), 317–337. https://doi.org/10.1177/0093650211398865

Mitchell, S. (2018). Narratives of resistance and repair in consumer society. *Third Text*, *32*(1), 55–67.

Murugesan, S. (2008). Harnessing green IT: Principles and practices. *IT Professional*, *10*(1), 24–33.

Norris, P. (2001). *Digital divide: Civic engagement, information poverty, and the Internet worldwide.* Cambridge, UK: Cambridge University Press.

Ragnedda, M., & Muschert, G. W. (Eds.). (2013). *The digital divide: The Internet and social inequality in international perspective.* New York, NY: Routledge.

Ribeiro, M., (2016) *How often should your company replace computers?* Retrieved from https://www.vbsitservices.com/2016/02/how-often-should-your-company-replace-computers/

Robinson, B. H. (2009). E-waste: An assessment of global production and environmental impacts. *Science of the Total Environment, 408*(2), 183–191.

Robinson, L. (2014). Endowed, entrepreneurial, and empowered-strivers: Doing a lot with a lot, doing a lot with a little. *Information, Communication & Society, 17*(5), 521–536.

Robinson, L., & Schulz, J. (2013). Net time negotiations within the family. *Information, Communication & Society, 16*(4), 542–560.

Rosner, D. K., & Ames, M. (2014). Designing for repair? Infrastructures and materialities of breakdown. In *Proceedings of the 17th ACM Conference on Computer Supported Cooperative Work & Social Computing* (pp. 319–331). ACM.

Sabbaghi, M., Cade, W., Behdad, S., & Bisantz, A. M. (2017). The current status of the consumer electronics repair industry in the US: A survey-based study. *Resources, Conservation and Recycling, 116*, 137–151.

Sabbaghi, M., Esmaeilian, B., Cade, W., Wiens, K., & Behdad, S. (2016). Business outcomes of product repairability: A survey-based study of consumer repair experiences. *Resources, Conservation and Recycling, 109*, 114–122.

Spicework.com (2018). *Data snapshot: The lifespan of computers and other tech in the workplace.* Retrieved from https://community.spiceworks.com/blog/3103-data-snapshot-the-lifespan-of-computers-and-other-tech-in-the-workplace

Spiezia, V. (2013). ICT investments and productivity. *OECD Journal: Economic Studies, 2012*(1), 199–211.

Van Deursen, A. J., & Helsper, E. J. (2015). The third-level digital divide: Who benefits most from being online?. In *Communication and Information Technologies Annual* (pp. 29–52). Emerald Group Publishing Limited.

Van Dijk, J. A. (2005). *The deepening divide: Inequality in the information society.* Newbury Park, CA: Sage Publications.

Van Dijk, J. A. (2006). Digital divide research, achievements and shortcomings. *Poetics, 34*(4–5), 221–235.

Velkova, J. (2018). Repairing and developing software infrastructures: The case of Morevna Project in Russia. *New Media & Society, 20*(6), 2145–2161. doi:10.1177/1461444817731922

Viswanath, K., & Kreuter, M. W. (2007). Health disparities, communication inequalities, and eHealth. *American Journal of Preventive Medicine, 32*(5), S131–S133.

Vogel, D. (2007). *The market for virtue: The potential and limits of corporate social responsibility.* Washington, DC: Brookings Institution Press.

Williams, E., Kahhat, R., Allenby, B., Kavazanjian, E., Kim, J., & Xu, M. (2008). Environmental, social, and economic implications of global reuse and recycling of personal computers. *Environmental Science & Technology, 42*(17), 6446–6454.

Yu, X. Z., Gao, Y., Wu, S. C., Zhang, H. B., Cheung, K. C., & Wong, M. H. (2006). Distribution of polycyclic aromatic hydrocarbons in soils at Guiyu area of China, affected by recycling of electronic waste using primitive technologies. *Chemosphere, 65*(9), 1500–1509.

6 When Pacing Is a Privilege

The Time Scale of Exclusion

Dawna I. Ballard and Ana M. Aguilar

A 20th-century ideal of the relationship between time and work suggested that the ability to pace oneself amid any number of tasks should be earned (and rewarded) to assure peak organizational efficiency (Thompson, 1967). A classic example of this was depicted in Charlie Chaplin's *Modern Times* (Chaplin, 1936) where the Little Tramp character was (out)paced by an accelerating assembly line, whose speed was determined by upper management. Even his eating pace was subject to an experimental "feeding machine," which posed serious threats to his health and safety. Further into the 20th century, as industrial time expanded beyond the factory, Jaques (1982) developed and employed psychometric tests to determine whether organizational members had the cognitive capacity to be good stewards of their time. He argued that individuals in varied positions across an organization should be assigned a proper *time span of discretion* in line with their stewardship potential (as reflected in their test scores). These early examples of pacing norms, and the related privilege and inclusion afforded to some members and denied to others, continue to influence the underlying design logics (Barbour, Gill, & Barge, 2018) of contemporary organizational structures.

Pacing structures are inherent in formal organizing, as McPhee and Zaug (2000) describe activity coordination as one of the four constitutive flows of organizing. The implications of time's constitutive role in organizing, however, are often overlooked when considering the topic of organizational exclusion/ inclusion. In practice, pacing is one of the primary ways to effect systematic exclusion (Bailey & Madden, 2017; Ryan & Kossek, 2008). Sharma (2014) describes how speed functions as ideological discourse, disciplining those unable to maintain the pace. Slow bodies, slow emotions, and slow professional processes exist throughout organizations and industries of all types (Berg & Seeber, 2016; Honore, 2004; Parkins, 2004; Slow Science Academy, 2010). Bodies grow slower through illness, pregnancy, and age, to name a few. The emotions and respective recovery processes associated with grief and trauma are also sometimes slow (Richardson, 2002). As well, the inevitable process of newcomer socialization and acculturation is slow and inconvenient relative to a routine pace (Gomez, 2009). To the extent that dominant Western, (post) industrial pacing norms demand speedy bodies, fast emotions, and truncated processes, entire classes of people and many more individuals will be excluded based on their demographic, health, occupational, or ability grouping (Jammaers, Zanoni, & Hardonk, 2016; Kossek & Lautsch, 2018; Mik-Meyer, 2016). In their discussion regarding how discourses of otherness limit inclusion, Ghorashi and Sabelis (2013) argue that "Creating space in organizational and communicative settings always entails taking 'time out' as well" (p. 83).

Temporally based exclusion and inclusion are not binary practices. For instance, organizations are unlikely to permanently exclude someone for having the flu and most recognize that newcomers require at least a degree of patience in order to become functioning members of the team. Rather, exclusion and inclusion exist on a continuum that unfolds over time and, thus, implicates particular time scales as sites of exclusion/inclusion. Our focus in this chapter is on considering how time scale and organizational temporality, more broadly, can function to include or exclude certain types of natural processes inherent in members' experiences, particularly those processes that arise in and through their work. We do this through applying a temporal stewardship perspective (Bluedorn & Waller, 2006) to the question of inclusion/exclusion in contemporary work and consider each of the three components of their model, in turn: *organizational effectiveness versus efficiency, wider participation*, and *more cognizant agency*.

Based on their model, in the pages that follow, first we describe the nature of the temporal commons and explore questions of effectiveness (versus efficiency) through the lens of time scale. Next, we identify a range of stakeholders whose interests and experiences must be brought to bear on the issue of temporal inclusion. Finally, we reflect on two classes of "slow" processes—both *professional* and *physiological*—that can be associated with exclusionary practices and consider the types of data that scholars and practitioners can use to foster greater agency and, ultimately, inclusion across varied types of work.

Finding Inclusion through Temporal Stewardship

Following a stakeholder approach, Bluedorn and Waller (2006) articulate the need for organizations and their members to engage in stewardship of *the temporal commons* in much the same way as other (tangible and intangible) public resources demand thoughtful and shared oversight. The temporal commons is "the shared conceptualization of time and the set of resultant values, beliefs, and behaviors regarding time, as created and applied by members of a culture-carrying collectivity ..." (p. 367). They argue that under the rise of privatization, the temporal commons has become subsumed under market-based metrics of efficiency that lead to a number of problems, including the exclusion of certain *times*. Their expanded conception of relevant stakeholders suggests an alternate stewardship model centered on organizational effectiveness (compared to efficiency), wider participation (rather than decision making on the part of only one set of stakeholders), and more cognizant agency (as opposed to unconscious contribution to existing power structures). We begin by exploring the relevance of choices made based on efficiency versus effectiveness for temporal inclusion.

The Time Scale of Efficiency and Effectiveness

Bluedorn and Waller's conceptualization of stewardship of the temporal commons is well-suited to examine how questions relating to exclusion can be illuminated through reconsidering the time scale through which we conceptualize "slow" processes—either professional or physiological—and their relationship to organizational effectiveness. To illustrate this point, consider how productivity is directly related to the pace of work. It is calculated based on the output generated per unit of input, with output measured in units of time—such as daily sales figures or units produced per week. Taylorism is built on this conception of productivity (1911). The challenge is that when stewardship decisions are based upon brief time scales, the choice between efficiency (e.g., faster) and effectiveness (e.g., better) appears quite costly. Effectiveness is seen as an expensive stewardship principle, because time is (conceived as) money (Ancona, Okhuysen, & Perlow, 2001). Viewed from a different perspective, if efficiency is chosen as a stewardship principle, the human costs (of injury, of ageist and ableist institutional cultures, of employee burnout) are also high. Thus, neither approach appears to be without major sacrifice.

When the choice of either efficiency or effectiveness appears high, choosing the least costly outcome makes sense. Within smaller windows of time, efficiency is likely to be seen as least costly. While injury, burnout, and turnover are high, they are long-term, not short-term, costs. Through normalizing these costs in particular professions and industries it becomes accepted as part of the "cost of business" rather than an issue of (im)proper stewardship. Consequently, certain problems are seen as intractable aspects of the professional timescape (Adam, 2004) that must be accounted for (in expected high rates of turnover, burnout, and injury, for example) rather than addressed through policies and norms (Stein, Alvarez, & McKee, 2014).

In contrast, if the time frame through which productivity is viewed becomes substantially enlarged, from daily or weekly figures, to—perhaps—a scale as large as mean (or median) employee tenure, then even discussions about efficiency (as well as effectiveness) will include the risks to employee turnover, ethics, absenteeism, presenteeism, health, commitment, and satisfaction, among others (Ballard & Webster, 2009; Barnes, Schaubroeck, Huth, Ghumman, & 2011; Barnes & Van Dyne, 2009; Kuhn, 2006). From this larger time scale, organizations might find that the most efficient and effective organizational practices are actually the practices that include (rather than exclude) more organizational members. Ballard and McVey (2014) illustrate how attention to the temporality of communication processes reveals opportunities for communication design efforts. Particularly, a focus on time scale offers a path to change how outcomes are measured and jobs are defined. Time scale sensitivity also facilitates the temporal inclusion of a range of professionally and physiologically driven processes (Zaheer, Albert, & Zaheer, 1999). We illustrate below through considering the time scale of an oft-cited topic with a great deal of recent scholarly, professional, and mainstream interest: Resilience (Buzzanell & Houston, 2018; Doerfel, Harris, Kwestel, & Kim, forthcoming; Richardson, 2002).

Despite the lack of consensus on the definition of resilience, the concept has piqued the interest of academics, practitioners, and the general public. As such, it is becoming a fundamental measure in evaluating new interventions and policies (Windle, Bennett, & Noyes, 2011). Gaining an understanding of how individuals, teams, and organizations can recover from trauma or disruptions is beneficial in creating interventions or implementing structural changes in organizations and communities. The concept of resilience, believed to originate in ecology (Batabyal, 1998), has been applied in a variety of social science disciplines, including communication. Early psychological research on resilience focused on traits that prevented "at risk" children from developing psychopathological disorders (Garmezy, 1993; Masten et al., 1999). The idea of resilience as a trait soon lost its popularity for a more complex understanding of resilience as a process (Richardson, 2002). It was no longer understood as something someone possessed or lacked but was something in which an entity engaged. The construct of resilience has moved far beyond its original focus of children and expanded to studying adults, teams, organizations, communities, and even nations (Afifi, 2018; Buzzanell & Houston, 2018; Doerfel & Haseki, 2013). Despite the increase in research on varying levels of analysis (from micro to macro), an inherent feature of the construct has been commonly overlooked: temporality.

Time is an integral part of resilience but little critique or theorizing has focused on what temporal assumptions exist in current conceptions of the term and its impact. In examining commonly used and highly cited definitions across social science disciplines, a pattern emerges in the language used to define resilience. The ability to bounce back from negative experiences (Block & Kremen, 1996) is echoed in thousands of articles as a defining feature of resilience. The idea of an entity "bouncing back" is referring to the temporal enactment of pace (Ballard & Seibold, 2003). Temporal enactments refer to "the way work group members 'perform' time" (p. 385) while pace specifically refers to the "tempo or rate of an activity" (p. 387, Ballard & Seibold, 2003). "Bouncing back" brings to mind the idea of throwing a rubber ball onto the floor, only for it to return to the person's hand in a matter of seconds. Bouncing back inherently implies a quick pace, meaning that if an entity is to be resilient it must do so in a quick manner. Thus, extant conceptions of resilience assume brief time scales and appear to be more focused on efficiency than effectiveness.

Some empirical work conceptualizes resilience as a process, thus implicitly acknowledging the temporality of the construct (Buzzanell & Houston, 2018; Doerfel, Lai, & Chewning, 2010). For instance, Doerfel et al. (forthcoming) discuss five distinct factors that indicate the resiliency of organizations which reflect temporal features. These factors include the organization's *robustness,* degrees of *redundancy,* how *resourceful* it is in identifying and prioritizing problems as well as being able to mobilize, *rapid* response and being *externally available* to stakeholders.

Nonetheless, the implied temporal features often suggest that resilience must be fast. For example, Windle, Bennett, and Noyes (2011) analyzed resilience scales for their psychometric properties. They narrowed down hundreds of scales until they had 19 that were commonly used throughout the articles. They analyzed and ultimately found three to have high validity and reliability. Of those three scales that were considered to have the highest validity and reliability, all contained mention of quick pace as a desirable factor (Campell-Sills & Stein, 2007; Friborg, Hjemdal, Rosenvinge, & Martinussen 2003; Smith et al., 2008).

If these scales all indicate that quick pace is a marker of being resilient then does it put resilience at odds with generally slower populations and forms of trauma that are slower to heal? Is "bouncing back" (i.e., resilience) from physiological trauma the same as healing, or does it imply that the entity is just attempting to operate as before? And are they doing so quickly? If resilience is, in fact, to be understood as a process, then having entities rush to function as they did before the trauma or disruption may do more harm than good (Richardson, 2002). When we think of physiological trauma, most things cannot be healed quickly—especially if the trauma is acute. For example, a broken bone will not heal overnight and trying to function as if the injury had not occurred may actually prolong the healing process and cause more long-term damage. Reducing the pressure to quickly function at the same capacity as before may afford access to better long-term recovery (Krause, Frank, Dasinger, Sullivan, & Sinclair, 2001). Doerfel et al. (2010) offer a large-scale longitudinal example of this finding in the city of New Orleans post-Hurricane Katrina. They found that the process of recovery occurred over a long span of time in various stages.

Krause and colleagues (2001) conducted an expansive literature review to answer questions regarding: (a) what factors affect individuals' time lost from work; (b) the rate at which they return to work; and (c) subsequent unemployment and changes in occupation after acute trauma. Their review found that increases in psychosocial job characteristics—such as time pressure, shift work, low control over work-rest schedule, and long work hours—were positively related to prolonged work disability. In addition, various other factors—such as the physical demands of their work and the social support they receive from coworkers and supervisors—were critical as well. The authors found that when these psychosocial job characteristics were lessened—less time pressure, less shift work, more control over their work-rest schedule, and more reasonable work hours—recovery rates improved. Despite the efficacy of temporal measures at promoting recovery, common temporal stewardship norms may mean these options are overlooked.

In many cases, individuals cannot engage in a true process of resilience but rather must attempt to function at their pre-trauma capacity as soon as possible regardless of their level of recovery (Briere, Kaltman & Green, 2008, p. 223). While this is true for acute trauma or disruptions, it is equally true for small, day-to-day trauma that occurs in the form of psychological stressors. If an entity cannot heal from smaller day-to-day issues due to their inability to manage their own pace, this becomes a form of cumulative trauma, which is "accumulated exposure to different types of traumatic events" (Briere et al., 2008, p. 223). Cumulative trauma is frequently studied among social work professionals, where case workers commonly experience secondary or vicarious trauma while simultaneously being overwhelmed by the pace in which they have to operate and the number of cases they must address (Nelson-Gardell & Harris, 2003). The accumulated trauma, the pressing pace, and the inability to fully recuperate all contribute to the high turnover rate within this occupation. Without the ability to manage one's pace in response to trauma, resilience is left for certain occupations and organizational members, excluding whole classes of bodies, work, and emotions.

To remedy this systemic exclusion, Bluedorn and Waller (2006) demonstrate how the issue of effectiveness versus efficiency rests, in part, upon the choice regarding which stakeholder interests are considered in decisions about the temporal commons. Below, we consider ways in which existing conceptions of stakeholders can be expanded in line with more inclusive time scales. Notably, reframing the temporality of the metrics themselves—performance, resilience, etc.—through a shift in time scale, offers a path to consider how multiple stakeholder interests, including employer interests, may intersect over time.

Expanded Time Scales Reveal Expanded Stakeholders

As described in the last section, common management metrics—such as efficiency, productivity, success, value—have a constitutive temporal aspect that implicitly guides a great deal of management theory (Ancona et al., 2001; Bailey, 2018). Even understandings of workplace wellness and health, such as resilience, are inherently (if implicitly) temporal in nature. These Western, (post)industrial conceptions of time commonly used to measure individual and organizational performance and health metrics are based on what Bluedorn (2002) describes as *fungible* time, where all times are essentially the same and are fully interchangeable. Within a fungible conception, time is defined by external measure, independent of persons and their relationships. This is contrasted with an *epochal* conception, where time is defined by a larger system of behavioral patterning: it exists in the context of *identities, relationships, and interactions* that can only be reckoned within broader expanses of time and reflects a story—with a beginning, middle, and end. Rather than representing a dichotomy, fungible and epochal times constitute a largely neglected duality that, together, offer more informed, fuller conceptions of human temporality.

Some aspects of work are best reckoned within fungible time, while others are better construed as epochal. Notably, the focus on identities, relationships, and interactions within an epochal conception is useful as we think about the relevant stakeholders for considering more inclusive organizational practices. Given Bluedorn's reference to epochality as reflecting a story, Browning's (1992) theoretical treatment of lists and stories as organizational communication helps to further elucidate the communicative implications of fungible and epochal temporal conceptions. His description of each reflects markedly different temporal conceptions which arise from different focal organizational stakeholders. Browning demonstrates that these two contrasting types of communication (i.e., lists and stories) direct attention to the process of (and differences across aspects of) organizing.

Within a fungible conception of time, lists (rather than stories) are used to guide and direct behavior and activities. As Browning (1992) describes, "The list is rooted in science and presented as a formula for action leading to controllable outcomes. It represents standards, accountability, and certainty … Lists are technical communication, progressive, and public; and once shared they extend a power base" (p. 281). Relying upon lists and the fungible time they represent leads to a focus on stakeholders based on what appear to be easily controllable outcomes. Stockholders will be included in the list because market performance is easy to measure—it is standardized and clear. Investors will also be included in the list because profits are easy to communicate. In many cases, however, the employee is not included as a stakeholder, but rather as an organizational resource (i.e., an input). Product and service inputs are viewed as easily controllable, while organizational members are not. Customers and clients have also traditionally been treated as resources, rather than stakeholders, because fully understanding customers has historically been so difficult and uncertain. While recent advances in artificial intelligence and computer learning are offering greater insight into this "black box," the long-term focus needed to consider customers and clients as stakeholders eludes most industries and organizations. There are notable exceptions in traditional firms, however (Hall, 1983; Scott, 1987). Both Hall (1983) and Scott (1987) contrasted the deeply relational foundation of commerce in traditional cultures with the owner-customer relationship that guided the development of industrial capitalism. In Hall's (1983) classic description of polychronic businesses, these close, long-term relationships were a hallmark.

In contrast, epochal conceptions of time are reflected in organizational stories, found in everyday discourse.

> … The story is romantic, humorous, tragic, and dramatic. It unfolds sequentially, with overlays, pockets of mystery, and the addition or deletion of performers … They reflect local knowledge, give coherence to group subcultures, change over time, and contain multiple voices. (Browning, 1992, p. 281).

While the measurement of fungible time is unaffected by context, which makes attention to broader time expanses unnecessary and irrelevant, epochal time conceptions necessarily depend upon broader time expanses in order to capture change, multiple voices, and the twists and turns of daily life. Thus, attention to the stories organizational members share—during the day, after work, during exit interviews—points directly to the relevant stakeholders with important roles in the shared stewardship of the temporal commons. The actors may be unruly and difficult to measure or quantify, but their stories are powerful and unmistakable in their import.

Within stories, we recognize that organizational members, themselves, are key organizational stakeholders: both employers and employees. Members' families are also stakeholders because their lives shape and are shaped by what happens at the organization—how many hours members work, when they must work, where they must work, whether they have sick leave, whether they have vacation time, the quality and safety of their working conditions, and their overall job stability (Perlow & Kelly, 2014). The communities within which organizations are located are also critical stakeholders. Around the country, citizens tell stories of initial hope and, later, broken trust when large companies receive support to expand into their cities. Semuels (2018) writes of her experience as a journalist reporting on Amazon:

> For local residents, starting work in this facility or one like it can seem like a blessing. At around $12 an hour, 40 hours a week, full-time jobs pay higher than many others in the region, and the benefits are also better than many other jobs in the industry. But workers are required to be on their feet all day, and receive scant time for bathroom breaks or lunch. They're pressured to meet certain production goals and are penalized by getting "written up"—the first step in getting fired—for not meeting them, they say. They're also allowed very little time off, and written up if they go over a certain amount of time off, these workers say, even if they get sick … As one worker, John Burgett, a current employee in Indiana who has detailed his experiences on the blog Amazon Emancipatory, told me, "It's very physically and emotionally grueling. They're walking a fine line in the community—everybody knows someone who's worked there, and no one says it's a good place to work."

Thus, in addition to organizations' investors, stockholders, and customers, their members, the communities in which they are located, the families of their members, and their customers, are all legitimate stakeholders within the temporal commons. Viewed from the metric of effectiveness (over efficiency), the interests of these stakeholders intersect. First, organizational members and their families want members to have healthy working conditions, livable policies, and living wages (including benefits). These strong working conditions, policies and wages translate to organizational members who report a greater intent to stay, increased satisfaction, more satisfied clients, and lower turnover—all of which support the organization and employer in their goals of cost savings and higher profits (Perlow, 2012). Additionally, research shows that the way organizational members are treated by management predicts the level of service quality they provide to clients and customers (Schneider, 1994). Therefore, employees', employers', and clients' interests are aligned. A satisfied customer or client base, particularly one that speaks highly of the organization to others, is also a boon to the organization's health and continued success. This meets the needs of investors and stockholders—who have interests aligned with growth and profits. Ultimately, enlarging an organization's stakeholders, through considering the epochal times reflected in stories contributes to greater inclusion and greater long-term organizational success. Below we explore ways to include the needs of these varied stakeholders through applying more cognizant agency, as Bluedorn and Waller suggest.

Cognizant Agency in Creating Metrics of Inclusion

The discussion of fungible and epochal times points toward a particular thesis about work and time embodied in common performance metrics: Fungible time reflects what Hassard (2002) describes as a *commodification thesis*, revealed in the equation of time with quantitative value. This commodification thesis is directly tied to the standards—of efficiency (versus effectiveness)—that Bluedorn and Waller (2006) challenge in their concern regarding stewardship of the temporal commons. They describe that, while effectiveness concerns goal attainment, efficiency is measured by the ratio of a system's output to its input:

> the efficiency or worth of time is in many ways today measured by the worth of transactions conducted or savings accrued, rather than the quality of experience, during that time. In other words, the worth of time in our market-driven culture is measured by its efficiency, to the exclusion of practically all other metrics.
>
> (p. 376)

It is this commodification thesis—and the concomitant focus on fungible time to the exclusion of epochal time—that leads to a stewardship of the temporal commons in ways that often exclude slow(er) processes.

Bailey (2018) offers a theoretical treatment of *waiting* which highlights how the commodification thesis construes slowness in organizations as inherently problematic. She notes that, this view "can paradoxically damage an organisation's ability to tackle problems or generate creative responses, as it imposes artificial constraints on the messy realities of organisational life, inhibiting the development of creative solutions" (p. 5). In contrast, within epochal understandings of organizational time, the delay of waiting for processes to unfold is seen as inherent to, and even healthy for, organizational functioning. Bailey goes on to describe the varied temporality of different types of work. Notably, as Bailey describes, there are both *professional* and *physiological* processes that shape and are shaped by the experience of waiting. We develop these distinctions next and identify key sources of data that shed light on each of these processes. We are especially interested in sources of data that support more agentic visions for temporal inclusion and stewardship of the temporal commons.

To better understand the impact of time scale on exclusionary organizational practices, consider the ways in which professional and physiological spheres of activity are interlocking processes rather than separate spheres of temporal experience (Bailey, 2018; Barnes et al., 2011; Richardson, 2002). It is impossible to establish boundaries around either process for two reasons. First, from a spillover perspective (Perrigino, Dunford, & Wilson, 2018), communication-based demands that derive from one's professional activities have real consequences for organizational members' physiological wellness; similarly, communication-based demands that originate from any number of physiological processes (emotional or otherwise) can also shape organizational members' professional agility. Second, however, the most ironic exclusion comes from ignoring the natural pace of the *physiological demands that organizational members face in carrying out their professional activities*. These demands are inherent in the work as opposed to simply being consequential for the work.

The problem of professionally focused demands creating physiological stress, or disruption, concerning organizational members' time, energy, resilience, and coping resources is not limited in scope or exceptional by any means (Manville, Akremi, Niezborala, & Mignonac, 2016; Pang, 2016). In 2016, 2.9 million organizational members across industries such as construction, transportation, manufacturing, oil and gas, and agriculture were injured on the job (Bureau of Labor Statistics, 2017). As well, recent work on rates of suicide among physicians shows how the work itself contributes to physiological trauma (Anderson, 2018). Research on social work (Yuill & Mueller-Hirth, 2018) and health care, more generally (Wang, 2018), athletic and military careers (Stein et al., 2014), and a range of blue-collar professions (Kreiner, Ashforth, & Sluss, 2006) indicates that the cause of slow physiological processes have professional origins. Thus, organizational chronemics—that is, the ways in which time and communication are bound together—often gives rise to the very demands that members must manage in order to maintain their resilience. As a result, the impact of professional and physiological demands that shape members' resilience is frequently separable in analytic terms only, as depicted in Figure 6.1: Organizational membership entails both professional and physiological demands.

Figure 6.1 also illustrates the ways in which time scale can include or exclude professional and physiological processes. We conceptualize professional processes, those driven by the work and/or the formal organization, as oriented toward either exploitation or exploration as theorized by March (1991). Each concept occupies a place on the continuum—rather than a dichotomy—of organizational learning processes. March argues that organizational processes more governed by exploitation will highlight and privilege efficiency, production, and execution. In contrast, processes driven by exploration will

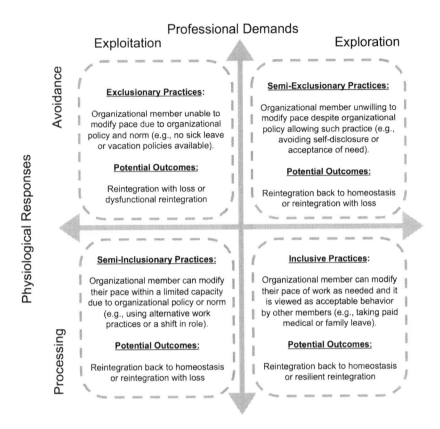

Figure 6.1 The impact of physiological responses and professional demands on resilience outcomes.

exhibit more flexibility, experimentation, innovation, and variation. He illustrates how a balance between the two is necessary for organizational effectiveness and survival. Notably, the time scale of each differs. Exploitation values speed, while exploration values deliberation. We use this continuum to characterize the temporality of professionally focused communication processes and their related outcomes, reflected in the horizontal axis.

We characterize the continuum of responses to physiological stressors (identified on the vertical axis) as ranging from *processing* to *avoidance*. On one end of the vertical axis, responding to physiological stressors—such as illness, injury, or trauma—through seeking needed medical treatment or communicating with others reflects a response of *processing*. In contrast, failing to communicate about or seek treatment for physiological stressors reflects an *avoidance* response. Richardson (2002) describes how individuals vary in their disposition to either process or avoid communicating about stressors—a decision which can shape their recovery and long-term resilience.

We also use March's (1991) terms to characterize a continuum of professional demands (on the horizontal axis) marked by organizations' orientations toward either exploitation or exploration. At one end of the continuum, organizations create policies that reflect the high value placed on risks which favor innovation and long-term rewards. This reflects a culture of exploration. In contrast, at the other end of the continuum, organizations maintain policies that reflect a "sink-or-swim" approach and place value on shorter term, easier to predict rewards. This reflects a bias toward exploitation.

While both approaches (avoidance versus processing and exploitation versus exploration) are continuous in nature, below we depict four types of practices and outcomes expected as a result of norms and policies that fall along the ends of each continuum. Some norms and policies lead to more exclusionary outcomes and other practices lead to more inclusive outcomes. This depicts the intersecting role of professional demands associated with particular organizational environments *and* physiological stressors associated with particular responses by individuals in an organization. Findings by Richardson (2002) assist with potential outcomes we identify in each quadrant. Following this discussion, we also describe multiple types of data, at varied time scales, and collected at various organizational levels, that provide a window into temporal inclusivity.

Exclusionary Practices and Outcomes

When organizational norms and policies privilege exploitation over exploration and individuals tend toward avoidance over processing related to the physiological stressors they face, slow processes will be excluded. For example, physician burnout and suicide (Anderson, 2018) is the highest among all occupations, in part, due to the long hours, chronic sleep deprivation, role strain, and personal isolation. The institutional culture among attending physicians leads to professional demands that reflect exploitation over exploration. The training model also leads to personal isolation and a high level of competition which makes avoidance a more likely response to physiological stressors than processing. Taken together, this means that organizational members will be unable to modify their pace and unwilling to violate institutional norms of seeking help. As a result, as physicians manage the demands of the physiological stressors they face, they are likely to develop burnout and/or substance abuse. Burnout reflects Richardson's (2002) description of *reintegration with loss*, situations in which people lose hope, motivation, and drive. Substance abuse is an example of *dysfunctional reintegration*, wherein individuals cope through substance abuse or other destructive behaviors to manage the professional-physiological demands placed on them (Richardson, 2002). In these cases, a range of human experience will be excluded from the organization (Jammaers et al., 2016).

Semi-Exclusionary Practices and Outcomes

In contrast, when organizational norms and policies value exploration and long-term gains, over exploitation marked by short-term wins, the institutional or organizational culture may afford their members greater resilience. Nonetheless, if the organizational member is more oriented toward avoidance than processing, self-exclusion may still result. In the case above, related to burnout and mental illness, an individual may still be unwilling to modify their pace despite organizational policies and norms which permit it. Rather than being driven by professional demands, an individual's personal disposition toward self-disclosure of illness or hardship can lead them to avoid processing the physiological stressors. This may take the form of not taking (allowable) vacation days or not utilizing formal leave policies, even when others use these policies without negative consequences. Passalacqua (2017) describes the role of personality and the problem of personal isolation in contributing to high burnout rates among physicians.

When the individual finally begins the process of addressing the issues that require their attention, their resiliency outcomes are likely to be the same as for the next quadrant—described as semi-inclusionary—although the reasons differ. A key distinction for the practices and outcomes in this semi-exclusionary quadrant, that makes them more exclusionary, is the norm setting function that they can have for others. As others witness these, essentially, *self*-exclusionary practices, tacit beliefs may form that serve to exclude behaviors focused on processing one's physiologically focused needs (Dyrbye et al., 2010).

Semi-Inclusionary Practices and Outcomes

In some cases, organizational norms and formal policies may privilege exploitation over exploration, but individuals persist in attempting to process the physiological demands they face. If alternative work practices are available (such as part-time work, job sharing, or telework, for example) or if shifting roles is permitted (such as with internal rotations), and the organizational member uses them, slow processes will be accommodated, but not accepted (Ballard & Gossett, 2007). In the physician burnout example described thus far, this might take the form of shifting roles (such as one's specialty). In other professions, it might take the form of temporarily shifting to part-time work. This highlights the economic privilege that might be associated with this particular practice. Minimum wage earners are unlikely to find any suitable options without adequate organizational policies that support medical leave or paid vacation time.

In the event that this is a viable option for an individual, the member will be able to modify their pace to a degree; however, they still risk reintegration with loss. In addition to burnout, this could take the form of depression based upon hurting one's chances for promotion or the feeling of unfilled professional goals. In the best case of this scenario, eventual *reintegration back to homeostasis* is possible. This means that things can eventually return to normal. Richardson (2002) describes, "The essence of reintegration back to homeostasis is to heal and 'just get past' a disruption" (p. 312). This is not always possible, such as in cases of permanent physical loss. In this case, inclusion will likely require a great deal of impression management work on the part of the organizational member. In these conditions, many may decide to simply withdraw given the efforts and coping resources it requires.

Inclusionary Practices and Outcomes

In the most temporally inclusive of all settings, organizational members can modify their pace of work (e.g., through paid medical or family leave) if needed and it is viewed as acceptable behavior by other members. When organizational norms and policies privilege exploration over exploitation *and* individuals tend toward processing (as opposed to avoiding) the physiological demands they face, slow processes will be included. In these cases, reintegration to homeostasis can be expected and even *resilient reintegration* is possible. Resilient reintegration occurs when individuals "experience some insight or growth *through* disruptions. The process is an introspective experience in identifying, accessing, and nurturing resilient qualities" (Richardson, 2002, p. 312, italics added). It also provides additional support to weather and recover successfully from future disruptions. When organizational members have access to and take sick leave or vacation time to deal with a professionally focused and/or physiologically focused disruption this reflects temporally inclusive behavior. In the case of epidemic physician burnout rates described earlier, offering paid medical leave as well as mental health resources and training in healthy coping strategies to physicians could help to minimize the recurrence of burnout.

Access to this level of inclusion, however, is rare in practice. Below we describe the types of organizational data that will help to identify and track changes in temporal inclusivity. A host of data can help to identify inclusionary/exclusionary practices and their related outcomes.

Finding Metrics that Help to Identify Temporal Exclusion/Inclusion Organizational Data

Objective measures of time-based indicators in an organization are a key resource in understanding temporal exclusion. Are alternative work practices, sick and family leave policies, and paid vacation time available? If so, the data collected should also include records of unused vacation time, days used of family and medical leave, and the use of alternative work practices. Are members who utilize these resources promoted and retained at similar levels? Additionally, records of hours worked, absenteeism, and turnover are important sources of organizational data. If an intervention is planned, large-scale (not personally identifying) data on organizational members' health (such as BMI, rates of hypertension, and chronic illness) can serve as a baseline to track the effectiveness of new policies or norms.

Multiple Performance Measures

Many organizations collect various forms of data on performance outcomes. In order to include multiple stakeholders, multiple types of performance measures are essential. Notably, these data must be longitudinal in nature—capturing three- to five-year time frames. This allows long-term processes to emerge, such as resilience and sustainable productivity. For publicly traded organizations, stock market performance over even longer time scales—such as a decade—is important depending upon the historicity and current volatility of the market. For privately held organizations, records of profits should be collected over similarly long time scales. News stories may also yield relevant information. From the member perspective, exit interviews can be invaluable. As well, exploring online "suck sites" or other forums where current and former organizational members describe their experiences may also offer insights (Gossett & Kilker, 2006). For current members, performance measures that include quarterly target goals met as well as feedback from client or customer surveys are important. Additionally, community surveys may be vital in certain situations. This may take the form of face-to-face or phone interviews or mail-based surveys in the surrounding area.

Self-Administered Scales

Finally, a number of highly reliable self-administered scales exist to capture subjective and intersubjective reports of temporal exclusion/inclusion. For instance, data on burnout, job satisfaction, and psychological safety help to assess the broader climate of inclusion. Measures of organizational and individual temporality are also available—including specific measures of pace or speed (Ballard & Seibold, 2004; Schriber & Gutek, 1987). When possible, cross-sectional data should be avoided (Ballard, Waller, & Tschan, 2008). Capturing members' reports over time, especially tied to the timing of other performance measures will help scholars and practitioners to understand larger trends of resilience and performance declines related to external pacers such as market volatility (McGlone, Merola, & McGlynn, 2017). Triangulating these varied types of data—self-administered scales, performance measures, and available organizational data—will offer an informed view of the culture of temporal inclusivity.

Conclusion

One vantage point from which to pursue the question of inclusion in organizing is to interrogate existing and alternative treatments of one of the central constitutive aspects of work and institutions: Time. For example, the increasing speed with which new employees are expected to create measurable value for the company, as compared to hiring organizational members based on demonstrated promise and trainability, leads to greater numbers of underemployed and unemployable mid- to late-career professionals (Gliner, 1999). Relatedly, routine layoffs have accompanied the trend toward demonstrating larger and larger quarterly profit margins (Fairhurst, Cooren, & Cahill, 2002). This truncated time scale drove the mortgage crisis, fueled by the desire to create illusory short-term investor profits. Similarly, recent protests by Walmart employees demanding better wages amid record profits for the retailer are fueled by executives' shortsighted conceptions of profitability and productivity (Miles, 2013).

There are mainstream examples of efforts to reconsider the temporality of how value creation occurs in 21st-century work. The LifeTwist Study, a report by The Futures Company (and commissioned by American Express), revealed that contemporary organizational members report a nonlinear path to career "success" that has altered their definitions of success compared to previous generations (Tugend, 2013). Relatedly, Arianna Huffington, editor in chief of the *Huffington Post*, hosted a gathering called "The Third Metric: Redefining Success Beyond Money & Power" where Missouri Senator Claire McCaskill stressed that:

> renewal and redefining success are not just for those at the top of the corporate or the political ladders. Because the destructive definition of success we're living (and dying) under affects people at every social and economic level. But those working two or three jobs are also those with the least leverage to insist on policies and workplace practices that allow for any kind of work-life balance. And, of course, by redefining success we'll end up with leaders able to make better decisions—which, of course, affect everybody. For example, we'll have leaders less likely to make the sorts of terrible and shortsighted decisions that led to the financial meltdown, and led to the misguided decision to respond to the ensuing crisis with austerity measures. (Huffington, 2013)

At the same event, Aetna CEO, Mark Bertolini described how company wellness programs—while costly in the short term—save companies money in the long term (Young, 2013).

As scholars and practitioners, Bluedorn and Waller (2006) draw our attention to the stewardship of *the temporal commons* that underlies these varied time-related sites of inclusion and exclusion. As such, it is an ideal means through which we can consider temporally based inclusion in organizing. Taking up this perspective points to three issues we develop in this chapter. First, the issue of time scale emerges as a key factor underlying temporal exclusion as well as a path to (re)consider the value of effectiveness over efficiency. We consider the traditional concept of productivity as well as its wellness-based companion, resilience, through a temporal lens. Next, we leverage these insights (derived from careful attention to time scale) as well as Browning's (1992) theory of lists and stories to identify key stakeholder interests that matter in any discussion of temporal inclusivity. Finally, we develop and elaborate on a model that highlights the interlocking nature of professionally focused and physiologically focused processes in developing more resilient organizational members.

In summary, conversations centered around stewardship of the temporal commons have the potential to create more temporally inclusive organizing structures. Nonetheless, contemporary repackaged conceptualizations of productivity abound: They simply mirror organizing norms designed to keep Chaplin's character in a loop of ever-greater value creation by utilizing new, human-centered discourse. As a result, common treatments of resilience, or even grit, valorize individual perseverance and striving in the face of remarkable obstacles (Duckworth, Peterson, Matthews, & Kelly, 2007). Rather than create more temporally inclusive workplaces, these constructs work to systematically exclude certain bodies, minds, and emotions from particular institutions (Jammaers et al., 2016; Kossek & Lautsch, 2018). Examples of this are found in primary and secondary education, social work, and law enforcement, to name a few (Yuill & Mueller-Hirth, 2018). This means that certain work will lack members with seniority (due to turnover), those with more non-work obligations (such as elder care and young families), as well as those with higher levels of concern for their own mental health.

Pioneering epidemiological research on John Henryism—a measure of "prolonged, high-effort coping with difficult psychosocial environmental stressors" (p. 167)—demonstrates that the impact of ignoring the long-term consequences of active coping leads to a host of physiological costs paid by the individual not the institution (James, 1994; Bennett et al., 2004). The John Henryism measurement scale includes items such as (a) *When things don't go the way I want them to, that just makes me work even harder*; (b) *I've always felt that I could make of my life pretty much what I wanted to make of it*; and (c) *Once I make up my mind to something, I stay with it until the job is completely done.*

James (1994) describes the genesis of this construct and resultant measure. In a series of related studies published in the early and mid-1970s—some field-based and others controlled laboratory experiments—researchers found that active, sustained coping (marked by cognitive and emotional engagement) with structural inequities led to increased heart rate and systolic blood pressure. In the late 1970s, informed by this stream of research, Syme (1979) proposed that certain forms of coping (i.e., prolonged and marked by high effort) could explain both the inverse relationship between hypertension and socioeconomic status and the increased risk for hypertension among African Americans. At the same time, James (1994) describes a chance encounter that led to the John Henryism construct.

It was my good fortune to come across this literature, and Syme's (1979) commentary, shortly after I had met a fascinating, retired Black farmer named *John Henry* Martin. His name could hardly have been more appropriate, since his life story (James, 1993) contained a number of features that evoked the legend of John Henry, the "steel-driving man" … known far and wide among late 19th century railroad and tunnel workers (Williams, 1983) for the remarkable physical strength and endurance he displayed in his work. John Henry beat a mechanical steam drill in a famous "steel-driving" contest pitting "man against machine." Moments after the contest ended, however, John Henry dropped dead from complete physical and mental exhaustion (Johnson, 1927; Williams, 1983). *John Henry* Martin, the retired Black farmer, also won an epic battle against "the machine." In his case, however, the "machine" was the ruthlessly exploitative sharecropping system of the rural South. Mr. Martin was born into an extremely poor, sharecropping family in 1907, in the Upper Piedmont region of the state of North Carolina. As a child, he was not able to attend school beyond the second grade; but, as an adult, he somehow taught himself to read and write.

Even more impressively, however, through unrelenting hard work and determination (i.e., effortful active coping), John Henry Martin—against tremendous odds—freed himself and his offspring from the debt bondage of the sharecropper system. Specifically, by the time he was 40 years of age, he owned 75 acres of fertile North Carolina farmland. Like the legendary "steel driver," however, John Henry Martin also paid a price for his victory. By his late 50s, he suffered from hypertension, arthritis, and a case of peptic ulcer disease so severe that 40% of his stomach had to be removed (James, 1993) … In tribute to John Henry Martin, and the larger historical drama that I believe his life story represents, I decided to provide a context—cultural as well as historical—for the active coping hypothesis by referring to it in my own work as the "John Henryism Hypothesis."

Since work on the John Henryism Hypothesis began, an entire body of work has repeatedly supported the idea that high-effort coping among disadvantaged populations—persevering against all odds—leads to physiological illness (Bennet et al., 2004). Thus, for certain groups, grit comes with a high cost. Instead, through the theory of TRIOS (Time, Rhythm, Improvisation, Orality, and Spirituality), Jones (2003) suggests that this sort of perseverance must be complemented by a reflexive understanding of one's larger temporal, cultural and even spiritual context. While individual resilience can be invaluable, the stewardship of the temporal commons relies upon a collective commitment to long-term, sustainable outcomes. Taking ever-greater time scales into account in our conceptions of key organizational constructs, like resilience and productivity, is critical to ensuring inclusive organizing.

References

Adam, B. (2004). *Time*. Cambridge, UK: Polity Press.
Afifi, T. D. (2018). Individual/relational resilience. *Journal of Applied Communication Research, 46*(1), 5–9, doi:10.1080/00909882.2018.1426707

Ancona, D. G., Okhuysen, G. A., Perlow, L. A. (2001). Taking time to integrate temporal research. *Academy of Management Review, 26*, 512–529.

Anderson, P. (2018, May 07). Physicians experience highest suicide rate of any profession. *Medscape.* Retrieved 8/30/18 from https://www.medscape.com/viewarticle/896257?nlid=122292_2051&src=WNL_mdplsnews_180511_mscpedit_psyc&uac=277137PV&spon=12&impID=1630261&faf=1#vp_1

Bailey, C. (2018). Waiting in organisations. *Time & Society,* Advance online publication. doi:10.1177/0961463X18794587

Bailey, C., & Madden, A. (2017). Time reclaimed: Temporality and meaningful work. *Work, Employment and Society, 31*(1), 3–18. doi:10.1177/0950017015604100

Ballard, D. I., & Gossett, L. M. (2007). Alternative times: The temporal perceptions, processes, and practices defining the non-standard work arrangement. In C. Beck (Ed.), *Communication yearbook, 31* (pp. 269–316). Mahwah, NJ: Lawrence Erlbaum Associates.

Ballard, D. I., & McVey, T. (2014). Measure twice, cut once: The temporality of communication design. *Journal of Applied Communication Research, 42*(2), 190–207. doi:10.1080/00909882.2013.874571

Ballard, D. I., & Seibold, D. R. (2003). Communicating and organizing in time: A meso level model of organizational temporality. *Management Communication Quarterly, 16*, 380–415.

Ballard, D. I., & Seibold, D. R. (2004). Organizational members' communication and temporal experience: Scale development and validation. *Communication Research, 31*, 135–172.

Ballard, D. I., Waller, M. J., & Tschan, F. (2008). All in the timing: Considering time at multiple stages of group research. *Small Group Communication, 39*, 328–351.

Ballard, D. I., & Webster, S. P. (2009). Time and time again: The search for meaning/fulness through popular discourse on the time and timing of work. *KronoScope: Journal for the Study of Time, 8*, 131–145.

Barbour, J. B., Gill, R., & Barge, J. K. (2018). Organizational communication design logics: A theory of communicative intervention and collective communication design. *Communication Theory, 28*, 332–353. doi:10.1093/ct/qtx005

Barnes, C. M., Schaubroeck, J., Huth, M., & Ghumman, S. (2011). Lack of sleep and unethical conduct. *Organizational Behavior and Human Decision Processes, 115*, 169–180.

Barnes, C. M., & Van Dyne, L. (2009). 'I'm tired': Differential effects of physical and emotional fatigue on workload management strategies. *Human Relations, 61*, 59–92.

Batabyal, A. A. (1998). The concept of resilience: Retrospect and prospect. *Environment and Development Economics, 3*(2), 221–262.

Bennett, G. G., Merritt, M. M., Sollers III, J. J., Edwards, C. L., Whitfield, K. E., Brandon, D. T., & Tucker, R. D. (2004). Stress, coping, and health outcomes among African-Americans: A review of the John Henryism hypothesis. *Psychology & Health, 19*(3), 369–383. doi:10.1080/0887044042000193505

Berg, M., & Seeber, B. K. (2016). *The slow professor: Challenging the culture of speed in the academy.* Toronto: University of Toronto Press.

Block, J., & Kremen, A. M. (1996). IQ and ego-resiliency: Conceptual and empirical connections and separateness. *Journal of Personality and Social Psychology, 70*, 340–361. doi:10.1037/0022-3514.70.2.349

Bluedorn, A. C. (2002). *The human organization of time: Temporal realities and experience.* Stanford, CA: Stanford Business Books.

Bluedorn, A. C., & Waller, M. J. (2006). The stewardship of the temporal commons. *Research in Organizational Behavior, 27,* 355–306. doi:10.1016/ S0191-3085(06)27009-6

Briere, J., Kaltman, S., & Green, B. L. (2008). Accumulated childhood trauma and symptom complexity. *Journal of Traumatic Stress, 21*(2), 223–226.

Browning, L. D. (1992). Lists and stories as organizational communication. *Communication Theory, 2,* 281–302.

Bureau of Labor Statistics. (2017, November 9). Employer-reported workplace injury and illnesses, 2016 [Press Release]. Retrieved from https://www.bls.gov/ news.release/osh.nr0.htm

Buzzanell, P. M., & Houston, J. B. (2018). Communication and resilience: Multilevel applications and insights–A Journal of Applied Communication Research forum. *Journal of Applied Communication Research, 46*(1), 1–4. doi:10.1080/00909 882.2017.1412086

Campell-Sills, L., & Stein, M. B. (2007). Psychometric analysis and refinement of the Connor-Davidson Resilience Scale (CD-RISC): Validation of a 10-item measure of resilience. *Journal of Traumatic Stress, 20*(6), 1019–1028. doi:10.1002/ jts.20271

Chaplin, C. (Producer), & Chaplin, C. (Director). (1936). *Modern times* [Motion picture]. United States: United Artists.

Doerfel, M. L., Harris, J. L., Kwestel, M., & Kim, M. (forthcoming). Crisis communication and organizational resilience. In F. Frandsen, & W. Johansen (Eds.), *Crisis communication* (Vol. 23). Berlin, Germany: Mouton de Gruyter.

Doerfel, M. L., & Haseki, M. (2013). Networks, disrupted: Media use as an organizing mechanism for rebuilding. *New Media & Society.* doi:10.1177/1461444 813505362

Doerfel, M. L., Lai, C. H., & Chewning, L. V. (2010). The evolutionary role of interorganizational communication: Modeling social capital in disaster contexts. *Human Communication Research, 36,* 125–162. doi:10.1111/j.1468-2958. 2010.01371.x

Duckworth, A. L., Peterson, C., Matthews, M. D., & Kelly, D. R. (2007). Grit: Perseverance and passion for long-term goals. *Journal of Personality and Social Psychology, 92*(6), 1087. doi:10.1037/0022-3514.92.6.1087

Dyrbye, L. N., Power, D. V., Massie, F. S., Eacker, A., Harper, W., Thomas, M. R., … Shanafelt, T. D. (2010). Factors associated with resilience to and recovery from burnout: A prospective, multi-institutional study of US medical students: Resilience in medical students. *Medical Education, 44*(10), 1016–1026. doi:10.1111/j.1365-2923.2010.03754.x

Fairhurst, G. T., Cooren, F., & Cahill, D. J. (2002). Discursiveness, contradiction, and unintended consequences in successive downsizings. *Management Communication Quarterly, 15,* 501–540. doi:10.1177/0893318902154001

Friborg, O., Hjemdal, O., Rosenvinge, J. H., & Martinussen, M. (2003). A new rating scale for adult resilience: What are the central protective resources behind healthy adjustment? *International Journal of Methods in Psychiatric Research, 12*(2), 65–76. doi:10.1002/mpr.143

Garmezy, N. (1993). Children in poverty: Resilience despite risk. *Psychiatry, 56*(1), 127–136. doi:10.1080/00332747.1993.11024627

Ghorashi, H., & Sabelis, I. (2013). Juggling difference and sameness: Rethinking strategies for diversity in organizations. *Scandinavian Journal of Management, 29*(1), 78–86. doi:10.1016/j.scaman.2012.11.002

Gliner, B. (Director). (1999). Time frenzy: Keeping up with tomorrow [Documentary]. United States: Films for the Humanities & Sciences.

Gómez, L. F. (2009). Time to socialize: Organizational socialization structures and temporality. *The Journal of Business Communication, 46*(2), 179–207. doi:10.1177/0021943608328077

Gossett, L. M., & Kilker, J. (2006). My job sucks: Examining counterinstitutional web sites as locations for organizational member voice, dissent, and resistance. *Management Communication Quarterly, 20*, 63–90.

Hall, E. T. (1983). *The dance of life*. Garden City, NY: Doubleday.

Hassard, J. (2002). Essai: Organizational time: Modern, symbolic and postmodern reflections. *Organization Studies, 23*(6), 885–892. doi:10.1177/0170840602236010

Honoré, C. (2004). *In praise of slowness: How a worldwide movement is challenging the cult of speed*. San Francisco, CA: Harper.

Huffington, A. (2013, June 14). Redefining success: Takeaways from our Third Metric Conference. *Huffington Post*. Retrieved from http://www.huffingtonpost.com/arianna-huffington/redefining-success-takeaway_b_3444007.html

James, S. A. (1994). John Henryism and the health of African-Americans. *Culture, Medicine and Psychiatry, 18*(2), 163–182.

Jammaers, E., Zanoni, P., & Hardonk, S. (2016). Constructing positive identities in ableist workplaces: Disabled employees' discursive practices engaging with the discourse of lower productivity. *Human Relations, 69*(6), 1365–1386. doi:10.1177/0018726715612901

Jaques, E. (1982). *The form of time*. London: Heinemann.

Johnson, G. B. (1927). *John Henry: Tracking down a Negro legend*. Chapel Hill, NC: University of North Carolina Press.

Jones, J.M. (2003). TRIOS: A psychological theory of the African legacy in American culture. *Journal of Social Issues, 59*, 217–242. doi:10.1111/1540-4560.t01-1-00014

Kossek, E. E., & Lautsch, B. A. (2018). Work–life flexibility for whom? Occupational status and work–life inequality in upper, middle, and lower level jobs. *Academy of Management Annals, 12*(1), 5–36. doi:10.5465/annals.2016.0059

Krause, N., Frank, J. W., Dasinger, L. K., Sullivan, T. J., & Sinclair, S. J. (2001). Determinants of duration of disability and return-to-work after work-related injury and illness: Challenges for future research. *American Journal of Industrial Medicine, 40*(4), 464–484. doi:10.1002/ajim.1116

Kreiner, G. E., Ashforth, B. E., & Sluss, D. M. (2006). Identity dynamics in occupational dirty work: Integrating social identity and system justification perspectives. *Organization Science, 17*(5), 527–676. doi:10.1287/orsc.1060.0208

Kuhn, T. (2006). A 'demented work ethic' and a 'lifestyle firm': Discourse, identity, and workplace time commitments. *Organization Studies* online first. doi:10.1177/0170840606067249

Manville, C., Akremi, A. E., Niezborala, M., & Mignonac, K. (2016). Injustice hurts, literally: The role of sleep and emotional exhaustion in the relationship between organizational justice and musculoskeletal disorders. *Human Relations, 69*(6), 1315–1339. doi:10.1177/0018726715615927

March, J. G. (1991). Exploration and exploitation in organizational learning. *Organization Science, 2*(1), 71–87. Retrieved from https://www.jstor.org/stable/2634940

Masten, A. S., Hubbard, J. J., Gest, S. D., Tellegen, A., Garmezy, N., & Ramirez, M. (1999). Competence in the context of adversity: Pathways to resilience and maladaptation from childhood to late adolescence. *Development and Psychopathology, 11*(1), 143–169.

McGlone, M. S., Merola, N. A., & McGlynn, J. (2017). Time is not on our side: Temporal agency in the Enron email dataset. In D. I. Ballard, & M. S. McGlone (Eds.), *Work pressures: New agendas in communication* (pp. 120–136). New York, NY: Routledge.

McPhee, R., & Zaug, P. (2000). The communicative constitution of organizations: A framework for explanation. *The Electronic Journal of Communication, 10*(1/2), 21–47.

Mik-Meyer, N. (2016). Othering, ableism and disability: A discursive analysis of co-workers' construction of colleagues with visible impairments. *Human Relations, 69*(6), 1341–1363. doi:10.1177/0018726715618454

Miles, K. (2013, November 8). Largest civil disobedience in Walmart history leads to more than 50 arrests. *Huffington Post.* Retrieved from http://www.huffingtonpost.com/2013/11/08/walmart-arrests_n_4227411.html

Nelson-Gardell, D., & Harris, D. (2003). Childhood abuse history, secondary traumatic stress, and child welfare workers. *Child Welfare, 82*(1), 1–26.

Pang, A. S. K. (2016). *Rest: Why you get more done when you work less.* New York, NY: Basic Books.

Parkins, W. (2004). Out of time: Fast subjects and slow living. *Time and Society, 13*(2–3), 363–382. doi:10.1177/0961463X04045662

Passalacqua, S. A. (2017). Occupational burnout and the case study of physicians. In D. I. Ballard, & M. S. McGlone (Eds.), *Work pressures: New agendas in communication* (pp. 111–130). New York, NY: Routledge.

Perlow, L. A. (2012). *Sleeping with your smartphone: How to break the 24/7 habit and change the way you work.* Boston, MA: Harvard Business Press.

Perlow, L. A., & Kelly, E. L. (2014). Toward a model of work redesign for better work and better life. *Work and Occupations, 41*(1), 111–134. doi:10.1177/0730888413516473

Perrigino, M. B., Dunford, B. B., & Wilson, K. S. (2018). Work–family backlash: The "dark side" of work–life balance (WLB) policies. *Academy of Management Annals, 12*(2), 600–630. doi:10.5465/annals.2016.0077

Richardson, G. E. (2002). The metatheory of resilience and resiliency. *Journal of Clinical Psychology, 58*, 307–321. doi:10.1002/jclp.10020

Ryan, A. M., & Kossek, E. E. (2008). Work-life policy implementation: Breaking down or creating barriers to inclusiveness? *Human Resource Management, 47*(2), 295–310. doi:10.1002/hrm.20213

Schneider, B. (1994). HRM—A service perspective: Towards a customer-focused HRM. *International Journal of Service Industry Management, 5*, 64–76.

Schriber, J. B., & Gutek, B. A. (1987). Some time dimensions of work: The measurement of an underlying dimension of organizational culture. *Journal of Applied Psychology, 72*, 642–650.

Scott, W. R. (1987). *Organizations: Rational, natural, & open systems.* Englewood Cliffs, NJ: Prentice Hall.

Semuels, A. (2018, February 1). What Amazon does to poor cities. *The Atlantic*. Retrieved from https://www.theatlantic.com/business/archive/2018/02/amazon-warehouses-poor-cities/552020/

Sharma, S. (2014). In the meantime: Temporality and cultural politics. Durham: Duke University Press.

The Slow Science Academy. (2010). *The slow science manifesto*. Retrieved October 23, 2014, from http://www.slow-science.org/

Smith, B. W., Dalen, J., Wiggins, K., Tooley, E., Christopher, P., & Bernard, J. (2008). The brief resilience scale: Assessing the ability to bounce back. *International Journal of Behavioural Medicine, 15*,194–200. doi:10.1080/10705500802222972

Stein, T. D., Alvarez, V. E., & McKee, A. C. (2014). Chronic traumatic encephalopathy: A spectrum of neuropathological changes following repetitive brain trauma in athletes and military personnel. *Alzheimer's Research & Therapy, 6*(4), 1–11.

Syme, S. L. (1979). Psychosocial determinants of hypertension. In E. Oresti, & C. Klint (Eds.), *Hypertension determinants, complications and intermention* (pp. 95–98). New York, NY: Grune and Stratton.

Taylor, F. W. (1911). *Scientific management*. New York, NY: Harper & Row. The Slow Science Manifesto: Retrieved from slow-science.org/slow-science-manifesto.pdf

Thompson, E. P. (1967). Time, work-discipline and industrial capitalism. *Past and Present, 38*, 56–97.

Tugend, A. (2013, June 14). A call for a movement to redefine the successful life. *The New York Times*. Retrieved from http://www.nytimes.com/2013/06/15/your-money/a-call-for-a-movement-to-redefine-the-successful-life.html?pagewanted=all&_r=0

Wang, C. (2018). Temporal dynamics in the daily lives of health practitioners. *Time & Society*, Advanced online publication. doi:10.1177/0961463X18787047

Williams, B. (1983). *John Henry: A bio-bibliography*. Westport, CT: Greenwood Press.

Windle, G., Bennett, K., & Noyes, J. (2011). A methodological review of resilience measurement scales. *Health and Quality of Life Outcomes, 9*(1), 8. doi:10.1186/1477-7525-9-8

Young, J. (2013, June 6). Company wellness programs may boost bottom lines, Aetna CEO Mark Bertolini says. *Huffington Post*. Retrieved from http://www.huffingtonpost.com/2013/06/06/company-wellness-programs-aetna-ceo_n_3398670.html

Yuill, C., & Mueller-Hirth, N. (2018). Paperwork, compassion and temporal conflicts in British social work. *Time & Society*, Advanced online publication. doi:10.1177/0961463X18785030

Zaheer, S., Albert, S., & Zaheer, A. (1999). Time scales and organizational theory. *Academy of Management Review, 24*, 725–741.

7 Creating the Being of Inclusion in Organizations

Sarah J. Tracy, Robert J. Razzante, and Katrina N. Hanna

Earlier this week we met with the board of trustees and I was the only African American woman in the room. There was an Ethiopian African man in the room who was of color, but I was the only African American female. In the room was a White male here and another White male there. Basically, there were three little brown specks in a room of like 30. It is one of those things that I don't let bother me as much. Sometimes you feel like [audible sigh], but you just shake it off.

> —Michelle, Black university administrator
> (Razzante & Tracy, 2019)

I feel like everything I say is thrown back at me! ... White people are being attacked and blamed, and we have to defend ourselves or just be used as punching bags. I give up! I am not saying anything else.

> —A White woman's comment in a cross-racial
> dialogue (DiAngelo, 2018, p. 99)

I always like our annual board of trustees meeting. There's a real mix of people there—queer, straight, Brown, Black, White. You get the picture. At our last meeting, people greeted each other with smiles, handshakes, and questions about their summer breaks. There was a newbie I didn't recognize. He seemed to be of Middle Eastern descent and uncertain of where to sit. I caught his eye, waved him over to my table, and introduced myself. Sure enough, he was the visiting scholar from Iran. Although he seemed not so interested in my research, I shrugged that off and invited him to join a book club I'm leading later this month.

> —Anonymous, hypothetical faculty member,
> hypothetical university

The snippets above show a slice of the being of exclusion and inclusion. Exclusion, as an experience, includes feelings of uncertainty, loneliness, dread, anger, and resentment. At an interactional level, exclusion might include being ignored, interrupted, bullied, blamed, attacked, or rebuffed. Inclusion, on the other hand, feels like connection, joy, and anticipation; it includes invitations, curious questions, and warm nonverbal communication in the form of eye contact, hand waves, and sharing physical space. Phenomenologically, inclusion feels good. And, materially, it goes beyond mere diversity. So, how might our research and scholarship best inspire, motivate, and create inclusion?

As we will review in this chapter, engaged communication scholars typically address issues of inclusion in terms of activities such as (1) focusing on a problem or dilemma related to exclusion that needs to be solved, (2) conducting research on this problem, (3) creating analyses that then may be applied to help shed light on the issue, and (4) developing diversity programs (Dempsey & Barge, 2014; Mease, 2012; Tracy, 2016). Such approaches are certainly useful for helping explain how and why *exclusion* takes place. However, we would argue that these approaches are limited in their ability to create the being of *inclusion*.

In this chapter, we discuss how scholarship and teaching could be practiced so as to create what we call the "being of inclusion." As will be fleshed out throughout this chapter, we put this phrase in quotation marks to indicate the specialized way we refer to "being" as the lived behavior and communication that results in people judging and feeling that a situation, person, or context is inclusive. This chapter outlines the limitations of merely "knowing about" inclusion at an epistemological level, as well as the restrictions of typical practical application activities for creating inclusion. As an alternative, we point to the promise of an ontological, phenomenological, phronetic, transformative (OPPT-in) "being" approach (Tracy & Donovan, 2018; Tracy, Franks, Brooks, & Hoffman, 2015). Such an approach highlights the value of several practices, including (1) the study of positive deviance (e.g., places where we see extraordinary connection, inclusion, or comradeship in action), (2) scholarly research that, through its thick description, inspires perspective taking and transformed behavior, and (3) pedagogy that asks students to practice and critically reflect on as-lived improvisation of talking and being that spark inclusion (e.g., practicing acknowledgement, micro affirmations, and authentic listening as well as communicating requests and demands in the face of injustice). We close this chapter by describing three programs that hold promise for creating the being of inclusion: *Free Listening, Civil Dialogue®* and *Storyscope*. Programs such as these and other activities associated with an OPPT-in approach may provide access for the doing and being of inclusion, social justice, and activism (Donovan & Tracy, 2017). First, we review some key issues regarding the being of exclusion and inclusion.

How Inclusion and Exclusion Manifest at Micro, Meso, and Macro Levels

A glimpse at the current research shows that practices of inclusion and exclusion are manifest at macro, meso, and micro levels (Ferdman, 2017). That is, inclusion and exclusion unfold within the interplay of varying ideologies, organizational practices, and interactional behavior. In what follows, we use the macro-, meso-, and micro-level framework to review just a slice of existing literature related to exclusion and inclusion.

Exclusion at Macro, Meso, and Micro Levels

Macro-level exclusion occurs through discursive formations that perpetuate larger ideologies of exclusion. Much research has recorded the macro-level discourses of whiteness (Nakayama & Martin, 2000) and color-blind ideology (Bonilla-Silva, 2014). Within the field of communication studies, organizational researchers have also focused on how discursive formations of sexism manifest through male executives' language use (Tracy & Rivera, 2010). Research focusing on macro-level discourses shows how larger structures and sedimented scripts perpetuate exclusionary practices.

Meso-level exclusion occurs through various organizational practices such as trainings, committees, and job requirements. A primary way that organizations have attempted to address issues of exclusion has been through instituting diversity programs. However, diversity training is often undertaken for business reasons, rather than for reasons of human dignity and social justice (Mease, 2012), and racism is often obscured precisely through the institutionalization of diversity. With such programs in place, executives can turn a blind eye to exclusionary practices and point to their diversity programs as proof that they are "doing something." Indeed, many commitments to diversity are "non-performative," meaning that they do not bring into being what they claim to create (Ahmed, 2012).

Even when diversity programs are successful at including typically marginalized peoples, they may still result in "peripheral inclusion" (Rennstam & Sullivan, 2018), a term used to describe the experience of being neither included nor excluded, but rather somewhere in the middle or are relegated to provide the "marginalized perspective." When marginalized peoples are tokenized, they often face challenges in succeeding in typical workplace tasks—which is the case, for example, with faculty members of color who are asked to be on so many committees that there is less time to devote to research and academic publication (Fryberg & Martínez, 2014; Rennstam & Sullivan, 2018). What's more, seeking inclusion oftentimes requires that marginalized people must fit into and therefore perpetuate a biased organizational structure—which is the case, for instance, with blue-collar unemployed job seekers of color who learn White middle-class communication norms in order to get hired (Gist-Mackey, 2018).

Finally, micro-level exclusion occurs through small group and interpersonal communicative behavior. In the context of workplace bullying, exclusion manifests when an employee feels left out, whispered or gossiped about, or not invited to important meetings (Lutgen-Sandvik & Tracy, 2012). Past research with transgender employees provide a vivid portrayal of what exclusion feels like. Among other things, transgender employees feel worried that revealing one's identity at work would be dangerous (Jones, under submission) and having "to pretend to be someone I'm not, or I'm not going to be able to find a job" (Eger, 2018, p. 278). In the context of whiteness studies, White fragility unfolds when White people feel unfairly attacked, and in response, become unstable, defensive, and aggressive in their communicative behavior (DiAngelo, 2018). As such, micro-level responses are informed by macro-level ways of thinking (i.e., whiteness ideology, color-blind ideology, meritocracy, etc.). In the context of whiteness studies, Ahmed (2007) notes that the experience of exclusion manifests in the body when a person of color is one of the few, if any, people of color in the organization—a "little brown speck" (Razzante & Tracy, 2019).

Inclusion at Macro, Meso, and Micro Levels

Macro discursive formations such as meritocracy, supposed color-blindness, and the Protestant work ethic seep into organizational policy and practice (see Fryberg & Martínez, 2014). As a response, institutions of higher education have incorporated macro-level messages of inclusive excellence (Bauman, Bustillos, Bensimon, Brown, & Bartee, 2005) which serve as "institutional speech acts" (Ahmed, 2012, p. 54) to encourage change. Indeed, for inclusion to become a hallmark of organizational culture, "diversity needs to be embedded in the symbolic and cultural fabric of the institution" (Williams, 2007, p. 12). Increasing numbers of organizations are instituting macro-level inclusionary messages, in the forms of commitments to civility, policies against workplace bullying, and training guides for inclusive leadership (Bourke & Dillon, 2016). However, rules-based approaches do not necessarily show *how* organizational leaders should create inclusive workplaces and, therefore, can end up being non-performative in action.

At the meso level, organizational leaders have made efforts to create inclusive environments where employees can voice their opinion in relation to organizational change (Barge, 2014). Researchers have documented case studies of organizational inclusion as related to positive organizational ethics (Sekerka et al., 2014), compassion organizing (Dutton et al., 2006; Frost, 1999), and organizational virtuousness (Lutgen-Sandvik, Hood, & Jacobson, 2016). Such research is focused on creating flourishing in organizations. However, it's often unclear how positive organizational ethics, compassion organizing, and organizational virtuousness might motivate material and embodied forms of difference in terms of social and cultural identity (Cooren, 2018).

Finally, we might consider micro-level interactions that promote inclusion. In the context of Black Lives Matter, Opie and Roberts (2017) suggest that members of organizations, especially Whites, adopt perspective taking when considering how racism influences people's different ways of engaging the world. The workplace bullying research suggests that bystanders (especially those of privileged status) can engage in conversational pivoting and enhanced positive communication when they encounter bullying at work (Razzante, Tracy, & Orbe, 2018). Co-cultural communication suggests that dominant group members can engage in conversational work that fosters inclusion by educating others, micro affirmations, and authentically articulating one's assumptions (see Orbe, 1998; Razzante & Orbe, 2018). And, research with girls of color and technology shows that, when organizational leaders open up discussions regarding the ways that people may be marginalized in some ways but privileged in others, that doing so helps form community (Ashcraft, Eger, & Scott, 2017). Collectively, these research findings illustrate a range of actionable paths toward inclusion, and as we explain next, we believe an OPPT-in approach can enhance and extend such work related to the being of inclusion.

OPPT-in into the Being of Inclusion

An OPPT-in approach provides a promising framework (Tracy & Donovan, 2018) for the being of inclusion. First, an **ontological** approach is concerned with the existential being of human being (Heidegger, 1927/1962). Human beings are not just objects in the world, or a collection of bones, organs, and flesh. Rather, their humanness comes through interaction, experience, and consciousness. Indeed, "the basic practical-moral problem in life is not what *to do*, but what *to be*" (Shotter, 1993, p. 118, italics in original). Ontological scholarship and pedagogy inform and inspire ways of being; "if we know *who to be*, then *what to do* falls into place" (Cunliffe, 2009, p. 94, italics in original).

An ontological-phenomenological model contrasts with banking (Freire, 2000) and epistemological (Souba, 2014) models of education. Epistemological models focus on conceptual knowledge, and banking models suggest that students (or readers of research) are passive containers ready to be filled with information. Such approaches tend to focus on analysis of hypothetical, historical, or external situations rather than examining one's own contextual experience. Third-person analyses of case studies, however, are not sufficient for creating virtuous action and being in the world (such as the being of inclusion). This becomes abundantly, if painfully clear when considering the question, "Do you *know* that exercise is good for you?" and realizing that all the knowledge in the world is not enough to motivate the being of exercise. This also becomes clear when considering the additional aspects of OPPT-in, including phenomenology, phronesis, and transformation.

In terms of the first P in OPPT-in, access to being is made possible through a **phenomenological** method in which first person, "on the court" learning is fostered rather than on third person, "from the stands" approaches (Erhard, Jensen, & Granger, 2012). As discussed in depth by Tracy and her colleagues (Tracy, 2016; Tracy & Donovan, 2018; Tracy et al. 2015), most organizational communication scholarship, even that which focuses on practical application, is focused on an epistemological third-person approach. Researchers begin with problems (e.g., workplace bullying, racism, and incivility), delineate how these problems manifest, and then provide recommendations that people, sometime in their future, might take up and apply. Although these approaches add to epistemological knowledge, they do not provide direct access to phenomenological, as-lived experience. The problems are "out-there" to be solved by someone else in some future hypothetical time.

A phenomenological approach provides direct access to specific ways of being in real time with tangible outcomes. Peoples' interpretations of the world and their actions are provided by the contexts, meanings, and assumptions that are embedded in our language (Hyde, 1994). Sometimes the words we have are not the words we need for transformation (Ashcraft, 2000); critical reflection on language and creating new linguistic alternatives provides access to new ways of being and interacting in the world. What's more, phenomenological access to a preferred way of being (such as the being of inclusion) lies not in acquiring knowledge or certain personal attributes. Instead, this being comes through discovering the frames of reference and contexts through which we engage with the world and, through language, recreating experiential contexts that will leave people exercising ways of being that serve themselves and others (Souba, 2014). Such access is crucial for practical wisdom, which leads to the next aspect of an OPPT-in approach.

The second P of OPPT-in refers to **phronesis**, variously translated as prudence or practical wisdom, a "true state, reasoned, and capable of action with regard to things that are good or bad for man" (Aristotle, trans. 1976, 1140a24-aa40b12). Phronesis is about appropriate and virtuous action in a particular situation, with choices deemed as useful (or not) in relation to specific values and interests of specific people in a specific scene; "phronesis goes beyond both analytical, scientific knowledge (episteme) and technical knowledge or know-how (techne) and involves judgements and decisions made in the manner of a virtuoso social and political actor" (Flyvbjerg, 2001, p. 2). Acontextual rules and theories lead to episteme, but enacting wise ways of being requires contextual apprenticeship, emulation, practice, and self-reflection.

The importance of intentional contextual practice, complete with its twists and turns, successes and failures, is also demonstrated in the skill acquisition research. As explained by Dreyfus & Dreyfus (2005), novices to any craft begin by learning rules and theories, and those who are at a level of competence *apply* these rules and theories to contextual cases. Applying theories to case studies is a very popular way in the field of communication of doing practical theory as "engaged reflection" (Barge, 2001). This type of practical theory unfolds by applying a theory to a case and using it iteratively with emergent data in the field to create new insight. Practical application requires learning the theories first (e.g., standpoint theory; critical theory; or muted group theory) and then laying these on top of real-world situations (such as exclusion or racism). Such an approach may be useful for creating *competence* in a preferred way of being (e.g., allowing a student or reader of a journal article to notice racism at work and make a decision to try conversational pivoting, for instance), but it does not create *expertise* or *phronesis* (e.g., the practical, intuitive wisdom of a workplace bullying bystander being skilled at when and how to intervene and conversationally pivot).

In short, for scholars (like ourselves) who are interested in creating expertise in being (and not just competence), the skill acquisition literature would suggest that *application* of epistemological knowledge is simply not enough to inspire transformation. This is because expertise requires embodied action, practice, and decision-making in context. Experts operate holistically rather than applying rules, guidelines, or theories.

> An expert does not calculate, or solve problems, or even think. He or she just does what normally works and, of course, it normally works. // If one asks an expert for the rules he or she is using, one will, in effect, force the expert to regress to the level of a beginner and state the rules learned in school.
>
> (Dreyfus & Dreyfus, 2005, p. 788)

To achieve expertise in being—whether that being is in sports, music, compassion, or the being of inclusion—requires intentional contextual practice. In terms of the being of inclusion, it means that people pay close attention to and honor silence, absence, suppression, and subtle nonverbal cues. Indeed, as Cruz's (2016) methodology of the traces so richly reveals, people are often reticent to openly talk about trauma. Identifying the residue of violence and upset—such as that which can accompany exclusion—requires close attention to context. It also means that organizational members (especially those who hold privileged status) benefit from immersion and interaction with those who are different, practicing invitations even if rejection is likely, crossing boundaries and entering unfamiliar ground, complicating oneself, and playing with the edges in life (Tracy & Trethewey, 2005). However, sole practice without reflection is not enough and is merely what Freire (2000) calls "activism." The practical wisdom of phronesis (similar to Freire's "praxis") requires action plus reflection of what is virtuous and appropriate, which leads to the final aspect of OPPT-in.

The T in OPPT-in stands for **transformative** learning. Based in large part on Freire's (2000) critical pedagogy, transformative learning is considered a liberatory pedagogical process in which readers or students can discover for themselves how to transform actions and frames of reference that have contributed to oppression, lack of freedom, or disempowerment. The critical-dialectical discourse aspect of transformative learning requires emotional intelligence, including "having an open mind, learning to listen empathetically, 'bracketing' premature judgment, and seeking common ground" (Mezirow, 2003, p. 60). To access the essence of experience, people need to be aware of their biases and habits, so that these lenses may be (if only temporarily) suspended—a process similar to phenomenological epoché (Orbe, 2009).

How is such reflexivity accomplished? People first must be able to talk freely about their own experiences, assumptions, and viewpoints. Then, through a process of critical self-reflexivity, people can examine the assumptions that guide their actions. As Cunliffe (2004) explains:

> Instead of applying theory to practice, critical reflexivity emphasizes praxis—questioning our own assumptions and taken-for-granted actions,

thinking about where/who we are and where/who we would like to be, challenging our conceptions of reality, and exploring new possibilities.

(p. 411)

Such questioning goes beyond self-reflexivity, in which people recognize the way they shape and are shaped by social experience, and instead involves a dialogue with ourselves in which we unsettle our assumptions, actions, and their impact on others, certain events, and in life as lived (Cunliffe, 2009). Critical self-reflexivity is virtually impossible to do by merely thinking on one's own, but rather benefits from collaborative relational interaction with others who listen, share, and ask questions. People often do not know what they think until they hear what they say (Weick, 2001).

Much of a transformative approach is accomplished via experiential learning in which students or readers of academic scholarship are inspired to focus on the "here and now" rather than the "there and then" of communication and behavior (Frey & White, 2012). Traditional epistemological and banking approaches to scholarship focus on observing, analyzing, and reflecting, whereas experiential learning surfaces and questions tacit knowledge in use right now; "learning is about 'moving with' rather than 'thinking about' ideas" (Tomkins & Ulus, 2016). In terms of the being of inclusion, then, transformative and experiential approaches would suggest that scholars need to go beyond analyzing problematic case studies to first recognizing and questioning the assumptions that guide peoples' ways of being in the world, and then motivating intentional contextual practice that might recreate the preferred future. So, what might this look like in terms of "being of inclusion" OPPT-in scholarship?

Creating the Being of Inclusion through OPPT-in

Studying and practicing expertise in action is a primary aspect of OPPT-in. Phronesis and practical wisdom are developed when we can learn from rich and thick case studies that show intuition and improvisation in context. However, most research aimed at creating inclusion focuses on analyzing problems (Tracy & Donovan, 2018). What's more, typical organizational communication and leadership classes focus on reading case studies of problematic or ethically questionable behavior. Case in point, a review of five popular collections of organizational communication case studies (Bisel, Kavya, & Tracy, 2018) found that most of them focused on ethically problematic situations, with only 22% of them focusing on exemplary issues to emulate (for an exception, see Lyon's 2017 collection of case studies in courageous organizational communication).

To create expertise in being, scholarship must do more than illuminate problems (like exclusion) but must also describe, cultivate, and inspire immersive experience in the practice of positive deviance and virtuoso craft practice. This is because when learners watch or are brought through scholarly thick description (Geertz, 1973) into the being of situations where people are especially good at something (whether that something is cooking or being inclusive), this can reduce the learner's random trials to the more valuable ones. One way to create an immersive phronetic experience is through writing richly and aesthetically about positively deviant situations in which people are especially compassionate or active in creating connection across difference, and then providing recommendations of what readers (especially those who are privileged) might practice themselves to imitate and create the preferred situation (Bisel et al., 2018). Indeed, "observation and imitation of the activity of an expert can replace a random search for better ways to act. In general, this is the advantage of being an apprentice" (Dreyfus & Dreyfus, 2005, p. 788). Related pedagogical activities could usefully include analyzing lives of Nobel Peace Prize winners or "wisdom witnessing" in which students are constantly on the lookout for and discuss inclusion in action, and/ or choosing "inclusive" role models and modeling ones values and actions likewise (Bruya & Ardelt, 2018, p. 242).

Students could also valuably reflect on how to employ aspects of their own privilege to *respond* to exclusion. As Brenda Allen (expert in issues of difference in organizational communication) pointed out at the 2017 Aspen Engaged Conference, there is a difference between being "response-able" and "responsible." An OPPT-in model might suggest that *responsible* privilege is a three-part process of *observing, listening,* and *responding*. First, in terms of **observing**, responsible privilege requires that people are present to the suffering that makes up exclusion and, what's more, take responsibility for the existence of walls of exclusion that they have themselves built and maintained, intentionally or not. Second, **listening** is the process of actively tuning in to the concerns of those who experience marginalization and exclusion. Finally, **responding** is the process of working alongside marginalized members, making requests for change, crafting new and inclusive spaces, and delivering tangible repercussions when demands for justice are not fulfilled. Each of the steps requires relational empathy, critical self-reflexivity, and the continual unsettling of assumptions.

What do these issues look like as lived? This poignant example from Sara Ahmed (2012) illustrates her responsible action in the face of an exclusionary wall.

An open call comes out for an academic event on power and resistance. A number of speakers are named on the call: all male speakers but one, all white speakers but one. Some of us point out the restriction. A wall comes up in the very denial of a wall. We begin with a friendly openness. It's an open call, they say. Take our places, they even say. Note here how the gesture of inclusion, which is also a promise of inclusion, can be offered in a way that negates a point about exclusion. To suggest incorporation as potential (come along as you *can* come along) prevents any acknowledgement that the open call was restricted as a call. How to respond? We point out publicly that the publicity of the call suggests the event is not open.

(pp. 178–179)

This example illustrates several aspects regarding responsible privilege. As we see in this example, Ahmed addresses an instance of exclusion by pointing it out, making it visible, and refusing to simply ignore the wall or "get over it." As a prominent female scholar of color, she responsibly (and courageously) takes action. This excerpt also illustrates that when people of privilege refuse to acknowledge the walls of exclusion they have created, or just expect that the disenfranchised will figure out a way to climb over them, it shuts down conversation and the potential for transformation. So, how might we cultivate alternative ways of being?

Toward Creating the Being of Inclusion: Free Listening, Story Circles, and Civil Dialogue

The being of inclusion can be inspired through "dialogic spaces" (Rule, 2004) where people (employees, students, co-researchers) can talk through and reflect upon a range of macro-level societal issues (such as the "isms" that create exclusion) and practice being with those with whom they might typically exclude. We offer Free Listening, Storyscope, and Civil Dialogue® as three meso-level activities in which people can practice micro-interactions related to the being of inclusion.

Free Listening

As demonstrated by Bourke and Dillon (2016), inclusive leadership includes six signature traits: cognizance, curiosity, courage, commitment, collaboration, and cultural intelligence. More specifically, each trait aims to develop the following elements of inclusion: fairness and respect, value and belonging, and confidence and inspiration. Listening can serve to cultivate the being of fairness and respect, value and belonging, and confidence and inspiration emerge. Additionally, people can practice listening as a way to experience curiosity and courage toward developing cognizance and cultural intelligence. Finally, as demonstrated by recent research, listening is a good place to start when working toward creating inclusive organizational environments (Broome et al., 2019).

Free Listening is a grassroots movement in which listeners stand in public, hold homemade signs that read "free listening," and then simply listen and ask questions to those people who approach the sign-holder and want to talk. Free listening is not about changing anyone's mind, agreeing, or disagreeing. Rather, it is an activity that invites people to share what is on their mind, while the free listener asks questions, is verbally and nonverbally present in an embodied way, and refrains from judgment or resistance to what the other is saying. What's more, this activity provides the "free listeners" with excellent practice related to relational empathy and the being of inclusion. A full description of the process and FAQs is available at https://urbanconfessional.org.

Communication instructors at Arizona State University have successfully incorporated Free Listening in a range of different classes and for different purposes including to cultivate authentic listening, connection, and compassion.

A related course assignment that uses Free Listening for creating the being of inclusion might spring from the tenets regarding responsible privilege described in the previous section: observe, listen, respond. Before engaging in this assignment, we encourage instructors to practice Free Listening multiple times themselves, practice it in the classroom (with half the students listening to the other half), and taking the students out together on campus to listen to at least somewhat familiar others. Many students will find Free Listening difficult even when talking to students who have a similar background, and practicing first in a collaborative and supportive atmosphere primes the wheels for listening to people that students do not typically include in their lives.

So how would a "being of inclusion" Free Listening event unfold? First, students could be asked to **observe** their life as lived and note situations in the community where they see problems regarding difference or exclusion. Or they may locate specific types of viewpoints, people, or ideas with whom they do not regularly interact (and therefore exclude) in their lives. This would help them determine physical locations where they could practice listening and being inclusive of ideas and people. Students would share what they have discovered and make connections with other students in their class who discovered similar places, ideas, and spaces.

Second, in small groups, students could go to this place (e.g., perhaps a rally for a political candidate with whom they disagree, or a parade for people who hold different values) and engage in 60–90 minutes of Free **Listening**. Third, before debriefing collectively, students could journal about their experience and critically reflect on the following: Who stopped by to talk? How did the conversations unfold? What did this experience feel like? How was this easy? How was this uncomfortable? What did you learn about your own ability to listen with or without resistance? What did you learn about the being of inclusion? After journaling, students could usefully debrief about the situation in class.

Fifth, students could be asked to **respond** by identifying three behaviors they would commit to practice that are related to listening and the being of inclusion (e.g., asking more questions rather than using blanket statements; using "I" language more than "you" language; spending more time listening than speaking; keeping their phone out of sight when sharing a meal with friends). Throughout the rest of the semester, students could practice their new behaviors, share their experiences (both the breakthroughs and breakdowns), and reflect on how these new behaviors impacted being of inclusion at micro, meso, and macro levels.

Storyscope Story Circles

Storyscope, a type of story circle, is another structured activity that might inspire the being of inclusion. To show and not just tell, consider a vivid thick description of how story circle might unfold:

> You are excited but nervous for your first Storyscope event. You know very few people and have no idea what story you will share. The host of

the event warmly greets you, offers a nametag, and provides a handout about the theme: *Change*. The evening's event begins with a short performance. A local artist reads her poetry, and you learn from others who have attended before that past performances include singing, dance, and interpretive readings.

As you reflect on the theme of change, you start jotting down some notes. The host encourages you to communicate in narrative form, with stories having a clear beginning, middle, and end. After another performance by a local artist, the group creates five or so small circles of chairs. A facilitator invites each in your group to take turns introducing yourself and shares some ground rules for your time together, such as keeping the story to three minutes, and finding a way to nonverbally acknowledge each other (so as not to noisily disrupt the other circles).

The story circle begins in silence. Most of your fellow six circle mates are staring at the floor while a couple of brave souls meet each other's eyes. The facilitator waits patiently with a warm, inviting smile. The woman to your right, sighs and clears her throat, "Alright, I'm happy to get this started." One by one, each member shares a story of change in their life. You are amazed to discover how different each story is even though they are bound by a common theme. You find yourself listening more intently to the person next to you share about the passing of her husband of 54 years. Inspired by her vulnerability, you suddenly feel more prepared to tell your story. After she finishes, the group acknowledges her with shimmering fingers and head bows. Clearing your throat and offering a tentative smile, you look up and begin narrating your story.

As shown in this description, Storyscope provides a space for bringing communities together through "personal and compelling stories around some of our more pressing issues" ("Storyscope," n.d.). By creating the space for people to come together and share their stories, story circles open discursive possibilities for connection and overcoming fear and ignorance about issues and people whom we typically exclude. This is because an individual story does not exist in isolation within a story circle. As each individual takes their turn, a "collective story emerges—larger, richer, and more complex. The things we have in common, as well as real differences, are brought to light" ("About story circles," 2018).

The creators of Storyscope thusly see how a story circle functions like a kaleidoscope—fluid and ever changing, yet vibrant as we individually twist and turn throughout life and then come into shared moments with others that add new dimensions. New dimensions require difference or disconnection. In this sense, disconnection is a learning tool; we learn from others when we see differences in their experiences. This disconnection then can lead to connection. Through such a practice, inclusion occurs during a story circle when someone is willing to exert effort to extend themselves to and towards another. This extension occurs through sharing, listening, and providing social support in communicative and embodied ways. Participants experience connection in that they all have stories related to the same topic, yet simultaneously witness how their experiences are unique and distinct, a process that emphasizes how one's own experience cannot be unproblematically generalized to others.

Civil Dialogue

In contrast to Storyscope, Civil Dialogue® begins from a place of difference: people come together to civilly talk through a divisive topic such as gun rights, political candidates, or health care. The expressed goal of Civil Dialogue® is to work within communities to

> instruct citizens of all cultures, groups, political, parties, religions, gener-ation, and belief systems that is it possible to sit down and cogently share ideas of disagreement, express themselves passionately, while really work-ing to understand why those who hold differing, perhaps even opposite opinions may well be as deeply convicted as themselves.
> (Genette, Olson, & Linde, 2018, p. 5)

Based on this goal, the creators have crafted a format that involves commu-nity members with the ongoing, sensemaking process of dialogue as a means for cultivating civility and critical communication practices.

A Civil Dialogue® event follows a consistent format (see Genette et al., 2018). Regardless of the place in which the dialogue takes place (e.g., a com-munity space, a classroom, a place of worship), the room is always set up with five empty chairs placed in a tight semicircle facing the audience and potential dialogue participants. After providing background information and a rationale for the dialogue, a trained facilitator reveals a provocative statement around which the dialogue will revolve (e.g., "Trump will make America great again"). At this time, the audience is also informed of the format's ground rules: (1) be passionate, not hostile, (2) focus on how the statement makes you feel, (3) avoid framing the dialogue as an argument, (4) use "I" language (conviction) not "You" language (implies critique), (5) use your own words, avoid slogans, (6) disagree without demonizing, (7) listen to create genuine dialogue and communication, (8), listen patiently, do not interrupt, and (9) be present when listening, do not plan what you want to say next. Next, five participants are invited to take one of the empty chairs facing the audience—each of which is sign-marked with an opinion regard-ing the provocative statement: from left to right, "Agree Strongly," "Agree Somewhat," "Neutral/Undecided," "Disagree Somewhat," and "Disagree Strongly."

After five participants take their seats, they are invited to talk through their opinion on the provocative statement and how they came to have that viewpoint. After each participant shares in turn, they have 10 minutes to freely dialogue with each other. After that, the facilitator turns to the larger audience for further reflections and questions. The facilitator encourages diverse viewpoints to be shared, and for people to speak up when they disagree with others. As such, this is not necessarily a "feel-good" type of experience, but instead one in which clashes of viewpoints can be discussed in a civil framework (Figure 7.1).

Understanding Civil Dialogue® through the lens of inclusion means acknowledging that, instead of affirmation or comfort, inclusion also relates to bravely sharing our opinions with those who differ. What's more, the framework encourages participants to speak up in resistance to issues and viewpoints in the world that they deem problematic (or exclusionary). Speaking openly about one's opinions within the format of dialogue invites us to think critically about what inclusion looks likes. More specifically, within this dialogic format, inclusion is something that requires practice, courage, and vulnerability to *be* with others who see the world differently.

As illustrated by the activities of Free Listening, Storyscope story circles, and Civil Dialogue®, the being of inclusion can manifest in a number of different ways. Free Listening asks us to set aside our own viewpoints and be with others so they feel heard. Story circles create connection across difference and the realization that even those from disparate walks of life may have something in common (e.g., stories of change). Civil Dialogue® provides participants with well-needed practice to civilly articulate their viewpoint on divisive issues among those who do not share their point of view. What each of these activities has in common are core communicative practices related to

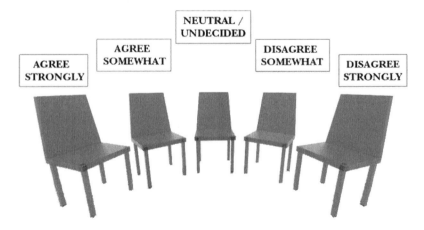

Figure 7.1 Inclusion relates to bravely sharing opinions with those who differ, as opposed to affirming and comforting communication.

the being of inclusion, such as bracketing presuppositions (if only temporarily), authentically listening, vulnerably sharing space with unfamiliar others, and openness to change.

Conclusion

Acts of inclusion and exclusion take place at macro, meso, and micro levels (Ferdman, 2017). What we propose in this chapter are several meso-level practices that can encourage the being of inclusion at the micro level. It is through micro-level interaction that we embrace the possibility for inclusivity to scale up to the macro level. Additionally, it is through such meso-level activities that people can begin to practice inclusivity through a phronetic, practically wise manner. Whether through Free Listening, Civil Dialogue®, or Storyscope story circles, such activities provide opportunities for people to practice and phenomenologically experience key communicative skills related to inclusion. What's more, they provide space for critical reflexivity in which participants might question their suppositions and ways of being. Finally, through such experiences, and through hearing and using new language, they may then see the world in new ways that allow for different possibilities rather than entrenched scripts of division and exclusion.

As discussed throughout this piece, to create the being of inclusion, scholars can usefully go beyond epistemological examination of problems to also practice scholarship that inspires authentic listening, generosity in spirit, and bravery. In addition to studying problematic situations, we can usefully examine positively deviant organizations and communicative interactions where inclusion is exemplified in living breathing color. For example, more research needs to be done on those organizations that practice radical inclusion (Johnson, 2019)—as opposed to periphery inclusion (Rennstam & Sullivan, 2018)—where marginalized groups are integral contributors to organizational decision making. Indeed, an OPPT-in approach suggests the importance of scholarship that goes beyond epistemological learning and third-person analysis of problematic exclusionary behavior in organizations. Such an approach inspires (1) research and analysis of positively deviant instances of inclusion, (2) intentional practice and critical reflection on as-lived behaviors that spark inclusion, and (3) structured programs that hold promise for creating the being of inclusion, such as Free Listening,[1] Civil Dialogue®,[2] and Storyscope[3] story circles.

Afterword From Sarah: A Moment of Critical Self-Reflexivity

In the end stages of drafting this chapter (in Fall, 2018), I was struck with the irony and hypocrisy of three white people writing about the being of inclusion. That led to further reflection, and a sober assessment: All but four of my 50-some co-authored publications are the result of white hands and all but two of the 40-some graduate students I have formally advised are white.

In getting clear for the first time on the wall of white bricks surrounding myself as a scholar, I alternately felt ashamed, astonished, disgusted, and clueless. I have held myself out to be an inclusive, mindful, and critically reflexive person. I have not intentionally made choices about who to work with based upon gender, race, sexual identity or orientation, ability, or age. Meanwhile, if I took a photo with all my coauthors and advisees, we would together constitute a wall of relatively privileged people—most of us white, female, heterosexual, and normatively attractive.

To have a blind spot of one's own bullshit revealed is a gloriously excruciating experience. It is one level of pain to discover we have been fooling others, and "far more unsettling to discover that we have fooled ourselves" (Hochschild, 1983, p. 47). Indeed, when I originally drafted this afterword in 2018, I could feel my face grimacing and my fingers fluttering up to my lips in uncertainty and shame. When I considered whether to include it in this chapter, I fretted about whether and when I should explicitly share the whiteness of my scholarship and teaching, and the ramifications of doing so.

In writing this chapter, listening and contributing to the 2019 #CommunicationSoWhite discussion, writing an article for a special issue on whiteness and merit (Tracy, 2019), and identifying and assigning more inclusive readings in my courses, I have spent at least 150 hours in the last year thinking, writing, and teaching about the importance of critical self-reflexivity, vulnerability, and taking responsibility for our own walls of exclusion. So, I am standing in the muck of such a revelation with these words from Tibetan Buddhist Pema Chödrön (2000):

> Rather than letting our negativity get the better of us, we could acknowledge that right now we feel like a piece of shit and not be squeamish about taking a good look. That's the compassionate thing to do. That's the brave thing to do. We could smell that piece of shit. We could feel it; what is its texture, color, and shape? We can explore the nature of that piece of shit. We can know the nature of dislike, shame, and embarrassment and not believe there's something wrong with that.
>
> (p. 50)

And we can also make our way through the shit and come out on the other side with some important change.

Alas, as I write now in 2020, I can stare with less fear and shame at the walls of exclusion in my own life—walls laid brick-by-well-intentioned brick – and do the rigorous work to recraft that wall. It can be a disorienting and cognitively dissonant space to stand. It is also one, though, that prompts action—both in destruction of privilege and recrafting the way I can know and teach. It is precisely a space of being that proponents of critical self-reflexivity and an OPPT-in approach would say is imperative for transformation, inclusion, and social justice.

Notes

1 See The Urban Confessional for more information on Free Listening at https://urbanconfessional.org/.
2 See the Institute for Civil Dialogue for more information at civil-dialogue. com.
3 Storyscope is an affiliate of the U.S. Department of Arts and Culture (usdac. us), a grassroots action network inciting creativity and social imagination to shape a culture of empathy, equity, and belonging.

References

Ahmed, S. (2007). A phenomenology of whiteness. *Feminist Theory, 8*(2), 149–168. doi:10.1177/1464700107078139

Ahmed, S. (2012). *On being included: Racism and diversity in institutional life.* Durham, NC: Duke University Press.

Aristotle. (trans. 1976). *The nicomachean ethics.* (J. A. K. Thomson, Trans.). Harmondsworth: Penguin.

Ashcraft, C. (2000). Naming knowledge: A language for reconstructing domestic violence and systemic gender inequity. *Women and Language, 23*(1), 3–10. Retrieved from https://search.proquest.com/openview/a992266cf8c8cef6ceb e6b67831a4e1e/1?pq-origsite=gscholar&cbl=31040

Ashcraft, C., Eger, E. K., & Scott, K. A. (2017). Becoming technosocial change agents: Intersectionality and culturally responsive pedagogies as vital resources for increasing girls' participation in computing. *Anthropology & Education Quarterly, 48*(3), 233–251. doi:10.1111/aeq.12197

Barge, J. K. (2001). Practical theory as mapping, engaged reflection, and transformative practice. *Communication Theory, 11*(1), 5–13. doi:10.1111/aeq.12197

Barge, J. K. (2014). Pivotal leadership and the art of conversation. *Leadership, 10*(1), 56–78. doi:10.1177/1742715013511739

Bisel, R. S., Kavya, P., Tracy, S. J. (2018). *Positive deviance case study as a method for organizational communication.* Presented at the annual meeting of the National Communication Association, Salt Lake City.

Bauman, G. L., Bustillos, L. T., Bensimon, E. M., Brown, C., & Bartee, R. D. (2005). Achieving equitable educational outcomes with all students: The institution's roles and responsibilities. *Association of American Colleges and Universities.* Retrieved from https://www.stetson.edu/other/alana-ia-caucus/ media/04%20%20Georgia%20Baumann,%20Equitable%20Educ%20 Outcomes.pdf

Bonilla-Silva, E. (2014). *Racism without racists: Color-blind racism and the persistence of racial inequality in America.* Lanham, MD: Rowman & Littlefield Pub.

Bourke, J., & Dillon, B. (2016). The six signature traits of inclusive leadership: Thriving in a diverse new world. *Deloitte University Press.* Retrieved from http:// dupress.deloitte.com/content/dam/dup-us-en/articles/six-signature-traitsof-inclusive-leadership/DUP-3046_Inclusive-leader_vFINAL.pdf

Broome, B., Derk, I., Razzante, R., Steiner, E., Taylor, J., & Zamora, A. (2019). Building an inclusive climate for intercultural dialogue: A participant-generated framework. *Negotiation and Conflict Management Research, 12*(3), 234–255. DOI: 10.1111/ncmr.1215.

Bruya, B., & Ardelt, M. (2018). Fostering wisdom in the classroom, part 1: A general theory of wisdom pedagogy. *Teaching Philosophy*, *41*(3), 239–253. doi:10.5840/teachphil201882889

Chödrön, P. (2000). *When things fall apart: Heart advice for difficult times*. Boston, MA: Shambhala Publications.

Cooren, F. (2018). Materializing communication: Making the case for a relational ontology. *Journal of Communication*, *68*(2), 278–288. doi:10.1093/joc/jqx014

Cruz, J. (2016). Following traces: An organizational ethnography in the midst of trauma. *Qualitative Research in Organizations and Management: An International Journal*, 11, 214–231. doi:10.1108/QROM-02-2016-1366

Cunliffe, A. L. (2004). On becoming a critically reflexive practitioner. *Journal of Management Education*, *28*(4), 407–426. doi:10.1177/1052562904264440

Cunliffe, A. L. (2009). The philosophical leader: On relationalism, ethics, and reflexivity—A critical perspective to teaching leadership. *Management Learning*, *40*(1), 87–101. doi:10.1177/1350507608099315

Dempsey, S. E., & Barge, J. K. (2014). Engaged scholarship and democracy. In L. L. Putnam & D. K. Mumby (Eds.), *The SAGE handbook of organizational communication: Advances in theory, research, and methods* (3rd ed., pp. 665–688). Los Angeles, CA: SAGE.

DiAngelo, R. (2018). *White fragility: Why it's so hard for White people to talk about racism*. Boston, MA: Beacon Press.

Donovan, M. C. J., & Tracy, S. J. (2017). Critical pedagogy meets transformation: Creating the being of communication activists. *Communication Education*, *66*(3), 378–380. doi: 10.1080/03634523.2017.1294254

Dreyfus, H. L., & Dreyfus, S. E. (2005). Peripheral vision: Expertise in real world contexts. *Organization Studies*, *26*(5), 779–792. doi: 10.1177/0170840605053102

Dutton, J. E., Worline, M. C., Frost, P. J., & Lilius, J. (2006). Explaining compassion organizing. *Administrative Science Quarterly*, *51*(1), 59–96. https://doi.org/10.2189/asqu.51.1.59

Eger, E. K. (2018). Transgender jobseekers navigating closeting communication. *Management Communication Quarterly*, *32*(2), 276–281. doi:10.1177/0893318917740226

Erhard, W., Jensen, M. C. and Granger, K. L. (2012). Creating leaders: An ontological/phenomenological model. In S. Snook, N. Nohria, & R. Khurana (Eds.), *The handbook for teaching leadership: Knowing, doing, and being* (pp. 245–262). Thousand Oaks, CA: SAGE.

Ferdman, B. M. (2017). Paradoxes of inclusion: Understanding and managing the tensions of diversity and multiculturalism. *Journal of Applied Behavioral Science*, *53*(2), 235–263. doi:10.1177/0021886317702608

Frey, L, R., & White, A, B. (2012). Promoting personal, interpersonal, and group growth through positive experiential encounter communication pedagogy. In T. J. Socha & M. J. Pitts (Eds.), *The positive side of interpersonal communication* (pp. 297–312). New York, NY: Peter Lang.

Fryberg, S., & Martínez, E. (2014). *The truly diverse faculty: New dialogues in American higher education*. New York: Springer.

Flyvbjerg, B. (2001). *Making social science matter: Why social inquiry fails and how it can succeed again*. New York: Cambridge University Press.

Freire, P. (2000). *Pedagogy of the oppressed*. New York: Bloomsbury Publishing.

Frost, P. J. (1999). Why compassion counts!. *Journal of Management Inquiry*, *8*, 127–133. doi:10.1177/105649269982004

Geertz, C. (1973). *The interpretation of cultures: Selected essays*. New York: Basic Books.

Gist-Mackey, A. N. (2018). (Dis)embodied job search communication training: Comparative critical ethnographic analysis of materiality and discourse during the unequal search for work. *Organization Studies*, (9), 1251–1275. doi:10.1177/0170840617736936

Genette, J., Olson, C. D., & Linde, J. (2018). *Hot topics, cool heads: A handbook for Civil Dialogue*. Dubuque, IA: Kendall Hunt.

Heidegger, M. (1962). *Being and time* (J. Macquarrie & E. Robinson, Trans.). San Francisco, CA: Harper and Row (Original work published in 1927).

Hochschild, A. R. (1983). *The managed heart: Commercialization of human feeling*. Berkeley, CA: University of California Press.

Human Communication, The Hugh Downs. (2018). About story circles. *The Empty Space: Current Performances*. Retrieved September 25, 2018, from https://humancommunication.clas.asu.edu/empty-space/current-performances.

Hyde, R. B. (1994). Listening authentically: A Heideggerian perspective on interpersonal communication. In K. Carter & M. Presnell (Eds.), *Interpretive approaches to interpersonal communication* (pp. 179–197). Albany, NY: SUNY Press.

Johnson, A. (2018). Radical inclusion in the movement for social change. Intersections of Civil, Critical, and Creative Communication (I-4C). Talk presented at the 2019 I-4C Research Collaborative Guest Lecture, Arizona State University, Tempe, US.

Jones, S. (In Press). Negotiating transgender identity at work: A movement to theorize a transgender standpoint epistemology. *Management Communication Quarterly*.

Lutgen-Sandvik, P., Hood, J. N., & Jacobson, R. P. (2016). The impact of positive organizational phenomena and workplace bullying on individual outcomes. *Journal of Managerial Issues*, *28*, 30–49.

Lutgen-Sandvik, P., & Tracy, S. J. (2012). Answering five key questions about workplace bullying: How communication scholarship provides thought leadership for transforming abuse at work. *Management Communication Quarterly*, *26*(1), 3–47. doi:10.1177/0893318911414400

Lyon, A. (2017). *Case studies in courageous organizational communication: Research and practice for effective workplaces*. New York: Peter Lang.

Mease, J. J. (2012). Reconsidering consultant's strategic use of the business case for diversity. *Journal of Applied Communication Research*, *40*(4), 1–19. doi:10.1080/00909882.2012.720380

Mezirow, J. (2003). Transformative learning as discourse. *Journal of Transformative Education*, *1*(1), 58–63. doi:10.1177/1541344603252172

Nakayama, T. & Martin, J. (2000). *Whiteness: The communication of social identity*. Thousand Oaks, CA: SAGE.

Opie, T., & Roberts, L. M. (2017). Do Black lives really matter in the workplace? Restorative justice as a means to reclaim humanity. *Equality, Diversity and Inclusion: An International Journal*, *36*(8), 707–719. doi:10.1108/EDI-07-2017-0149

Orbe, M. P. (1998). *Constructing co-cultural theory: An explication of culture, power, and communication*. Thousand Oaks, CA: SAGE.

Orbe, M. P. (2009). Phenomenology. In S. W. Littlejohn & K. A. Foss (Eds.), *Encyclopedia of communication theory* (pp. 750–751). Thousand Oaks, CA: SAGE.

Razzante, R., & Orbe, M. (2018). Two sides of the same coin: Conceptualizing dominant group theory in the context of co-cultural theory. *Communication Theory*, *28*(3), 354–375. doi:10.1093/ct/qtx008

Razzante, R., & Tracy, S. J. (2019). Co-cultural theory: Performing emotional labor from a position of exclusion. In C. J. Liberman, A. S. Rancer, & T. A. Avtgis (Eds.), *Casing communication theory* (pp. 117–130). Dubuque, IA: Kendall Hunt.

Razzante, R. J., Tracy, S. J., & Orbe, M. P. (2018). How dominant group members can transform workplace bullying. In R. West & C. Beck (Eds.), *Routledge Handbook of Communication and Bullying* (pp. 46–56). London: Routledge.

Rennstam, J., & Sullivan, K. R. (2018). Peripheral inclusion through informal silencing and voice—A study of LGB officers in the Swedish police. *Gender, Work & Organization, 25*(2), 177–194. doi:10.1111/gwao.12194

Rule, P. (2004). Dialogic spaces: Adult education projects and social engagement. *International Journal of Lifelong Education, 23*, 319–334.

Sekerka, L., Comer, D., & Godwin, L. (2014). Positive organizational ethics: Cultivating and sustaining moral performance. *Journal of Business Ethics, 119*(4), 435–444. doi:10.1007/s10551-013-1911-z

Shotter, J. (1993). *Conversational realities: Constructing life through language.* London: SAGE.

Souba, W. W. (2014). The phenomenology of leadership. *Open Journal of Leadership, 3*, 77–105. Retrieved from http://file.scirp.org/pdf/OJL_201412 1616584278.pdf

Storyscope. (n.d.). Home. *StoryScope: A Story Circles Project.* Retrieved September 25, 2018, from http://www.storyscopeproject.com/

Tomkins, L., & Ulus, E. (2016). 'Oh, was that "experiential learning"?!' Spaces, synergies and surprises with Kolb's learning cycle. *Management Learning, 47*(2), 158–178. doi:10.1177/1350507615587451

Tracy, S. J. (2019). A short soliloquy on merit. *Departures in Critical Qualitative Research*, 8:4, 46–48.

Tracy, S. J. (2016). Practical application in organizational communication: A historical snapshot and challenge for the future. *Management Communication Quarterly, 31*(1). doi:10.1177/0893318916675736

Tracy, S. J., & Donovan, M. C. J. (2018). Moving from practical application to expert craft practice in organizational communication: A review of the past and OPPT-ing into the future. In P. J. Salem & E. Timmerman (Eds.), *Transformative practices and research in organizational communication* (pp. 202–220). Hershey, PA: IGI Global.

Tracy, S. J., Franks, T., Brooks, M. M., & Hoffman, T. K. (2015). An OPPT-in approach to relational and emotional organizational communication pedagogy. *Management Communication Quarterly, 29*(2), 322–328. doi:10.1177/0893318915571350

Tracy, S. J., & Rivera, K. D. (2010). Endorsing equity and applauding stay-at-home moms: How male voices on work-life reveal aversive sexism and flickers of transformation. *Management Communication Quarterly, 24*(1), 3–43. doi:10.1177/0893318909352248

Tracy, S. J., & Trethewey, A. (2005). Fracturing the real-self↔fake-self dichotomy: Moving toward crystallized organizational identities. *Communication Theory, 15*(2), 168–195. doi:10.1111/j.1468-2885.2005.tb00331.x

Weick, K. E. (2001). *Making sense of the organization.* Malden, MA: Blackwell Business.

Williams, D. A. (2007). Achieving inclusive excellence: Strategies for creating real and sustainable change in quality and diversity. *About Campus, 12*(1), 8–14. doi:10.1002/abc.198

Part II
Top-Down Approaches

8 The Politics of Inclusion and Exclusion among Professions and Professionals

Joshua B. Barbour, Shelbey L. Rolison, and Jared T. Jensen

Professionals and professions navigate multiple dimensions of inclusion and exclusion in the conduct of their work. Professionals name and adjudicate who may be considered members of professions, who gets access to services, and what sorts of work and expertise count. Professionals exercise authority over others that stems from their education and certification, legal and cultural standing, relationships with other professionals, and the material conduct of their work. Professions develop, defend, and institutionalize domains of work (Ashcraft, 2013; Meisenbach, 2008). Communication scholarship focused on professions and professionals has demonstrated that the study of professions can shed valuable light on the politics of expert and expertise difference, which center on issues of inclusion and exclusion (Ashcraft, 2013; Barbour & Lammers, 2015; Cheney & Ashcraft, 2007; Meisenbach, 2008; Mitra, 2015). Such politics include efforts to define and ascribe types of work as professional and others as amateur, expertise as more or less relevant to or encumbering of problems, and people as more or less deserving of and in control of organizational resources (Barbour, Sommer, & Gill, 2016).

Negotiating competing rationales for action is at the center of professional work. Professionals as experts are those who have distinctive capacities for solving particular organizational problems (or at least those individuals thought to have such capacities) (Kuhn & Jackson, 2008; Treem, 2012), and professional work revolves around deciding whose expertise ought to be legitimate or authoritative in any given moment (Barbour, Sommer, et al., 2016; Kuhn & Rennstam, 2016). Cheney and Ashcraft (2007) underscored expertise, division of labor, and the normative-ethical obligation as key in the study of professions. Lammers and Garcia (2009) explicated how the concept of "profession" has developed in communication research, detailing emotional neutrality, a body of knowledge, formal standards of conduct, service orientation, social status, self-control, social control, formal associations, and professional identity as all characteristic of professionalism. Cheney and Ashcraft contended that although ethical obligation, akin to the service orientation highlighted by Lammers and Garcia, is an integral characteristic of professionalization, professionals simultaneously elevate and downplay ethical commitments, which Cheney and Ashcraft argued "may function, deliberately or unwittingly, to naturalize the exclusion of particular social groups" (p. 152). Central to exclusion is the creation, development, and exercise of "both material and symbolic boundaries—that is, barriers to Othered bodies as well as the norms, values, practices, aesthetics, and so forth, associated with them" (Ashcraft, Muhr, Rennstam, & Sullivan, 2012, p. 470). For example, negotiating expertise difference is essential in interdisciplinary problem solving and innovation, and at the same time, it can also involve wars of faith that degrade and exclude (Barbour & James, 2015; Thompson, 2009). Communication research and theory can and should offer insights for professionals' and professions' more enlightened negotiation of dynamics of inclusion and exclusion.

In this chapter, we review communication scholarship focused on professions, professionals, and professionalization. Two questions guide this review: First, how has communication scholarship on professionals and professional work examined issues of inclusion and exclusion? Second, what strategies for negotiating inclusion and exclusion does this scholarship forward? This review centers on four boundaries inherent to professional work along which important issues of inclusion and exclusion are negotiated: (1) Membership— who can claim to be a professional and who cannot? (2) Work—what counts as meaningful, professional work? (3) Organization—how are professionals at once members of organizational and occupational groups? (4) Knowing— who can know what professionals know and how do professionals negotiate interdisciplinarity? Through this review, we argue that professionals and professions perform, defend, and can remake these boundaries. We highlight the stakeholders affected by issues of inclusion and exclusion at these boundaries and forward an agenda for future scholarship focused on (a) the types of data and methods valuable for investigating these phenomena and (b) how communication scholarship focused on professions and professionals can contribute.

Membership

Navigating issues of inclusion and exclusion requires problematizing the notion of the "professional" in the first place. Professional identity is a distinctive subset of occupational identity, which Meisenbach (2008) defined as a "shifting, material, and discursive framing of image and practices associated with a particular type of work" (p. 263), drawing on Ashcraft (2007) and Alvesson and Willmott (2002). Per this scholarship, we conceptualize all occupations as professionalized to varying degrees. A "professional" is typically seen as a worker in an occupation that has achieved a measure of status and formal organization, but this scholarship emphasizes that occupational identity is at once constituted through interaction in the day-to-day lives of workers and informed by and constructed in historical and cultural action (Ashcraft, 2007; Barrett & Dailey, 2018; Kuhn et al., 2008; Mitra, 2015). The category "professional" tends to align with elite status, studies of professionals tend to focus on the privileged, and this convergence should be interrogated (e.g., Agarwal & Buzzanell, 2015; Novak, 2016).

Membership is a boundary that by definition ascribes who is included and who is excluded in practice and in the macrodiscursive construction of the occupation (Allen, 2010; Ashcraft, 2013; Barbour & Lammers, 2015). Professions organize to make contrasts among those who are legitimate members and those who are not (Ashcraft et al., 2012; Meisenbach, 2008). Membership in a profession has benefits, such as insulation from organizational instability, expertise, access to clients, social status, and networking. Professionalization, a category of institutionalization, involves an ongoing defense of the profession that is intertwined with the processes of identification and produces socially constructed and agreed upon notions of who is in and who is out (Ashcraft, 2013; Garcia & Barbour, 2018; Meisenbach, 2008).

All occupations can be understood as professionalizing or rejecting professionalization to some degree. In professionalizing, workers lay claim to specific jurisdictions of practice. The ongoing dispute of those jurisdictional boundaries constitutes the history of professions and determines their futures (Abbott, 1988). To gain social status, occupations formalize, which enables a profession to develop and adjudicate criteria that members must meet to become and remain members (Ashcraft et al., 2012). Determining the hurdles to, and standards of, membership makes it easier for a profession to decide those who are rightfully in and those who are appropriately out (Lammers & Garcia, 2009). The development and protection of those barriers may not sit well with all professions, especially those focused on serving the public good or committed to egalitarianism (Garcia & Barbour, 2018).

Efforts to define, protect, and defend professions manifest in the negotiation of who may be a member. Abbott (1988) recounted psychiatry's battle in the early 20th century to infiltrate work otherwise dominated by lawyers, clergy, and social workers. Psychiatry prevailed until the 1970s when psychotherapy erupted in popularity and social workers, once again, infiltrated psychiatry's jurisdictional space. More recently, Norander, Mazer, and Bates (2011) documented osteopathic students' fight to keep their Doctor of Osteopathy (OD) degree designation. Despite the prestige of the allopathic MD degree, OD students saw themselves as something more, and they highly identified with the distinct work practices that an OD manages. Garcia and Barbour (2018) found that librarians managed threats to their profession by privileging work practices as "librarian-related" and requiring "The Degree," the masters of library science. Over time, specialization within a profession can also become fragmented, which redistributes the locus of control and rekindles efforts to define the boundaries of membership (Scott, 2008).

These examples elucidate the communicative work involved in carving out categories of work and workers, and how being a professional involves a broader constitution and negotiation of identity. The principal identity work of the professional may be making it clear that they are the professionals and that others are not—who may access the powers of membership and who may not. Individuals construct professional selves that originate in the early socialization phases of professional training and are further developed as they are immersed in the rules, language, skills, and work of the profession. The construction of the professional self can involve identification with degrees, certifications, and experiences that set them apart and offer useful proof of their affiliation, expertise, and educational background (Garcia & Barbour, 2018; Norander et al., 2011). In doing so, professionals signal their superiority and reinforce boundaries between insiders and outsiders (Ashcraft, 2013).

These boundaries are bound up with history and culture (Cheney & Ashcraft, 2007). Macrodiscursive constructions of gender, race, social class, sexuality, (dis)ability, national-origin, and age shape and are shaped by who can be a professional (Allen, 2010; Ashcraft, 2013). For example, Ashcraft (2007) analyzed concerted efforts to define the nature of flying, in which the airlines and pilot union worked together to construct the expert, male, professional "pilot" we know today while excluding the casual, hobbyist "ladyflier." Such constructions can persist despite efforts to deconstruct or reconstruct them, as can be seen, for example, in efforts to recruit women and underrepresented groups into science, technology, engineering, and math (Jahn & Myers, 2014; Kisselburgh, Berkelaar, & Buzzanell, 2009). In a study of efforts to diversify information technology industries, McDonald and Kuhn (2016) found contradictions among official occupational branding that casts the work as welcoming to women and unofficial occupational branding that casts it as hostile. They argued the contradictions could be managed by broadening concerns beyond just increasing the number of women in IT to also include challenging the culture of hostility itself and by focusing less on occupational branding interventions and more on interventions into the material conditions of the work.

What constitutes professionalism is also defined through cultural discourse intertwined with constructions of gender, race, social class, sexuality, (dis)ability, national-origin, and age (Allen, 2010; Ashcraft, 2013). Professional membership is enforced through cultural designations of who can do what work (Mitra, 2015). The gender, race, social class, sexuality, (dis)ability, national-origin, and age of professions are evident in the "image" of the profession; the public discourse associated with the profession, and marketed and constructed to evoke identity attributes (Ashcraft, 2013). Ashcraft (2007) found that despite an early push of female celebrity pilots, the historical predominance of masculine characteristics attributed to pilots was accomplished through advertising campaigns that suggested that men belong in the cockpit and women belong in the cabin or on the pilot's arm. Women may be excluded from male-dominated professions and simultaneously included as semi-professional counterparts. Women in Tsetsura's (2010) study of public relations found that gendered professional identities derived, in part, from contrasting definitions of what "real work" and "women's work" looked like.

The notion of profession converges with other forms of elite privilege as well. Novak's (2016) study of Streetwise vendors, for example, shows how the societal construction of professional work excludes forms of work from professional status even though it may be professionalized (see also, Garcia &

Barbour, 2018; Meisenbach, 2008). The construction of who can do what work has implications not just for systemic differences in wages but also the

> distribution of voice, risk, opportunity, sleep, mental and physical health and health care, exposure to violence, access to quality food and housing, to resources of all kinds, experiences of dignity and shame, of authority and deference, intergenerational and community thriving, security and precarity, even life expectancy, and more.
>
> (Kuhn, Ashcraft, & Cooren, 2017, pp. 163–164)

The fragmented and multifaceted nature of social identities complicates efforts to deconstruct and reconstruct who ought to be included or excluded (Allen, 2010; Mease, 2016). Intersectionality involves the compounding and transformation of societal privilege and disadvantage inherent to overlapping social identities (Holvino, 2010). Researches at the nexus of identity and professional membership have tended to focus on particular social identities or categories of identity related to professional work (e.g., Barbour, Gill, & Dean, 2016; Barbour & James, 2015; Chinn & Barbour, 2013; Garcia & Barbour, 2018), while sidestepping the complexities of intersectionality that are inescapable for the humans that inhabit them (Masri, 2019). This critique notwithstanding, a rich array of communication scholarship tackles intersectionality in the defining, navigating, and changing professional membership (e.g., Allen, 2010; Linabary, Long, Mouton, Rao, & Buzzanell, 2016; Malvini Redden & Scarduzio, 2018; McDonald, 2015; Mitra, 2015; Wells, Gill, & McDonald, 2015).

The communication literature's notion of a "third space" is another important site for the negotiation of professional membership (Ganesh & McAllum, 2012). The third space is an ill-defined organizational position that refers to roles individuals inhabit beyond their primary work, including clubs, choirs, and religious groups, and it has been particularly well-studied in communication research on volunteering (McNamee & Peterson, 2014). Ganesh and McAllum (2012) argued that holding professionalism and volunteerism in tension enables scholars to examine their "gendered, discursive, and contingent" performances (p. 153). Doing so can reveal important contrasts: Volunteers receive limited training and tend to engage in low-status, unpaid, paraprofessional labor. Moreover, volunteers operate in a third space literally, in that they perform work in locations removed from paid employees (Ashcraft & Kedrowicz, 2002), and figuratively, in that their volunteer work role is complemented with other life roles, jobs, and personal responsibilities. To underscore the tension here, volunteering can be excluding in that the volunteer is understood in opposition to the worker or working professional (Barbour & Manly, 2016), and yet having the freedom, resources, and time to volunteer involves its own sorts of privilege (Chinn & Barbour, 2013). Nonprofit organizations rely on the work of volunteers, and yet volunteers typically have no legal obligation to or financial dependence on the organization. Membership boundaries are fluid, and individuals can decide their membership in terms of how participation serves their higher-order identities (Meisenbach & Kramer, 2014). These forms of privilege notwithstanding, to be a volunteer is also to be understood as an amateur (Agarwal & Buzzanell, 2015; Chinn & Barbour, 2013; Ganesh & McAllum, 2012).

In sum, professionals and professions draw the membership boundaries to protect and defend the profession. They navigate this boundary in their communication by advocating for the profession, claiming jurisdiction, indicating their credentials, and framing work as specialized and elite. At the same time, communication research has demonstrated that professions and professionals can transcend and remake such boundaries also while making clear that the agency for doing so itself bound up with constructions of gender, race, social class, sexuality, (dis)ability, national-origin, and age and the material realities of difference (Allen, 2010; Kuhn et al., 2017; Mitra, 2015). Journalists can carve out fluid, entrepreneurial career trajectories where they rely on individual resources rather than occupational consciousness (Davidson & Meyers, 2016). Volunteer disaster responders can resist and shift professional logics of preparedness (Barbour & Manly, 2016), and move beyond the professional/amateur dichotomy by drawing on "network identification connections—familial, ideological, and spiritual—that empower individuals to construct their identities in transformative ways" (Agarwal & Buzzanell, 2015, p. 422). Workers can assign meaning to what they do through egalitarian work structures and cultural discourse, rather than occupational distinctions (Barrett & Dailey, 2018). These examples suggest that the macrolevel constructions of professions can be altered even as they are constrained by differing access to the privileges of professional status. As professions seek to define membership, the boundary for what constitutes membership can be transformed.

Work

Entwined with negotiating professional membership is the negotiation of what counts as professional work and how it comes to have meaning. Professionals and professions help define what counts as meaningful work. As such, professions are also bound by the meanings attributed to the type of work that the professional performs. Disentangling tasks that professionals perform from tasks that non-professionals perform can highlight inclusionary and exclusionary work practices. Professional work can be called "real work" in opposition to other forms of work, such as volunteering (Ganesh & McAllum, 2012; McNamee & Peterson, 2014); restaurant work that is considered "art" or "manual labor" (Kuhn et al., 2008); or work that is helpful or related to the profession but not professional (Ashcraft, 2007; Ganesh & McAllum, 2012; Tsetsura, 2010).

Central to being a professional is defending the work that only professionals can do. For example, in their study of volunteer preparedness organizing, Barbour and Manly (2016) found that volunteer coordinators designed and developed a majority of the planning associated with disaster preparedness response with little input from volunteers even as they acknowledge the need and importance of volunteer engagement and input. In this context, plans required expertise, knowledge, training, and certification. At the same time, volunteers and coordinators rhetorically shifted what counted as volunteer work to accomplish locally important tasks while attending to macrolevel logics of preparation and profession. Along these lines, Garcia and Barbour (2018) found that librarians leveraged specific work practices to communicate expertise and delineate librarian and staff roles. Librarian work included building, curating, teaching, and programming; non-librarian work included routine questions and checking out books, tasks that support staff were allowed to handle. Support staff reinforced these associations with librarian professionalism when they deferred to librarians for help when asked by patrons to perform work outside of their domain. In this example, professionals and paraprofessionals enacted the boundaries ascribed to professional work.

Professionals carve out particular types of work as belonging to the profession in part to make it meaningful. Barrett and Dailey (2018) examined professional identity management and meaningful work in relation to national cultural discourses in Norway. They found that workers in Norway were undergoing significant cultural professional change at the intersection of meaningful work defined by (a) their historical commitment to workers' rights and collective values and (b) masculine work performances aligned with an economic era of oil. Workers transitioning to strict hierarchies, less autonomy, and more competition drew on macro-discourses of meaningful work as other-oriented, less superficial, and including time for personal reflection to delineate the scope of their work. Individuals expressed professional identities that were intertwined with traditional Norwegian values and culture rather than specific occupations or organizations. The cultural discourse surrounding the changing of the social landscape informed their professional identities.

The definition of professional work, like membership, interacts with additional lines of difference. Professional identity is, in part, shaped by region (Gill & Larson, 2014). Identity work is enmeshed in professional status, and so too is the perception of work status. Leonardi and Rodriguez-Lluesma (2013) found that engineers in Mexico were perceived as lower-status by counterparts in India and the United States. Mexican engineers did similar work, and sought to alter how they were perceived. They did so by behaving in ways stereotypical to engineers, which counter-productively reinforced a low-status perception. The geographical and the cultural-communicative divides between Mexico, India, and the United States influenced the ability to claim work as professional. Against the backdrop of the immigration debate in the US, Wells, Gill, and McDonald's (2015) study of scientists on H-1B visas also found that national identity drove the scientists experience of what Wells et al. termed an intersectional "netting," "a patterned weave that can be intermittently basic and/or complex; capable of folding in on itself, becoming tangled, and also providing order and familiarity" (p. 549). The meaning of what it meant to do scientific work, a key element of professional identity, depended on the weave of gender, national origin, and body.

Professionals draw a boundary around what constitutes professional work versus non-professional work. Professional work may be altered by changes in practice including routinization, standardization, and mechanization (Scott, 2008). At the same time, professionals govern what is considered work only they can do and work that is subordinate, for example, what sort of work can be automated and work cannot (Bailey & Leonardi, 2015). They privilege some work practices as high-status and exercise dominion over them, and they follow stereotypical perceptions about what professional work looks like. However, much like the negotiation of membership, communication scholars have identified ways in which this boundary is traversed. For example, Meisenbach (2008) found that fundraisers used discursive frames (i.e. mission, coordinating, magical framing) to accommodate but also resist stigmatized meanings and practices of their work. Treem (2012, 2016) found that public relations professionals could cultivate perceptions of expertise. These examples show that the boundary of what constitutes professional work may be reinforced and also contested through communication.

Organization

Professions are distinct from the organizations in which professionals work in that they are substantiated by specialized activities, distinct knowledge, and enduring influence that continues to exist beyond particular organizations (Lammers & Garcia, 2009). This knowledge and technical ability becomes institutionalized through its transcendence beyond the work groups and organizations in which it is performed (Freidson, 1986; Scott, 2008), as does the identity associated with being a professional and its influence on organizational members' expectations of each other, behavior, work conditions, and emotions (Lammers & Garcia, 2009). However, even as professional work is distinct from an organizational context, professionals often conduct their work within specific organizations, and professions cannot easily be disentangled from the particular organizational forms they take. Professionals must situate themselves in networks of complementary roles, as purpose and meaning cannot be established in work without viewing it against the broader context in which it is embedded (Sluss & Ashforth, 2007).

Within organizational spaces, professionals form groups to coordinate knowledge and skill; these groups hold distinctive organizational *and* professional characteristics. The collaboration involved in professional work can blur professional and organizational boundaries. Collaborative work hinges on the ways in which professionals negotiate their membership of interorganizational groups, as well as how those groups negotiate and utilize knowledge in the midst of barriers and opportunities posed by their interdisciplinarity (Barley, 2015; Barley, Leonardi, & Bailey, 2012). Although collaboration necessitates inclusion of others' efforts and ideas, groups must also exercise exclusion by establishing role-related boundaries to manage threats to the professional identities nested within them (Barbour & James, 2015; Harrison, Smith, Greenwell, & Stephens, 2018; McNeil, Mitchell, & Parker, 2013).

Workers' attachments to professions demand an intensive and exclusive socialization process distinct from but related to the organizations in which they work (Lammers, Atouba, & Carlson, 2013). The socialization process may rely on standards of conduct, appearance, and discourse established by the nature of the work, while simultaneously being bound by the reality that professions hold implicit and explicit expectations associated with gender, race, and class (Ashcraft, 2013; Cheney & Ashcraft, 2007). For example, the ability of healthcare professionals to coordinate their knowledge and practice is further complicated by the extensive profession-specific socialization process they endure, which often results in fundamentally different understandings of patient-care and the roles and processes necessary for effective collaboration.

Professionals form and negotiate their identity in tandem with other targets of identification (Scott, 1997, 1999). Professional and organizational goals are distinct and may not be commensurate (Gossett, 2002). Workers may identify strongly with their profession as a source of pride and co-workers as a source of emotional support, and not define themselves in terms of the organization in which they work. Scott (1997) found that although more local targets tended to be associated with higher identification, occupational identifications were comparatively resistant to the effects of geographic dispersion. Russo (1998) found that journalists reported significantly higher identification with the profession of journalism than with their employing newspaper. Lammers and colleagues (2013) found that veterinarians working in a poison control center reported varying degrees of attachment with their organization, group, and profession, and that the veterinarians were able to draw on their professional identity to buffer against workplace stress and burnout.

Professionals form work-related identities based on the tasks they perform and responsibilities they hold. Workers might be excluded from certain professional duties when they are promoted to management or when they must meet the demands of other related work (Garcia & Barbour, 2018). Such exclusion may degrade their attachment to the profession in favor of the organization (Lammers et al., 2013). In contrast, members may actually wish to be excluded from certain domains of work, and in an effort to do so, strategically present themselves in a negative fashion to deter their inclusion (Leonardi & Treem, 2012). Frandsen (2012) found that financial professionals managed the stigma associated with working at a firm with a very poor reputation by "cynically distancing" themselves, at once bolstering their identity as professionals and sustaining the firm's negative image. Professionals may heighten the boundary between the profession and the organization when working in organizations whose purpose does not reflect the nature of the profession or when they do not identify with the organization's mission.

Knowing

Boundaries between domains of knowledge offer a fourth site of professional inclusion and exclusion. Professional work is frequently associated with claims of expertise, as these groups may hold the power to determine who has the legitimacy to operate in various domains of work (Lammers & Garcia, 2009). Professional membership is at times treated as tantamount to holding a given body of knowledge (Jarvenpaa & Majchrzak, 2008; Lammers & Krikorian, 1997; Majchrzak, Jarvenpaa, & Hollingshead, 2007). The variety of professions has grown significantly since their initial rise in the early 19th century due to the progressive differentiation of knowledge in society and the bureaucratic expansion of the state's power and functions necessitating the professionalization of these functions (Larson, 1979). At the same time, the rise of the professions has included and excluded different sorts of work as work knowing (e.g., paid work done by elites) or not (e.g., unpaid work, women's work, craft work, slave labor)—boundaries reflected in the professional groups most often studied.

Professionals enact performances to communicate that their work is distinctive to the profession that center on what they know that others do not (Treem, 2012, 2016). Lammers and Garcia (2009) argued that professionals provide, seek, and share knowledge to be regarded as professionals. Communicating domain knowledge to others reinforces and substantiates boundaries of professional inclusion. Professional status is secured not only by the appropriation of specific knowledge as an exclusive area of work, but also the designation of that knowledge as legitimate (Cheney & Ashcraft, 2007; Treem, 2012).

Professionals' expertise is communicatively performed and negotiated (Treem & Leonardi, 2016). Professionals' knowing centers on distinctive capacities for solving particular organizational problems (or at least those individuals thought to have such capacities) (Kuhn & Jackson, 2008; Kuhn & Rennstam, 2016). At the same time, professionals' ability to claim what they know as known is grounded in institutionalized, macrolevel structures (Ashcraft, 2013; Barbour & Lammers, 2015; Cheney & Ashcraft, 2007; Lammers & Barbour, 2006). Professionals must negotiate boundaries in knowing between who can legitimately claim to know what and who has expertise (Barbour, Sommer, et al., 2016). Professional work centers on deciding whose expertise ought to be legitimate, encumbering, or authoritative in any given moment. Navigating the boundaries of inclusion and exclusion related to knowing has to do with answering questions of who can claim what they know as legitimate; who can encumber the actions of others by virtue of that knowledge and its enshrinement in laws, professional standards, regulatory frameworks and policies, and organizational rules; and who has authority in and across organizations (Barbour, Sommer, et al., 2016).

Associations of knowledge with specific professions provide expectations about who does what work (Barley, 1996; Lammers & Krikorian, 1997). Professionals claim identity in part through efforts to exclude others from accessing an area of knowledge or expertise (see blackboxing in, Reed, 1996). At the same time, professionals can create objects such as graphs, charts, figures to manage communication across different knowledge domains (Barley, 2015; Barley et al., 2012). The negotiation of different forms, claims, and commitments to knowing are central to successful interprofessional communication (Apker, Propp, & Zabava Ford, 2005; Apker, Ptacek, Beach, & Wears, 2016) and interdisciplinary collaboration (Barbour & James, 2015; Barley & Weickum, 2017; Thompson, 2009).

Negotiating Inclusion and Exclusion

Looking across research at these boundaries, professionals and professions negotiate inclusion and exclusion in multiple ways. Professionals (re)construct their work and the profession, as they explain and frame the field for others. They can maintain but also correct stereotypes and taken-for-granted notions of difference, and they preview issues of inclusion and exclusion in giving newcomers a sense of what a domain of work entails. They include and exclude as they construct and perform the identity of the good worker, professional, and the work worth knowing. Though at times constrained by local organizational rules and requirements, they can exercise a degree of autonomy over the work they do and where they spend their time. They have some ability to redesign work and its related domains of knowing expressed along or apart from power, status, and embodied forms of difference.

Salient Organizational Stakeholders

The management of difference at these boundaries of inclusion and exclusion has implications for the professionals themselves; their managers and leaders; professional societies and trade associations; apprentices, residents, trainees, and students joining the profession; allied occupations and voluntary groups; the organizations in which they work; and the clients who rely on professional services and expertise. Relationships considered in the literature described above include the professional and volunteer, professionals and managers, the doctor and the nurse, the librarian and the staff, the engineer and the craft, and situations that bring together multiple professions (e.g., scientists, regulators, engineers, and project managers, Barbour & James, 2015). The key is that thinking in terms of these relationships brings the boundaries and dynamics of inclusion and exclusion into relief.

Implications for the clients and subjects of professional work have received less attention in communicative study of the professions; although, the study of professional work is often grounded in improving it to benefit them. It can be difficult to study professions and professionals while at the same time studying the implications for those who they serve. This difficulty notwithstanding communication research has demonstrated the value of doing so. For example, this boundary can be seen in work on interprofessional communication in healthcare contexts wherein models of more effective collaborative work among multiple medical specialties and occupational groups can improve patient care and reduce medical errors (Apker et al., 2005, 2016; Dean, Gill, & Barbour, 2016; Eisenberg et al., 2005; Harrison et al., 2018; Real, Bardach, & Bardach, 2016). Treem's (2012, 2016) work provides another example, of how, in this case, public relations workers communicate their expertise to clients, client-focused advocacy for work that lacks strong ties to an institutionalized occupation. This work shows how these professionals make their work visible for clients in practices such as repurposing previously perfected work.

These exemplars suggest a few takeaways for considering the organizational stakeholders of the study of professions and professionals for issues of inclusion and exclusion. Research should continue to explore and practice must grapple with the relational and power-laden nature of the dynamics among stakeholders. In considering who can access and benefit from professional services and expertise, although it can be difficult to do so, existing research provides a warrant for considering the implications of how professionals and professions negotiate issues of inclusion and exclusion for those they serve, including how professionals reveal or conceal work from those they serve.

Data, Methods, and Research Foci

Investigating issues of inclusion and exclusion can reveal the role and power of professions and professionals in controlling the permeability of the boundaries of membership, work, organization, and knowing. Data particularly useful to communication scholars includes research focused on professional work practices (Bailey & Leonardi, 2015; Leonardi, 2015; Treem, 2012), which can reveal not just the nature of the professional work but also what is at stake as professionals negotiate how work ought to be done and by whom. Likewise, data about professionals' efforts to design and discipline their communication may reveal how dynamics of inclusion and exclusion scale up from micro- to macro-level patterns and offer a site for intervention (Barbour & Gill, 2017; Barbour, Gill, & Barge, 2018). Previous scholarship has also tried to understand the multilevel nature of professions and professional work (Ashcraft, 2013; Ashforth, Rogers, & Corley, 2011; Barbour & Lammers, 2007), which requires a focus on the actual work of a profession and its macrolevel construction (Ashcraft, 2007). Longitudinal, historical, multiorganizational research should be of particular value for doing so (Lammers & Barbour, 2006) as well as research focused on occupations in times of change (Meisenbach, 2008) or disruption (Garcia & Barbour, 2018). In the communicative study of professions and professionals, survey-based scholarship has also emphasized understanding professionals' attachment to various targets of identification (Barbour & Lammers, 2007; Lammers et al., 2013; Scott, 1997; Scott & Timmerman, 1999). Research should not conflate attachment to the profession with the internalization of external constructions of a profession or the holding of beliefs typical for most professionals (Scott, Corman, & Cheney, 1998). Instead, research should consider how membership in, attachment to, and beliefs about a profession and professional work are related but independent constructs (Barbour & Lammers, 2015).

The Contributions of the Communicative Study of Professions and Professionals to Problems of Exclusion and Inclusion

The communicative study of professions, professionals, professional work, and the efforts of professionals to negotiate membership, work, organizational, and knowledge boundaries can provide useful strategies. First, we should acknowledge that the nature of professional work grounded in institutionalized organizational arrangements may make reconstruction more difficult. Institutions resist change (Lammers & Barbour, 2006). By focusing on the tensions and contradictions inherent to institutionalized work, including issues of inclusion and exclusion (Creed, DeJordy, & Lok, 2010), communication research can identify strategies for more adaptively navigating those tensions and the efficacy of communication efforts for reimagining established professional boundaries (Barbour & Manly, 2016; Bisel, Kramer, & Banas, 2016).

Communication research focused on professions, professionals, and professionalism already demonstrates the possibilities along these lines. For example, funding and policy guidance may constrain the work of professionals and volunteers in disaster preparation and response, but organizers can nonetheless reconstruct volunteer work, volunteering, and who can volunteer (Ganesh & McAllum, 2012) and in part by drawing on the very institutional logics that constrain (Barbour & Manly, 2016). Who counts as a volunteer and who counts as a professional can be shifting by riffing on institutional contradictions to redraw membership boundaries. Legal mandates for interdisciplinary collaboration in, for example environmental protection and waste management, can make collaborative problem solving more difficult. Legal and regulatory frameworks may sublimate conflicts between domains of knowing, and yet communicative strategies such as meta-communicating about competing premises for action can ameliorate the difficulties (Barbour & James, 2015). The historical construction or image of profession may constrain what seems like legitimate professional work and who seems a legitimate professional (Ashcraft, 2007), and these constraints may be built into the very spaces in which professionals work (Dean et al., 2016), but they are constructed and so can be deconstructed and reconstructed (Allen, 2010; Ashcraft, 2000; Ashcraft, 2013; Mease, 2016). Who gets to work and speak where can be challenged by reimagining spaces hand in hand with understandings of the professional role expectations ascribed to them (Barbour, Gill, et al., 2016).

A principal contribution of communication research on professions and professionals to problems of inclusion and exclusion should be to identify the sorts of communication strategies, practices, and interventions described above that can make for more competent professional and interprofessional communication for the understanding and reconstruction of expertise difference. Doing so requires refining not just the practice of individuals but of collectives and not just professionals but professions (Thompson, 2009). The macrolevel construction of a profession may be marshalled to reinforce, accommodate, or resist organizational circumstances. Take, for example, the Mexican engineers who altered their own work discourses based on the perceived status they associated with their international colleagues (Leonardi & Rodriguez-Lluesma, 2013). In doing so, they challenged but also reinforced racially-driven assumptions surrounding their profession. A key risk in the rhetorical construction of a profession is to avoid bolstering one form of work at the expense of another. Elsewhere, in response to hegemonic masculinization of professions, Turner and Norwood (2014) advocated for a shift in the discourse of workplace breastfeeding, reconceptualizing it towards a public and essential need. This shift could serve to empower new mothers while at the same time pushing them to subordinate their own interests and biological needs to function as "good workers."

Recent writing on automation has highlighted that professional work traditionally thought of beyond machines may not be much longer (Brynjolfsson & McAfee, 2016; Stone et al., 2016), and at the same time, the established professions have worked to construct autonomous, machine workers as augmenting rather than replacing professionals (Topol, 2019). Communication research shows that professions and professionals shape the lived reality of advances in the technologies of work; the technologies and nature of work change together (Bailey & Leonardi, 2015; Leonardi, 2012). Communication research must help ensure that the future of work does not recapitulate historical inequities of inclusion and exclusion (Lepore, 2019), and it will be in the professions where this story unfolds.

Looking beyond traditional professions, workers can empower themselves through discourse in their pursuit of legitimacy. Volunteers, service-workers, fundraisers, and educators can speak their legitimacy into existence over the course of their day-to-day work (Barbour & Manly, 2016; Treem, 2012; Meisenbach, 2008; Barrett & Dailey, 2018). These threads of research suggest that individuals and organizations must reflect on institutionalized discursive messaging if they wish to act against the exclusionary aspects of professional work. By acknowledging, discussing, and challenging how we conceptualize, discuss, and reinforce exclusionary aspects of professional practice, we may begin to remove the barriers that deprive people and work from professional legitimacy. Leaders and advocacy organizations should cultivate professional cultures that reinforce and create space for discourse that aids in democratic definition of membership. At the same time, professionals and professions need to wrestle with the tension inherent to inclusivity that runs counter to the very nature of professional status, which centers on exclusivity. Doing may seem to risk the dilution of professional power, but elite status should not be confused with professional competence. Professionals can preserve what makes a profession special without reifying historical divides. Failure to manage the dynamics of inclusion and exclusion may be most undermining where the risks to the profession are technological or where societal trust in the profession has eroded.

Furthermore, research and practice should identify resources and strategies that may be used by the clients served by professionals. Doing so would prompt questions such as, who gets to count themselves as a client of a particular profession, what issues of inclusion and exclusion do individuals face when they seek the services of professionals, and what sort of legal, financial, and social barriers prevent access to professional services? The exclusivity of professions is itself scaffolded by a lack of research focused on the experience of the client. Medicine, the most frequently professional domain where movements such as patient centered care and collaborative caregiving (Dean et al., 2016) are about redefining the implicated professions by redefining their relationship to each other and to those who they serve. Doing so may also serve to bolster society's trust in the profession while grappling with the changing technologies of medical work (Timmermans & Berg, 2003; Topol, 2019).

Research should take up a more explicit focus on the boundaries of inclusion and exclusion highlighted in this review—membership, work, organization, and knowing. Failing to do so may exacerbate problems of inclusion and exclusion. This research should ask how particular boundaries involve, implicate, and overlap others. It should reveal the key tensions and contradictions inherent to those boundaries as they may offer purchase for efforts aimed at reconstruction, and in doing so, it may help identify and test strategies for negotiating inclusion and exclusion.

References

Abbott, A. D. (1988). *The system of professions: An essay on the division of expert labor.* Chicago, IL: University of Chicago Press.

Agarwal, V., & Buzzanell, P. M. (2015). Communicative reconstruction of resilience labor: Identity/identification in disaster-relief workers. *Journal of Applied Communication Research, 43,* 408–428.

Allen, B. J. (2010). *Difference matters: Communicating social identity* (2nd ed.). Prospect Heights, IL: Waveland Press.

Alvesson, M., & Willmott, H. (2002). Idenity regulation as organizational control: Reproducing the appropriate individual. *Journal of Management Studies, 39,* 619–644.

Apker, J., Propp, K. M., & Zabava Ford, W. (2005). Negotiating status and identity tensions in healthcare team interactions: An exploration of nurse role dialectics. *Journal of Applied Communication Research, 33,* 93–115. doi:10.1080/00909880500044620

Apker, J., Ptacek, J., Beach, C., & Wears, R. (2016). Exploring role dialectics in inter-service admission handoffs: A qualitative analysis of physician communication. *Journal of Applied Communication Research, 44,* 399–414. doi:10.1080/00909882.2016.1225164

Ashcraft, K. L. (2000). Empowering "professional" relationships: Organizational communication meets feminist practice. *Management Communication Quarterly, 13,* 347–392.

Ashcraft, K. L. (2007). Appreciating the 'work' of discourse: Occupational identity and difference as organizing mechanisms in the case of commercial airline pilots. *Discourse & Communication, 1,* 9–36.

Ashcraft, K. L. (2013). The glass slipper: "Incorporating" occupational identity in management studies. *Academy of Management Review, 38,* 6–31.

Ashcraft, K. L., & Kedrowicz, A. (2002). Self-direction or social support? Nonprofit empowerment and the tacit employment contract of organizational communication studies. *Communication Monographs, 69,* 88–110. doi:10.1080/03637750216538

Ashcraft, K. L., Muhr, S. L., Rennstam, J., & Sullivan, K. (2012). Professionalization as a branding activity: Occupational identity and the dialectic of inclusivity-exclusivity. *Gender, Work & Organization, 19,* 467–488. doi:10.1111/j.1468-0432.2012.00600.x

Ashforth, B. E., Rogers, K. M., & Corley, K. G. (2011). Identity in oganizations: Exploring cross-level dynamics. *Organization Science, 22,* 1144–1156.

Bailey, D. E., & Leonardi, P. M. (2015). *Technology choices: Why occupations differ in their embrace of new technology.* Cambridge, MA: The MIT Press.

Barbour, J. B., & Gill, R. (2017). Questioning as regulatory work practice: The communicative accomplishment of reliability for the safety oversight of nuclear power plants. *Communication Monographs, 84,* 466–487. doi:10.1080/03637751.2017.1322212

Barbour, J. B., Gill, R., & Barge, J. K. (2018). Organizational communication design logics: A theory of communicative intervention and collective communication design. *Communication Theory, 28,* 332–353. doi:10.1093/ct/qtx005

Barbour, J. B., Gill, R., & Dean, M. (2016). Work space, gendered occupations, and the organization of health: Redesigning emergency department communication. In T. Harrison & E. Williams (Eds.), *Organizations, communication, and health* (pp. 101–118). New York, NY: Routledge.

Barbour, J. B., & James, E. P. (2015). Collaboration for compliance: Identity tensions in the interorganizational and interdisciplinary regulation of a toxic waste facility. *Journal of Applied Communication Research, 43,* 363–384. doi:10.1080/00909882.2015.1083601

Barbour, J. B., & Lammers, J. C. (2007). Health care institutions, communication, and physicians' experience of managed care: A multilevel analysis. *Management Communication Quarterly, 21,* 201–231. doi:10.1177/0893318907308747

Barbour, J. B., & Lammers, J. C. (2015). Measuring professional identity: A review of the literature and a multilevel confirmatory factor analysis of professional identity constructs. *Journal of Professions and Organization, 2,* 38–60. doi:10.1093/jpo/jou009

Barbour, J. B., & Manly, J. N. (2016). Redefining disaster preparedness: Institutional contradictions and praxis in volunteer responder organizing. *Management Communication Quarterly, 30,* 333–361. doi:10.1177/0893318916629101

Barbour, J. B., Sommer, P., & Gill, R. (2016). Technical, arcane, interpersonal, and embodied expertise. In J. W. Treem & P. M. Leonardi (Eds.), *Expertise, communication, and organizing* (pp. 44–59). Oxford: Oxford University Press.

Barley, S. R. (1996). Technicians in the workplace: Ethnographic evidence for bringing work into organizational studies. *Administrative Science Quarterly, 41,* 404–441. doi:10.2307/2393937

Barley, W. C. (2015). Anticipatory work: How the need to represent knowledge across boundaries shapes work practices within them. *Organization Science, 26,* 1612–1628. doi:10.1287/orsc.2015.1012

Barley, W. C., Leonardi, P. M., & Bailey, D. E. (2012). Engineering objects for collaboration: Strategies of ambiguity and clarity at knowledge boundaries. *Human Communication Research, 38,* 280–308. doi:10.1111/j.1468–2958.2012.01430.x

Barley, W. C., & Weickum, N. R. (2017). The work gap: A structured review of collaborative teamwork research from 2005 to 2015. *Annals of the International Communication Association, 41,* 136–167. doi:10.1080/23808985.2017.1322912

Barrett, A. K., & Dailey, S. (2018). A new normal? Competing national cultural discourses and workers' constructions of identity and meaningful work in Norway. *Communication Monographs, 85,* 284–307. doi:10.1080/03637751.2017.1372587

Bisel, R. S., Kramer, M. W., & Banas, J. A. (2016). Scaling up to institutional entrepreneurship: A life history of an elite training gymnastics organization. *Human Relations, 70,* 410–435. doi:10.1177/0018726716658964

Brynjolfsson, E., & McAfee, A. (2016). *The second machine age: Work, progress, and prosperity in a time of brilliant technologies.* New York, NY: W.W. Norton & Company.

Cheney, G., & Ashcraft, K. L. (2007). Considering "The Professional" in communication studies: Implications for theory and research within and beyond the boundaries of organizational communication. *Communication Theory, 17,* 146–175.

Chinn, J. N., & Barbour, J. B. (2013). Negotiating aging and agedness in volunteer disaster response teams. In M. Kramer, L. Gossett, & L. Lewis (Eds.), *Volunteering and communication: Studies from multiple contexts* (pp. 231–249). New York: Peter Lang.

Creed, W. E. D., DeJordy, R., & Lok, J. (2010). Being the change: Resolving institutional contradictions through identity work. *Academy of Management Journal, 53,* 1336–1364. doi:10.5465/AMJ.2010.57318357

Davidson, R., & Meyers, O. (2016). Toward a typology of journalism careers: Conceptualizing Israeli journalists' occupational trajectories. *Communication, Culture and Critique, 9,* 193–211. doi:10.1111/cccr.12103

Dean, M., Gill, R., & Barbour, J. B. (2016). s Investigating interprofessional communication, collaboration, professional roles, and physical space at EmergiCare. *Health Communication, 31,* 1506–1516. doi:10.1080/10410236.2015.1089457

Eisenberg, E. M., Murphy, A. G., Sutcliffe, K. M., Wears, R., Schenkel, S., Perry, S., & Vanderhoef, M. (2005). Communication in emergency medicine: Implications for patient safety. *Communication Monographs, 72,* 390–413.

Frandsen, S. (2012). Organizational image, identification, and cynical distance: Prestigious professionals in a low-prestige organization. *Management Communication Quarterly, 26,* 351–376. doi:10.1177/0893318912438692

Freidson, E. (1986). *Professional powers.* Chicago, IL: The University of Chicago Press.

Ganesh, S., & McAllum, K. (2012). Volunteering and professionalization: Trends in tension? *Management Communication Quarterly, 26,* 152–158. doi:10.1177/0893318911423762

Garcia, M. A., & Barbour, J. B. (2018). "Ask a professional—Ask a librarian": Librarianship and the chronic struggle for professional status. *Management Communication Quarterly, 32*, 565–592. doi:10.1177/0893318918776798

Gill, R., & Larson, G. S. (2014). Making the ideal (local) entrepreneur: Place and the regional development of high-tech entrepreneurial identity. *Human Relations, 67*(5), 519–542. doi:10.1177/0018726713496829

Gossett, L. M. (2002). Kept at arm's length: Questioning the organizational desirability of member identification. *Communication Monographs, 69*, 385–404.

Harrison, M. A., Smith, W. R., Greenwell, M. R., & Stephens, K. K. (2018). Frontline employees in the health clinic: Impression management multiplexing when performing in-the-round. *Communication Monographs, 85*, 309–330. doi:10.1080/03637751.2018.1429638

Holvino, E. (2010). Intersections: The simultaneity of race, cender and class in organization studies. *Gender, Work & Organization, 17*, 248–277. doi:10.1111/j.1468-0432.2008.00400.x

Jahn, J. L. S., & Myers, K. K. (2014). Vocational anticipatory socialization of adolescents: Messages, sources, and frameworks that Influence interest in STEM careers. *Journal of Applied Communication Research, 42*, 85–106. doi:10.1080/0090 9882.2013.874568

Jarvenpaa, S. L., & Majchrzak, A. (2008). Knowledge collaboration among professionals protecting national security: Role of transactive memories in ego-centered knowledge networks. *Organization Science, 19*, 260–276.

Kisselburgh, L. G., Berkelaar, B. L., & Buzzanell, P. M. (2009). Discourse, gender, and the meaning of work: Rearticulating science, technology, and engineering careers through communicative lenses. In C. S. Beck (Ed.), *Communication Yearbook 33* (pp. 259–299). Mahwah, NJ: Lawrence Erlbaum.

Kuhn, T., Ashcraft, K. L., & Cooren, F. (2017). *The work of communication: Relational perspectives on working and organizing in contemporary capitalism.* New York, NY: Routledge.

Kuhn, T., Golden, A. G., Jorgenson, J., Buzzanell, P. M., Berkelaar, B. L., Kisselburgh, L. G., . . . Cruz, D. (2008). Cultural discourses and discursive resources for meaning/ful work: Constructing and disrupting identities in contemporary capitalism. *Management Communication Quarterly, 22*, 162–171. doi:10.1177/0893318908318262

Kuhn, T., & Jackson, M. (2008). Accomplishing knowledge: A framework for investigating knowing in organizations. *Management Communication Quarterly, 21*, 454–485. doi:10.1177/0893318907313710

Kuhn, T., & Rennstam, J. (2016). Expertise as a practical accomplishment among objects and values. In J. W. Treem & P. M. Leonardi (Eds.), *Expertise, communication, and organizing* (pp. 25–43). Oxford: Oxford University Press.

Lammers, J. C., Atouba, Y., & Carlson, E. J. (2013). Which identities matter? A mixed-method study of group, organizational, and professional identities and their relationship to burnout. *Management Communication Quarterly, 27*, 503–536.

Lammers, J. C., & Barbour, J. B. (2006). An institutional theory of organizational communication. *Communication Theory, 16*, 356–377. doi:10.1111/j.1468-2885.2006.00274.x

Lammers, J. C., & Garcia, M. A. (2009). Exploring the concept of "profession" for organizational communication research: Institutional influences in a veterinary organization. *Management Communication Quarterly, 22*, 357–384.

Lammers, J. C., & Krikorian, D. H. (1997). Theoretical extension and operationalization of the bona fide group construct with an application to surgical teams. *Journal of Applied Communication Research, 25*, 17–38.

Larson, M. S. (1979). *The rise of professionalism: A sociological analysis* (1st pbk. printing ed.). Berkeley, CA: University of California Press.

Leonardi, P. M. (2012). *Car crashes without cars: Lessons about simulation technology and organizational change from automotive design*. Cambridge, MA: MIT Press.

Leonardi, P. M. (2015). Studying work practices in organizations: Theoretical considerations and empirical guidelines. *Annals of the International Communication Association, 39*, 235–273. doi:10.1080/23808985.2015.11679177

Leonardi, P. M., & Rodriguez-Lluesma, C. (2013). Occupational stereotypes, perceived status differences, and intercultural communication in global organizations. *Communication Monographs, 80*, 478–502. doi:10.1080/03637751.2013.828155

Leonardi, P. M., & Treem, J. W. (2012). Knowledge management technology as a stage for strategic self-presentation: Implications for knowledge sharing in organizations. *Information and Organization, 22*, 37–59. doi:10.1016/j.infoandorg.2011.10.003

Lepore, J. (2019). Are robots competing for your job? Probably, but don't count yourself out. *The New Yorker*. Retrieved from https://www.newyorker.com/magazine/2019/03/04/are-robots-competing-for-your-job

Linabary, J. R., Long, Z., Mouton, A., Rao, R. L., & Buzzanell, P. M. (2016). Embracing tensions in feminist organizational communication pedagogies. *Communication Education*, 1–23. doi:10.1080/03634523.2016.1257818

Majchrzak, A., Jarvenpaa, S. L., & Hollingshead, A. B. (2007). Coordinating expertise among emergent groups responding to disasters. *Organization Science, 18*, 147–161.

Malvini Redden, S., & Scarduzio, J. A. (2018). A different type of dirty work: Hidden taint, intersectionality, and emotion management in bureaucratic organizations. *Communication Monographs, 85*, 224–244. doi:10.1080/03637751.2017.1394580

Masri, H. (2019). Communication studies' hollow intersectionality rhetoric. *Women's Studies in Communication, 42*, 417–421. doi:10.1080/07491409.2019.1682916

McDonald, J. (2015). Organizational communication meets Queer Theory: Theorizing relations of "difference" differently. *Communication Theory, 25*(3), 310–329. doi:10.1111/comt.12060

McDonald, J., & Kuhn, T. R. (2016). Occupational branding for diversity: Managing discursive contradictions. *Journal of Applied Communication Research, 44*, 101–117. doi:10.1080/00909882.2016.1155725

McNamee, L. G., & Peterson, B. L. (2014). Reconciling "Third space/place" toward a complementary dialectical understanding of volunteer management. *Management Communication Quarterly, 28*, 214–243.

McNeil, K. A., Mitchell, R. J., & Parker, V. (2013). Interprofessional practice and professional identity threat. *Health Sociology Review, 22*, 291–307. doi:10.5172/hesr.2013.22.3.291

Mease, J. J. (2016). Embracing discursive paradox: Consultants navigating the constitutive tensions of diversity work. *Management Communication Quarterly, 30*, 59–83. doi:10.1177/0893318915604239

Meisenbach, R. J. (2008). Materiality, discourse, and (dis)empowerment in occupational identity negotiation among higher education fund-raisers. *Management Communication Quarterly, 22*, 258–287.

Meisenbach, R. J., & Kramer, M. (2014). Exploring nested identities: Voluntary membership, social category identity, and identification in a community choir. *Management Communication Quarterly, 28*, 187–213.

Mitra, R. (2015). Proposing a culture-centered approach to career scholarship: The example of subsistence careers in the US Arctic. *Human Relations, 68*, 1813–1835. doi:10.1177/0018726715570100

Norander, S., Mazer, J. P., & Bates, B. R. (2011). "D.O. or Die": Identity negotiation among osteophathic medical students. *Health Communication, 26*, 59–70. doi:10.1080/10410236.2011.527622

Novak, D. R. (2016). Democratic work at an organization-society boundary: Sociomateriality and the communicative instantiation. *Management Communication Quarterly, 30*, 218–244. doi:10.1177/0893318915622455

Real, K., Bardach, S. H., & Bardach, D. R. (2016). The role of the built environment: How decentralized nurse stations shape communication, patient care processes, and patient outcomes. *Health Communication*, 1–14. doi:10.1080/1041 0236.2016.1239302

Reed, M. I. (1996). Expert power and control in late modernity: An empirical review and theoretical synthesis. *Organization Studies, 17*, 573–597.

Russo, T. C. (1998). Organizational and professional identification: A case of newspaper journalists. *Management Communication Quarterly, 12*, 72–111.

Scott, C. R. (1997). Identification with multiple targets in a geographically dispersed organization. *Management Communication Quarterly, 10*, 491–522.

Scott, C. R. (1999). The impact of physical and discursive anonymity of group members' multiple identification during computer-supported decision making. *Western Journal of Communication, 63*, 456–487.

Scott, C. R., Corman, S. R., & Cheney, G. (1998). Development of a structurational model of identification in the organization. *Communication Theory, 8*, 298–336. doi:10.1111/j.1468–2885.1998.tb00223.x

Scott, C. R., & Timmerman, C. E. (1999). Communication techology use and multiple workplace identifications among organizational teleworkers wth varied degrees of virtuality. *IEEE Transactions on Professional Communication, 42*, 240–260.

Scott, W. R. (2008). Lords of the dance: Professionals as institutional agents. *Organization Studies, 29*, 219–238. doi:10.1177/0170840607088151

Sluss, D. M., & Ashforth, B. E. (2007). Relational identity and identification: Defining ourselves through work relationships. *Academy of Management Review, 32*, 9–32.

Stone, P., Brooks, R., Brynjolfsson, E., Calo, R., Etzioni, O., Hager, G., . . . Teller, A. (2016). *"Artificial intelligence and life in 2030." One hundred year study on artificial intelligence: Report of the 2015–2016 study panel*, Stanford, CA. Retrieved from http://ai100.stanford.edu/2016-report

Thompson, J. L. (2009). Building collective communication competence in interdisciplinary research teams. *Journal of Applied Communication Research, 37*, 278–297.

Timmermans, S., & Berg, M. (2003). *The gold standard: The challenge of evidence-based medicine and standardization in health care*. Philadelphia, PA: Temple University Press.

Topol, E. J. (2019). High-performance medicine: The convergence of human and artificial intelligence. *Nature Medicine, 25*, 44–56. doi:10.1038/s41591-018-0300-7

Treem, J. W. (2012). Communicating expertise: Knowledge performances in professional-service firms. *Communication Monographs, 79*, 23–47. doi:10.1080/0 3637751.2011.646487

Treem, J. W. (2016). How organizations communicate expertise without experts: Practices and performances of knowledge-intensive firms. *Management Communication Quarterly, 30*, 503–531. doi:10.1177/0893318916635750

Treem, J. W., & Leonardi, P. M. (2016). *Expertise, communication, and organizing.* Oxford: Oxford University Press.

Tsetsura, K. (2010). Is public relations a real job? How female practitioners construct the profession. *Journal of Public Relations Research, 23*, 1–23. doi:10.1080/1 062726x.2010.504763

Turner, P. K., & Norwood, K. (2014). 'I had the luxury . . .': Organizational breastfeeding support as privatized privilege. *Human Relations, 67*, 849–874. doi:10.1177/0018726713507730

Wells, C., Gill, R., & McDonald, J. (2015). "Us foreigners": Intersectionality in a scientific organization. *Equality, Diversity and Inclusion: An International Journal, 34*, 539–553. doi:10.1108/EDI-12-2014-0086

9 Moving Beyond Inclusion

Lessons from the Graduate Certificate in Participatory Research at the University of North Carolina at Chapel Hill

Patricia S. Parker, Dorothy Holland, Jean Dennison, Sara H. Smith, and Melvin Jackson

In this chapter, inclusion is interrogated at the level of knowledge production in academic research. In our many years working in universities we have seen that efforts focused broadly on "diversity" and "inclusion" have failed to shift the academy in significant ways. Rather, as Ahmed (2012) has argued, the language of inclusion and diversity has been deployed as *nonperformative* terms, that is, terms that are used and promoted in order to avoid doing the work of transformative justice that the university requires. It is not enough to get different people into the room and to give everyone equal space, when academic disciplines are so clearly premised on and geared toward majority interests. We must, as Megan Ybarra argues, "be the killjoy who argues not only for admission into graduate school (i.e., inclusion), but also argues that classes, classrooms and reading lists should change with their arrival (i.e., transformation)" (2019, p. 8, following Ahmed, 2010). Academic spaces, even when diverse and inclusive, too often continue to be driven by majority values and commitments that make marginalized students feel unsafe, unwelcome, or at best, uninterested in the academy.

The Graduate Certificate in Participatory Research at the University of North Carolina at Chapel Hill was intended as a transformative intervention into the University, creating more space for social justice values, commitments, and strategies. This chapter presents a reprint of an article about the Certificate that was first published in 2017 (Parker, Holland, Dennison, Smith, & Jackson). Some parts of the original article, including the title, have been adapted to fit the format and themes of the current volume.

When Rachel Gelfand[1] began contemplating her MA research in the American Studies Department at the University of North Carolina at Chapel Hill, she had already begun to question the applicability of traditional methodologies to her project and felt the need to experiment. A historian with a background in oral history, radio, and social justice activism, she asked, "how do archives function in the transmission of gay and lesbian history?" "What if," she thought, "I begin with the assumption that archives are living and emerging, rather than static and stowed away in dusty library basements down rarely entered hallways?" "What if I researched this project *collaboratively* with the person who has been archived?" These were not the sorts of questions Rachel had heard anyone asking in her department. She faced the common concerns that graduate students and faculty researchers in the academy encounter when they challenge academic norms: "Will I find a mentor who can guide me through the research process? What if I do the research and it is rejected by the academy—either in completing the degree or finding a faculty or research position?"

Rachel's concerns highlight the limitations of the academy, as currently configured, to address the urgent questions of our times. The radical departures and reconfigurations of academic strictures that are necessary to accommodate emerging forms of research, particularly those guided by social justice methodologies, require critical shifts in university culture. There have been decades of interdisciplinary critiques of academic cultures as colonizing spaces that operate to maintain "Euro-American hegemonies at the level of thinking and therefore in the larger material world" (Davies, Gadsby, Peterson, & Williams, 2003, p. ix). There is a rich and developing literature on indigenous knowledge production (Bishop, 1998; Denzin, Lincoln, & Smith, 2008; L. T. Smith, 2012), as well as critical pedagogy for liberation that highlights the linkages between challenging power structures, new approaches to research, and diversifying educational spaces (Brown & Strega, 2005; Freire, 1996; hooks, 2014). However, there is less elaboration on how we might actually shift these institutional spaces, particularly in the academy itself. In the Freirian tradition of "making the road while walking it" (Horton et al. 1990, p. 3), the present chapter describes one academic community's ongoing efforts to utilize this vibrant and rigorous scholarship as a basis for our (four faculty members' and one community member's) intervention into the space of the university.

The Graduate Certificate in Participatory Research at the University of North Carolina at Chapel Hill is an interdisciplinary certificate program for graduate students, like Rachel, who desire training in the theoretical basis, rationale, methodologies, challenges, and motivations for carrying out research in equitable partnership with, instead of on, communities (Table 9.1).

From its inception, the Certificate was envisioned as an institutional mechanism for transforming the academy, toward a social justice-focused space. In this process we are committed to recognizing and transforming the systems of power that perpetually create majority perspectives, building pathways through and into the academy for marginalized students and faculty, and bringing the communities with which we work more fully into the research process at all stages.

At the core of our approach is an understanding that inclusive education systems are part of colonial projects that attempt to assimilate indigenous and other minority populations and agendas, thus facilitating the systems of power that operate through majority white institutions (Esson et al., 2017; Johnson, Joseph-Salisbury, & Kamunge, 2019; Lomawaima & McCarty, 2006).

Table 9.1 Certificate Participation by School, Discipline, Inclusivity, and Local/
Global Reach-2016

Feature	Certificate Participation
Student College or School Affiliation	73% College of Arts and Sciences 27% Schools of Public Health, Medicine, and Social Work
Student Disciplinary Affiliation ($N = 26$)	26% Anthropology 16% Communication 16% Geography 16% Music 11% American Studies 5% Anthropology/Archaeology 5% City and Regional Planning 5% Religious Studies
Student Inclusivity ($N = 26$)	50% Graduate students of color
Board Member Affiliation ($N = 11$)	6 Board members from College of Arts and Sciences 3 Board members from School of Public Health 1 Board member from School of Medicine 1 Community Expert as board member and Co-Director
Board Inclusivity ($N = 11$)	36% Board members of color
Local and Global Reach of Student Projects ($N = 26$)	38% of student projects are in North Carolina 19% are in other parts of the United States 38% are in other parts of the world

Including native peoples, in particular, in American education systems has worked as part of what Patrick Wolfe (2006) has termed settler colonialism's logic of elimination. This persistent set of colonial structures attempts to erase native presence through not just genocide but also intermarriage, forced language and cultural assimilation, stereotypes, land privatization, and, importantly, systems of education. Through this process of elimination, settlers are able to claim native land as empty of other political entities and thus rightfully their own. To shift university spaces today, we must move beyond inclusion within assimilative education spaces, toward growing the spaces within the academy that enable marginalized students, faculty, and communities to thrive.

Unlike the majority of research spaces, objectivity and contributing to existing academic knowledge production were not among our core commitments in designing the Certificate. Instead, we were, and remain, committed to asking the questions that matter most to the communities we wanted to work with/for, building the kinds of relationships needed to understand how to answer those questions, and to questioning how the knowledge we create might reinforce/shift systems of power. We understand the performance of objectivity as a tool for maintaining existing systems of power and hoped that a focus on participatory research could disrupt existing systems of power both in and outside the academy. In shifting our approach to and commitments around research, we hoped that we could transform the academy and its relationship to challenging systems of power.

Central to this project is a commitment to disrupting the ways in which knowledge has been and continues to be used as a form of colonization and other systems of power (L. T. Smith, 2012). This means articulating knowledge as it emanates from a wide variety of sources, rather than from what Anaheed Al-Hardan describes as gatekeeping theory used "to reinforce an intellectual class hierarchy in the academy, and with it, a colonial and Eurocentric 'ego-politics of knowledge'" (Al-Hardan, 2014, p. 64; see also L. T. Smith, 2012). This means recognizing the artificiality of theory's Eurocentric origins and the clear limits of its applicability. It also means exposing the limitations of normative models and privileging the wider applicability of differently situated theories. This represents a paradigmatic shift that has profound implications for research practices and the space of the academy.

As founders[2] of the Graduate Certificate in Participatory Research, our aim in this chapter is to outline the critical process that informed the development of the Certificate and, in doing so, demonstrate three critical practices that have been vital to our efforts toward building a social justice-focused space in the academy: (a) establishing different gatekeeping standards; (b) building more hospitable spaces for marginalized students; and (c) providing training for research traditions that engage participants as co-producers of knowledge. After detailing the development of the Certificate and the needs and challenges that prompted its initiatives and core course, we elaborate each of these critical practices through a set of lessons we have learned. This chapter concludes with calls for creating additional academic and community spaces that challenge existing power dynamics, enable marginalized people to thrive in the academy, disrupt binary thinking about "the community" and "the academy," and work to ensure the future of indigenous people (Tuck & Yang, 2012) as well as that of other marginalized peoples.

The Graduate Certificate in Participatory Research: Not the Usual Certificate

The Graduate Certificate in Participatory Research at the University of North Carolina at Chapel Hill emerged from the intellectual, ethical, and activist concerns of faculty, students, and community members who led its formation. The Certificate took shape in an era of high interest in "engaged scholarship" on the part of a Chancellor of the University and several other campus leaders. It built on a long history of pioneering work in participatory research in the School of Public Health (Holland, Powell, Eng, & Drew, 2010) and benefited from the faculty support program of the Carolina Center for Public Service, an organization founded at UNC-CH in 1999. In the early 2000s, the faculty and graduate students interested in using and developing participatory/collaborative methodologies were scattered across departments and units across the campus. They were not coalesced academically in a way that served graduate students or provided for the collective development of an in-depth, self-conscious praxis to guide pedagogy and research. In 2007, Holland from Anthropology and Geni Eng from Public Health developed an interdisciplinary faculty seminar that brought together 30 faculty and graduate students for a series of meetings to examine the intellectual traditions and ethical concerns motivating and guiding engaged scholarship at UNC.[3] Those seminars were important steps toward the Certificate program that would eventually coordinate courses from across campus. The Certificate draws primarily from the expertise of faculty and graduate students in the College of Arts and Sciences, but also from the professional schools such as Public Health and Social Work, as well as community experts. Eng, Holland, and Parker (from Communication) were all organizers or members of that seminar and part of the subsequent founding group of the Certificate.

The organic, multiple-year process of creating the Certificate replicates the participatory praxis we wanted to champion, reflecting one of several ways it differs from other certificates on UNC's and other campuses. Graduate certificates generally develop in response to an interdisciplinary need for specific conceptual, content, and/or methodological training across disciplines. They are usually aimed at including more people in existing spaces on campus. The Certificate in Participatory Research has been premised differently from the beginning. It was about creating a new space, one which from its conception was driven by diverse faculty and toward social justice aims. It was and continues to be a faculty/student/community-generated entity offering an academic credential in a paradigm of scholarship that pursues four distinctive central commitments: (a) interdisciplinarity and diversity; (b) community knowledge as necessary for, and constitutive of, productive research; (c) the valuing of research for the purpose of action, particularly to disrupt ongoing colonial forces; and (d) a conceptual and ethical framework for a social justice praxis. These underlying commitments require specific resources, training, and institutional shifts not necessary in other certificate programs. As discussed below, gaining approval for the Certificate, creating special initiatives to support student training, and developing a paradigm shifting core course reveal some of the challenges and possibilities of creating different spaces within an often-rigid institutional structure.

Co-Producing the Certificate Proposal

Commitments to participatory design, interdisciplinarity, and social justice guided the development of the Certificate proposal that was eventually approved by the University administration. Bringing together disciplines with different prototypes for participatory research and faculty/graduate students with different racial and ethnicity-related experiences called for mutually respectful and open dialogue. For two years, the organizing team conducted a series of interviews[4] and meetings with faculty and graduate students from several disciplines and units to discuss the motivation, foundation, and requirements of the Certificate, which informed the development and production of a written proposal for the University administration.

It was clear in these initial interviews that different faculty had concerns about the participatory research of faculty in different disciplines based on their methodologies, critical stance, and theories of social change. Voicing these concerns was necessary but could have resulted in polarization.[5] However, the 2007 faculty seminar had begun a process of building relationships and of listening and respecting the visions of different disciplines and how each in its own ways contributes to critical stances about participatory research. The collaborative approach was another means of building relationships. Listening and being respectful was and continues to be extremely important. This does not mean a lack of common principles. In the faculty seminar, for example, some participants espoused social entrepreneurial approaches. In the critical discussion that followed, the consensus was that the existing models of social entrepreneurism were not forms of productive social justice participatory research.

Community members were central to the Certificate development process, and communities were recognized in Certificate materials as necessary co-producers of knowledge. Most of the involved faculty and graduate students had long-term relationships with community groups and change efforts and indeed saw the Certificate as producing researchers that could work alongside these groups. Our colleagues in Public Health had pioneered the practice of engaging community leaders and members (referred to as "community experts") as co-equal participants on research teams and intervention projects. In the development of the Certificate, it was a community expert, Melvin Jackson, then Executive Director of Strengthening the Black Family, a not-for-profit organization in Raleigh, North Carolina, who became central to the process of institutionalizing a community voice in the Certificate. The relationships built between him and Holland allowed him to pointedly question her about a year into the process about how community input was to be accomplished in the Certificate.

Jackson became an integral part of the founding of the Certificate and the Community Co-Director of the Certificate's advisory board. Alongside Holland, who serves as founding director, Jackson has led the board in the considerable effort that the Certificate makes to develop community experts as important shapers of Certificate activities. An important part of the vision of the Certificate Program is to bring faculty and students from across campus together with community experts who know about the strengths and historically specific challenges and opportunities facing their communities. From this perspective, community mentors, faculty, and students together co-produce ways to bridge the gap between disciplinary knowledge and the lived knowledge, acquired wisdom, and "ways of doing" in their communities (Robertson, 2012).

The Certificate Initiatives

Student training in participatory research praxis is accomplished via three initiatives and two required courses, each designed to build relationships and intellectual spaces that bring students into the intentional learning community created on campus and beyond. The *Community Expert Initiative*, led by Jackson, facilitates Certificate students' engagement with community members, providing opportunities for community-led mentoring and relationship building. Community experts often are the first to acquaint students with the kind of "refusal" that is taking place with regard to university research (e.g., Simpson, 2007, 2014; Tuck & Yang, 2018). Certificate students learn that their challenge is not only to master disciplinary knowledge and research skills but also to learn how to connect the skills and knowledge they bring to the table with local knowledge and vice versa and to never take the participation of a community for granted. They learn, for example, to shape research questions in communication with a community and that an obligatory first step is identifying others in the community who are concerned about, if not already organized to address, the problems and/or opportunities that the graduate student seeks to engage. Similar to other knowledge-producers in the academy, community experts receive honoraria when their work involves sharing specialized knowledge, such as during class visits and campus workshops.

The *Seed Grant Initiative* supports students through participatory research relationships. As of 2016, the Certificate has awarded 16 seed grants for a variety of projects.[6] Seed grant winners work with input from fellow seed grant winners, from community experts, both locally and at their research location, and faculty. They make subsequent presentations to other Certificate students and faculty. The size of these seed grants is small, currently $1,200, but it is enough to help students get started and provides a context where it is easy to obtain mentoring from many sources.

The *Participatory Research Workshop Forums* is a student-led initiative inspired by the workshop portion of the core course (discussed later). Seed grant winners and indeed anyone on campus with a dilemma in participatory research can avail themselves of the workshop forums. During these forums students seek feedback on a specific issue they are struggling with in their project from a group of approximately eight faculty members and students, who offer them suggestions, support, and guidance. Student desires to continue the kind of interdisciplinary and critically supportive community created by the Certificate, speaks to the success of these initiatives and the importance of this work in establishing new spaces on campus that value and support different kinds of scholarship and thus different kinds of scholars.

Finally, two required courses help guide student training in participatory research praxis. The one credit-hour introductory course, *"Current Issues in Participatory Research,"* seeks to bring students into the community of participatory researchers on campus. The course incorporates field trips, guest speakers, and class discussion to acquaint students with UNC-CH faculty, community experts, and student colleagues engaged in participatory research. Students hear about the problems, dilemmas, and successes of ongoing projects, are exposed to a variety of methodologies, and get acquainted with each other and the range of participants in the community. The class also works in teams to collaboratively produce resources for the Certificate website (e.g., funding sources and exemplary articles). The students also get practice in creating a project idea and workshopping it with fellow students. The important messages of the course are that participatory research differs by discipline, that disciplinary differences are of value, and that each student needs to be active in creating their own identity as a participatory researcher.

The three credit-hour core course, *"Decolonizing Methodologies,"* serves as the central node of the Certificate.[7] At the time of this writing, the core course has been taught each spring since 2014. The course is designed to accommodate 20 students, with each instructor creating a disciplinary special topics course ("Decolonizing Methodologies") of ten enrolled students. Like the rest of the Certificate, the goal of the class has been to move beyond an inclusion-based model of graduate education, whereby students are literally disciplined into particular kinds of methodologies based on the history of the field that they are being trained in. Instead, the goal has been to grow the space on campus that is run collaboratively, that privileges the needs of a more diverse segment of students, and that prioritizes relationships to communities.

The Core Course

Once the university approved the Certificate, we began the work of building the core course. With support from UNC's Arts and Sciences Interdisciplinary Initiatives Team Teaching grant, and the contributions of PhD student Pavithra Vasudevan, Smith and Dennison hosted a workshop in fall 2013, which was intended as the first event in an iterative process to refine objectives and materials for the core course. Given the focus of the Certificate, it was important not only that the core course was co-taught and thus inherently interdisciplinary, but that it was itself developed through a participatory process. Over 40 graduate students and faculty members participated in the two-hour workshop, bringing their various disciplinary perspectives to a discussion of the central goals, readings, and assignments that would be required within the course.

Several key elements from the workshop and subsequent discussions guided the design of the core course and continue to ground its role in creating a social justice space on campus. First, participants in the course explore the differences between indigenous, postcolonial, and participatory approaches to fieldwork. For example, we examine Linda Smith's critiques of postcolonial approaches, which argue that for many indigenous peoples "post-colonialism is viewed as a convenient invention of Western intellectuals which re-inscribes their power to define the world" (1999, p. 14). While postcolonialism seeks to understand what colonialism has done in the world, social justice work seeks to acknowledge and disrupt ongoing colonial approaches to and understandings of knowledge. The goal is to work with ongoing processes that are enabling communities to, as Dennison writes, "pick up the pieces of the current moment and create their own original patterns for the future" (2013, p. 117).

Second, developing, reflecting upon, and teaching critical praxis is, along with the development of a social justice pedagogy, a central purpose of the core course. As the course is co-taught by pairs of faculty from different fields rotating for two-year stints, common ideas of praxis must be worked out. Gavin Smith argues that praxis is "the ability of people as collective subjects to become a force in history, not merely the objects of other people's history" (G. Smith, 2014, p. 23). Pulling from Gramsci (Crehan, 2002; Gramsci, 1992) we are particularly interested in the encouragement of students coming from indigenous, working-class, and other marginalized backgrounds who wish to engage in scholarship in support of their own or other communities' liberation, and approaches that provide communities with the analyses they request about the instruments and mechanisms of power (Nonini, in press). Through the core course, everyone involved engages in a dynamic debate about new work and ideas on praxis such as Leslie Robertson's idea of "social projects," Dennison and Holland's (in preparation) ideas of Emergent Anthropology, and Parker's work on concretizing Black feminist liberatory antiracist philosophies for collective organizing (Parker, 2016).

For us, creating a course that seeks to foster a social justice approach to research means going beyond the first stages of thinking critically about research, in which students may question the ethics of research and endeavor to be "good" researchers. In the casual parlance of class, we discuss the importance of distinguishing between careful methods and "not being a jerk" in the field as well as deeper and more challenging critiques that question the very foundations and categories of knowledge itself (Chakrabarty, 2008; L. T. Smith, 2012). Central to this project is asking what projects our research is serving and deeply interrogating what our commitments are. This includes asking ourselves questions such as "What does my research do to challenge existing power dynamics" or "how does my work repatriate indigenous land and life?"

Finally, in the face of these challenges, the course is designed to maintain a stubborn sense of hope in the possibility of a space for social justice in the academy. This presents a challenge given the nature of the critique, but through a novel classroom strategy—"inspiration presentations," we attempt to leave space for hope in the difficult work of social justice. Each week we ask students to start the class by presenting on a project that they find inspirational. These projects come from the work of artists, academics, community activists, and projects that blur these boundaries; in the spring of 2016, for instance, they included presentations on activist-artist Favianna Rodriguez, the youth-led organization Yole!Africa, the Abounaddara Syrian filmmakers, and one student's own struggle and engagement with Pascha Bueno Hansen's suggestion that she use her own research to heal her colonial wounds. Hope, a central thread of all social justice efforts, is at the center of the core course's teaching.

We now turn to three critical practices that frame the lessons we learned from both the successes and challenges in developing the Certificate, including its initiatives and the core course.

Transforming the University: Critical Practices

In creating the Graduate Certificate and its core course, we took seriously Linda Tuhiwai Smith's lessons from the process of decolonizing methodologies: "... it is not enough to hope or desire change. System change requires capability, leadership, support, time, courage, reflexivity, determination and compassion. It is hard work and the outcome often seems a distant vision" (2012, xii). Here, we elaborate on three critical practices that we believe can help concretize visions of creating a social justice space that will enable marginalized graduate students and faculty to thrive in the academy.

Critical Practice 1: Establishing Different Gatekeeping Standards

Academic gatekeeping sets limits around not only what kind of research is acceptable but also who is drawn to the academy in the first place. A relational and power/knowledge production process, academic gatekeeping determines what kinds of research counts, what research purposes are legitimate, whose research gets funded, and even who is treated as a (potentially) serious contributor to the academy in the first place. The archive that interested Rachel involved Vicki Gabriner, co-founder of the Atlanta Lesbian/Feminist Alliance (ALFA), and a close family friend. Rachel was raised by lesbian mothers and is queer herself, so her methodological experiments in how archives function in the transmission of gay and lesbian history took on a personal importance, as is often the case for students and faculty, especially those living through marginalized positionalities.

Against the grain of how research has historically been described, research interests for marginalized students often arise from deeply personal and political experiences. If told enough times that your approach to research is not "objective" or "rigorous" enough, you are likely to shift your project or seek out a space outside of academia where you can do this work. The academy frequently does not provide the institutional affirmation, guidance, and resources to support the kinds of research that Rachel was attempting. The excitement that Rachel felt about pursuing unconventional research might easily have been quelled by uneasiness and self-censorship if faculty and fellow students had responded to her from the normalizing practices of tradition. How many potentially transformational projects die on the vine as students are told their projects are too dangerous to their careers?

The Certificate in Participatory Research, however, was set up to privilege, not exclude, such clear commitments to and relationships with the communities we are working with. In shifting gatekeeping mechanisms to focus on the strength of one's ties, rather than the distance from the research, our goal was to ultimately transform what the university could be. In her first semester at UNC, as she was beginning to form the seeds for what eventually became a discipline-shaping collaborative archival research project, Rachel met Anthropology professor Jean Dennison, who encouraged Rachel to register in the core course she was co-teaching as part of the new Graduate Certificate in Participatory Research at UNC-CH. With mentoring and support from her advisor, Sharon Holland, a Professor in American Studies, Rachel signed up for the Certificate, joined its one-hour required course, and enrolled the following spring.

Too often, students and younger faculty seeking social justice approaches to research are bolstered only by chance encounters with sympathetic research mentors, or worse, discouraged by unwelcoming settings where influential faculty persuade them that their research goals are out of step with established academic pursuits. These same students and faculty are often, although certainly not always, coming from a place of vulnerability vis-à-vis the university due to their own subject positioning, by being non-white or non-normative in terms of their gender, class, or religion (Puwar, 2004; Gutiérrez y Muhs, Niemann, González, & Harris, 2012). If we as academics are really committed to diversifying who inhabits academia, we must establish different academic gatekeeping criteria that shift the standards of research. This is not about making it less rigorous, however, but about including clear research commitments and strong relationships as part of what makes good research.

The founders of the Certificate, while coming from a wide variety of disciplines, including Anthropology, Communication, Public Health, Religious Studies, Geography, and Nutrition, often felt the limitations of the current structure of academia personally and through our research relationships. We knew the challenges we faced in pursuing participatory social justice approaches at a major research university. In fulfilling the publication, teaching, and university service requirements for tenure and promotion, there was little time left for a hallmark of participatory research: long-term collaborative research with communities outside the academy. Respect for community knowledge and interest in the co-production of knowledge were novel concepts that were neither valued nor fostered in many parts of the university. The founders sought to not only create standards in the academy that would not carve out space for students wishing to do collaborative research but also enable a community of critical scholars to push this work further and deeper, a space in which the shared goal of challenging existing power dynamics from differently situated disciplines and perspectives was paramount.

Connecting with Existing Movements

Challenging the ways in which "engaged scholarship" was seen as less relevant or useful than "traditional research" meant strategically connecting to and influencing the wider conversations about the role of the University.

As with other universities, UNC-CH was inspired in the 1990s by national and statewide conversations about the purposes of public colleges and universities and the call to help improve community life and educate students for civic and social responsibility (Boyer, 1996).[8] Campus Compact, a national higher education association with state and regional chapters, emerged as an organizing channel for campus-based civic engagement at UNC-CH with a mission of nurturing students' citizenship skills and forging effective community/university partnerships. These developments and others encouraged initiatives at UNC-CH to expand the university's role to place a greater emphasis on engaging communities. All of this momentum facilitated the development of the Certificate. We were able to build upon the changes underway and push them toward our own goals of social justice and participatory research, in order to create space and legitimacy for the Certificate.

We have continued to stress these traditions and the intellectual ferment underway in participatory research through events such as panel discussions hosted by the Certificate (see videos on http://participatoryresearch.web. unc.edu) and publications (see Grimes & Parker, 2009). While engagement continues to be a debated term at UNC-CH, the core mission of the university to serve communities in the state is a key tool for explaining the importance of social justice participatory work. As we would learn, however, the legibility of participatory research as an intellectual endeavor did not guarantee the legibility of all parts of the Certificate nor was it guaranteed that it would be a high priority for institutional support.

Create Institutional Legibility for Participatory Research Praxis

A key lesson for shifting academic gatekeeping involves the necessity of creating a recognized space for social justice-focused participatory research training in the intellectual and ethical life of the university. We asked ourselves: What is the best institutional vehicle for training graduate students in social justice-focused research praxis? Should there be a stand-alone department, a center or institute, or perhaps occasional workshops? The tendency in universities to make "applied research," "service endeavors," and "engaged scholarship" a second-class knowledge endeavor is a distinctive problem for our vision and hopes for participatory research.

The vision for participatory research is one that prioritizes the synergy of disciplinary grounding coupled with a collaborative, social justice praxis. This led us to use the Certificate as a means to transform the university, but through standards that could be accessed from across the University. We see disciplinary grounding and interdisciplinary cross-fertilization as key to maintaining the dynamism of participatory research methods and theory. The Certificate seeks to build an intellectual and praxis community that learns and develops from each other. At UNC-CH we have multiple clusters of nationally recognized participatory researchers and community experts, from performance ethnography in Communication (e.g., Craft, 2015; Pollock, 2005, 2010) to action research (e.g., Price, Gittell, & Ferman, 2011) and collaborative archaeology in Anthropology (e.g., Agbe-Davis, 2011), to art making in post-conflict zones in Music (e.g., Ndaliko, 2016), to model community partnerships in Health Behavior (e.g., Schaal et al., 2016). Our goal is to increase the number of trained researchers and community experts who know how to bring the power of collaborative research to communities. A Certificate seemed the best vehicle possible for breaking down disciplinary silos, ensuring intellectual and ethical rigor for participatory endeavors, effectively concentrating university resources for graduate training of marginalized individuals, and integrating participatory concerns into the university as a whole.

Critical Practice 2: Building More Hospitable Spaces for Marginalized Students

The second practice we find critical in this work is a conscious effort to transform the space of the University so that underrepresented minority and other marginalized students feel not just safe but also valued. The core course has proven to be especially attractive to students of color, with over 50% of participants identifying in this way through the first three years of the course. In this first three-year period, there were also eight different departments represented by students and a mix of MA and PhD students. These different kinds of diversity have a number of important implications for how the course climate develops and the extent to which different perspectives open up, rather than close down, conversations inflected with race and power.

Challenging Systems of Power in the Classroom

First, identity difference brings immediacy to our need to challenge (call in) structures of power (white privilege, class privilege, patriarchy, heteronormativity, settler colonialism) circulating in the classroom and throughout the course. Instructors for this class are faced with the typical social justice paradox: the course can *only* work with the premise of a safe space, but it must also be a place where students can challenge the way power dynamics play out in and outside the classroom. Our lesson plans for the first day of class are instructive. As a closing activity for the last half of the class, we ask the students to circle up for a "think-pair-share" activity. Students write their response to three questions: (a) What scares you about doing decolonizing work in the academy? (b) What institutional constraints have you encountered? (c) What gives you hope? Then they share their responses in pairs and share some of their common or most compelling responses in the larger circle.

The ensuing conversation usually identifies some of the challenges of how structures of power circulate and whose knowledge counts. In 2016, among other concerns, students asked questions about how to find mentors who could advocate for social justice projects, how to acknowledge privilege, be critically reflexive, but still be productive. This includes how to avoid being either paralyzed by realizations of privilege or being overconfident in your status (as similarly identified or as an ally). The co-teachers use this opportunity to draw out particular challenges of engaging in a diverse classroom and working against the presumptions of white privilege, patriarchy, heteronormativity, and settler colonialism. Thus, a vital lesson is that professors must find strategies for "calling in" students without shutting down productive conversation. For example, students rarely come to class fully understanding how "objectivity" has long supported white privilege or how instincts to "save others" are steeped in deep colonial processes (see, e.g., Abu-Lughod, 2002). Depending on teacher strengths, student personalities, and classroom dynamics, this "calling in" will sometimes happen in the moment, and at other times in written feedback on class assignments/performance.

Disrupting the Pretense of Expertise

One of the most important components of creating a more hospitable classroom is directly challenging the ways research projects are talked about in the course. During the final third of the core class students workshop a specific problem they are facing in their research. This problem-based focus was designed because too often in academia we are taught to gloss over or veer away from methodological challenges we face, particularly in research proposals where we are trying to convince a committee we are ready to do research or are the best person to receive limited grant funds. We ask students to be as specific as possible with the problem and to provide the necessary background to allow their peers to help them think through their problem. A workshop problem can be anything from navigating a practical logistical problem to interrogating students' assumptions about incorporating their expertise with community knowledge.

Prior to class, students must identify and circulate to the class a relevant reading that will provide the class with some needed context in addition to writing a two-page single-spaced description of the problem that they want to work on. This assignment includes a very brief one-paragraph description of their research questions and methods, and the remainder of the paper is to be comprised of a preliminary and frank assessment of the problem they face. During class, students spend 5–10 minutes on a concise statement of the workshop problem, mostly devoted to answering any clarifying questions their peers have about the problem they are facing.

For ten minutes, their peers then work in pairs to reflect on and brainstorm around the workshop problem, filling out a worksheet that asks the following questions (among others): What question or challenge does the person identify? What do you see as the most engaging aspect of this person's project? Why? Can you think of a different way to phrase or frame that problem? What suggestions do you have for how they might approach this problem in a thoughtful and productive manner? During this same time, the co-instructors meet with the student to provide their own feedback on the problem.

The peer groups then take five minutes to report back about their conversation and the student collects all of the written feedback. The presenter is encouraged to be an active listener throughout this process but can ask clarifying questions as needed or at the end. Students often focus on one central problem for their research that speaks to a larger question; for instance: "How do I do political work in my hometown, across the racial border that I was socialized into?" "How do I work with people seeking healthcare, when the medical establishment has been a site of violence for them and for their families?" "How do I do work in an ethically responsible manner and follow my political commitments when that requires me to disagree with dissertation committee feedback?"

Allowing students to have a place to explore their own research in an environment where they don't have to have all the answers, the workshop process creates a space for healthy and deep critique. In our experience, this is a radical space, because it strips away some of the pretense of perfection that we are encouraged to have in other types of academic spaces and creates a collaborative space where everyone is working together to brainstorm around the presented problems. Instructors can also help create this space throughout the course by refusing the role as experts throughout the class, acting more as facilitators who are developing the social justice potential of everyone in the room, including themselves.

Critical Practice 3: Providing Training for Research Traditions that Engage Participants as Co-Producers of Knowledge

Our final critical practice is to provide training for and practice in research traditions that engage participants as co-producers of knowledge, rather than as sources of data. When Rachel began the *Decolonizing Methodolog*ies course, she had a broad array of topics she was interested in, including lesbian feminist studies and critical Holocaust studies. As is the nature of graduate school, her research project was taking shape through the conversations and experiences in her courses. As part of an Introduction to Oral History class during the same semester, Rachel had conducted a traditional life history style interview with Vicki Gabriner, co-founder of the ALFA, who was also her family friend and mentor. She successfully crafted an application for a seed grant from the Graduate Certificate in Participatory Research to fund her travel to do collaborative research with Vicki over the summer, traveling to the various archives where Vicki's materials were housed, including her home. The research emerged as a rich and nuanced account of an embodied engagement with the archive. Vicki served as the community expert as they traveled to each of the archive sites and co-authored papers about their interpretations, which they each presented at conferences. This research became the foundation for her dissertation titled *Queer Intergeneration: Visual, Aural, and Archival Forms of Remembering.*

Rachel's story demonstrates the potential in projects that transgress borders of insider/outsider in knowledge production, and the importance of privileging methodologies whereby students bring their own backgrounds and commitments to the research process. The focus on participatory methods in the core class and throughout her certificate process enabled her to practice the kinds of relational knowledge production that would form the core of her dissertation research. Students bring potential, forward momentum, and embodied knowledge to the center of knowledge production when they embark on dissertation research, and it is our responsibility to not only make space for them, and create a hospitable environment, but also to provide them with a wide range of tools and strategies to bring to their work.

Retrofit the University to Support Community Involvement

Creating respect for community knowledge in university research, in the training of Certificate students, and in leadership is a vital aspect of recruiting and supporting marginalized students. Feeling like the knowledge that grounds your work and the kinds of places you center have space in the academy can drastically alter a student's feelings about their own place in the University. This work of bringing community into the university, however, often pushes against many existing structures set up in the academy. Community members, aside from those who are donors, have had few recognized roles in the university. Indeed, the process of incorporating community presence has met with institutional friction, especially when it comes to compensating community experts for their time and expertise. Homeland Security requirements, for example, specify that community people working as independent contractors serving as researchers, as visiting classroom teachers, or as mentors to Certificate students must complete costly annual background checks. Thus, a core lesson is that university procedures and arrangements will often need retrofitting.

Translate Participatory Research across Disciplines

The core course serves as a space for disrupting institutional barriers to collaborative, participatory research practice through its inherent interdisciplinarity. Interdisciplinarity challenges students toward more critical reflexivity about their own disciplines and research projects. This kind of reflection begins to take root on the very first day of the core course, for example. As we sit in a circle and participants share their name, department/discipline, and research topics (including the co-instructors, who go last), the energy is palpable. Several students have commented that this is the most interdisciplinary-diverse classroom they have *ever* encountered and share their excitement for the opportunity to learn from/about other disciplines. On the other hand, there are some students who have yet to define their projects, or whose disciplines have little support for the kinds of social justice work they want to do. These students share their feelings of trepidation as they see students who are further along in the development of their projects and who seem to have institutional support for their work. There are also some latent critiques students have of how other disciplines have historically approached problems, so it is vital to help students recognize the assets and contributions different disciplines can make to shared problems.

For instance, what does it mean to bring social justice into musicology? How does a field that emphasizes scientific outcomes understand performance ethnography research products and their contribution to social justice efforts? Students speak from their individual departmental experiences and can share strategies that have worked to navigate the sometimes difficult terrain of gaining committee acceptance or departmental approval. Learning to speak across disciplines can be helpful in this regard, as can learning the ways that disciplines vary in working as part of social justice efforts.

Teaching students how to think through different approaches to social justice research has also forced us to move through *all* the spaces that comprise knowledge production: the kitchen table, at which a research interview might take place, but also the classroom, where graduate students and undergraduate students are trained, and, equally as crucial, the conference room in which tenure and hiring decisions are made and dissertations defended. Thus, a vital lesson for all involved in the social justice project is to understand what forms of destabilization and disruption need to occur within the institutional setting itself, before students even design their projects. If we had only focused on the "field" as the site at which research happens, we would have missed these crucial spaces, which contain epistemic violence and exclusion as well as generative conversation and dialogue.

Provide Multiple and Varied Research Tools for Co-Producing Knowledge

Midway through the core course, different traditions of knowledge co-production are interrogated for what they offer us as tools. Specifically, we look at different strategies around collaboration and activist engagement (Hale, 2001; Moses, 2001; Sangtin Writers Collective & Nagar, 2006), ethnographic methods archives (Chapman & Berggren, 2005; Pollack, 2003; Sheftel & Zembrzycki, 2010; Simpson, 2014), discourse, text, and context (DeVun & McClure, 2014; LeGreco & Tracy, 2009; Williams, 2010) and crucial arts-based inquiry (Cahill, 2006; Castleden & Garvin, 2008; Conrad, 2014; Dennison, 2015). With each of these articles we talk about what the limitations and potentials of these approaches for the described research are and what aspects of these approaches would be useful for our own research projects. Having as many tools available to us as possible seems to be one of the most vital aspects of social justice research, since the communities we are working with will often necessitate different approaches to the co-production of knowledge. Described above, the required "inspiration presentations" is another way the course provides class participants with a wide variety of methodologies for knowledge co-production. Opening up not just who we see as knowledge producers, but what kinds of forms knowledge production can take, these presentations are a vital part of the course.

Create Intentional Learning Communities

Students entering the certificate frequently express concern about meeting the standards of participatory research, especially as they are navigating their graduate programs. Not only must they have some confidence about how to design and conduct research, but they also must have confidence about building relationships and co-creating projects with people in a community. While they may have developed social justice-based stances toward those with whom they are doing research, they are often overcome by questions about how to put those stances into practice. Thus, an important lesson, built into the design of the Certificate, is to create intentional learning communities to support graduate students' development as participatory researchers. The Certificate's three current initiatives discussed earlier—the *Seed Grant Initiative*, the *Community Expert Initiative*, and the *Participatory Research Workshop Forums*—along with the required courses, all help students navigate these challenges.

The *Seed Grant* and *Community Expert Initiatives*, in particular, have been fundamental in helping students conceptualize and venture forth in many of the different parts of a participatory research project. Seed grants have been used for preliminary research to help develop research questions with the community they want to work with (rather than just in conversation with academics), to lay the groundwork for collaboration with community organizations, and to demonstrate the feasibility of unconventional projects, thus assisting the applicant in securing funding for participatory components of their MA thesis or dissertation research from relevant sources. Applicants often get help from Board members and from the Director and Co-Director in shaping their idea for a project. There is a definite effort to model respect for community expertise both by the consultative and mentoring roles played by the community experts, by their visits to courses that are part of the program, including the core course, and by the fact that seed grant winners are encouraged to identify a community expert in the community of their own project and can access extra funding for an honorarium for the community expert. These initiatives, however, require funding, which has itself been an institutional barrier to be overcome.

Translate Participatory Research to Potential Donors

Raising money for the Certificate has taught us several lessons and is still a matter of uncertainty. As in other instances, the question of funding acutely exposes the limits of the academy. The hurdles to funding the Certificate demonstrate in particular the narrow definitions of what the academy does and who is recognized as participants. The Certificate was given three-year start-up grants by two administrative offices at UNC-CH. These grants allowed the Certificate to develop initiatives to bring in community experts and to offer 4–6 seed grants per year. One of the internal sources explicitly channeled the funding to parts of the program other than the Community Expert Initiative, the stated reason being that compensating community people would be hard to justify given the office's research mandate. Three years later, our effort to raise money from two other administrative units for community experts met a more encouraging response from one unit while for the other and more crucial source, community engagement was nowhere on the priority list. Efforts to gain inclusion in the roster of projects presented to the donors of the university have also run into the problem of illegibility. Professional fundraisers we consulted told us that donors do not yet understand the idea of community-engaged research. We are still in the process of crafting a narrative about the importance of this research that will appeal to donors and become legible to the academy.

Discussion

Moving beyond inclusion toward transforming the academy into a space of social justice involves working with, overcoming, and confronting persistent institutional practices. It means reshaping or dismantling the structures of power that have made different modes of living and world-making impossible, rather than seeking to simply open the gates but expect new scholars to reshape themselves for survival. It further demands creating new pedagogies and educational spaces and changing relations between university researchers and those with whom they collaborate. It means insisting that knowledge production should be working toward community and group well-being. We have in this chapter concentrated on critical practices we undertook to meet institutional barriers and provide through the core course and initiatives such as the seed grants, an intentional learning community that supports graduate students seeking to do participatory social justice research. We explain three critical practices: (a) establishing different gatekeeping standards; (b) building more hospitable spaces for marginalized students; and (c) providing training for research traditions that engage participants as co-producers of knowledge.

The Certificate draws students from diverse disciplines and social, ethnic, and racial backgrounds by providing them to the community and tools both understand the logic and intent of participatory methodologies and further their own transformation to researchers who are part of the process of social justice knowledge production. In this work, we are recognizing how all knowledge comes out of particularly positioned perspectives and that peoples from spaces of oppression frequently have different and vital questions they want research to address. Attention is paid to these issues in the intentional learning community created by the Certificate activities. These activities provide a foundation for the researchers we train to deal with, among other things, the symbolic violence leveled against them by conventional researchers and proponents of existing gatekeeping mechanisms both in and outside the university.

Perhaps one of the most important lessons from our experiences with the Certificate and its core course is that creating a social justice space on campus requires the intentional creation of spaces that allow not only for dissent, disruption, and critique but also for hope, care, and vulnerability. These are the sorts of spaces that participatory research can help to create for the co-production of knowledge in community spaces as well. The surprise with which students have greeted this endeavor demonstrates the degree to which such spaces continue to be lacking (at least on our campus). In spring 2016, one student wrote on their evaluation form that,

> the space to work through research problems, be creative with solutions, and openly discuss matters that may be sensitive were perhaps my favorite elements of the course; please never let these go! All graduate students— at any level—need a course like this!

Though comments like these are gratifying in that they demonstrate the utility of the course and Certificate itself, they also suggest broader challenges faced by the academy. Surely being creative with solutions and being open to the discussion of difficult topics ought to be fundamental to any graduate program. Likewise, the way that the course draws students of color is a signal to us about the ways the academy needs to transform.

All of us still in the academy, whether in a tenured or more contingent position, must strive to see our current position in the academy as a starting point on a lifelong trajectory toward social justice. It is vital to work on what *is* possible, and to keep both a short-term and long-term vision in mind. Our hope is for the Certificate to be just a beginning. By continually keeping multiple horizons in view, our intention is that we are all doing what we can now, recognizing the constraints that we are under, and planning for a future in which we continue to hone our skills of openness, care, and critique, so that as we progress through our careers we can also be working for a more just and fundamentally different form of knowledge production than the one that is hegemonic today. Perhaps as a PhD student, we can work with a community-based organization and receive feedback on our research plans, and hope to divert some of the research energies toward furthering the goals of that organization. But as we move into tenure-track jobs or into non-academic career paths, we could consider more radical forms of intervention into the academy or organizations we work for through considerations of things like hiring practices, institutional racism, or theoretical challenges to Eurocentric knowledge. The important thing is to consider what is possible for us at each stage of our career and to have a set of driving principles and commitments that are kept in view as we navigate the academy.

In all of these projects it is also vital not to lose sight of the goal of breaking the settler colonial triad (Tuck & Yang, 2012). The fact is that historical and ongoing forms of black oppression, native land theft and colonization, and global hegemony continue to be woven into the questions scientists ask, the projects that are funded, the methods that are used, the findings that are deemed valid, and the scholars who are graduated, hired, promoted, and honored. It is only by creating new academic spaces whereby structures of power are interrogated, different voices are heard, and community engagement is privileged that we can alter this cycle. Without spaces of accountability and engagement, there is no hope of creating a social justice space on campus.

Notes

1 Thanks to Rachel for allowing us to tell her story and for reviewing the manuscript.
2 The authors, four of whom were members of the founding Board, participated in the participatory process through which a core group of some 15 faculty, 10 graduate students, and 2 community experts created the design of the Certificate and core course.
3 The six "models of engaged scholarship" salient on UNC's campus during that period are described in Holland et al. (2010).
4 The idea of a Certificate originated in a university/community partnership, a SPARC (Sustained Participatory Action Research Collaboration), formed between a group of researchers at UNC-CH and a non-profit in a rural county in North Carolina. Holland and leaders at the non-profit were thinking of creating an off-campus center in the county that would host long-term residential stays for graduate students who would learn participatory research on projects in the county. The leaders of the non-profit, Gabe Cumming and Carla Norwood, who are a story in their own right, having decided to return to Carla's home county and devote their university training in ecology to helping to economically revitalize the area, had developed an important participatory research process called Community Voice (Cumming & Norwood 2012, Cumming & Holland 2013). Cumming, along with Claire Novotony, one of the first archaeology grad students from UNC-CH to champion participatory methods, carried out the early interviews mentioned above in the text. From the interviews and meetings with graduate students about the residency program, the sad news came that the graduate students strongly doubted the feasibility of students with commitments to research in other locales relocating to the rural site for several months. That idea was dropped from the design of the Certificate.
5 Some polarization did happen among the graduate students who attended the first iteration of the one-hour required course, "Current Issues in Participatory Research." In subsequent versions of the course, polarization was avoided by explicitly discussing the varying engagements of different disciplines with making social change and why those in public health might need to persuade through "scientific" evidence.
6 Examples are featured on the Certificate's website, http://participatoryresearch. web.unc.edu.
7 The official requirements for the Certificate are ten hours of course credit that include the three-credit core course, a three-credit elective, a three-credit practicum, and the one credit for the community-building, gateway course to

the Certificate, "Current Issues in Participatory Research." While all four of these courses have their purposes, we focus on the core course as the exemplar of social justice praxis. For more information on the requirements, go to the Certificate website: http://participatoryresearch.web.unc.edu.

8 He also called for the transformation of the university to lower the walls between academic units and to overcome the insular behaviors between disciplines. Boyer's call was taken seriously at UNC-CH by some units, e.g., led by Ruel Tyson, the Academic Leadership Program at the Institute for the Arts and Humanities Faculty Fellowship, opened Holland's eyes in 2003 to different ways to conceptualize leadership in the university.

References

Abu-Lughod, L. (2002). Do Muslim women really need saving? Anthropological reflections on cultural relativism and its others. *American Anthropologist, 104*(3), 783–790.

Agbe-Davis, A. S. (2011). Inside, outside, upside-down: Approaches to "community" archaeology in Chicago. *Archaeologies: Journal of the World Archaeological Congress, 7*(3), 574–595.

Ahmed, S. (2010). *The promise of happiness.* Durham, NC: Duke University Press.

Ahmed, S. (2012). *On being included: Racism and diversity in institutional life.* Durham, NC: Duke University Press.

Al-Hardan, A. (2014). Decolonizing research on Palestinians: Towards critical epistemologies and research practices. *Qualitative Inquiry, 20*(1), 61–71.

Bishop, R. (1998). Freeing ourselves from neo-colonial domination in research: A Maori approach to creating knowledge. *International Journal of Qualitative Studies in Education, 11*(2), 199–219.

Boyer, E. (1996). The scholarship of engagement. *Journal of Public Service and Outreach, 1*(1), 11–20.

Brown, L. A., & Strega, S. (2005). *Research as resistance: Critical, indigenous and anti-oppressive approaches.* Toronto: Canadian Scholars' Press.

Cahill, C. (2006). "At risk"? The fed up honeys re-present the gentrification of the lower east side. *Women's Studies Quarterly, 34*(1/2), 334–363.

Castleden, H., & Garvin, T. (2008). Modifying photovoice for community-based participatory indigenous research. *Social Science & Medicine, 66*(6), 1393–1405.

Chakrabarty, D. (2008). *Provincializing Europe: Postcolonial thought and historical difference.* Princeton, NJ: Princeton University Press.

Chapman, R. R., & Berggren, J. R. (2005). Radical contextualization: Contributions to an anthropology of racial/ethnic health disparities. *Health, 9*(2), 145–167.

Conrad, D. (2014). Lock "em up…" but where's the key? Transformative drama with incarcerated youth. *Journal of Contemporary Issues in Education, 8*(2), 4–18.

Craft, A. (2015). *When the devil knocks: The Congo tradition and the politics of blackness in twentieth-century Panama.* Columbus, OH: The Ohio State University Press.

Crehan, K. A. (2002). *Gramsci, culture and anthropology.* Berkeley: University of California Press.

Cruz, M. R. (2008). What if I just cite Graciela? Working toward decolonizing knowledge through a critical ethnography. *Qualitative Inquiry, 14*(4), 651–658.

Cumming, G., & Norwood, C. (2012). The community voice method: Using participatory research and filmmaking to foster dialog about changing landscapes. *Landscape and Urban Planning*, 105, 434–44.

Cumming, G., & Holland, D. (2013). Growing Local/Buying Local: Challenging Pessimism and Social Division through Narratives of Possibility. *Progressive Planning*, No. 195 (Spring). 42–45.

Davies, C. B., Gadsby, M., Peterson, C. F., & Williams, H. (2003). *Decolonizing the academy: African diaspora studies*. Trenton, NJ: Africa World Press.

Dennison, J. (2013). Stitching osage governance into the future. *American Indian Culture and Research Journal*, *37*(2), 115–128.

Dennison, J. (2015). Situating graphic anthropology. *Visual Anthropology, 28*(1), 88–108.

Denzin, N. K., Lincoln, Y. S., & Smith, L. T. (2008). *Handbook of critical and indigenous methodologies*. Los Angeles, CA: Sage.

DeVun, L., & McClure, M. J. (2014). Archives behaving badly. *Radical History Review, 2014*(120), 121–130.

Esson, J., Noxolo, P., Baxter, R., Daley, P., & Byron, M. (2017). The 2017 RGS-IBG chair's theme: Decolonising geographical knowledges, or reproducing coloniality? *Area*, *49*(3), 384–388.

Fine, M. (1994). Dis-stance and other stances: Negotiations of power inside feminist research. In A. Gitlin (Ed.), *Power and method: Political activism and educational research* (pp. 13–35). London: Routledge.

Freire, P. (1996). *Pedagogy of the oppressed (revised)*. New York, NY: Continuum.

Gramsci, A. (1992). *Prison notebooks*. New York, NY: Columbia University Press.

Grimes, D. S., & Parker, P. S. (2009). Imagining organizational communication as a decolonizing project: In conversation with Broadfoot, Munshi, Mumby, and Stohl. *Management Communication Quarterly*, *22*(3), 502–511.

Gutiérrez y Muhs, G., Niemann, Y. F., González, C. G., & Harris, A. P. (2012). *Presumed incompetent: The intersections of race and class for women in academia*. Boulder: University Press of Colorado.

Hale, C. R. (2001). What is activist research. *Social Science Research Council*, *2*(1–2), 13–15.

Holland, D., Powell, D. E., Eng, E., & Drew, G. (2010). Models of engaged scholarship: An interdisciplinary discussion. *Collaborative Anthropologies*, *3*(1), 1–36.

hooks, B. (2014). *Teaching to transgress*. New York, NY: Routledge.

Horton, M., Bell, B., Gaventa, J., & Peters, J. M. 1990. *We make the road by walking: Conversations on education and social change*. Philadelphia, PA: Temple University Press.

Johnson, A., Joseph-Salisbury, R., & Kamunge, B. (2019). *The fire now: Anti-racist scholarship in times of explicit racial violence*. London: Zed.

LeGreco, M., & Tracy, S. J. (2009). Discourse tracing as qualitative practice. *Qualitative Inquiry*, *15*(9), 1516–1543.

Moses, R. (2001). *The algebra project*. Boston, MA: Beacon Press.

Ndaliko, C. R. (2016). *Necessary noise: Music, film, and charitable imperialism in the East of Congo*. Oxford, UK: Oxford University Press.

Nonini, D. (2018). Praxis. In H. Callan (Ed.), *The international encyclopedia of anthropology*. Hoboken, NJ: Wiley-Blackwell.

Parker, P. S. (2016, December 4). Black feminist praxis and social justice activism: Toward catalytic validity in research with communities. Paper presented at the Feminisms Here and Now Conference, Chapel Hill, NC.

Pollack, S. (2003). Focus-group methodology in research with incarcerated women: Race, power, and collective experience. *Affilia, 18*(4), 461–472.

Pollock, D. (2005). *Remembering: Oral history performance.* New York, NY: Palgrave Macmillan.

Pollock, D. (2010). Doorjambs and the promise of engaged scholarship. *Quarterly Journal of Speech, 96*(4), 462–468.

Price, C., Gittell, M., & Ferman, B. (2011). Community organizing, relationships, collaboration, and research: Lessons from the fund for community organizing initiative. In R. Gittell, & K. Newman (Eds.), *Activist scholar: Selected works of Marilyn Gittell* (pp. 235–261). Thousand Oaks, CA: SAGE Publications.

Puwar, N. (2004). *Space invaders: Race, gender and bodies out of place.* Oxford and New York, NY: Berg.

Robertson, L. A., & Kwagu"l Gixsam Clan (2012). *Standing up with Ga'axsta'las: Jane constance cook and the politics of memory, church, and custom.* Vancouver, CA: University of British Columbia Press.

Sangtin Writers Collective, & Nagar, R. (2006). *Playing with fire: Feminist thought and activism through seven lives in India.* Minneapolis: University of Minnesota Press.

Schaal, J., Lightfoot, A. F., Black, K. Z., Stein, K., Baker White, S., Cothern, C., … Eng, E. (2016). Community-guided focus group analysis on cancer disparities. *Progress in Community Health Partnerships: Research, Education, Action, 10*(1), 159–167.

Sheftel, A., & Zembrzycki, S. (2010). Only human: A reflection on the ethical and methodological challenges of working with "difficult" stories. *Oral History Review, 37*(2), 191–214.

Simpson, A. (2007, December). On ethnographic refusal: Indigeneity, "voice" and colonial citizenship. *Junctures: The Journal for Thematic Dialogue,* (9), 67–80.

Simpson, A. (2014). *Mohawk interruptus: Political life across the borders of settler states.* Durham, NC: Duke University Press.

Smith, G. (2014). *Intellectuals and (counter-) politics: Essays in historical realism* (Vol. 12). New York, NY: Berghahn Books.

Smith, L. T. (1999). Decolonizing methodologies. London: Zed Books, Ltd.

Smith, L. T. (2012). *Decolonizing methodologies: Research and indigenous peoples* (2nd ed.). New York, NY: Zed.

Tuck, E., & Yang, K. W. (2012). Decolonization is not a metaphor. *Decolonization: Indigeneity, Education & Society, 1*(1), 1–40.

Tuck, E., & Yang, K. W. (2018). R-words: Refusing research. In D. Paris, & M. T. Winn (Eds.), *Humaninzing research* (pp. 223–248). London: SAGE Publications.

Williams, J. R. (2010). Doing feminist-demography. *International Journal of Social Research Methodology, 13*, 197–210.

Wolfe, P. (2006). Settler colonialism and the elimination of the native. *Journal of Genocide Research, 8*(4), 387–409.

Ybarra, M. (2019). On becoming a LatinX geographies killjoy. *Society and Space:* January 23. https://societyandspace.org/2019/01/23/on-becoming-a-latinx-geographies-killjoy/

10 Organizing for Sustainability

Including and Engaging Diverse Stakeholders

Rahul Mitra

During the summer of 2014, I made my first trip to Alaska to begin collecting data for a research project on the management of natural resources, given the all-too-real impacts of climate change in the circumpolar regions of the world (Mitra, 2015, 2018b). My goal was to interview individuals affiliated with key organizations involved in these decisions and policies, with an eye toward their communicative practices. Along the way, I was fortunate to join a policy tour seeking feedback from local communities on federal laws and regulations, attended conferences on Arctic energy and natural resource management, and on polar law. These experiences were immeasurably useful in helping me—a non-Arctic resident of the United States (US)—understand the confluence of local and global, social and technical, expert and grassroots discourses that framed natural resource management in the Arctic. Most importantly, these experiences showcased some of the intrigues and intricacies of stakeholder inclusion and engagement when it comes to sustainable organizing.

Stakeholder inclusion and engagement are twin problematic—if promising—concepts in the organizational communication literature. At their most laudatory, stakeholder inclusion means bringing diverse actors to the table, listening to their voices, and implementing their inputs in organizational actions and policies (Mitchell, Van Buren, Greenwood, & Freeman, 2015), whereas engagement emphasizes a proactive and rich communicative process whereby organizations actively seek out stakeholder inputs and involve them in every stage of their operations (Waters, Burnett, Lamm, & Lucas, 2009). Nevertheless, examples abound wherein inclusion and engagement are inauthentic claims made by organizational conveners, so that although invited to the table stakeholders are never truly listened to, or perhaps are devalued at every turn, and engagement becomes akin to one-way messaging rather than interactive, dialogic, and substantial (Deetz, 2010). In my understanding of stakeholder inclusion, I thus prioritize the empowerment of stakeholders to articulate their own concerns, partnership relations that recognize stakeholder interests and voices, and listening to these voices at every stage from conceptualization to evaluation.

I began this chapter with my recollection of the Arctic project to highlight two complementary dictums of stakeholder inclusion in the context of sustainable organizing. First, being guided by principles of inclusion is not only the ethically superior course of action, it is also by far the most pragmatic option. Instances of sustainable organizing—such as natural resource management, environmental corporate social responsibility, enacting climate change mitigation (and adaptation), and curbing waste—depend crucially on stakeholder adoption, and without ensuring diverse and inclusive participation, the much-vaunted objective simply falls flat. This was the clear reasoning behind the five-site policy tour on which I accompanied federal and state policymakers over 2014–2015, who were tasked with shaping the US agenda as it took over the rotating chair of the multi-country Arctic Council (Young, 2005). Given the slew of strategy issues at stake (e.g., national security, new shipping routes) and the fragile ecosystem's unpredictable geography, policymakers recognized that involving multiple civic and institutional stakeholders would be vital to their agenda, lest derailment occur later, costing much time, money, and social capital.

Second, including (or not) diverse stakeholders can change the very meaning of sustainability in such situations. During a community feedback session in Nome, the discussion turned suddenly from a criticism of oil and gas multinational companies to fiercely attacking environmental activists. That shift took me by surprise, as I had assumed that such groups would be regarded favorably by local communities, but as I listened to the angry remarks it began to make sense: Although Big Oil was roundly criticized for encroaching on native lands and not adequately sharing their wealth with local tribes, environmental activists were often seen as agitating to prevent oil exploration which halted *all* compensation to the tribes, regardless of how paltry they may have seemed. Moreover, because the most prominent environmentalist groups were from outside Alaska (e.g., Greenpeace), they were seen as "outsiders" focused on merely protecting the environment while ignoring the age-old interdependence of tribal culture and nature. Thus, from the perspective of local communities, neither Big Oil nor environmentalists provided a truly viable vision of sustainable organizing in the Arctic. As one participant angrily remarked, to cheers from the assemblage, "Our homes are not a national park for people in Washington! Real people live and work here!" (See Image 10.1).

In the remainder of this chapter, I first address these tensional meanings of sustainable organizing. Then, recalling the different ways organizational communication scholarship has hitherto examined sustainability, I discuss some implications for including diverse stakeholders, as per each of these traditions. Specifically, I consider how these organizational communication traditions conceptualize stakeholder interests and enactment and outline questions to guide future scholarship on stakeholder inclusion for sustainable organizing.

Image 10.1 Conservation and commerce in Alaska, where "real people" live and work.

Defining (and Contesting) Sustainability

The most widely adopted institutional definition of sustainability comes from the United Nations (UN), through its 1987 report, *Our Common Future*. The report was also called the Brundtland Report, after its principal architect Norwegian Prime Minister Gro Harlem Brundtland, who chaired the World Commission on Environment and Development, which produced the document. The commission was tasked with synthesizing and codifying a series of intense discussions on how the environment and social development intersected among national and international policymakers. The report eventually defined "sustainable development" as development that meets the needs of the present without jeopardizing future generations' growth and prosperity (Brundtland, 1987). This definition was also influenced by earlier developments, such as the 1972 UN Conference on the Human Environment in Stockholm, the 1980 World Conservation Strategy, Pinochet's environmental conservation movement in the US, and Rachel Carson's book "Silent Spring" (Ganesh, 2007; Killingsworth & Palmer, 1992).

Although the Brundtland (1987) report was mainly concerned with the role of national governments and international aid agencies, both large corporations and small businesses were implicated because of their role in economic growth processes, environmental impacts, and employment conditions crucial to development. Thus, overarching organizations and standards like the World Business Council for Sustainable Development, the UN Global Compact, Global Reporting Initiative (GRI) and CEO Water Mandate, were formed to encourage business leaders to adopt sustainability principles. Peterson (1997) observes astutely that one of the reasons sustainable development appealed to such leaders was because it "offer[ed] a conceptualization of ecological integrity which includes humanity. Rather than attempting to displace anthropocentric perspectives with ecocentric perspectives (or vice versa), it suggests integrating human concerns into the larger biosphere" (p. 1). Nevertheless, given the range and number of potential stakeholders and their potentially competing interests, sustainability means many different things to different actors.

Symbols and Substance

The debate over sustainability goes much deeper than the relatively superficial "planet versus profits"—or its sibling, the "people versus planet versus profits"—dilemma. Rather, sustainability discourse is characterized by broader tensions related to stakeholder involvement (e.g., elites versus grassroots, community versus corporation), scope (e.g., global impacts of climate change versus localized environmental impacts), measures (e.g., quantification and implementation of sustainability measures), and accountability (e.g., democratic, mandatory, or voluntary enforcement), to mention but a few. Sustainability discourse is thus characterized by multiple, often-competing stakeholder voices and interests, giving rise to different sets of meaning that make sense according to stakeholders' diverse positionalities (Mitra & Buzzanell, 2018; Stevens, 2006). Indeed, despite these tensions—or perhaps, because of them—a veritable "profession" of management consultancies, communication firms, design houses, credit traders, architects, certification bodies, think tanks, higher education organizations, and nonprofit organizations has sprung up (Danaher, Biggs, & Mark, 2007; Signitzer & Prexl, 2008; Tams & Marshall, 2011). Peterson (1997) noted, "the discourse surrounding sustainable development is difficult to analyze, for it has become a metadiscourse in which the claims to provide insight can only be evaluated in terms of the discourse itself" (p. 29).

On the one hand, some critics argue that sustainability is merely the latest in a long line of management fashions, destined to be short-lived despite the hoopla, and often used as "greenwashing" (Munshi & Kurian, 2005; Plec & Pettenger, 2012), or inauthentic messaging to sway consumers and regulators, but resulting in few meaningful outcomes. On the other hand, "some fashions last longer than others … with some even becoming relatively permanent fixtures" (Zorn & Collins, 2007, p. 413). In some cases, mere public articulations of sustainability agendas can mobilize stakeholders and force organizations (and politicians) to action, regardless of their original intent. At stake, therefore, are tensions between symbolic and substantive sustainability (Schons & Steinmeier, 2016), and to what extent critics and stakeholders hold symbols to be significant in the material world. If symbols are key, then even greenwashing can create openings for real change; nevertheless, if substance eschews symbolic action (i.e., communication) and focuses on tangible materials alone, then signaling sustainability values by itself is unimpressive. For Schons and Steinmeier (2016), this tension requires a dialectical resolution—symbolic sustainability lacking tangible follow-through will not satisfy stakeholders for long, even as the most substantive results might as well be nonexistent if organizations do not engage stakeholders through symbolic action.

Mainstream and Radical Approaches

Possibly the most fundamental tension at stake concerns the relationship of sustainability with the dominant sociopolitical-economic system—Late Capitalism (i.e., the current era of rampant socioeconomic inequality, systemic injustice, ethical failures, and environmental crises like oil spills). The "mainstreaming" approach, often derided as "soft" sustainability, adopts a long-term view of sustainability's scope and (eventual) outcomes and seeks to include them *within* the mainstream or dominant capitalist system, rather than changing the system entirely (Dangelico & Pujari, 2010). By mainstreaming sustainability within existing business practices, or so the argument goes, corporations can realize long-term savings (or "eco-efficiency") and generate margins, not just on the traditional bottom line but on the more broadly conceptualized "triple bottom line" that comprises economic, social, and environmental markers (Elkington, 1998; Vogel, 2005). Proponents of mainstreaming thus highlight the multi-phase implementation of sustainability in day-to-day organizational operations (e.g., "green manufacturing" to minimize pollution and raw material waste), domestic and international regulations (e.g., implementing supply chain standards and values such as "fair trade"), market restrictions (e.g., carbon taxes for polluting companies), and multi-stakeholder initiatives and certification groups that hold organizations accountable (van Marrewijk & Werre, 2003).

Nevertheless, mainstreaming lacks teeth for acolytes of an alternative, radical or "hard" version of sustainability, which holds that such accountability measures are inherently unfair or weak because they are constrained by the dominant capitalist system (Prasad & Elmes, 2005). For instance, green manufacturing lacks strong regulation and is adopted by a disproportionately low number of companies worldwide, strict supply chain standards often result in the impoverishment of firms in developing countries who must accede to demands of powerful multinational companies, carbon taxes have not only failed to be rolled out but are also inadequate to contain the impact of greenhouse gases, and multi-stakeholder certification groups tend to operate as advisory bodies alone. Worryingly, for critics, mainstreaming approaches foster the notion of sustainability as always "in progress," without specifying a clear goal or end-point, and avoid fixing responsibility (Milne, Kearins, & Walton, 2006). Thus, the radical approach envisages the disruption of Late Capitalism's structures and processes and urges a deeply critical revisioning of its social institutions to prioritize social justice and environmental well-being (Kendall, 2008). This would include not merely stronger regulation of the market and greater accountability to impacted communities (not just fiduciary stakeholders), but a fundamental rethinking of civil society and its institutions.

Despite their differences, mainstreaming and radical approaches to sustainable organizing prioritize stakeholder diversity and inclusion. Both perspectives value coalition-building for action on environmental problems, trust-building with communities for long-term engagement, and listening to grassroots voices to accomplish long-term goals. However, mainstreaming proponents believe that existing liberal democratic forums and measures can equalize power disparities and foster stakeholder engagement, whereas radical sustainability rejects these same institutions as inadequate to the task and urges newer frameworks to privilege marginalized grassroots voices. For instance, radical sustainability proponents urge the use of eco-feminist and eco-material perspectives, which are attuned to how women and social minorities bear the brunt of environmental degradation (Merchant, 2005), and which increasingly center the environment itself as an active stakeholder (Driscoll & Starik, 2004), respectively.

Organizational Communication and Sustainability

Various sub-fields of the communication discipline have studied intersections among social collectives and the environment. Organizational communication scholars, in particular, have used multiple methods to examine how different organizations make environmental decisions and policies, mobilize partnerships and broader networks to accomplish these goals, and engage with customers and impacted communities (e.g., Allen, 2016; Bullis & Ie, 2007; Jaworska, 2018; Mitra & Buzzanell, 2018; Norton, Sias, & Brown, 2011; O'Connor & Gronewold, 2012).

Sustainability, as defined by Brundtland (1987), fits within the "organization-society relationship" problematic, which—along with problematics of voice, rationality, and the nature of the organization itself (Mumby & Stohl, 1996)—helps articulate the nature of the organizational communication sub-field. Thus, organizing for sustainable development "underscores the recognition that organizational boundaries are permeable and in flux and the dividing line between organizations and society can easily be drawn … [so that] society, culture, organizations, and communication are inextricably and reciprocally bound" (p. 65). This is evident when one considers the creation, maintenance, and dissolution of multi-stakeholder initiatives that organize around environmental management (Livesey, Hartman, Stafford, & Shearer, 2009; Mitra, 2018a), or the global supply chains that link disparate organizations with both competing and cooperative goals regarding the natural materials they use (Allen, Walker, & Brady, 2012; Ban, 2018). Moreover, even the organization problematic becomes pertinent with sustainable organizing, when we consider how it disrupts "the very notion of organization" (Mumby & Stohl, 1996, p. 62) and embodies the "shift from treating organizations as reified structures to a focus on communication practices and processes" (p. 64) with its centering of stakeholder inclusion.

Nevertheless, as I have observed elsewhere, "organizational communication research has rarely embraced the term 'sustainability' itself, even when
studying the management of scarce resources for organizing systems" (Mitra,
2017, p. 2337). None of the exemplars cited by Mumby and Stohl (1996) to
illustrate the field's problematics pertain to environmental issues. The same
is true for Broadfoot and Munshi's (2007) rejoinder, which called for more
diverse voices and alternative rationalities to theorize organizational communication. The only time the word "environment" appeared in Broadfoot and
Munshi's treatise was when they urged attention to social justice organizing
by indigenous communities, such as the Chiapas of Mexico. Although this
example could be probed further to highlight connections among indigenous
organizing, neoliberal interests, and environmental exploitation, these were
left unpacked.

The inclusion of "sustainability and sustainable development" as a chapter
in the recent *International Encyclopedia of Organizational Communication* (Scott &
Lewis, 2017) is thus a testament to how rapidly the topic has attracted attention in the field. This was influenced perhaps by the widespread impacts of
climate change, increasingly experienced in everyday life (e.g., floods, wild-
fires) and documented in detail by urgent policy texts, such as the US Government's Fourth National Climate Assessment (see https://www.globalchange.
gov/nca4). To better align organizational communication research with these
broader developments, Mitra and Buzzanell (2015) proposed a uniquely communicative definition of sustainability as "organizing practices—grounded in
communicative action—that go beyond the preservation of the status quo to
consider the contingencies and novel re-combinations possible, as social entities negotiate a complex-risk-laden world" (p. 133). They not only extended
the Brundtland (1987) definition with a more nuanced understanding of entangled social-environmental-institutional risks but also emphasized stakeholder inclusion to unpack these risks and design new frameworks for both
research and practice.

In the next section, I outline how organizational communication research
can better address stakeholder inclusion for sustainable organizing.

Stakeholder Inclusion for Sustainable Organizing/ Communicating

In a previous review of organizational communication scholarship discussing sustainability, I traced four main traditions that adopt different yet intersecting meanings (Mitra, 2017). These include sustainability as long-term
organizational viability given the existence of multiple operating tensions;
sustainability as environmental corporate social responsibility (CSR) practices; sustainability as corporations' broader environmental impacts; and
sustainability as resilience of complex adaptive systems. Here, I outline how
stakeholder inclusion may be conceptualized in each of these scholarship traditions, arranging them along two parameters of stakeholder inclusion, as

Figure 10.2 Stakeholder inclusion for sustainable organizing traditions.

shown in Figure 10.2. Along the vertical axis, I consider the *primary stake-holder interests being served*, ranging from the interests of the organization itself to broader, more collective social and ecological interests. The second parameter is the *locus of enactment*, traced on the horizontal axis, which might range from the organization itself to a broader dispersal of stakeholders. For each tradition (or quadrant), I propose research questions to help guide scholars studying stakeholder inclusion toward sustainable organizing.

Quadrant 1: Inclusion for Organizational Viability

The largest tradition of organizational communication scholarship that addresses sustainability tends to downplay environmental impacts, while focusing on the organization's continued viability as a for-profit corporation, nonprofit, or other form of collective entity. These researchers examine *how the organization can sustain itself* vis-à-vis multiple tensions stemming from stakeholders as diverse as shareholders, employers, top management, government regulators, supply chain partners, nonprofit partners, and consumers. At the macro level, viability might involve various organizational mission-related tensions for multi-stakeholder initiatives (e.g., Koschmann, 2013), while at the meso level, departmental or inter-group tensions might be evident (e.g., Mitra & Fyke, 2017), and at the micro level, viability of individual values with the organization's identity might be at stake (e.g., D'Enbeau & Buzzanell, 2011).

Seen through the lens of stakeholder interests and locus of enactment, research in this vein fits generally in the first quadrant (top, left of Figure 10.2). Typically, enactment is seen to be top-down and managerial, with the primary interests served being that of the organization overseeing the accomplishment of sustainability. During my fieldwork in Alaska referenced earlier in this chapter, for instance, several representatives of for-profit extraction-based companies were concerned about the viability of their organization and their industry (whether salmon fishing, mining, or oil-and-gas). They recognized the need for sustainability initiatives to preserve these natural resources for long-term harvesting, so that their business could continue, but also grappled with the likely revenue losses they would incur upon meaningful implementation of sustainability initiatives. At the same time, several environmentalist organizations and coalitions were also concerned with their own continued viability, not just more sustainable management of natural resources, in the face of government regulation and corporate pushback. The interpretation of sustainability as organizational viability thus tends to be the most insular and organization-centered, rather than considering external stakeholders and the environment. Rather than eschewing inclusion altogether, viability is more focused on its primary or internal stakeholders and core values, for longevity of the organization itself.

Thus, inclusion-oriented organizational communication scholars might address the following questions for organizations focusing on sustainability as viability:

First, *for whom does (and should) the organization sustain itself?* How diverse are the primary stakeholders that the organization is most concerned with? How inclusive are the organization's employment practices, with regard to hiring, socialization, promotion, and firing (for instance)? How does inclusion (or the lack thereof) shape the organization's viability in terms of work productivity, efficiency, revenues, and reputation? For shareholders, who are both internal and external stakeholders for publicly traded corporations, and who might be driven by competing agendas (e.g., impact investing), how do organizational members and decision-makers orient their practices to these relationships?

Second, *what core organizational values and practices are (and should be) sustained?* How diverse are the parameters of success whereby member inclusion is gauged? Are they somewhat open-ended, flexible, and suited to a global multicultural workplace, or do they remain overly insular, traditional, and narrow? Do the organizations' core values and identity resonate with newer members of the workforce and with 21st-century customers and investors, and how are these potential tensions managed? At stake is the relatively fluid notion of stakeholder interest—how might sustainability as organizational viability require the ongoing alignment of organizational missions with broader interests and values?

Third, *what new modes of organizing become apparent, as organizations pursue sustainability-as-viability?* With interconnected media technologies, supply chains, and markets, even the most insular organizations and management teams must recognize that traditional boundaries are no longer watertight (if they ever were). Interconnected social-ecological conditions affect stakeholders' behavior, commitment, organizational identification, and interactions with others. New organizing modes, like the "gig economy," recasts workers as both independent and subservient to managerial diktats, prompting protests, lawsuits, and government regulation that interrogates existing practices (Prassl, 2018). Under these circumstances, how are both "organization" and "inclusion" redefined and contested?

Quadrant 2: Inclusion for CSR

A second tradition sees sustainability as akin to environmental CSR practices (e.g., member volunteerism with the Sierra Club, philanthropy to environmental causes). Scholars examine how and to what degree organizations define their triple bottom line, how the business case for CSR is made, and to what extent "corporate social performance" aligns with traditional parameters of corporate success, such as profits, revenues, and brand value (e.g., Hoffman & Kristensen, 2017; O'Connor & Gronewold, 2012; Pal & Jenkins, 2014). As CSR, sustainable organizing is squarely within the mainstreaming approach, working from within extant socioeconomic structures, but also vulnerable to charges of greenwashing. Since CSR is often shelved by organizational leadership in favor of profit generation (Kallio, 2007) and thus depends largely on managerial discretion, sustainability might not be very substantive. Moreover, since CSR is largely voluntary (except in India), it is hard to hold organizations accountable for not meeting their sustainability goals under this framework.

In terms of stakeholder inclusion, sustainability as CSR is a mixed bag, occupying the top right quadrant of Figure 10.2. Depending on market structures, regulatory environments, and organizational missions, this notion of sustainability involves a small or large mix of stakeholders to make key implementation decisions. CSR is meant to display organizational commitment to particular causes and stakeholders and thus enshrines *its* interests above all others. Even when a company consults with nonprofits, certification groups, and local governments about its campaign to ethically source natural materials, these actions are essentially made to better its own self-interest—to ward off government regulations, consumer activism, and a potential fall in share prices due to negative publicity and bad sales. The CSR effort will also be swayed by its impact on the company's bottom line. In my Arctic project, for instance, this was evident not just with Big Oil but also the privately owned for-profit Alaskan native companies, which struggled to balance their bottom line with their broader identity as socially responsible companies representing local shareholders (Mitra, 2018b).

Thus, we might ask of organizational communication research in this CSR tradition:

First, *who gets to design the environmental CSR agenda, and how?* There is a need to interrogate the processes of inclusion underlying CSR claims of dispersed decision-making. Probing the power dynamics and relational networks shaping decision-making for sustainability is key, so that we can trace who is invited to participate and to what degree. The emergence of employee volunteerism as a key CSR practice ought to be further probed, especially in terms of how and whether this "voluntary" practice is positioned vis-à-vis employer directives, and how CSR branding might appropriate employee work as representative of the organization's own virtue (Cycyota, Ferrante, & Schroeder, 2016).

Second, *how are supply and demand chains impacted by sustainability as CSR?* Even as suppliers, vendors, subsidiaries, and distributors are key organizational stakeholders, they are also impacted by ethical codes, CSR practices, and changes to manufacturing procedures imposed from above, to be in compliance with global sustainability principles (Allen et al., 2012). Thus, how are these relationships and impacts negotiated on the ground, and how are inputs from demand and supply chain actors included in larger decision-making? Since these chain actors are linked to their own local stakeholders and ecosystems, so that there are broader "third generation" CSR impacts (Stohl, Stohl, & Popova, 2009) reverberating along the chain, scholars should examine these in more depth.

Third, *how do intersecting local and global policies shape the impact of sustainability on interconnected communities?* Crucial to excavate are stories from "the field," different locations both near and far from organizational sites, since contemporary organizations (and CSR) are widespread in their intended and unintended impacts (Luken & Stares, 2005). Researchers should examine how CSR policies, laws, regulations, and standards (where present) in different parts of the world unfold in practice and impact stakeholders. In some contexts, for instance, domestic policies might not specifically consider the plight of indigenous communities who might be marginalized as "nomadic" by their own state (Ban, 2018).

Quadrant 3: Inclusion for Environmental Impact

The communicative attempts of organizations seeking to address their broader environmental impacts constitute a third tradition focused on sustainable organizing. Rather than reduce environmental impact to CSR initiatives or a firm's strategic interests, the goal here is unpack how everyday organizational actions create environmental problems (Allen, 2016; Frandsen & Johansen, 2011; Hossain, Islam, Momin, Nahar, & Alam, 2018; Livesey et al., 2009). Moreover, there is the hope that by adopting broad changes to the "usual way" of organizing, such as sustainable manufacturing processes and/or technologies (e.g., carbon capture), reshaping supply chains, and pursuing new products and services, some of these negative impacts might be mitigated. This tradition hews most closely to Brundtland's (1987) vision, wherein corporations voluntarily change their extant practices and support broader policy transformations to address climate change. There is often, however, a gap between sustainability rhetoric and reality due to inauthentic greenwashing, interorganizational conflicts, exaggeration of claims, or downplaying the severity and unpredictability of environmental change (Ihlen, 2009; Jaworska, 2018).

Stakeholder inclusion for sustainability as broader environmental impact tends to fall in the bottom left quadrant of Figure 10.2. Compared to the prior two traditions' emphasis on organizational interests, this strand acknowledges the social-ecological interests that must guide sustainable organizing. Both global initiatives (e.g., UN Global Compact, CEO Water Mandate) and local programs (e.g., pollution clean-up, community development) are guided by the realization that organizations are embedded in complex webs of social and environmental relations. Nevertheless, most of these efforts are driven top-down by corporate actors (or government and nonprofit elites aligned with corporate interests), who rarely cede decision-making agency to grass-roots stakeholders. For instance, while the US Arctic Council policy tour that I attended hosted public forums in five locations across Alaska, and was expressly geared to include discussion on different social and environmental issues affecting these communities, the speaker list was carefully compiled in consultation with elite nonprofit and corporate actors—many of whom have offices in Anchorage rather than the other four (much smaller) locations. Forum attendees were carefully vetted, and both the messaging and distribution of results from the forums were tightly controlled.

The environmental impact tradition prompts the following questions related to inclusion:

First, *what tensions arise (and how) when social-ecological interests are avowed although decision-making is not participatory?* Even as corporate actors collaborate with multiple stakeholders from the nonprofit, government, and civic sectors, it would be instructive to trace the processes and structures of decision-making and implementation to examine whose interests are truly being served. How are stakeholder actions, values, and agendas appropriated when the locus of enactment remains dominated by corporate actors; conversely, might less powerful stakeholders subvert dominant structures to accomplish their own values? Who receives key information across the collaboration network, how, and what might they accomplish (or not) with such information? How do stakeholders mobilize across time and space to ensure their interests are addressed, even when facilitated by elite actors?

Second, *how is environmental justice framed, marginalized, and/or naturalized?* Thus, how do widely adopted definitions of "impact" recognize unequal access to and availability of natural resources, or privileged access to forums designed to address these very inequities (e.g., commodity roundtables organized by global organizations)? Even as environmental justice rhetoric is increasingly adopted in elite lexicons, how does this rhetoric align with the concerns and lived experiences of grassroots communities? It thus becomes valuable to both deconstruct and re-construct meanings of environmental justice, allowing for multiple plurivocal discourses that might not readily fit traditionally preferred or elite timelines.

Third, *how is nature an active stakeholder when considering environmental impact?* Useful counters to traditional corporation-centered models of sustainable organizing might include eco-materialist and eco-feminist frameworks that recognize various nonhuman stakeholders capable of action, in conjunction with human actors or on their own, to shape environmental impact (e.g., Driscoll & Starik, 2004; Mitra, 2016). Engaging deeply with grassroots communities might reveal more nuanced frames on the role of such "natural stakeholders," reframing them from passive *tabula rasa* to co-actors of environmental action (Rich, 2016). Concerted efforts to protect endangered species might incorporate indigenous knowledge about their lifespan and behaviors, enabling more sustained conservation (Liles et al., 2015). Moreover, interrogating the power dynamics around natural stakeholders, how might gendering such stakeholders in public discourse as "feminine" (e.g., Mother Earth) or "masculine" (e.g., wild forest fires) shape efforts to mitigate environmental impact?

Quadrant 4: Inclusion for Systemic Resilience

Viewing sustainability as systemic resilience is perhaps the most radical tradition considered thus far. Whereas the environmental impact tradition might sometimes adopt a systemic view and suggest changes to extant social practices, it largely refrains from rethinking the underlying socioeconomic system in place and advocates mainstreaming sustainability. In contrast, this fourth tradition of systemic resilience prioritizes new forms of thinking, designing, communicating, and organizing that disrupt deeply entrenched norms, holding them responsible for perpetuating climate change and other (interconnected) environmental risks (Nyberg, Wright, & Kirk, 2018; Tregidga, Kearins, & Milne, 2013). Systemic resilience must span across macro, meso, and micro levels of social action, with attention paid to how local sites and interactions can network with broader global discourses and coalitions (Kalonaityte, 2018; Mitra, 2018a). Explicitly future-oriented and rooted in grassroots, the goal of resilience is to enable dispersed stakeholders to enact their own best practices that might then connect across time and space, creating multiple layers of vigilance and adaptability to withstand social-ecological shocks (Carlson, 2018; Kurian et al., 2014).

Systemic resilience requires both dispersed stakeholder enactment and attention to diverse social-ecological interests, as shown in Figure 10.2 (bottom, right quadrant). This tradition examines how collaborations in various contexts engage stakeholders, the politics of coalition-building for sustainable development, and the structures whereby such coalitions produce more institutionalized initiatives for long-term viability. Stakeholder inclusion in this tradition disrupts the liberal humanist separation of nature and culture and urges new articulations of subjectivity, rationality, and voice that do not seek to contain conflict but embrace the contestation of key concepts. In my Alaska research, despite significant material challenges, some actors were able to enact sustainable management of natural resources when they reframed key practices of decision-making, building trust with grassroots communities, and managing risk (Mitra, 2018b). For instance, several federal agencies decided (informally) to be less restrictive while enforcing land use jurisdiction policies for interconnected tracts, which enabled more efficient use of their scarce resources. This shift would have been impossible if the coalition partners had not recognized recurrent "creative tensions" (p. 421), and chosen to adapt to them accordingly.

Questions for scholarship extending this tradition include:

First, *how can diverse stakeholders be engaged for socio-environmental resilience across the system?* Rather than see stakeholder connections as entirely altruistic, symbiotic, or otherwise beneficial, further research is warranted on the nature of these complex relations—specifically, how they are formed, their sociomaterial bases and their broader implications keeping in mind the power dynamics at stake. How are these relationships negotiated, what factors shape sustainable organizing priorities with respect to grassroots and marginalized voices, and what sociopolitical values become foregrounded as a result? Finally, how do these relationships evolve over time, in different local and global spaces, to enact adaptability and resilience?

Second, *how do stakeholders assess socio-environmental resilience and risk across the system?* Recognizing the competing interests and values at stake, it becomes important to trace the logic(s) and coalitions that enable systemic action. How are these interests and values formed, deliberated, and contested by stakeholders over time? How do they inform decision-making and enactment of system-wide organizing for sustainable development, especially in the face of impending risks? For instance, with rising sea levels in high-end coastal cities like Miami, how do real estate developers, community organizations, policymakers, and activists engage in assessments of risk and resilience? Which set of ethics—long versus short term, property values versus human safety—wins out in the court of public opinion, and how are they framed to win over proponents (e.g., painting concerned actors as alarmist fear-mongers)? Who can access vital resources to survive impending risks, and what discursive and material boundaries privilege certain actors over others (e.g., urban cores versus wealthy suburbs)?

Third, *how can we critique new modes of sustainable organizing to ensure they remain inclusive and radical?* Despite their focus on reimagining extant social, political, and economic structures to better address rapid environmental risks (e.g., Kalonaityte, 2018), scholars and activists should remain vigilant that these structures do not reproduce the inequalities and excesses of Late Capitalism or set into motion new modes of oppression. It becomes crucial to continually evaluate the merits and demerits of new ideas, technologies, and skill sets, while pushing policymakers, organizations, and civic groups to ensure these systemic solutions empower hitherto marginalized stakeholders—both human and natural. Such vigilance is crucial to ensure both stakeholder inclusion and the transformative potential of radical measures designed for systemic resilience (Carlson, 2018).

Necessary and/or Sufficient?

I began this chapter with a brief foray into my research project examining sustainable organizing in the US Arctic, specifically in the context of natural resource management by a variety of for-profit, nonprofit, and government agencies (Mitra, 2015, 2018b). Although I described how stakeholder inclusion was centered in that project—and through the preceding sections of this chapter, I have tried to show how it becomes evident for sustainable organizing more generally—it may be useful to consider whether stakeholder inclusion is indeed absolutely necessary, or even sufficient, for sustainable organizing.

Consider a couple of examples from that Arctic project:

- Example 1: Prominent environmentalist nonprofit organizations often found themselves at odds not just with representatives of powerful extraction-based industries in the state, which provided a disproportionate number of jobs (e.g., Big Oil, salmon fisheries, mining), but also most ordinary citizens, most of whom were closely connected to their local environments and engaged in hunting or fishing. Most of these environmentalist nonprofits were easily portrayed as "outsiders" from Washington, DC, rather than local actors, who had little in common with the Alaskan people. This was exacerbated by political polarization, so that in generally Republican party-leaning Alaska, the outsider environmentalists were perceived as both colonists from DC and aligned with President Obama's Democratic Party. Moreover, the environmentalists' own discourse prioritized conservation of pristine Arctic land- and water-scapes, protecting polar bears and other at-risk living creatures, and eradicating fossil fuel drilling altogether. Most residents interpreted these acts as erasing their social history in the state, ignoring the dependence of native cultures on hunting (viz., both subsistence and recreational), and destroying their livelihood without offering a viable alternative, respectively.
- Example 2: In contrast to this general air of suspicion accorded to most environmentalist organizations, the Pebble Mine initiative has consistently faced an antagonistic coalition of Alaska native communities, urban residents, environmentalists, for-profit allies, and state and federal agencies, for decades (Greenberg, 2018). The Bristol Bay region, where the large mining operation was proposed, is the site of one of the world's largest and most valuable salmon runs. The mines thus pit powerful interests against each other. Rather than being a traditional (and overly simplistic) economic versus environmental debate, Pebble's opponents successfully framed the issue as vital to the social, environmental, and economic fabric of the region and garnered supporters from across the political and geographical spectrum.

Stakeholder inclusion is crucial to sustainable organizing in both examples. In Example 1, despite the best (?) of intentions, most environmentalist nonprofits failed to attract a broad coalition of supporters, because they could not resist the stereotype of "DC tree-huggers." In some cases, these DC nonprofits were justifiably critiqued for ethnocentric presumptions that ignored indigenous customs such as subsistence. However, in Example 2, engaging a broad coalition proved strategic both for garnering widespread popular support and because it enabled Pebble's opponents to work with Republican *and* Democratic politicians over the years.

Stakeholder inclusion thus certainly seems *necessary*, on two major counts. First, meaningful inclusion is pragmatic, because inauthentic or incompetent attempts at engaging stakeholders will end up creating far more obstacles to the goal of sustainable organizing (Example 1). Omission of efforts to include diverse stakeholders is simply not an option, especially with far greater interconnections among local and global activists, politicians, media, and corporations. Second, stakeholder inclusion is necessary because it uncovers alternative meanings and discourses of sustainability, the environment, and social-ecological relationships that might ensure both more efficient and socially just mechanisms of sustainable organizing. Rather than restrict organizations and stakeholders in binaries (e.g., economic *versus* environmental), inclusion allows the overlapping of boundaries and generation of new paths forward, while still maintaining tensions across meanings (e.g., environmental *is/not* economic), as with Example 2. Even if stakeholder inclusion uncovers oppositional meanings and power injustices, it provides members an opportunity to address these disparities early on, rather than attempt to ignore such injustices in the vain hope they will be immaterial.

But, while stakeholder inclusion may be necessary for sustainable organizing, its *sufficiency* might be debated. Sufficiency would mean that the very act of stakeholder inclusion would stimulate enactment of system-wide collaboration toward sustainability and address deep-seated power disparities and social injustices. Instances of greenwashing demonstrate, however, that collaboration can sometimes lead to endless deliberation, privileging symbolic over substantive sustainability (Schons & Steinmeier, 2016). This would accomplish neither radical nor mainstreaming modes of sustainability—it would be quite hollow, in fact. Two recent texts show us the limitations of stakeholder inclusion that remains willfully blind to the realities of power relations—the US Fourth National Climate Assessment I cited earlier, and the Green New Deal introduced by Progressive Democrats in Congress (Kurtzleben, 2019). Whereas the Climate Assessment might be considered a "mainstreaming" (Dangelico & Pujari, 2010) approach drawing on existing socioeconomic institutions, the Green New Deal goes a "radical" (Merchant, 2005) step further and urges rewriting the social contract of these institutions altogether to privilege social and environmental justice. Although both texts call for urgent action involving multiple stakeholders across government, industry, and civil society, they recognize that long drawn-out modes of inclusion and engagement will simply not suffice and have been abused for decades by powerful interests who want to maintain the fossil fuel status quo. The architects of both the Climate Assessment and the Green New Deal seem to aver that stakeholder inclusion is rarely sufficient for sustainable organizing on its own.

Conclusion

Sustainable organizing blends various foundational themes of organizational communication—not just the sub-field's organization-society problematic but also problematics of voice, rationality, and nature of organizing/organization—which center stakeholder inclusion. In this chapter, I trace how key traditions of sustainable organizing within organizational communication fare in terms of their attention to stakeholder interest and locus of enactment (Figure 10.2). For each tradition, I suggest questions to interrogate these practices further, so as to both avoid complacency and continually critique extant norms and modes of organizing. These two parameters—stakeholder interests and locus of enactment—are certainly not the only consequential standards of sustainable organizing, and future research might well extend this framework by identifying others that also matter (if not more, in some contexts). Nevertheless, they address both the structures and processes of stakeholder inclusion, and the dialectical interplay between them that both impedes and enables sustainable organizing.

References

Allen, M. (2016). *Strategic communication for sustainable organizations*. New York, NY: Springer.

Allen, M. W., Walker, K. L., & Brady, R. (2012). Sustainability discourse within a supply chain relationship: Mapping convergence and divergence. *International Journal of Business Communication, 49*, 210–236.

Ban, Z. (2018). Mobilities, communication, and Asia: Tracing the discourse of migrant labor in China: Mobility, fixity, and displacement in the workshop of the world. *International Journal of Communication, 12*, 3979–3996.

Broadfoot, K., & Munshi, D. (2007). Diverse voices and alternative rationalities: Imagining forms of postcolonial organizational communication. *Management Communication Quarterly, 21*, 249, 267.

Brundtland, H. (1987). *Our common future*. Oxford, UK: Oxford University Press for the World Commission on Environment and Development.

Bullis, C., & Ie, F. (2007). Corporate environmentalism. In S. May, G. Cheney, & J. Roper (Eds.), *The debate over corporate social responsibility* (pp. 321–335). New York, NY: Oxford University Press.

Carlson, E. (2018). Vigilant resilience: The possibilities for renewal through preparedness. *Corporate Communications, 23*, 212–225.

Cycyota, C., Ferrante, C. J., & Schroeder, J. M. (2016). Corporate social responsibility and employee volunteerism: What do the best companies do? *Business Horizons, 59*, 321–329.

Danaher, K., Biggs, S., & Mark, J. (2007). *Building the green economy: Success stories from the grass roots*. Sausalito, CA: PoliPointPress.

Dangelico, M., & Pujari, D. (2010). Mainstreaming green product innovation: Why and how companies integrate environmental sustainability. *Journal of Business Ethics, 95*, 471–486.

Deetz, S. (2010). Politically attentive relational constructionism (PARC): Making a difference in a pluralistic, interdependent world. In D. Carbaugh, & P. M. Buzzanell (Eds.), *Distinctive qualities in Communication research* (pp. 32–52). New York, NY: Routledge.

D'Enbeau, S., & Buzzanell, P. M. (2011). Selling (out) feminism: Sustainability of ideology viability tensions in a competitive marketplace. *Communication Monographs, 78*, 27–52.

Driscoll, C., & Starik, M. (2004). The primordial stakeholder: Advancing the conceptual consideration of stakeholder status for the natural environment. *Journal of Business Ethics, 49*, 55–73.

Elkington, J. (1998). *Cannibals with forks: The triple bottom line of 21st century business.* Gabriola Island: New Society.

Frandsen, F., & Johansen, W. (2011). Rhetoric, climate change, and corporate identity management. *Management Communication Quarterly, 25*, 511–530.

Ganesh, S. (2007). Sustainable development discourse and the global economy: Promoting responsibility, containing change. In S. May, G. Cheney, & J. Roper (Eds.), *The debate over corporate social responsibility* (pp. 379–390). New York, NY: Oxford University Press.

Greenberg, P. (2018, June 28). The future of Alaska's Pebble Mine—and it's salmon. *High Country News.* Retrieved from https://www.hcn.org/articles/climate-desk-the-future-of-alaska-pebble-mine-and-its-wild-sockeye-salmon

Hoffman, J., & Kristensen, M. E. (2017). Sustainable oil and profitable wind: The communication of corporate responsibilities as inverted positioning. *Nordicom Review, 38*(2), 79–96.

Hossain, M., Islam, M. T., Momin, M. A., Nahar, S., & Alam, M. S. (2018). Understanding communication of sustainability reporting: Application of symbolic convergence theory (SCT). *Journal of Business Ethics.* Advance online publication. doi:10.1007/s10551-018-3874-6

Ihlen, Ø. (2009). Business and climate change: The climate response of the world's 30 largest corporations. *Environmental Communication, 3*, 244–262.

Jaworska, S. (2018). Change but no climate change: Discourses of climate change in corporate social responsibility reporting in the oil industry. *International Journal of Business Communication, 55*, 194–219.

Kallio, T. J. (2007). Taboos in corporate social responsibility discourse. *Journal of Business Ethics, 74*, 165–175.

Kalonaityte, V. (2018). When rivers go to court: The Anthropocene in organization studies through the lens of Jacques Ranciere. *Organization, 25*, 517–532.

Kendall, B. E. (2008). Personae and natural capitalism: Negotiating politics and constituencies in a rhetoric of sustainability. *Environmental Communication, 2*, 59–77.

Killingsworth, M. J., & Palmer, J. S. (1992). *Ecospeak: Rhetoric and environmental politics in America.* Carbondale: Southern Illinois University Press.

Koschmann, M. A. (2013). The communicative constitution of collective identity in interorganizational collaboration. *Management Communication Quarterly, 27*, 61–89.

Kurian, P. A., Munshi, D., & Bartlett, R. V. (2014). Sustainable citizenship for a technological world: negotiating deliberative dialectics. *Citizenship Studies, 18*(3–4), 435–451. doi:10.1080/13621025.2014.905284

Kurtzleben, D. (2019, February 7). Rep. Alexandria Ocasio-Cortez releases Green New Deal outline. *NPR.* Retrieved from https://www.npr.org/2019/02/07/691997301/rep-alexandria-ocasio-cortez-releases-green-new-deal-outline

Liles, M. J., Peterson, M. J., Lincoln, Y. S., Sminoff, J. A., Gaos, A. R., & Peterson, T. R. (2015). Connecting international priorities with human well-being in low income regions: Lessons from hawksbill turtle conservation in El Salvador. *Local Environment, 20*, 1383–1404.

Livesey, S. M., Hartman, C. L., Stafford, E. R., & Shearer, M. (2009). Performing sustainable development through eco-collaboration. *The International Journal of Business Communication, 46*, 423–454.

Luken, R., & Stares, R. (2005). Small business responsibility in developing countries: A threat or an opportunity? *Business Strategy and the Environment, 14*, 38–53.

Merchant, C. (2005). *Radical ecology: The search for a livable world* (2nd ed.). New York, NY: Routledge.

Milne, M. J., Kearins, K., & Walton, S. (2006). Creating adventures in Wonderland: The journey metaphor and environmental sustainability. *Organization, 13*, 801–839.

Mitchell, R. K., Van Buren, H. J., Greenwood, M., & Freeman, R. E. (2015). Stakeholder inclusion and accounting for stakeholders. *Journal of Management Studies, 52*, 851–877.

Mitra, R. (2015). Proposing a culture-centered approach to career scholarship: The example of subsistence careers in the US Arctic. *Human Relations, 68*, 1813–1835.

Mitra, R. (2016). Re-constituting "America": The clean energy economy ventriloquized. *Environmental Communication, 10*, 269–288.

Mitra, R. (2017). Sustainability and sustainable development. In C. R. Scott., & L. K. Lewis (Eds.), *International encyclopedia of organizational communication, Vol. 4* (pp. 2337–2346). Malden, MA: Wiley-Blackwell.

Mitra, R. (2018a). Communicative management of tensions by multi-stakeholder initiatives (MSIs) for water resilience. *Corporate Communications: An International Journal, 23*, 257–273.

Mitra, R. (2018b). Natural resource management in the U.S. Arctic: Sustainable organizing through communicative practices. *Management Communication Quarterly, 32*, 398–430.

Mitra, R., & Buzzanell, P. M. (2015). Introduction: Organizing/communicating sustainably. *Management Communication Quarterly, 29*, 130–134.

Mitra, R., & Buzzanell, P. M. (2018). Implementing sustainability in organizations: How practitioners discursively position work. *Management Communication Quarterly, 32*, 172–201.

Mitra, R., & Fyke, J. (2017). Purpose-driven consultancies' negotiation of organizational tensions. *Journal of Applied Communication Research, 45*, 140–159.

Mumby, D. K., & Stohl, C. (1996). Disciplining organizational communication studies. *Management Communication Quarterly, 10*, 50–72.

Munshi, D., & Kurian, P. (2005). Imperializing spin cycles: A postcolonial look at public relations, greenwashing, and the separation of publics. *Public Relations Review, 31*, 513–520.

Norton, T., Sias, P., & Brown, S. (2011). Experiencing and managing uncertainty about climate change. *Journal of Applied Communication Change, 39*, 290–309.

Nyberg, D., Wright, C., & Kirk, J. (2018). Dash for gas: Climate change, hegemony and the scalar politics of fracking in the UK. *British Journal of Management, 29*, 235–251.

O'Connor, A., & Gronewold, K. L. (2012). Black gold, green earth: An analysis of the petroleum industry's CSR environmental sustainability discourse. *Management Communication Quarterly, 27*, 210–236.

Pal, M., & Jenkins, J. J. (2014). Reimagining sustainability: An interrogation of the Corporate Knights' Global 100. *Environmental Communication, 8*, 388–405.

Peterson, T. R. (1997). *Sharing the earth: The rhetoric of sustainable development.* Columbia, SC: University of South Carolina Press.

Plec, E., & Pettenger, M. (2012). Greenwashing consumption: The didactic framing of Exxon-Mobil's energy solutions. *Environmental Communication, 6,* 459–476.

Prasad, P., & Elmes, M. (2005). In the name of the practical: Unearthing the hegemony of pragmatics in the discourse of environmental management. *Journal of Management Studies, 42,* 845–867.

Prassl, J. (2018). *Humans as a service: The promise and perils of work in the gig economy.* New York, NY: Oxford University Press.

Rich, J. L. (2016). *Nature at work: An eco-sensible study of professional identity making in the fracking industry.* Unpublished dissertation at the University of North Carolina at Chapel Hill, NC.

Schons, L., & Steinmeier, M. (2016). Walk the talk? How symbolic and substantive CSR actions affect firm performance depending on stakeholder proximity. *Corporate Social Responsibility and Environmental Management, 23,* 358–372.

Scott, C., & Lewis, L. (Eds.) (2017). *The International Encyclopedia of Organizational Communication.* Malden, MA: John Wiley & Sons.

Signitzer, B., & Prexl, A. (2008). Corporate sustainability communications: Aspects of theory and professionalization. *Journal of Public Relations Research, 20,* 1–19.

Stevens, S. M. (2006). Activist rhetorics and the struggle for meaning: The case of "sustainability" in the reticulate public sphere. *Rhetoric Review, 25,* 297–315.

Stohl, C., Stohl, M., & Popova, L. (2009). A new generation of corporate codes of ethics. *Journal of Business Ethics, 90,* 607–622.

Tams, S., & Marshall, J. (2011). Responsible careers: Systemic reflexivity in shifting landscapes. *Human Relations, 64,* 109–131.

Tregidga, H., Kearins, K., & Milne, M. (2013). The politics of knowing "organizational sustainable development." *Organization & Environment, 26,* 102–129.

Van Marrewijk, M., & Werre, M. (2003). Multiple levels of corporate sustainability. *Journal of Business Ethics, 44,* 107–119.

Vogel, D. (2005). *The market for virtue: The potential and limits of corporate social responsibility.* Washington, DC: Brookings Institute Press.

Waters, R. D., Burnett, E., Lamm, A., & Lucas, J. (2009). Engaging stakeholders through social networking: How nonprofit organizations are using Facebook. *Public Relations Review, 35,* 102–106.

Young, O. R. (2005). Governing the Arctic: From cold war theater to mosaic of cooperation. *Global Governance: A Review of Multilateralism and International Organizations, 11,* 9–15.

Zorn, T. E., Jr., & Collins, E. (2007). Is sustainability sustainable? Corporate social responsibility, sustainable business, and management fashion. In S. May, G. Cheney, & J. Roper (Eds.), *The debate over corporate social responsibility* (pp. 405–416). New York, NY: Oxford University Press.

11 Toward Financial Inclusion

Pitfalls in Illustrating and Discussing Financial Inclusion

Odile Vallée

Since they first emerged in the early 1970s, the structured financial products and services on offer to disadvantaged and marginalized groups have multiplied and become more complex (Ledgerwood, 1999). Microcredit, which focused on savings and loans, grew into microfinance and now provides a wider range of financial and insurance services (Armendariz de Aghion & Morduch, 2005). The microfinance sector brings together particular economic, political, ideological and ethical questions related to access to financial products and support (Johnson, 2009). As such, microfinance discourses are subject to controversy, tension, and conflict. Sector stakeholders and third parties debate the various players' intentions, their practices and how the debate is framed (Roodman, 2012). Between the 1970s and the 2000s, the prevailing way of framing the debate on the role and effects of microfinance was "microcredit as a means of fighting poverty"; this has now been superseded by "financial inclusion" (Johnson, 2009; Taylor, 2012) that can be defined as "a process that ensures the ease of access, availability and usage of the formal financial system for all members of an economy" (Sarma, 2008, p. 3).

This chapter adopts a semiotic approach to examine financial documents using a framework of inclusion/exclusion. It examines financial inclusion through its manifestation and expression in graphic forms and discursive structures. Inclusion, and especially financial inclusion, is a nuanced process which is hard to record. Inclusion can be described, measured, and explained when it occurs in an observable form, and when its effects are enacted. It holds four particular strands of meaning. First, "inclusion" implies a relationship, potentially hierarchical, between two or more groups, determined by barriers or thresholds. These barriers and thresholds are more or less porous and may be breached by mechanisms that ease or hinder circulation among groups. If they can be pinpointed, these movements across group boundaries—in either direction—can be identified and measured. Second, inclusion portrays a situation where individuals may be identified as a part of a group (included) or not (excluded). Third, inclusion applies to an action suggesting that a group has potential power wielded by those performing acts of including others or not, both in their practice and in their underlying reasons for doing so. Finally, inclusion can be seen through the lens of the value—either positive or negative—attributed to the processes behind it, and to its objective of attracting individuals on the margins of society into a regulated space, and keeping them there in the long term. To apply reasoning based on inclusion is to invoke its corollary: exclusion. Exclusion is imbued with a negative value. Inclusion, therefore, draws individuals toward the center, cumulatively and positively; it seeks to tip the balance between inclusion and exclusion, in favor of the former; it draws attention to how access to the purported indicators of "included" status is granted or denied.

The idea of financial inclusion can be seen in two reports, which provide a starting point. *By the Numbers: Benchmarking Progress Toward Financial Inclusion (BTN)* (Kelly & Rhyne, 2015) and *Financial Inclusion Hype vs. Reality: Deconstructing the 2017 Findex Results* (Rhyne & Kelly, 2018) offer an initial framework for assessing inclusion in the financial sector, particularly when it comes to micro-loan servicing and access to such services. These reports provide quantitative evidence of financial inclusion, discuss its aims, and anticipate future development scenarios. The reports were drafted collectively by the Center for Financial Inclusion (CFI), the research arm of Accion International (Accion), a global non-profit organization and major player in the micro-financial sector. Accion was established in 1961. It champions the empowerment of people who are left out of the formal financial system and advocates a revolution in financial services aimed at them. Both reports, signed off by the Center's Managing Director and Research Director, are retrospective analyses of the quantitative results from eight years of action in the sector, taken by stakeholders on the ground.

These reports are interesting to analyze because of the material they capture and embody in an institutionalized, textualized, and condensed report form. The reports are the outcome of a collective, constructive communication process which updates the semantic characteristics of the concept of inclusion and opens up a new angle from which to observe a normative, and paradoxically exclusionary, force: the desire for inclusion. The act of writing these reports encompasses five distinct actions which promote a particular perspective on financial inclusion. These reports represent one stakeholder's statement, speaking out on the issue of financial inclusion. They transform and publish an existing data set which they analyze and comment on. The reports represent action which clients and stakeholders take on the ground in the sector and make it visible in the discourse. The reports are an interpretation of that action. Lastly, they bring matters to life and feed into a multi-stakeholder debate, proposing directions their action could take. Foucault (1980) asserted that discourse serves to constitute knowledge and through social relations that model aspects of knowledge, power is negotiated and reified. Through relational discursive practices, status, capacity to enact models, and underlying values get revealed. In the financial sector, this can be seen in these reports, which examine these six aspects of discourse, namely, integration, relations, models, status, capacity, and values. Such reports ask, to what extent do the graphical forms and discursive structures expressing the financial inclusion framework embody its aim to integrate (**integration**), its relational and process-based nature (**relations**), its practical side (**models**), its classificatory aspect (**status**), its capacity for action (**capacity**), and its ethical and normative aspect (**values**)? My semiotic and discursive analysis of the two reports adopts these concepts as a lens to investigate reservoirs of meaning for the concept of inclusion, within a defined space. This space illustrates the way in which seldom-discussed graphical and discursive structures exert a normative and performative influence on the financial inclusion-based processes of representation and of debating microfinance: on the practices used, the stakeholders' roles, and the scope of microfinance.

Having identified the stakeholders and the issues raised by the definitions of financial inclusion, this chapter will move on to investigate three significant aspects of the CFI reports: the issue of measuring financial inclusion; the issue of bank account use; and the mechanisms for and role played by scenarios.

Framing the Debate: Who Defines the Terms, and What is at Stake?

Microfinance has emerged against the backdrop of a long history in which development policy aims to include the poorest people in the market (Fouillet et al., 2016) and in society as a whole. Among the main indicators of development set out by international organizations are a gradual reduction in the extent of poverty and the efficiency of measures taken to improve quality of life (UNDP, 1999–2015).

Microcredit, and more recently microfinance, has been both praised and criticized (Johnson, 2009; Roodman, 2012). The polarized debate addresses practices and propositions. It discusses competing justifications for the economic and social acceptability of microfinance. It delimits and directs the scope for action taken by microfinance stakeholders and the roles allocated to financial products and services: in combating poverty; in customers' economic and even political empowerment; and in financial inclusion (Roodman, 2012). In other words, these debates amount to whether or not the financial services are efficient and fulfill the differentiated promises claimed by the players. It is either regarded/evidenced as helpful or considered neutral or plainly harmful. In an increasingly financialized environment, the organization and implementation of appropriate financial intermediaries is a major issue for society. The action and debates surrounding the practice of microfinance have a strong ideological component, as well as major implications for politics and power (Doligez, Bastiaensen, Bédécarrats, & Labie, 2016). Financial exclusion also results from highly complex processes that call for a concerted response to mobilize all of the relevant stakeholders (Doligez et al., 2016).

With regard to the framework of definitions, development stakeholders include in their definitions of financial inclusion nuances that necessarily change its scope. For example, Table 11.1 reviews definitions by three stakeholders, each with a different status: The World Bank (WB); the Consultative Group to Assist the Poor (CGAP), a think tank created in international partnership between more than 30 public and private bodies, all development stakeholders at local, inter-regional and international levels; and the CFI. Their definitions show how ambitious their financial inclusion plans are. At

Table 11.1 Definitions of Financial Inclusion

Organization	Definition of Financial Inclusion
World Bank	"Financial inclusion means that individuals and businesses have access to useful and affordable financial products and services that meet their needs—transactions, payments, savings, credit and insurance—delivered in a responsible and sustainable way." (https://www.worldbank.org/en/topic/financialinclusion)
CGAP (Consultative Group to Assist the Poor)	"Financial inclusion means that households and businesses have access to and can effectively use appropriate financial services. Such services must be provided responsibly and sustainably, in a well-regulated environment." (http://www.cgap.org/topics/financial-inclusion)
CFI (Center for Financial Inclusion)	"The CFI advocates for the following definition of full financial inclusion: Financial inclusion is a state in which everyone who can use them has access to a range of quality financial services at affordable prices, with convenience, dignity and consumer protection, delivered by a range of providers in a stable competitive market to financially capable clients. This definition derives from the conviction that the purpose of promoting financial inclusion is to enable people to use financial services to better manage their lives." (Kelly & Rhyne, 2015, pp. 6–7)

the very least, each definition covers access to and use of formal financial services provided by official banking institutions. The definitions add ethical imperatives relating to price, quality of service, and consumer protection. Market regulation is underpinned by the freedom of the market and by protective measures taken by nation states. Finally, the CFI's exhaustive definition of financial inclusion states that it aims to build customers' capacity to "better manage their lives."

The CFI adds to its definition of financial inclusion by outlining its vision for a financially inclusive world, which raises the bar for what is required of the financial services provided. These must go beyond simple "access" and adapt to needs as expressed by clients. It frames service providers' actions on ethics and holds them accountable:

> Partial and poor-quality services are not enough: we believe financial services should match clients' needs, provide good value for money and be designed to avoid causing harm. Our vision for financial inclusion goes beyond access to include quality, affordability, appropriateness, convenience, and consumer protection and empowerment.
> (https://www.centerforfinancialinclusion.org/about/mission/)

Performativity refers to the ways in which ideas are not just expressed, but mediated in a way such that stakeholders or other interested parties may observe the source's articulation of those ideas. As regards performativity (Austin, 1962), these definitions create a positive reading and interpretation of the process of financial inclusion and provide a gauge by which to assess the gap between discourse and practice. There nevertheless remain several points which require detailed investigation: the type of stakeholders promoting the logic of financial inclusion; conceptions of the market and the roles of stakeholders in it; and the appropriateness of overarching intervention in tackling different contexts. Researchers analyze the approach taken by financial inclusion as the latest manifestation of a financial liberalization agenda which began several decades ago. Marcus Taylor (2012) considers that the change in scale and quest for sustainability in microfinance activities have been expressed in a discourse that promotes financial inclusion as a "global moral imperative" and microfinance as a "universally applicable tool" with which everyday risks can be regulated (Taylor, 2012, p. 601). Taylor exposes the organizational power of this universalizing discourse, which removes the relevant context: the local situations from which poverty, inequality, and marginalization arise. He critically analyzes the problematic aspects of what he refers to as the "discourse," the "narrative," and the "paradigm" of financial inclusion. Taylor's analysis deconstructs and calls into question the performative effects of the financial inclusion discourse. This discourse creates a fictitious, unequivocal target group, the "financially excluded"—a solid, decontextualized object of development work which justifies creating an institutional ecosystem comprising stakeholders with the capacity to address its needs. This target group as characterized above blurs our detailed understanding of local processes that create distinctions in society, and of institutional processes that create and reproduce poverty, inequality, and marginalization in individuals. Taylor goes on to state that the paradigm of financial inclusion, which takes into account criticisms of microfinance's claim to reduce poverty, transforms the role of microfinance and narrows its ambitions. He states that its products and services are no longer a means of moving out of poverty, but are instead the instruments of "consumption smoothing": for instance, access to credit provides the "financial security" necessary for facing life's ups and downs. Taylor argues that, despite these altered ambitions, the paradigm of financial inclusion gains legitimacy by articulating two moral imperatives: the need to integrate excluded individuals by means of formal financial ties and the need to reduce their vulnerability. Both of these factors stimulate top-down action oblivious to the practical constraints on the ground and to the strategies for action taken by people categorized as financially excluded.

The specific case of the consequences of the agrarian change process in rural India illustrates the limitations of the financial inclusion paradigm, which goes so far as to produce "'adverse inclusion,' i.e. incorporation into a cycle of indebtedness" (Taylor, 2012, p. 608). Taylor also underscores the inconsistency of a formal/informal dichotomy, only strengthened by a paradigm of inclusion that overvalues fictitious rationality and removes the informal practices found within formal finance mechanisms. Although the access to resources opened up by subsidized and commercial microfinance is necessary, he states that effective policy relies on an understanding and integration of the problems that rural social movements constantly highlight. Here, Taylor brings in the political issue of the type of stakeholder considered relevant, and the role these stakeholders play in framing the debate and discussing social and institutional processes that are factors in exclusion.

From another perspective, Susan Johnson (2013) also sets out a critical analysis of the claim that the financial products and services on offer are inclusive. She examines the disjuncture between the discourse supporting the logic of inclusive financial markets, and the complexity of the processes observed on the ground. Johnson analyzes the "Making Markets Work for the Poor" (M4P). The M4P approach was activated by donors willing to retain a poverty focus that stands out in a policy context focused on the wider institutional development framework. The M4P draws up a roadmap for development stakeholders promoting "Finance for All." Johnson identifies and clarifies the "analytical disjuncture" between the theoretical principles of New Institutional Economics, which actually backs the financial inclusion agenda, and the theoretical perspective development stakeholders claim to take on social exclusion. The former is based on a legacy understanding of poverty that solely considers the lack of income as a defining criterion, while the latter relies on a relational understanding of poverty that acknowledges its multidimensionality and includes its consequences on self-esteem, social ties and networks, and social inclusion over time and across generations. The author takes the example of gender relations and the processes of exclusion which these unleash and goes on to formulate an analytical framework which is also an effective means of understanding inclusivity in financial markets. Her analysis points up contradictions between the supply and the demand for financial services. The supply side develops an ecosystem of institutions and commercial organizations and calibrates a model that "enables them to work with the mainstream financial sector, but retains poverty focus" (Johnson, 2013, p. S37).

However, Johnson states that exclusion is not merely a function of the way markets are structured. According to her analysis, the inclusivity perspective is focused on creating opportunity, to the detriment of taking into account the way in which local legal and sociocultural factors such as race, gender, and ethnicity affect processes of exclusion and permeate the way markets operate. Johnson's approach is to produce an analytical framework that can incorporate questions of power—and the strategies for action and resistance subsequently triggered—which restrict both any action taken by "excluded" individuals and their fair and effective integration into the market. Indeed, Johnson insists on broadening the scope of needs to be addressed and the type of stakeholders and arguments to be considered. She stipulates that training and education designed for excluded groups, in particular for women and minorities, should be included in interventions from inception. She points out "struggles for rights" (Johnson, 2013, p. 349) as a crucial springboard to influence regulatory structures.

In a nutshell, Johnson states that the theoretical framework on which the WB's financial mediation activity is based defines poverty as being residual and does not take into account the "multi-dimensional terms on which [groups of people] are either apparently excluded or incorporated" (Johnson, 2013, p. S42), as a relational approach to poverty would. Taylor, on the other hand, emphasizes that the narrative of financial inclusion produces one, universalized agent—"the financially excluded" (Taylor, 2012). The diverse individuals included in this category are stripped of their individual features and reduced to a single characteristic: exclusion from formal financial ties. Thus this object of development, the agent in the narrative, may symbolically be manipulated and discussed by the narrators. Johnson and Taylor both underline the need to develop the agency of groups affected by exclusion on multiple fronts, an agency which is not accounted for in the mechanisms for defining and framing the supply and distribution of financial products and services. Both indicate, without expanding on the issue, that it is important to broaden the range of stakeholders and arguments to be considered. The dynamics of the target groups' struggles for their rights must be taken into account. Their involvement in the processes that determine the products and services on offer to them will bring about a shift in the logic, from top-down to bottom-up.

The above-mentioned works frame our observations and investigations of expert discourse on financial inclusion and our questioning of the normative issues at play. As highlighted in the introduction, the semantic reservoir for "inclusion" translates to its aim to integrate (**integration**); its relational and processual nature (**relations**); its practical side as embodied by tools and models (**models**); its classificatory aspect (**status**); its capacity for action (**capacity**); and its ethical and normative aspect (**values**). Andersen and Born (2000) define semantic reservoir as meaning that is co-constructed through communication. The concreteness of meaning happens as ideas get communicated and in that communication, their meaning is recursively built up. As such, multiple meanings get condensed into single forms, building a reservoir from which to draw, generating the terms and conditions for sense-making (Luhmann, 1992; Neisig, 2017). Johnson and Taylor provide critical analysis that sheds light on potential alternative ways to activate this semantic reservoir and engage stakeholders. I contend that being open and receptive to the various people who are "excluded" can shift the interpretations currently applied by institutional public policy and commercial stakeholders (Table 11.2, column B) toward alternative interpretations stimulated by widening the voices effectively associated with the discussion (Table 11.2, column C). In this way, for instance, departing from a position of undifferentiation, the integration dimension of financial inclusion could acknowledge local multidimensional specificities. Also, capacity could be regarded as distributed among heterogeneous actors instead of being concentrated between few institutional ones. These shifts could have practical consequences for the design of financial products and services, the nature of stakeholders included, and the conditions of debate. The suggested adjectives associated with the semantic reservoir for inclusion in the table below each embody a hypothesis to be verified for the nature of this movement.

Table 11.2 Possible Meanings of the Semantic Reservoir Surrounding "Inclusion"

A	B	C
Semantic Reservoir for "Inclusion"	*Interpretations in Active Use*	*Alternative Interpretations*
Integration	Undifferentiated	Individualized
Relations	Hierarchical	Circular
Models	Prescribed	Discussed
Status	Unidimensional	Multidimensional
Capacity	Concentrated	Distributed
Values	Normative	Subjective

In contrast to the works cited previously, the present chapter will not explore the underlying concepts of poverty that color the discourse on international institutions and organizations active in financial inclusion. Instead, I focus on the distinct formats (graphic forms and discursive structures) that are mobilized in order to discuss the issue. These update and promote a naturalization of the semantic reservoir surrounding the term "inclusion." The formats also symbolically crystallize tensions inherent in the interpretations of the semantic reservoir derived from the analyses by Taylor and Johnson and can potentially also show them being resolved. These discrete formats will be analyzed on the basis of two reports produced by the CFI. They are loci in which the CFI speaks out and asserts its role in embodying the thinking of international players in financial inclusion. This role as claimed intermediary is underpinned by an act of representation. In other words, the stakeholders are described and put into context regarding the state of practices and behaviors in the areas where the financial inclusion dynamic operates. The reports are based on a database compiled and made available by the WB. The WB's published data-gathering methodology[1] attests to the real, "representative" individuals behind the statistics. Thus, the number of Taylor's "financially excluded" emerges not from findings on the ground, but from these reports, in the form of aggregated data that have been compiled, decompiled, recompiled, and interpreted by the CFI. These reports occupy an interesting position as they speak for and address institutional and private stakeholders. This allows for the investigation of the vision of financial inclusion through the graphical forms and discursive structures that facilitate discussion.

Case Study: CFI Reports on Financial Inclusion

The Organization

Accion is a global non-profit organization with headquarters in the US. It has 501(c)(3) non-profit organization status there. The organization was founded in 1961, which makes it a long-established player in microfinance. Accion organizes its work around four focal points. The first of these is *Advise*, advising financial service providers. In the second, *Invest*, Accion invests in microfinance institutions and Fintech (financial technology) startups by acquiring shares in them. The third point is *Influence*: influencing industry stakeholders, leaders, and regulators. The organization generates insights and research, engages stakeholders in collaboration, and does advocacy work. Accion's fourth focus is *Partner*: developing institutional partnerships to promote emerging, innovative markets, products, and services.

The "Influence" work is done by a separate entity, the CFI, which describes itself as an action-oriented think tank. Accion International and the CFI facilitate debate about financial inclusion. The CFI describes the task of promoting financial inclusion as follows:

> The global financial inclusion movement has been gathering steam for about a decade. Policy leaders and financial authorities everywhere are striving to construct the enabling conditions for inclusion. (...). The collective goal is to provide historically excluded populations [with] access to financial services they can use to improve their lives.
>
> (Rhyne & Kelly, 2018, p. 2)

Against this backdrop, Accion and the CFI launched the FI2020 network, a "global multi-stakeholder movement to achieve full inclusion, using the year 2020 as a focal point to achieve inclusion" (Financial Inclusion Week 2020 Roundup, November 2–6, 2015). A framework report titled *Seizing the Moment: On the Road to Financial Inclusion* (STM) published in 2014 summarized the results of a series of working groups, webinars, and other research conducted in 2013. These results are stated in a series of five themed roadmaps,[2] each of which operates as a set of recommendations drawn up collaboratively by the stakeholders, for the stakeholders. These are intended as open forums for interactions to engage with actors and help shape a shared vision of financial inclusion.

These roadmaps provide a framework for the analyses produced by the CFI, documenting the progress made on the ground toward financial inclusion; they look into the drivers behind it and identify problematic aspects of it. Following from this work, the CFI produced two 30-page reports, published three years apart (Kelly & Rhyne, 2015; Rhyne & Kelly, 2018), based predominantly on data from the Global Findex (GF).[3] The GF is a compilation of results from a global survey launched by the WB in 2011. It is a database of declarative international data gathered in line with a survey protocol ensuring that different areas and data from different survey periods are comparable. The database was launched with funding from the Bill and Melinda Gates Foundation. It is published every three years and has three main characteristics: its size, its international aspect, and the nature of the data. These allow us to view the issue of financial inclusion from a demand-side perspective. The survey seeks to record clients' needs, their particular difficulties, and the use made of the tools and services on offer. The survey and the mechanism for circulating its results were both produced in a collaborative context. Although the WB produces a report in its own name which describes and analyzes the state of financial inclusion around the world, the file of raw data output from the survey is made public, which in turn provides multiple opportunities for drawing up indicators, mapping areas, practices, and stakeholders. Thus, the WB offers anyone the opportunity to adapt the data and to manipulate it by generating indicators, graphs, and graphic representations giving comparisons and establishing relationships that give new meaning to the raw figures.

In its role of influencer and source of knowledge, the CFI utilizes these data to feed into two reports intended for stakeholders in the financial inclusion movement. These reports foster sector stakeholder engagement with a thought experiment. As a thought experiment, it is a speculative exercise that locates the future of financial inclusion in a timeline for action which is identified as part of a long-established joint project. For several years, the CFI at Accion has engaged in a thought experiment with participants across the financial inclusion sector. We have asked stakeholders to consider one question: could full financial inclusion be possible by the year 2020 (Kelly & Rhyne, 2015, p. 5)?

As both reports are publications and statements the CFI has made, they enable CFI to make active choices about representing and interpreting the results of the GF survey. These in turn make active use of the semantic reservoir surrounding inclusion. As noted above, the associated semantic reservoir of inclusion has six characteristics: integration, relations, models, status, capacity, and values. When these reports embody and discuss the state of progress made in financial inclusion processes by mobilizing graphic and discursive forms which enable the audience to read and interpret it, they are opening up particular perspectives for launching a discussion. In so doing, the reports and associated discussions help shape its semantic reservoir.

The Reports' Aims and the Issues at Stake

The BTN and FIHR reports produce an evaluative and prescriptive discourse that encompasses and analyzes eight years of financial inclusion expectations and practices. Across a three-year span, they move from prospective optimism to stark and factual disappointment. The authors assign three aims to the reports: taking stock of the progress indicators toward total financial inclusion; issuing predictive hypotheses for the future; and proposing corrective actions to spur stakeholders into action and enable continued progress toward financial inclusion. The gap between the two periods for which the status and determiners of financial inclusion are analyzed is evident in the reports' titles and also in the differences between their structures. BTN is arranged into three parts: findings on and predictions for financial inclusion by 2020; analysis of how people are using their access to financial services; and analysis of the institutional and legal infrastructure best suited to supporting progress on financial inclusion. FIHR focuses on the factual data that emerge from the GF: "This report looks first at accounts, then at product use, and finally at customer outcomes. The commentary is limited, allowing the data to speak for itself" (Rhyne & Kelly, 2018, p. 3). The reports clearly emerge from the tension between, on the one hand, producing a descriptive operational update on the state of financial inclusion (and by comparison exclusion) based on empirical data and, on the other hand, commenting on and interpreting the data by following strands found within them, i.e. the prescriptive production of projections based on "several rather heroic assumptions" (Kelly & Rhyne, 2015, p. 6). These anticipate particular courses of action and are made to spark discussion because, as the authors say, "in our view, the best use of this report is to provoke further questions" (Kelly & Rhyne, 2015, p. 6). The following analysis looks at three prominent, ambivalent aspects: the importance of quantitative measurements; account use as interpreted by a range of graphical forms in the reports; and predictive discursive structures, which are grouped together in the category scenarios. These aspects reinforce a trend toward updating the semantic characteristics of inclusion and are also the locus of movement in the reservoir of meaning.

The Question of Measuring Financial Inclusion: Building a Register of "Objectivity"

Financial inclusion can be constructed visually; it can be broken down and naturalized in graphical and discursive forms, such as the descriptive commentary on the data and the anticipatory projections which mark out the range of possibilities "objectively" based on the GF, which is presented as "the most comprehensive and authoritative demand-side picture of global financial service use" (Rhyne & Kelly, 2018, p. 2). Expressed in quantitative terms, inclusion appears to be synonymous with monitoring, channelling financial flows through formal, official circuits that can be checked and counted. Inclusion can be measured and evaluated using numbered criteria and indicators, presented in graphics and tables. The major, emblematic indicator of inclusion is having a bank account:

> Accounts are the most convenient marker for financial inclusion, and, particularly in high income countries, they are seen as the financial hub around which other financial services are organized. Access to an account takes a person from "unbanked" to "banked," an important threshold for both government and service providers. So, it is not surprising that accounts are the focal point for measuring progress in financial inclusion.
> (Kelly & Rhyne, 2015, p. 8)

The bank account also provides the material for anticipatory projections: the type of account (traditional or digital), its geographic location or institution, how accessible it is, who owns it, and how it is used, all allow a complex set of indicators to be established. These indicators designate achievements to be preserved, setting out corrective action to be taken if necessary.

The choice of indicators and their translation into graphics and tables establishes a hierarchy of the criteria to prioritize and directs attention toward trends and levers to be operated. The data seek to express the scale of international public policy and of policy locally, where the stories "play out." The macro level of aggregation summarizes nations and regions and constructs comparisons between areas, while the micro level addresses how services are distributed among and adopted by customers. The data merge situations that are potentially irreconcilable due to the wide range of social, economic, political, and cultural mechanisms that produce and contribute to positions of poverty. The data permit future projections that obscure the structural logic of exclusion contained in gender, class, and age relations as highlighted by Johnson (2013). The selection and implementation of graphics for the cover of the reports provides an interesting example of the tensions embodied in the integrative aspect of financial inclusion (integration). From a whole range of possible representations, the authors chose not to select visual or photographic representations of places or stakeholders, customers, or providers of financial services.[4] Instead, the graphics chosen for the covers are stylized representations of financial exclusion status, broken down by country. For BTN, the diagram does not name the regions and countries in question; it shows the projected size of the population that may still be financially excluded in 2020, the target date for near-complete inclusion. This cover illustration, listed as Figure 8 in the report, features in detail and with commentary on page 15—at the end of the first chapter and before the analysis of how people use their access to services (Figure 11.1).

The commentary emphasizes the critical role that regional development banks and political entities like the European Union will play in pushing past this final milestone on the road to total inclusion. For FIHR, the cover diagram does show the names of countries, ordered according to region and sorted according to their share of the total. It represents the geographical distribution of people whose bank accounts were dormant in 2017. After the introduction, this diagram is inserted into the body of the report as a central finding, whose nuances and consequences are unraveled in a series of 27 graphics, tables, and snapshots with commentary, showing countries with typical characteristics. This choice of cover images embodies the resolute focus on quantitative measurements and integration. While the graphic in the BTN report suggests that overarching, uniform action is being taken, the reappearance of the country names as a contextual variable in the FIHR report, and switching the indicator from the number of people excluded to the number of dormant accounts, reintroduce differentiation.

The Question of Bank Account Use: A Central Variable in Shifting the Semantics of Inclusion

The question of account use and the differences in use between high income and developing economies elicits a series of puzzled comments, from the BTN report onward, and draws attention to this crucial area of tension:

> These figures raise fundamental questions about the difference between financial access and full financial inclusion … This observation calls into

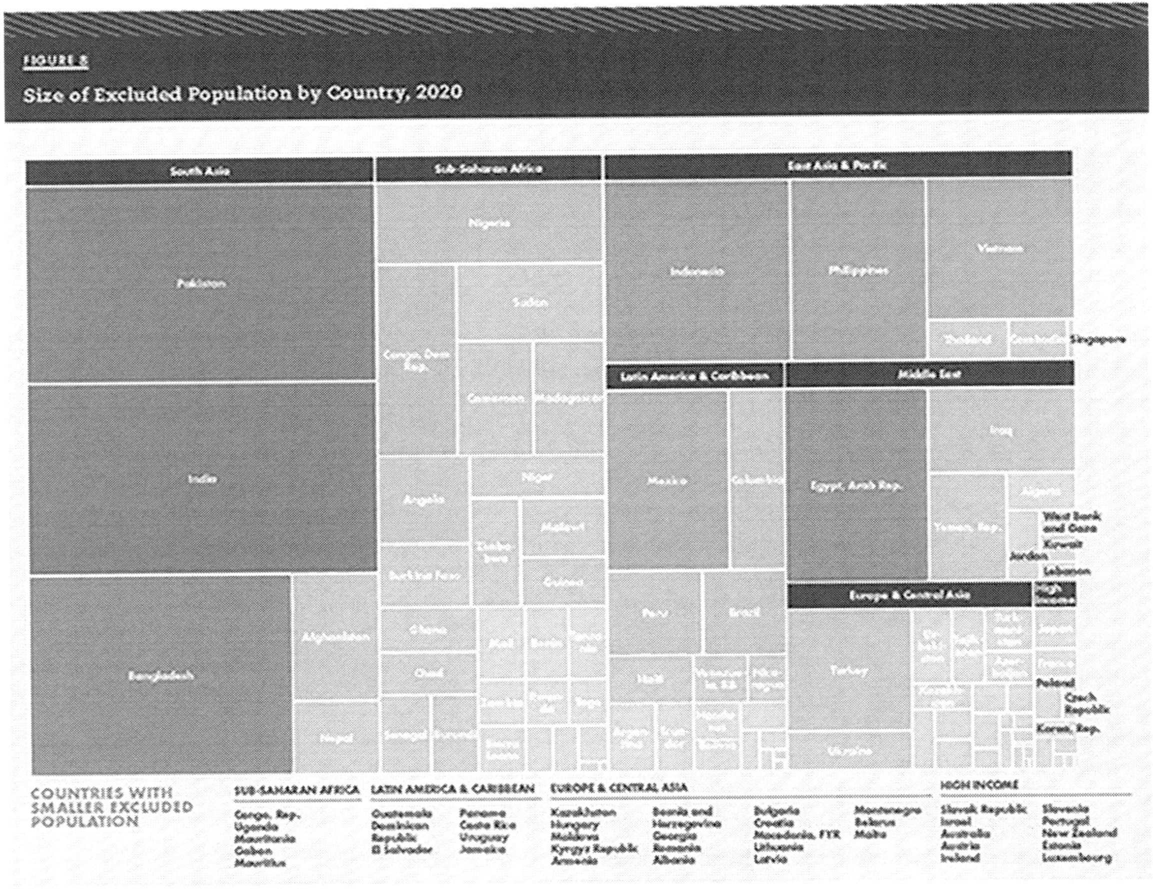
FIGURE 5
Size of Excluded Population by Country, 2020
South Asia
Pakistan
India
Bangladesh
Afghanistan
Nepal
Sub-Saharan Africa
Nigeria
Sudan
Congo, Dem. Rep.
Cameroon
Madagascar
Angola
Niger
Malawi
Zimbabwe
Burkina Faso
Guinea
Ghana
Mali
Benin
Chad
Zambia
Togo
Senegal
Burundi
East Asia & Pacific
Indonesia
Philippines
Vietnam
Thailand
Cambodia
Singapore
Latin America & Caribbean
Mexico
Colombia
Peru
Brazil
Haiti
Nicaragua
Middle East
Egypt, Arab Rep.
Iraq
Algeria
Yemen, Rep.
West Bank and Gaza
Kuwait
Jordan
Lebanon
Europe & Central Asia
Turkey
Ukraine
High income
Japan
France
Poland
Czech Republic
Korea, Rep.
COUNTRIES WITH SMALLER EXCLUDED POPULATION
SUB-SAHARAN AFRICA
Congo, Rep.
Uganda
Mauritania
Gabon
Mauritius
LATIN AMERICA & CARIBBEAN
Guatemala
Dominican Republic
El Salvador
Panama
Costa Rica
Uruguay
Jamaica
EUROPE & CENTRAL ASIA
Kazakhstan
Hungary
Moldova
Kyrgyz Republic
Armenia
Bosnia and Herzegovina
Georgia
Romania
Albania
Bulgaria
Croatia
Macedonia, FYR
Lithuania
Latvia
Montenegro
Belarus
Malta
HIGH INCOME
Slovak Republic
Israel
Australia
Austria
Ireland
Slovenia
Portugal
New Zealand
Estonia
Luxembourg

Source: Author projections based on Global Findex (2015) and UN World Population Prospects (2012).

question a presumption that access to an account will trigger greater inclusion … Before drawing firm conclusions, it will be important to uncover more about how people are using their accounts. Perhaps there are explanations other than dormancy and low usage … Further exploration of Findex microdata will be needed to gain greater understanding of account use.

(Kelly & Rhyne, 2015, p. 19)

Identifying dormant accounts and the difficulty of ascertaining the drivers of account use beyond the statements people have made form the basis of the GF survey. In its assessments, the GF survey thus points to the logic and strategies that can circumvent the inclusivity mechanism. Such strategies can be seen elsewhere. For example, spaces such as the financial notebooks that Collins et al. (2009) analyze make explicit how complex the arrangements and financial flows in poorer households are and make it untenable to maintain a strict dichotomy between formal and informal. Equally, the visual images of financial inclusion produced as entries in the 2018 CGAP photography competition, which might demonstrate aspects of development other than financial inclusion, are evidence of the "subject matter" of inclusion "resisting" being captured unequivocally in semiotic form.

The question of account use shifts the focus of action from public stakeholders and private service providers onto their clients, accompanied by a concomitant shift in the capacity for action. Inclusion as a variable is no longer the ability to access a functional, ethical bank account. Instead, inclusion has become the social, political, economic, and cultural conditions that influence the integration of an account into the individuals' own financial management. Neither graphics showing the distribution of account use broken down according to gender, nor sociodemographic criteria missing from BTN and introduced into FIHR are capably of allowing one to fully grasp the social, political, economic, and cultural conditions.

As evidenced in the above analyses, the contents of the two financial reports illustrate a symbolic shift in the capacity for action from the development institutions and service providers to their clients, as well as the vanishing point for their use of these services. The projections drawn up in the BTN report constitute a "scenario" for development in the inclusion situation. If this scenario is realized, it will bring about an adaptation of the services, the main vector of financial inclusion, to suit those segments of the population that are hardest to reach. The report states this as follows:

We urge readers to consider the projections here as one possible scenario (based on the best readily available data) and to focus more on the implications of the scenario than on the specific numbers. In that scenario, financial exclusion looks much different in 2020 than it looks today. Exclusion will be more hidden—in harder-to-reach population segments, in slow-growth countries, and in products that are not actively used to improve lives. Emphasis will turn to "leaving no one behind" and to offering services that make a real difference.

(Kelly & Rhyne, 2015, p. 6)

This scenario brings the question of financial inclusion back to the practical and logistical issues of formulating and distributing services appropriate to the residual share of the population that is hardest to reach.

The FIHR report attests that it is puzzled:

The 2017 results suggest a need for the financial inclusion community to reconsider assumptions about the levers of change and recalibrate expectations to a somewhat more modest level. Analysts will need to dig deeper to understand the causes of the relatively tepid performance in the past three years, and that may lead us to question some of the hypotheses that underpin financial inclusion efforts. For one thing, it will be important to consider the broader context in which change is occurring, recognizing that deliberate efforts to increase inclusion are not the only forces creating change, and possibly not even the most important. Another avenue of investigation will be analysis of the interplay of broad forces (political, economic, technological) and specific inclusion efforts in individual countries where the story is playing out. Most importantly, we will need to think critically about what drives usage and how financial services offer value to customers.

(Rhyne & Kelly, 2018, p. 3)

The hypotheses underlying the production of the scenarios (roadmaps) for the change currently in use, on which the targets for financial inclusion are themselves implicitly based, need to be investigated. The CFI's statement draws attention to possible parameters which need to be factored into such considerations: the political, economic, and technological forces at work and the factors driving use of the financial services on offer. Even if the terms in which the question is couched require rethinking, there is no indication that the type of stakeholders involved in the process or the methods for discussing it may be called into question.

Rethinking the Mechanism and Role of the "Scenario"

BTN states that it has constructed a scenario for development in the level of financial inclusion, based on a representative vision of end customers' needs, complete with figures. Three years later, FIHR encountered the issue of account use but abandoned and called into question its projections. Doing so indicates the crucial symbolic nature of projections as a practice. The practice of using scenarios as a means of anticipating and speculating on possible outcomes manifests itself in various ways in the BTN report. It manifests itself in the interrogative format of the chapter titles. It is also seen in extending the graph and histogram projections out to 2020, through the speculative questions with which the descriptive commentaries on the graphics end, and in the selective analyses which single out typical case studies illustrating the "variety of paths to financial access" (Kelly & Rhyne, 2015, p. 14).

Angela Wilkinson and Esther Eidinow (2008) propose a framework for analyzing the mechanism by which scenarios are drawn up by both public and private sector stakeholders, in the aim of collaboratively reaching an understanding—not of the issue of financial inclusion but of environmental change, which is just as complex. Their conclusions provide interesting perspectives on how we might conceive of this discursive structure and its practical implications as a space in which interpretations within the semantic reservoir for inclusion are shifting.

Scenarios are structured models for interpreting the future, as distinct from projections, predictions, and forecasts. Wilkinson and Eidinow emphasize their interestingly multidimensional and more unstable nature. For, they result from discursive processes and, thus, involve interactions between different types of knowledge.

The authors identify three main types of scenarios: (a) problem-focused, (b) actor-centric, and (c) reflexive-interventionist or multi-agent-based. Each of these scenarios is based on an underlying view of the knowledge considered to be relevant, the stakeholders, and the process for drawing up and discussing the options. Scenarios of the "problem-focused" variety look ahead to a knowable future, favor factual data, and reject value judgments likely to influence stakeholders. Scenarios of the "actor-centric" variety involve stakeholders' interpretations and are based on consensus, produced through interactive discussion. The third type of scenario, reflexive-interventionist or multi-agent-based, is designed around an action research mode. An action research mode mobilizes the whole range of available knowledge (quantitative, qualitative, expert, and local). This type incorporates characteristics from the context in which action takes place, as well as the relationships among stakeholders, and accepts contradictions. Wilkinson and Eidinow (2008) assert that such scenarios aim change participants' thinking to be more collaborative and action-oriented. In particular, Wilkinson and Eidinow underline the epistemological differences associated with these three types of scenarios that establish "truth" by admitting and employing knowledge of distinct sorts, and a variety of interlocutors and methods—whether based on scientific data or on consensus emerging from discussion.

The third type of scenario removes non-expert knowledge from its scope when it is transposed into a financial inclusion setting. It also removes the claims of groups agitating for rights (Johnson, 2013; Taylor, 2012) and offers an invitation to revisit a multitude of actions, including (a) the modes for constructing and expressing shared horizons for action; (b) the nature of knowledge employed; and (c) the possible tensions or even conflicts between perspectives and ideologies embodied "behind the scenes" in the graphic forms and discursive structures mobilized for explanation and interpretation purposes. In particular, we must think about representing and integrating people who are "excluded" into the reflection process, in a way that reaches beyond their status as customers whose expectations are explained and aggregated by interaction with a representative survey. The CFI reports avoid the trap of employing a gendered, racialized iconography of customers, which will always be imperfect and problematic (Vallée, 2017; Yartey & Birzescu, 2015). Nevertheless, the "financially excluded" who can so conveniently be presented in figures remain evanescent, intangible, and resistant to cross-tabulation of data. They force us to question the means by which their "words" and needs have been integrated into the process for formulating the services proposed in order to understand and acknowledge their practices in this area. The semiotics of these discrete forms feed into a conception of financial inclusion. This conception is quantitative and can be governed and taken out of context. This also helps highlight the need to shift the terms of the questions. How can the logic of inclusion and inclusivity avoid being thought of as merely the opposite of unequivocal exclusion, and instead invite reflection on creating the conditions for what is possible, on diverse perspectives and practices?

Notes

1 See: https://globalfindex.worldbank.org/
2 The five roadmaps are: Financial Capability; Addressing Customer Needs; Technology (-enabled business models); Credit Reporting; Consumer Protection (*Seizing the Moment: On the Road to Financial Inclusion*, CFI, 2014).
3 There are other sources involved in the BTN report: the EIU Global Microscope 2014, UN income and population growth data, World Development Indicators, IMF data on the supply of financial services, Alliance for Financial Inclusion data on national commitments to financial inclusion, and GSMA State of the Industry data on mobile financial service providers (Kelly & Rhyne, 2015, p. 5).
4 As an alternative means of documenting financial inclusion, the CGAP launched a photography competition, which was held for the 12th time in 2018. This brings together many photographers who want to illustrate financial inclusion through "original and compelling images." In its own words, the 2017 edition "invited submissions in four key areas that are instrumental to advancing financial inclusion: Innovations in Digital Finance, Creating Opportunities for People in Crisis, Building Sustainable Livelihoods, and Connecting People and Services" (http://photocontest.cgap.org/).

References

Andersen, N., & Born, A. (2000). Complexity and change: Two "semantic tricks" in the triumphant oscillating organization. *Systemic Practice and Action Research*, *13*(3), 297–328. doi:10.1023/A:1009511026806
Armendariz de Aghion, B., & Morduch, J. (2005). *The economics of microfinance*. Cambridge, MA: MIT Press.

Austin, J. L. (1962). *How to do things with words*. Cambridge, MA: Harvard University Press.

Collins, D., Morduch, J., Rutherford, S., & Ruthven, O. (2009). *Portfolios of the poor: How the world's poor live on $2 a day*. Princeton, NJ: Princeton University Press.

Doligez, F., Bastiaensen, J., Bédécarrats, F., & Labie, M., (2016). L'inclusion financière, nouvel avatar de la libéralisation financière? Introduction. *Revue Tiers Monde, 225*(1), 9–20. doi:10.3917/rtm.225.0009

Foucault, M. (1980). *Power/knowledge: Selected interviews and other writings, 1972–1977* (C. Gordon, Ed.). New York: Pantheon Books.

Fouillet, C., Guérin, I., Morvant-Roux, S., & Servet, J. M. (2016). De gré ou de force: Le microcrédit comme dispositif néolibéral. *Revue Tiers Monde, 1*, 21–48.

Johnson, S. (2009). Microfinance is dead! Long live microfinance! Critical reflections on two decades of microfinance policy and practice. *Enterprise Development and Microfinance, 20*(4), 291–303.

Johnson, S. (2013). From microfinance to inclusive financial markets: The challenge of social regulation. *Oxford Development Studies, 41*(sup1), S35–S52. doi:10.1080/113600818.2012.734799

Kelly, S. E., & Rhyne, E. (2015). *By the numbers: Benchmarking progress towards financial inclusion*. Center for Financial Inclusion/ACCION, June 2015.

Ledgerwood, J. 1999. *Microfinance handbook: An institutional and financial perspective*. Washington, DC: World Bank.

Luhmann, N. (1992). What is communication? *Communication Theory, 2*(3), 251–259. doi:10.1111/j.1468-2885.1992.tb00042.x

Neisig, M. (2017). Transition in complex polycentric contexts: Trusting and multifunctional semantics. *Systems Research and Behavioral Science, 34*(2), 163–181. doi:10.1002/sres.2450

Rhyne, E., & Kelly, S. E. (2018). *Financial inclusion hype vs. reality: Deconstructing the 2017 Findex results*. Center for Financial Inclusion/ACCION, May 2018.

Roodman, D. (2012). *Due diligence: An impertinent inquiry into microfinance*. Washington, DC: Center for Global Development. United Nations Development Program (UNDP). *Human Development Reports*, from 1999 to 2015.

Sarma, M. (2008). *Index of financial inclusion*. Working paper no 25. Indian Council for research on International Economic Relations.

Taylor, M. (2012). The antinomies of "financial inclusion": Debt, distress and the workings of Indian microfinance. *Journal of Agrarian Change, 12*(4), 601–610.

Vallée, O. (2017). La microfinance et ses portraits: Médiations paradoxales de la parole des "pauvres." *Etudes de Communication, 48*, 55–70.

Wilkinson, A., & Eidinow, E. (2008). Evolving practices in environmental scenarios: A new scenario typology. *Environmental Research Letters, 3*, 045017.

Yartey, F. N. A., & Birzescu, A. N. (2015). Surveillance of the poor in a socio-financial enclosure: A critical analysis of Zidisha.org. *Development in Practice, 25*(8), 1131–1145.

12 Design of Meaningful Work in Diversity and Inclusion

Enactment of Inclusionary Engineering Design and Partnerships in Rural Ghana

Patrice M. Buzzanell

Overview of Meaningful Work

Diversity and inclusion are organized and communicated processes that constitute a form of work often falling under the aegis of meaningful work. In this overview, I first discuss (a) work and its meaningfulness, noting that its politicized nature is associated with difference, with both positive and detrimental consequences. I conclude this section with a note about the (b) multilayered nature, questions, and contradictions in meaningful work.

First, with regard to work and its meaningfulness, work traditionally has been conceptualized as obligations to make a living and as self-fulfillment; however, recent theorizing considers how and where people choose to engage in or forfeit economic and voluntary labor such as in the sharing and gig economies (Fayard, 2019). Meaningful work explores the nature, value, and quality of jobs, occupations, and industries in different contexts. Linked to individual and corporate well-being (Cheney, Zorn, Planalp, & Lair, 2008), meaningfulness connects the symbolic nature of work with the doing of tasks and occupations in particular material and cultural conditions. Although seemingly straightforward, meaningfulness of work is contested because it is politicized in its assumptions about what counts as good work (Gardner, Csikszentmihalyi, & Damon, 2001). Of importance is who, or what roles, have the power to determine not only what labor is worthy but also how labor produces outcomes (un)favorable to workers (Fayard, 2019). Meaningfulness of work is also politicized in assumptions of how work is configured or segregated along lines of race/ethnicities, class, sexuality, ability, and gender. Thus, meaningfulness is socially constructed and embodied (Gabor, 2013), individual and communal (Lips-Wiersma & Wright, 2012), subjective and objective (Wolf, 2010), narcissistic or condescending and desirable (Lair, Shenoy, McClellan, & McGuire, 2008), fixed and shifting in contexts over time (e.g., too little or too much, Florian, Costas, & Kärreman, 2018), and threaded with socio-historical continuities and discontinuities reliant upon and generative through difference (e.g., religious origins, national cultural distinctions, and generational differences, Barrett & Dailey, 2018; Bernstein, 1997; Ciulla,

2000; Long, 2016; Long, Buzzanell, & Kuang, 2016; Shenoy-Packer & Buzzanell, 2013). Of importance to this essay is that work and its meanings depend on who does this labor, why and how they do it, and whether the labor is considered as appropriate for them. As an example, diversity and inclusion work often falls to women and people of color which connotes that it is not as valuable as other kinds of labor and that majority members need not feel ownership for diversity and inclusion efforts.

Regardless, individuals and groups engaging in the meaningful work of diversity and inclusion may accrue varied positive and negative outcomes. Positive outcomes include productivity, life satisfaction, well-being, and work commitment (Allan, Batz-Barbarich, Sterling, & Tay, 2018). These positive outcomes result from feelings of personal fulfillment, happiness, and satisfaction in seeing how particular kinds of labor shape personal lives and organizations (for origins and consequences of meaningfulness in work and happiness, see Baumeister, Vohs, Aaker, & Garbinsky, 2013; Berkelaar & Buzzanell, 2015). For instance, engaging in work that constitutes supportive organizational cultures for members who may face stigmatization and structural discrimination because of their disabilities can enhance their well-being, career advancement, and organizational contributions (Moloney, Brown, Ciciurkaite, & Foley, 2018; Wilson-Kovacs, Ryan, Haslam, & Rabinovich, 2008). Those performing diversity and inclusion work, notably organizational or diversity catalysts, also benefit from meaningful work (e.g., Strum, 2007).

However, the drive to own and enact meaningfulness has a "dark side" or negative outcomes. This drive can have detrimental consequences, surfacing the power and control dynamics riddled throughout meaningfulness of work scholarship and practice. When people view work as meaningful or a "calling" then such perceptions can correspond with long hours with little to no pay, underemployment and long-term financial results, and work devotion, as well as ongoing inattention to physical, emotional, and spiritual well-being (Allan, Rolniak, & Bouchard, 2018; Blair-Loy & Cech, 2017; Bunderson & Thompson, 2009). With diversity and inclusion work, it is often those who are different who bear the burden of change efforts not only in terms of time and effort but also in being pigeon-holed in narrow organizational tracks with little potential for advancement, assumptions that their work is done to benefit themselves and others like them, and sometimes few resources for this work.

Second, with respect to meaningful work's nature, questions, and contradictions, meaningful work is conceptualized and operationalized in multilayered and intersecting ways at micro (individuals' meanings and meaningfulness), meso (occupational and institutional work status, rewards, quality, functional area), and macro (societal symbolic meanings, popular cultural discourses) levels with each interlocked and having profound material and ethical consequences. As a multi-level example, organizational members and leaders can increase the correspondence of daily activities with meaningful work by connecting ordinary, even "menial," tasks with aspirational goals, much as President Kennedy and NASA leaders associated daily engineering and maintenance tasks with the objective of "putting a man on the moon" (Carton, 2018). As Carton (2018) demonstrates, meaningfulness was accomplished through framing of activities and their significance for achieving one national goal. Explicating the meaningfulness of work draws attention to a series of questions. Such questions ask: who determines meaningfulness; how material and human agents interact in pursuit of meaningfulness; when and how do individuals, communities, and researchers determine that work is meaningful; what work does meaningfulness do for the contemporary neoliberal political economy; and how does meaningfulness "walk the line" between becoming and commodified. At its core, then, meaningfulness is inherently tensional or paradoxical (Bailey et al., 2018; Mitra & Buzzanell, 2017). These questions and contradictions provide the background to this chapter on the meaningfulness and design of diversity and inclusion work. Specifically, these questions come into play when examining first (a) the meaningfulness of diversity and inclusion work and then (b) diversity and inclusion through a design lens, specifically one situated within human-centered design (HCD). This chapter concludes with (c) communication practices for enhancing the design of meaningful diversity and inclusion work.

Meaningfulness of Diversity and Inclusion Work

In discussing the meaningfulness of diversity and inclusion work, primary considerations are (a) how diversity and inclusion are constructed as meaningful broadly and in specific contexts, (b) how diversity and inclusion labor is constrained and enabled, and (c) how diversity and inclusion as meaningful work constitute a design challenge.

How Diversity and Inclusion Are Constructed as Meaningful

Diversity and inclusion work aims to create greater representation of marginalized groups and greater opportunity for full and consequential organizational participation. Participation includes having voice in everyday decisions and in deliberations about structures, rewards, and the very logics for why and how organizational and societal members do things. In other words, diversity connotes representation, and inclusion is aligned with belongingness, dialogue, incorporation of different logics, and understanding of the politicized nature of employment and personal life activities. Assumptions underlying this labor aligned with diversity and inclusion are that everyone doing such labor is aiming for the same goals, and that particular individuals and organizational units are more attuned to the nuances of this work because of their identity group memberships, particularly if they are members of marginalized groups. As noted earlier, such an approach places an unjust burden on Others (marginalized group members) and enables majority members to abdicate the responsibility (e.g., Allen, 2000).

Given different conceptualizations and assumptions, the goals of diversity and inclusion vary. Such variation is associated with broad meanings and meaningfulness of diversity and inclusion work. Although entangled, the goals can be sorted into ideal types: business, moral, and demographic. For instance, diversity and inclusion work is described as meaningful when it produces new insights or resources into organizational processes and returns on investments in terms of innovative products and services and alternative (yet productive) ways of doing things. For instance, automobile safety, seat belts, and crash-test "dummies" had been based on masculine bodies for decades. In considering how women's bodies might change over their lifespans, a mechanical engineer named Laura Thackray who worked for Volvo™ created "Linda" in 2002, the world's first dummy who could simulate various stages of pregnancy and lead to more complicated safety considerations for women, men, and children (Schiebinger & Schraudner, 2011). In discussing this and other innovations, Schiebinger and Schraudner (2011) advocate not only for representation and inclusion of gendered considerations into safety and technological designs but also for gender equality through this business case for diversity and inclusion. The meaningfulness of diversity and inclusion work in this instance is multifaceted but provides a mainstreaming strategy (i.e., one in which advocacy for change and inclusion of marginalized group interests is explicitly aligned with core community or organizational values, Buzzanell, 1994) situated within Volvo's and society's concerns about safety. Similarly, statistical analyses of a national sample of business data indicated that there can be different profit points with gender and racial diversity correlating with increased sales revenue, more customers, and greater relative profits, but with racial diversity adding to greater market share (Herring, 2009).

In the business case, the meaningfulness of diversity and inclusion work—representation of diverse stakeholders whose input alters business systems and results—can increase innovation, corporate social responsibility, and profit maximization. Here, the focus is on goal attainment through linear thinking that adding diversity and inclusion as an entity or variable into business systems can solve concerns for and problems of short- and long-term growth and sustainability. The work is not simply recruiting, retaining, promoting, and incorporating diversity into business systems but also "management" of diversity and inclusion itself.

Similar to the business case is demography. Rather than focusing on profit and growth, the demographic case for diversity and inclusion requires anticipating, developing strategies for, and forecasting or projecting the location and consequences of population shifts in all sectors. From political polls and targeted consumer marketing strategies to anticipated changes in higher education demand by locale and curriculum (e.g., Bransberger, 2018), the meaningfulness of such work is in providing the products and services that are presumably desired and/or needed by certain population segments and the satisfaction (and career attainment) associated with correct predictions.

Questions about how one capitalizes on demographic shifts in representation and how to create the optimal mix of heterogeneity for teams and other collectivities—changing numbers and networks—to achieve desirable results become paramount in this approach (e.g., Reagans & Zuckerman, 2001). For instance, much has been written about women's membership on Boards of Directors and in C-Suites (Kossek & Buzzanell, 2018), but research is still uncovering how, why, and in what cases such difference produces preferred results. Scholarship has shown that it is not simply adding women to the mix of top officers, but women's numbers in positions of authority, women's credibility and means of corporate ascent, and women's deployment of influence in ways that are gendered in feminine and masculine ways that matter. Besides these interactional and structural dynamics, how long and how people work together moves beyond surface-level, numerical representations of diversity (Harrison, Price, & Bell, 1998). By challenging why, where, and how demography should and could make a difference, meaningfulness of diversity and inclusion work from a vantage point of demography can open up structural opportunities for numerically underrepresented groups.

Finally, there is the moral argument that all workers should have opportunities to learn, display their competence, and ascend in their careers. Such opportunities benefit everyone—from individuals and communities through organizations, nations, and the global labor force. The argument goes like this: If provided resources that their socio-political-economic-cultural backgrounds have not routinely afforded, then marginalized group members can achieve better living standards, increased health and well-being, and recognition that their good work deserves. It is the right thing to do. The moral argument is akin to social justice or movements advocating for equal opportunity to health, education, well-being, justice, and opportunity. The moral case relies upon empathy, ethics of justice and care, and willingness to reallocate funds and material goods to under-resourced people. It may seem contradictory to organizational mandates toward profit, growth, sustainability, and competitiveness in today's neoliberal world (Tomlinson & Schwabenland, 2010). Diversity and inclusion work might be considered meaningful from the moral perspective when individuals recognize that their advantages in life multiply from the moment they were born into financially secure homes with adequate food, housing, education, safety, and attachments. These individuals may labor to use their privilege to benefit others.

Thus meaningfulness of diversity and inclusion work is often wrapped around three critical imperatives: business and economic, demographic, and moral. Indeed, many organizations incorporate ideals of "inclusion" in their discourses (Dobusch, Dobusch, & Muller-Seitz, 2019). For scholars and practitioners, the underlying premises that leaders can leverage diversity for strategic business objectives and outcomes (business case), for proportionally matching the population in which companies are located (demographic case), or for showcasing the greater good to which the organization is aligned (moral and social justice case; Corporate Social Responsibility) is alluring. Ideal cases are often complicated and used in diversity and inclusion discourses simultaneously. Therefore, those doing diversity and inclusion work can create identifications with one or more of these logics and with the organizations promoting participatory goals. Organizations' intentional strategies have led scrutiny of membership, adding incentives for recruiting difference, instituting legal measures and organizational policies, and routinizing practices to create more equitable workplaces and systems.

In sum, how diversity and inclusion are constructed as meaningful is dependent upon the goal of diversity and inclusion efforts. In turn, this goal affects how workers envision their efforts as meaningful and how efforts are instantiated in structures and interactions.

How Diversity and Inclusion Labor Is Constrained and Enabled

In this section, the nature of diversity and inclusion practices and agents is examined. Next, I argue that diversity and inclusion is a wicked problem for which conventional approaches would and should be ineffective.

First, for those who engage in paid and unpaid work in diversity and inclusion, the problems can seem unsurmountable, the traction of particular remedies can seem tenuous, the effects of efforts can do more harm than good, and the work itself can be exhausting because of intensive, even extreme, commitments (e.g., Kossek & Buzzanell, 2018; Romani, Holck, & Risberg, 2019). The nature of this work with its ups and downs can occur regardless of the individual's and collective's goals. Even where measureable progress has been made, side effects and unintended consequences lessen perceptions of success. For instance, deep gender conflicts, corporate discourses and routines, and everyday practices can replicate masculine organizing and ideal worker norms despite family-friendly policies and other efforts to increase and legitimize diversity and inclusion efforts (Martin, 1990). Well-intentioned efforts by human resource and diversity and inclusion experts can construct "others" as needing (and perhaps not deserving of) help without fully anticipating that these others might not necessarily fit the current hierarchical structure nor wish to do so (Romani et al., 2019; see also Acker, 2006). Black and brown bodies may need to perform and voice assimilation into the white hierarchy of academe or other organizations (Dar, 2018), without benefit of other organizational members' acknowledgment of their own responsibilities and roles to assist organizational newcomers (Allen, 2000; see also Sue et al., 2019). Scholarship is replete with strategies to adapt diversity and inclusion best practices (e.g., Dass & Parker, 1999), yet recommended changes in policy, leadership, and rules (Mitchneck, Smith, & Latimer, 2016) also require careful attention to interactions and organizational culture with few traditional measures of success.

Thus, from the perspective of those who labor on behalf of diversity and inclusion, the work may see few noticeable and seemingly sustainable gains, particularly if the work itself is relegated to human resource managers, chief diversity officers and staff, and directors of centers or initiatives for specific cultural groups (e.g., Center for Muslim Students; Networks or Societies for Women in Engineering). Framing diversity and inclusion from business, demographic, and/or moral lenses focuses attention on the costs of such work personally, organizationally, and societally. The costs can include the disheartening prospect that there seems to be little to no progress despite millions of dollars, time and energy, and well-constructed programs that logically should produce positive results. One reason for this relative lack of progress is because diversity and inclusion are entangled in webs of wicked problems, whose causes and effects are deeply embedded in inequality regimes (Acker, 2006), and whose effects and practices are not easily measured. Instead, framing diversity and inclusion as a wicked problem for which conventional approaches would and should be ineffective can lessen detrimental effects and enable workers to retain hope.

How Diversity and Inclusion as Meaningful Work Constitute a Design Challenge

This chapter positions diversity and inclusion as wicked problems for which the typical remedies are inadequate. This positioning enables scholars and practitioners to rethink diversity and inclusion efforts as naturally contradictory and messy rather than as rational and with singular solutions (e.g., to break the glass ceiling, increase numbers, Buzzanell 1995). Design provides the theoretical and practical underpinnings for a robust process of change, which requires attention to dialogue, images and identity, cultural humility, and deviation amplifying efforts. Design thinking is "a process for creative problem solving" that "starts with taking action and understanding the right questions. It's about embracing simple mindset shifts and tackling problems from a new direction" using empathy (understanding users' needs), ideation (generating ideas), experimentation (testing and prototyping) (IDEO, n.d.). HCD works with the users to generate (temporarily) solutions. Communication as Design (CaD) "happens when there is an intervention into some ongoing activity through the invention of techniques, devices, and procedures that aim to redesign interactivity and thus shape the possibilities for communication" (Aakhus, 2007, p. 112). In other words, CaD examines what those who shape communication do, or, put differently, what happens linguistically and interactively when people engage in conversation. Design thinking, HCD, and CaD overlap and interrelate as they focus on problems around products and services, what human users need, and how communication becomes possible, respectively. To make my argument, namely, that diversity and inclusion as meaningful work constitute a design challenge, I conceptualize wicked problems, then present reasons why diversity and inclusion are wicked problems.

Wicked problems are thorny issues, intractable problems with complex interdependencies such that efforts to solve one aspect create and/or surface other problems in the same and/or different forms (Rittel & Webber, 1973, 1974;

see also Camillus, 2008). Wicked problems have no easy or one-step solutions but are rife with deeply embedded contradictions, conflicts, and seemingly incompatible value propositions, often with incomplete information. Although presumably unique to a context, they often are not understood until a solution has been implemented and reveals the nature of the problem. As such, wicked problems are incredibly resistant to change. Resistance to change occurs because wicked problems and their manifestations, such as inequalities based on difference are embedded within the ideological scaffolding of societies and organizations, such that hypercompetitive and individualistic neoliberal systems prioritize profit regardless of stated social responsibilities and missions (Fyke & Buzzanell, 2013). Examples of wicked problems are many: poverty, climate change, unsustainable food systems, inadequate and unclean water, environmental destruction, and energy needs. These grand global challenges become visible in specific circumstances. Individuals and communities that suffer from poverty also have unsustainable food, water, health, and educational systems. Focusing on one aspect ignores the remaining manifestations of poverty but also does not get to the underlying causes of the conditions.

Second, there are multiple reasons as to why diversity and inclusion are wicked problems. Some of these issues center around understandings about who should and should not deserve treatment that some consider "special" or for which some consider others "undeserving." Such notions about competitiveness, individualism, privatization, and choice being the center of one's decision making and career considerations are part of neoliberal logics through which societal members discredit structural constraints on others' lives. In addition, people adhere to particular beliefs about themselves and others without even seeing what they are saying or doing.

To illustrate this point about people not seeing what they are saying or doing, some interview excerpts from people who would likely consider themselves well-intentioned might provide support (see also Sue et al., 2019). For instance, the following quote is an example of a male engineering student who verbally affirmed gender equality then began talking about an engineer who is a woman. For this quote, gender is the targeted source of difference and difficulty for this student. Other forms of difference—race, religion, disability, class, nationality, sexuality, able-bodiness, and so on—might be easily substituted for gender. He remarked: "... usually the criteria for women is a little lower than men, to help get more women into the field ..." (Arendt et al., 2014). From the same dataset, another male engineering student discussed recruitment of women into engineering. He argued that women should not be treated as "special." In other words, they should not need to be recruited into engineering: "Because, sure you can have a lot of people, but I think quality is more important that quantity. So if they're [women are] not interested, maybe they shouldn't be in it in the first place." In this case, the engineer denied any form of sexism or prejudice: "I'm all for gender neutrality."

These engineers used quality and commitment arguments to affirm their own and other men's rightful places in engineering, much as individuals call upon merit, meritocracy, and excellence claims and proofs that can bolster men's and diminish women's cases for recruitment, retention, and promotion (e.g., Seron, Silbey, Cech, & Rubineau, 2018). When meritocracy is invoked and promoted in an organizational culture, men paradoxically are preferred over equally qualified women (Castilla & Bernard, 2010) and men are given the benefit of the doubt with regard to positional criteria often making excuses for men who fall short of expectations but holding women to strict standards (van den Brink & Benschop, 2012). Thus, the meaningful work of diversity and inclusion is cultural and ideological, rather than rational and straightforward.

Furthermore, the contradictions evident in male engineering students' everyday talk are entangled with gendered, societal, occupational, and other tensions subsumed within difference and privilege dynamics:

> *… we have to embrace that there are less women in engineering and that's fine.* It's not to say that women can't be engineers or they're going to be inferior engineers; I just think we *need to be honest with them* and say "Hey, there are less of you guys, but you have all the opportunities in the world. There are *all kinds of programs for you.*"
>
> (Arendt et al., 2014, emphases added)

> That's kind of an interesting point just because like do they want to be treated equally or do they not want to be treated equally? That's the big thing I've always kind of struggled with because it seems like sometimes *they're always, you know, fighting for equal rights, but at the same time, I don't think they should have equal rights.* That's a personal thing, but I think that we should maybe *embrace that they are different,* you know?
>
> (Arendt et al., 2014, emphases added)

Their statements are not reliant on these men not being around women. They have mothers, sisters, cousins, and classmates who are women; they interact with bright and capable women daily. They simply do not see how their interests have been cultivated, or how they have gone to career development and skill building "special" programs their entire lives. To admit that they have benefited from such cultivation and investment by others means that they have not made their accomplishments by themselves. Admitting that others have helped them along the way could be perceived as diminishing their own individual talents and self-efficacy. In a competitive occupation with clearly delineated markers of success, these engineering students can (mostly) speak diversity talk but cannot seem to enact inclusion.

In short, diversity and inclusion are wicked problems. This stance moves away from a static view of meaningful work to a focus on the subtle ways in which meaningful work shifts and incorporates reflexivity and change. Instead, meaningfulness of diversity and inclusion work can be viewed as part of a "becoming" process of change (see Bryer, 2019). Becoming is mirrored in where, when, and how people are located and co-oriented, namely, in the *what*

that diversity and inclusion "becomes" and *how* this work becomes meaningful to people at different times.

The wicked problem of diversity and inclusion work requires processes that
are messy, contradictory, and oriented toward multiple iterations. Multiple iterations can then be viewed as a given, not as a failure. Such processes involve
design thinking and HCD (see Buzzanell, 2014, 2016, 2017), as well as CaD
(Aakhus, 2007) to orient toward prototype solutions, co-design with human
users, and rely upon communication as constitutive of realities.

Diversity and Inclusion through a Design Lens

Wicked problems like diversity and inclusion require solutions that address
their complicated nature. As a result, meaningful diversity and inclusion work
are best addressed using a design lens, specifically one situated within design
thinking, HCD, and CaD. Design thinking processes to derive solutions involve articulating problems, needs, and interests of potential users; developing
specifications; prototyping; critiquing and testing; and formulating solutions.
Design aims to gather sufficient data and engage in iterative sensemaking to
avoid design fixation (premature closure) and achieve sustainable solutions and
processes (Buzzanell & Zoltowski, 2014). HCD integrates diverse stakeholders, particularly acknowledged and potential users of solutions, into design
processes to ensure that the different iterations suit users' needs and interests
(Krippendorff, 2005; Zoltowski, Oakes, & Cardella, 2012). These stakeholders
would be those who want and resist solutions, those who seem to voice opposi-
tions and those who are often forgotten or neglected in change processes (e.g.,
Cooren, 2001; Waymer & Heath, 2007). Jackson and Aakhus (2014) note that
"situating a design enterprise within communication scholarship involves,
first, seeing theories as design languages that express the potential designabil-
ity of communication and that suggest principles for design" (p. 131).

Regardless of its variations, as Radcliffe and Fosmire (2014, see also Atman, Eris, McDonnell, Cardella, & Borgford-Parnell, 2014) assert, design is
a recursive activity that results in artifacts--physical or virtual, involving both
existing information and generation of new information and knowledge. They
maintain that design is both creative and disciplined. Design is done through
leaps of imagination, intuitive insight, and idea synthesis. But design is also
accomplished through careful attention to detail, knowledge of scientific principles, the ability to model complex systems, judgment, good understanding
of how things can be made, and the ability to work under severe time constraints, with incomplete information, and limited resources. These tensions
within the nature of design itself match the requirements for explicating and
constructing solutions for meaningful diversity and inclusion work.

Because HCD is grounded in human interaction and interests, it adds even
more complexity to design thinking. HCD is an ontological process in which
design is created and implemented **with** project partners and other "users"
for features that bear upon human health and well-being. As a result, HCD

requires empathy and reflection. In its ideal form and over time, empathy emerges from working directly with users (or project partners) and from considering both technical and socio-historical cultural aspects (Zoltowski et al., 2012). Cultural humility (aka critical empathy) is:

> This process begins by first *noticing* the outside, becoming aware of it and recognizing its value and its worth. This is emphatic awareness. In this process I notice that the other is "not me," and this awareness creates my *own* sense of otherness in the face of *their* otherness. In recognizing the subjectivity of the other I am also acknowledging the social constructedness of her existence.
>
> (Remke, 2006, p. 104)

This process makes both parties vulnerable by asking the reasons, historical-cultural understandings, and rich context as designers and researchers enter each other's worlds. It also makes all design team members vulnerable to mistakes, failures, and their own reflections on the entire design process that enable the final outcome to best fit users' interests even if only temporarily (Buzzanell & Long, 2016).

Although essential to successful HCD, empathy and care often are seen as incommensurate with the technical expertise for which engineers are trained and in which they focus for design considerations (Strobel, Hess, Pan, & Morris, 2013; Walther, Miller, & Socchaka, 2017). A primary consideration would be where and how might diversity and inclusion, as embodied by actual and potential users, be integrated into design processes such that designers develop the capacity for critical empathy and sustainable design (Surma-Aho, Björklund, & Hölttä-Otto, 2018; Zoltowski et al., 2012). A primary contention of this essay, then, is that empathy, reflexivity, diversity, and inclusion are essential to HCD, and in turn, HCD is needed to make meaningful diversity and inclusion in organizational life. A contention that follows, then, is that design in communication can build effective campaigns for change, manage conflicts, foster collaboration and deliberation, and articulate and assess everyday practices to achieve societal goals (see Jackson & Aakhus, 2014; see also Aakhus & Harrison, 2016; Aakhus & Jackson, 2005).

Communication Practices for the Design of Meaningful Diversity and Inclusion Work

The central arguments are that the meaningfulness of diversity and inclusion is linked to particular goals, but that the work itself is entangled in and confounded by wicked problems for which there are no easy solutions. These wicked problems indicate that the issues are ideological and contradictory rather than rational. They require confronting identity characteristics and societal structures that many people are unwilling to accept, let alone remedy. As a result, diversity and inclusion cannot be achieved with a problem-solution orientation. Instead, diversity and inclusion require expanded HCD processes that incorporate (a) paradox and reflexivity and (b) an ontological lens.

Paradox and Reflexivity

HCD begins with just trying to figure out what the problem is and who the users of the design are. Often the stated problems are not what the actual design addresses. Often the stated problems are too specific (fix, build, or create something) or too broad (increase diversity and inclusion). For instance, in our engineering design team working on water, energy, education, and sanitation in two rural villages in Ghana (see Buzzanell, 2014, 2016), the original problem, namely, that a well pump needed to be fixed, was not really the main concern. It was, however, a symptom of the underlying issues. Instead, our team learned that there were many cultural, gendered, and political issues that had to be considered in our designs. These issues called into question tacit assumptions that designers took for granted as they entered into the design space physically, discursively, and through online capabilities. These tacit assumptions became phrased as questions: why would people drink and cook with unsanitary groundwater? Why would villagers take essential parts of the water pump knowing that dismantling the equipment would harm themselves and others? Why wouldn't villagers use mosquito nets and other protections knowing that malaria, dengue fever, and Zika are mosquito-borne diseases? Why was the single-room classroom empty when elders professed desires for children's education and sent older children to other areas for education? Why would villagers continue to use an open-latrine trench for human waste that overflowed when it rained? Why were only men talking during the initial data gathering and site visit(s) despite the much greater numbers of women in public gatherings? Such questions exposed paradoxes that seem to create seemingly impossible choices linked to ironic and inconsistent outcomes (see also related processes of contradiction, irony, dialectics, and tensions; Putnam, Fairhurst, & Banghart, 2016). For our discovery, research, specifications, and prototyping phases, what is it that has been seemingly functional from villagers' perspectives that we could analyze, translate or replicate, and fold into our designs (i.e., what could provide starting points for local deviating amplifying loops in systems of change, see Buzzanell, Meisenbach, & Remke, 2008)?

Some of the questions above and the paradoxes embedded within behaviors and relationships were based on daily needs and timeworn routines (water, income, tradition, workarounds when educational and health services were unavailable). They resulted in both desired and unintended detrimental consequences. Moreover, our very design processes posed questions rooted in both present and past that formed paradoxical spaces. Why would these villagers even consider working with us (even though we had approvals from the Ghanaian ministries and tribal chiefs)? What might design interventions mean for the traditional ways of interacting, resolving conflicts, and allocating resources? How did it make sense for the villagers and for us (as designers and as mostly white US-born individuals) to work in a postcolonial/colonizing space where some of the most horrific slavery episodes happened at the "slave castles" in nearby Cape Coast? How might we best honor the dignity of the villagers and the integrity and sustainability of our designs? How would we as designers even make a dent in all the different needs and interests that the villagers brought to us as part of our discovery and problem specifications phases? If we could not "solve the problem," then have we failed?

The cultural, gendered, and political considerations increased not simply in number but in complexity and nuance. For example, some issues included who had access to water, when, and where. One village elder held the pump key and doled out pump water at specific times. Otherwise, village members used the unsanitary groundwater through which animals walked and insects alighted. On the one hand this elder restricted access to relatively (albeit untested) clean pump water; on the other hand, this elder was mandated to allot water so all could have some when well water was available. Other considerations involved reasons why pump mechanisms might have been stolen (i.e., copper was valuable and could be resold), and why women and young children made up most of the population (i.e., there was little work for adults and no regular education and medical care for children because teachers and health care providers would not stay in villages where there was no safe water, no electricity or cell phone access, no showers or use of toilets, no roads enabling easy access to the villages, and extreme poverty). At every encounter during the design process, understandings shifted as designers learned more about human interactions in the village, the constraints experienced by villagers on a daily basis, and the opportunities that they had and created given their resources.

As our team moved through design thinking phases from problem and specifications development through solutions, our designers unearthed many social and ethical considerations that impacted what we and the villagers co-designed, what materials were used, and how sustainable these efforts would be. As implied by HCD, the progression from technical and user-centered design to socio-technical and user-generated design involved much reflection about assumptions, relationships, and potential and unintended consequences and paradoxes of our activities. This example of the Ghanaian villages and HCD experiences is analogous to diversity and inclusion work in higher education and in other contexts. For instance, members of underrepresented groups might not have confidence in or access those entrusted with their health care, education, careers, and safety given documented accounts and media depictions where they were harmed (e.g., Tuskagee Syphilis Study; high school guidance counselors who track students into vocational paths and the military despite abilities and talents for professional careers; police who routinely stop and physically injure or kill black men and women for "traffic violations" or simply for being in the wrong place at the wrong time; brown people and refugees who are detained at national borders or deported because they are not in preferred classifications for visas). Members of majority groups may see their involvement in social justice programs as curtailing their own opportunities. Why would anyone create and participate in train- ing and/or programs, networking sessions, or other interventions when the problems seem so vast, the consequences so contradictory, and the observable progress so little? For diversity and inclusion, design dynamics are tensional and riddled with contradictions that surface on different levels ranging from individual beliefs that one acts in inclusionary and merit-based ways through the neoliberal dynamics in which organizations, including US institutions of higher education, are embedded. Diversity and inclusion may be perceived as contributing indirectly or actually antithetical to the overarching purposes (contributions to metrics that increase competitiveness, rankings of excel- lence, profit, and growth).

An Ontological Lens

As implied in the last section, design is accomplished through being and do- ing. Through design, individuals and collectivities delve into the nature of things and how other people and non-human agents, such as the village well, racial and national make up of stakeholders, and other material conditions, act upon each other (e.g., Tolbert, Buzzanell, Zoltowski, Cummings, & Car- della, 2016). Ideally in HCD there is no fixed relationship between design recipients and design creators. Instead, different stakeholders co-construct their understandings and their possibilities for solutions through interactions in which some elements become more or less salient based on design phase and based on greater understandings of the complexities surrounding change.

Thus, the meaningfulness of diversity and inclusion work to make deep- seated change in ideological and institutional structures can only come about when people engage in HCD processes. Such processes encourage them to ad- mit what they do not know, question what they think they know, challenge the nature of their worlds, and live with tensions about identity and expertise. At the core is the shift in the nature of things to a focus on what beings (designers, users, and other stakeholders) must consider non-negotiable responsibilities within interactions and structures created through practice. This shift creates the need to evaluate ontological hierarchies that link being and interpretation and that often replicate Western dualisms and epistemic closure (e.g., Other- ing difference and disavowing responsibilities, Borgerson, 2001).

For diversity issues, as mentioned earlier, representation can seem fairly simple: increase numbers with the contested rationale that critical mass and ascent of Others into occupations or the C-Suite leads to change in structural inequalities (e.g., see Kossek & Buzzanell, 2018; see also Buzzanell, 1995). However, for inclusion, practices and power struggles are much more difficult. This work basically asks everyone to disrupt and overturn their systems of being, meaning, and doing that shape and embody their most fundamental beliefs and values. Inclusion cannot be accomplished overnight, nor can stan- dardized metrics account for change based on singular or even multiple inter- ventions. Wicked problems are neither time-bound nor linear. As one possible solution or prototype is developed, the understanding of the problem and the needed criteria for solutions change. These points mean that design for meaningful diversity and inclusion work has no end, cannot be "fixed," and cannot be considered a "problem." But this design can be charted through attention to linguistic and interactional shifts in particular cultures.

For the rural Ghanaian designers, we wrote reflections after each encounter, shared our understandings, continuously asked questions, and sought to provide resources to indicate that we knew that villagers' time and expertise were valuable. These ongoing spirals of individual and shared reflections were coupled with ongoing consultations with an advisory board of civil engineers, anthropologists, specialists (academic and non-academic) in difference and advocacy, and others.

However, there are more insidious threats to the work of diversity and inclusion and its meaningfulness. With meaningful work, especially when framed as a calling, the "dark" side can involve different processes and outcomes. Some of these potentially detrimental features can include willingness to accept little to no pay and underemployment in terms of skill and education utilization; discouragement or feeling as though there is no progress and that the problem will never go away; inability to take a break or refrain from such work even temporarily; and social justice and/or "racial battle fatigue" (a chronic state of psychological, physiological, and emotional/behavioral distress, Smith, Hung, & Franklin, 2011, pp. 68–69; see also Allan et al., 2018; Bailey et al., 2018; Berkelaar & Buzzanell, 2015). In the case of the Ghanaian water-energy-education-sanitation team, the issues and complexities often seemed overwhelming to the point that there were times when it was difficult to figure out where to begin. However, design assists by providing a frame for recognizing that diversity and inclusion work is ongoing and that failure (or almost imperceptible moves forward) is part of the process.

Design also means that everyone is part of the process. Involving everyone requires understanding how potential users in specific locales grapple with how they understand, implement, and redesign their discursive and material practices for cultural change that then can become transferrable to other communities or organizational units through design processes. In this endeavor, Aakhus' (2007) second strategy in CaD studies is essential because it focuses on "how forms of communication that were once difficult, impossible, or unimagined came to be" (p. 116). Meaningful diversity and inclusion work necessitates co-design that pull people through iterative processes and prototypes toward seemingly unimagined futures.

Closing

In closing, the nature of diversity and inclusion work challenges its meaningfulness and contributions to goals. Rather than framing diversity and inclusion as a problem that can be solved, framing diversity and inclusion as wicked problems requiring messy, tensional, and iterative processes of doing, being, and becoming known as design can help construct and sustain efforts. Meaningfulness and meanings of diversity and inclusion work shift in contradictory ways whereby people admit and learn from their inevitable mistakes and develop expertise in identifying and challenging everyday privilege and marginalization through design. Design enables diversity and inclusion work to continue with hope. In design "failure" equals prototypes not ready for full implementation, and sustainability is associated with time frames that are indeterminate. Thus, the wicked problems of diversity and inclusion evident in the incredibly complex and entangled social problems that are so difficult to solve can be changed through design.

References

Aakhus, M. (2007). Communication as design. *Communication Monographs, 74*, 112–117. doi:10.1080/03637750701196383

Aakhus, M., & Harrison, T. (2016). Design thinking about communication in health system innovation. In T. Harrison, & E. Williams (Eds.), *Organizations, health, and communication* (pp. 402–419). New York, NY: Routledge.

Aakhus, M., & Jackson, S. (2005). Technology, interaction, and design. In K. Fitch, & R. Sanders (Eds.), *Handbook of language and social interaction* (pp. 411–436). Mahwah, NJ: LEA.

Acker, J. (2006). Inequality regimes: Gender, class, and race in organizations. *Gender & Society, 20*, 441–464. doi:10.1177/0891243206289499

Allan, B. A., Batz-Barbarich, C., Sterling, H., & Tay, L. (2018). Outcomes of meaningful work: A meta-analysis. *Journal of Management Studies, 56*, 500–528. doi:10.1111/joms.12406

Allan, B. A., Rolniak, J. R., & Bouchard, L. (2018, online). Underemployment and well-being: Exploring the dark side of meaningful work. *Journal of Career Development.* doi:10.1177/0894845318819861

Allen, B. J. (2000). "Learning the ropes": A black feminist standpoint analysis. In P. M. Buzzanell (Ed.), *Rethinking organizational and managerial communication from feminist perspectives* (pp. 177–208). Thousand Oaks, CA: Sage.

Arendt, C., Dohrman, R., Buzzanell, P. M., Rajan, P., O'Connor, E., Litera, N., & Armstrong, C. (2014, November). *Discourses of elitism and exclusion: Relating engineering self-efficacy and subtle sexism.* Paper presented to the National Communication Association, Chicago, IL.

Atman, C., Eris, O., McDonnell, J., Cardella, M., & Borgford-Parnell, J. (2014). Engineering design education. In A. Johri, & B. Olds (Eds.), *Cambridge handbook of engineering education research* (pp. 201–226). Cambridge, UK: Cambridge University Press.

Bailey, C., Lips-Wiersma, M., Madden, A., Yeoman, R., Thompson, M., & Chalofsky, N. (2018). The five paradoxes of meaningful work: Introduction to the special issue "Meaningful Work: Prospects for the 21st Century." *Journal of Management Studies.* doi:10.1111/joms.12422

Barrett, A., & Dailey, S. (2018). A new normal? Competing national cultural discourses and workers' constructions of identity and meaningful work in Norway. *Communication Monographs, 85*, 284–307. doi:10.1080/03637751.2017.1372587

Baumeister, R., Vohs, K., Aaker, J., & Garbinsky, E. (2013). Some key differences between a happy life and a meaningful life. *The Journal of Positive Psychology, 8*, 505–516. doi:10.1080/17439760.2013.830764

Berkelaar, B., & Buzzanell, P. M. (2015). Bait and switch or double-edged sword? The (sometimes) failed promises of calling. *Human Relations, 68*, 157–178. doi:10.1177/0018726714526265

Bernstein, P. (1997). *American work values: Their origin and development.* Albany, NY: SUNY Press.

Blair-Loy, M., & Cech, E. (2017, March). Demands and devotion: Cultural meanings of work and overload among women researchers and professionals in science and technology industries. *Sociological Forum, 32*, 5–27. doi:10.1111/socf.12315

Borgerson, J. (2001). Feminist ethical ontology: Contesting "the bare givenness of intersubjectivity." *Feminist Theory, 2*, 173–187. doi:10.1177/14647000122229460

Bransberger, P. (2018, July 24). Demographics, high school graduates & higher education demand. *Knocking at the college door.* Available through the Western Interstate Commission for Higher Education at www.knocking.wiche.edu

Bryer, A. (2019). Making organizations more inclusive: The work of belonging. *Organization Studies.* doi:10.1177/0170840618814576

Bunderson, J., & Thompson, J. (2009). The call of the wild: Zookeepers, callings, and the double-edged sword of deeply meaningful work. *Administrative Science Quarterly, 54*, 32–57. doi:10.2189/asqu.2009.54.1.32

Buzzanell, P. M. (1994). Gaining a voice: Feminist organizational communication theorizing. *Management Communication Quarterly, 7*, 339–383. doi:10.1177/0893318994007004001

Buzzanell, P. M. (1995). Reframing the glass ceiling as a socially constructed process: Implications for understanding and change. *Communication Monographs, 62*, 327–354. doi:10.1080/03637759509376366

Buzzanell, P. M. (2014). Reflections on global engineering design and intercultural competence: The Case of Ghana. In X. Dai, & G. M. Chen (Eds.), *Intercultural communication competence: Conceptualization and its development in contexts and interactions* (pp. 315–334). Newcastle upon Tyne: Cambridge Scholars Publishing.

Buzzanell, P. M. (2016, September). *Beyond prejudices and stereotyping of other cultures: Constituting interventions for inclusion through design thinking.* Keynote address to the I-Come'16: International Communication Regional Conference in Malaysia on "Exploring Communication: Beyond nation cultural adaptation, images and identity." Kuala Lumpur, Malaysia.

Buzzanell, P. M. (2017). Constituting intercultural harmony by design thinking: Conflict management in, for, and about diversity and inclusion work. In X. Dai, & G. M. Chen (Eds.), *Conflict management and intercultural harmony* (pp. 66–84). New York, NY: Routledge.

Buzzanell, P. M., & Long, Z. (2016). Learning expertise in engineering design work: Creating space for experts to make mistakes. In J. Treem, & P. Leonardi (Eds.), *Communication, expertise, and organizing* (pp. 168–188). Oxford, UK: Oxford University Press.

Buzzanell, P. M., Meisenbach, R., & Remke, R. (2008). Women, leadership, and dissent. In S. Banks (Ed.), *Dissent and the failure of leadership* (pp. 119–134). Northampton, MA: Edward Elgar Publishing Inc.

Buzzanell, P. M., & Zoltowski, C. (2014). Get your message across: The art of gathering and sharing information. In D. Radcliffe, & M. Fosmire (Eds.), *Integrating information into engineering design* (pp. 159–170). West Lafayette, IN: Purdue University Press.

Camillus, J. C. (2008). Strategy as a wicked problem. *Harvard Business Review, 86,* 99–106.

Carton, A. (2018). "I'm not mopping the floors, I'm putting a man on the moon": How NASA leaders enhanced the meaningfulness of work by changing the meaning of work. *Administrative Science Quarterly, 63,* 323–369. doi:10.1177/0001839217713748

Castilla, E., & Benard, S. (2010). The paradox of meritocracy in organizations. *Administrative Science Quarterly, 55,* 543–676. doi:10.2189/asqu.2010.55.4.543

Cheney, G., Zorn, T., Planalp, S., & Lair, D. (2008). Meaningful work and personal/social well-being organizational communication engages the meanings of work. *Annals of the International Communication Association, 32,* 137–185. doi:10.1080/23808985.2008.11679077

Ciulla, J. (2000). *The working life: The promise and betrayal of modern work.* New York, NY: Crown Publishing Group.

Cooren, F. (2001). Translation and articulation in the organization of coalitions: The Great Whale River case. *Communication Theory, 11,* 178–200. doi:10.1111/j.1468-2885.2001.tb00238.x

Dar, S. (2018). The masque of Blackness: Or, performing assimilation in the white academe. *Organization, 26,* 432–446. doi:10.1177/1350508418805280

Dass, P., & Parker, B. (1999). Strategies for managing human resource diversity: From resistance to learning. *Academy of Management Perspectives, 13,* 68–80. Retrieved from http://www.jstor.org/stable/4165541

Dobusch, L., Dobusch, L., & Muller-Seitz, G. (2019). Closing for the benefit of openness: The case of Wikimedia's open strategy process. *Organization Studies, 40,* 343–370. doi:10.1177/0170840617736930

Fayard, A. L. (2019, online). Notes on the meaning of work: Labor, work, and action in the 21st Century. *Journal of Management Inquiry.* doi:10.1177/1056492619841705

Florian, M., Costas, J., & Kärreman, D. (2018). Struggling with meaningfulness when context shifts: Volunteer work in a German refugee shelter. *Journal of Management Studies.* doi:10.1111/joms.12410

Fyke, J. P., & Buzzanell, P. M. (2013). The ethics of conscious capitalism: Wicked problems in leading change and changing leaders. *Human Relations, 66,* 1619–1643. doi:10.1177/0018726713485306

Gabor, E. (2013). "Tuning" the body of the classical musician: An embodied approach to vocational anticipatory socialization. *Qualitative Research in Organizations and Management: An International Journal, 8,* 206–223. doi:10.1108/QROM-05-2012-1068

Gardner, H., Csikszentmihalyi, M., & Damon, W. (2001). *Doing good work: When excellence and ethics meet.* New York, NY: Basic Books.

Harrison, D., Price, K., & Bell, M. (1998). Beyond relational demography: Time and the effects of surface-and deep-level diversity on work group cohesion. *Academy of Management Journal, 41,* 96–107. doi:10.5465/256901

Herring, C. (2009). Does diversity pay?: Race, gender, and the business case for diversity. *American Sociological Review, 74,* 208–224. doi:10.1177/000312240907400203

IDEO. (n.d.). *What is design thinking?* Retrieved from https://www.ideou.com/blogs/inspiration/what-is-design-thinking

Jackson, S., & Aakhus, M. (2014). Becoming more reflective about the role of design in communication. *Journal of Applied Communication Research, 42,* 125–134. doi:10-1080/00909882.2014.882009

Krippendorff, K. (2005). *The semantic turn: A new foundation for design.* Boca Raton, FL: CRC Press.

Kossek, E., & Buzzanell, P. M. (2018). Women's career equality and leadership in organizations: Creating an evidence-based positive change. *Human Resource Management, 57,* 813–822. doi:10.1002/hrm.21936

Lair, D., Shenoy, S., McClellan, J., & McGuire, T. (2008). The politics of meaning/ful work: Navigating the tensions of narcissism and condescension while finding meaning in work. *Management Communication Quarterly, 22,* 172–180. doi:10.1177/0893318908318263

Lips-Wiersma, M. & Wright, S. (2012). Measuring the meaning of meaningful work: Development and validation of the Comprehensive Meaningful Work Scale (CMWS). *Group and Organization Management, 37,* 655–685.

Long, Z. (2016). A Feminist ventriloquial analysis of *hao gongzuo* ("good work"): Politicizing Chinese Post-1980s women's meanings of work. *Women's Studies in Communication, 39,* 422–441. doi:10.1080/07491409.2016.1224991

Long, Z., Buzzanell, P. M., & Kuang, K. (2016). Positioning work amid discontinuities and continuities: Chinese Post80s workers' dialogical constructions of meanings of work. *Management Communication Quarterly, 30,* 532–556. doi:10.1177/0893318916636237

Martin, J. (1990). Deconstructing organizational taboos: The suppression of gender conflict in organizations. *Organization Science, 1,* 339–359. doi:10.1287/orsc.1.4.339

Mitchneck, B., Smith, J., & Latimer, M. (2016). A recipe for change: Creating a more inclusive academy. *Science, 352*(6282), 148–149. doi:10.1126/science.aad8493

Mitra, R., & Buzzanell, P. M. (2017). Communicative tensions of meaningful work: The case of sustainability practitioners. *Human Relations, 70,* 594–616. doi:10.1177/0018726716663288

Moloney, M., Brown, R., Ciciurkaite, G., & Foley, S. (2018). "Going the extra mile": Disclosure, accommodation, and stigma management among working women with disabilities. *Deviant Behavior,* 1–15. doi:10.1080/01639625.2018.1445445

Putnam, L. L., Fairhurst, G., & Banghart, S. (2016). Contradictions, dialectics, and paradoxes in organizations: A constitutive approach. *Academy of Management Annals, 10,* 65–172. doi:10.5465/19416520.2016.1162421

Radcliffe, D., & Fosmire, M. (Eds.). (2014). *Integrating information into engineering design.* West Lafayette, IN: Purdue University Press.

Reagans, R., & Zuckerman, E. (2001). Networks, diversity, and productivity: The social capital of corporate R&D teams. *Organization Science, 12,* 502–517. doi:10.1287/orsc.12.4.502.10637

Remke, R. V. (2006). *(Ir)Rationalities at work: The logics, heart, and soul of Head Start.* Unpublished doctoral dissertation, Purdue University, W. Lafayette, IN.

Rittel, H., & Webber, M. (1973). Dilemmas in a general theory of planning. *Policy Sciences, 4,* 155–169. doi:10.1007/BF01405730

Rittel, H., & Webber, M. (1974). Wicked problems. *Man-Made Futures, 26,* 272–280.

Romani, L., Holck, L., & Risberg, A. (2019). Benevolent discrimination: Explaining how human resources professionals can be blind to the harm of diversity initiatives. *Organization, 26,* 371–390. doi:10.1177/1350508418812585

Schiebinger, L., & Schraudner, M. (2011). Interdisciplinary approaches to achieving gendered innovations in science, medicine, and engineering. *Interdisciplinary Science Reviews, 36,* 154–167. doi:10.1179/030801811X13013181961518

Seron, C., Silbey, S., Cech, E., & Rubineau, B. (2018). "I am not a feminist, but…": Hegemony of a meritocratic ideology and the limits of critique among women in engineering. *Work and Occupations, 45*, 131–167. doi:10.1177/0730888418759774

Shenoy-Packer, S., & Buzzanell, P. M. (2013). Meanings of work among Hindu Indian women: Contextualizing meaningfulness and materialities of work through dharma and karma. *Journal of Communication & Religion, 36*, 149–172.

Smith, W., Hung, M., & Franklin, J. (2011). Racial battle fatigue and the miseducation of Black men: Microaggressions, societal problems and environmental stress. *The Journal of Negro Education, 80*, 63–82. Retrieved from https://www.jstor.org/stable/41341106

Strobel, J., Hess, J., Pan, R., & Morris, C. (2013). Empathy and care within engineering: Qualitative perspectives from engineering faculty and practicing engineers. *Engineering Studies, 5*, 137–159. doi:10.1080/19378629.2013.814136

Strum, S. (2007). The pivotal role of organizational catalysts. In A. Stewart, J. Malley, & D. LaVaque-Manty (Eds.), *Transforming science and engineering: Advancing academic women* (pp. 262–280). Ann Arbor: University of Michigan Press.

Sue, D. W., Alsaidi, S., Awad, M., Glaeser, E., Calle, C., & Mendez, N. (2019). Disarming racial microaggressions: Microintervention strategies for targets, white allies, and bystanders. *American Psychologist, 74*, 128–142. doi:10.1037/amp0000296

Surma-Aho, A., Björklund, T., & Höltta-Otto, K. (2018, August). An analysis of designer empathy in the early phases of design projects. *DS 91: Proceedings of NordDesign 2018*. Linköping, Sweden.

Tolbert, D., Buzzanell, P. M., Zoltowski, C., Cummings, A., & Cardella, M. (2016). Giving and responding to feedback through visualizations in design critiques. *Co-Design: International Journal of CoCreation in Design and the Arts, 12*, 26–38. doi:10.1080/15710882.2015.1135244

Tomlinson, F., & Schwabenland, C. (2010). Reconciling competing discourses of diversity? The UK non-profit sector between social justice and the business case. *Organization, 17*, 101–121. doi:10.1177/1350508409350237

Van den Brink, M., & Benschop, Y. (2012). Gender practices in the construction of academic excellence: Sheep with five legs. *Organization, 19*, 507–524. doi:10.1177/1350508411414293

Walther, J., Miller, S., & Sochacka, N. (2017). A model of empathy in engineering as a core skill, practice orientation, and professional way of being. *Journal of Engineering Education, 106*, 123–148. doi:10.1002/jee.2015

Waymer, D., & Heath, R. (2007). Emergent agents: The forgotten publics in crisis communication and issues management research. *Journal of Applied Communication Research, 35*, 88–108. doi:10.1080/00909880601065730

Wilson-Kovacs, D., Ryan, M. K., Haslam, S. A., & Rabinovich, A. (2008). 'Just because you can get a wheelchair in the building doesn't necessarily mean that you can still participate': Barriers to the career advancement of disabled professionals. *Disability & Society, 23*, 705–717. doi:10.1080/09687590802469198

Wolf, S. (2010). *Meaning in life and why it matters*. Princeton, NJ: Princeton University Press.

Zoltowski, C., Oakes, W., & Cardella, M. (2012). Students' ways of experiencing human-centered design. *Journal of Engineering Education, 101*, 28–59. doi:10.1002/j.2168-9830.2012.tb00040.x

13 #CommSoWEIRD

The Question of Sample
Representativeness
in Interpersonal
Communication Research

Walid A. Afifi and Monica Cornejo

There has long been criticism across social scientific disciplines regarding the unrepresentativeness of the samples and related data upon which disciplinary knowledge bases have been built. In the past decade, that conversation has been aided by the devotion of a substantial portion of an issue in *Behavioral and Brain Sciences* on this question. There, Henrich, Heine, and Norenzayan (2010) argued that knowledge within the social sciences has been almost exclusively tied to samples that come from Western, Educated, Industrialized, Rich, and Democratic (WEIRD) societies. The conversation about disciplinary inclusivity and diversity, including sample representativeness, within the discipline of Communication has also had a long history (see e.g., Shuter, 1976) and renewed fervor (e.g., Soliz & Phillips, 2018). As part of an effort to contribute to that discussion, this chapter offers a window into the level of sample representativeness within Interpersonal Communication research, as reflected by manuscripts published in several Communication journals during the past five years (2013–2018). A brief review of the literature tied to the question of sample diversity in the social sciences, generally, and the Communication discipline, specifically, helps contextualize the conversation to which we hope to contribute.

Sample Representativeness in the Disciplines of Psychology and Communication

A central commitment of the social scientific method is to make sure that the sample is inclusive of the range of people to which the scientists want their findings to generalize. This notion is captured through the concept of sample representativeness (e.g., Cohen & Nagel, 1934). It is also rooted in discussions of inclusion criteria. In medical research, clarity about inclusion (and exclusion) criteria is critical to the credibility of any design (e.g., Velasco, 2010). For example, results from a clinical trial can only speak to the effects of the tested procedure or drug (i.e., intervention) on populations that were among those included in the sample of trial participants. Of course, the same logic relates to the social sciences: the results of an investigation (in some cases, an intervention) only apply to populations represented in the study sample. Even with the strongest scientific designs—ones able to address most or all concerns with internal and external validity—the ability to make generalizable claims about behavior ultimately rests on the representativeness of the sample. Sample representativeness (and by extension, inclusiveness) is a scientific axiology. Failing to have a sample that fairly represents the population to which the researcher wishes to generalize violates a central tenant of the scientific method (Davern, 2008).

Unfortunately, budding social scientists learn early on that this criterion, while taught as an essential part of science and the related production of knowledge, is summarily ignored by the vast majority of published social scientists. For example, Arnett (2008) found that 96% of all participants in studies published in six leading Psychology journals (from 2003 to 2007) lived in Western Industrialized countries and the vast majority of samples included only college students. As Henrich et al. (2010) note, based on Arnett's data, "a randomly selected American undergraduate is more than 4,000 times more likely to be a research participant than is a randomly selected person from outside of the West" (p. 63). In a follow-up analysis, Rad, Martingano, and Ginges (2018) examined the samples found in *Psychological Science* in both 2014 and 2017 and concluded that little has changed since publication of Arnett's piece. For example, they found that "almost 85% of the world population comprises less than 7% of samples" in the 2017 issues they coded (p. 11043). Indeed, the evidence shows that the bulk of social scientific "knowledge" about human behavior is formed from samples that fail to meet a criterion essential for validity: sample representativeness.

Communication scholars have long critiqued the field for a lack of representativeness in its research. As early as 1968, the Speech Association of America's (now National Communication Association) ad hoc committee on social relevance wrote a "Manifesto to the Speech Profession," that started with a question: "Are we a field aimed only at the perpetuation of white, middle class standards and concepts …?" (see Davis, 1995). Eight years later, Shuter (1976) criticized the area of small group communication for being almost exclusively about "white, middle-class American subjects" (p. 5). In the 1980s, Putnam (1982) called for a "'shake-up' in communication research" (p. 7) to be more representative of women's experiences. In the 1990s, Hecht, Ribeau, and Sedano (1990) noted "inherent cultural biases" (p. 32) in communication research, and Allen (1995) argued that "scholars have used knowledge about one group (white males) to generalize to all groups" (p. 145). She continued by suggesting that the literature reflects a situation in which "the dominant group is accepted as the reference group" (p. 145). At approximately the same time, Parker and ogilvie (1996) critiqued the dominance of the white male voice in the literature on leadership, offered an alternative theoretical approach which addressed the African-American leadership experience, and called for additional research that "detail[ed] the reality of African-American women being subjected to the simultaneous oppressions of racism and sexism"

(p. 207; see also Parker, 2001). These critiques have continued. Hendrix (2005) penned a powerful essay that identified the ways in which disciplinary gate-keepers contribute to the muting of race-related research by scholars of color in Communication, and Hendrix and Wilson's (2014) analysis of articles appearing in *Communication Education* over a 13-year span (2000–2013) led to the conclusion that "typical publications assume white classrooms and white professors" (p. 406). In a similar vein, Orbe and Allen's (2008) analysis of articles published in the *Journal of Applied Communication Research* and studying "race" over a 30-year period (1973–2005) revealed that the samples were "predominantly White" (p. 203) and that even the literature on race is "best described as White scholarship" (p. 205).

Sample Representativeness in Interpersonal Communication

Although an updated, broad-based content analysis that spoke to the question of sample representativeness across the entire field of Communication is needed, this chapter takes on that question for the sub-area of Interpersonal Communication. Why restrict the analysis to a sub-area? Because we believe that each sub-area of the discipline may be characterized by different degrees of sample representativeness, based partly on different levels of internationalization and historical commitments to community engaged knowledge, and an analysis that investigates this question across the entire discipline is beyond the scope of this chapter. Why this sub-area? Because it is among the largest and most impactful areas of study in the discipline of Communication (as judged by division membership in the Interpersonal Communication divisions of the discipline's associations, and the frequency of its scholars among the discipline's Distinguished Scholars and Fellows list), and it is an area in which calls for greater inclusivity have been made for decades.

Indeed, Interpersonal Communication scholars have long been identifying the need for greater inclusivity and diversity in the samples studied. For example, Hecht and Ribeau (1984) wrote that "America's changing demographic profile represents a unique challenge: to make interpersonal communication theory and definitions of communicative effectiveness reflect ethnic diversity" (p. 136) and Lannamann (1991), in a piece titled "Interpersonal communication as ideological practice" cautioned that "the discipline is at risk of reifying what are essentially cultural forms of thought and treating them as if they represent natural facts" (p. 187). Relatedly, Houston (2002) did a comprehensive historical review of the small number of studies addressing African-Americans' interpersonal communication patterns and concluded that "communication scholars have created the impression that the masses of African Americans are preoccupied with how to talk and relate to White people and have inadvertently centered Whiteness in African American interpersonal scholarship" (p. 37). More recently, Davis (in press), echoing earlier critiques, argued that white American experiences represent that epicenter of interpersonal communication research, even in cases where the role of culture is examined. Specifically, she noted that "the few studies focused on race or ethnicity situate whiteness as the normal and natural way of being at the onset of the study" (Davis, in press, p. 30), and Chevrette (2013) critiqued the problem with white-centric knowledge within relational communication research, encouraging scholars to "[shift] focus to populations frequently omitted from dominant conceptions of relationships and families" (p. 184).

Despite these analyses and calls for demographic diversity within samples, no content analysis of the samples within the interpersonal communication, writ large, has been conducted, to our knowledge. The goal of this analysis is to offer empirical insight into the level of diversity (or lack thereof) in the samples currently being used to create knowledge within the interpersonal communication domain. Specifically, we forward the following research question:

RQ: What are the characteristics of the samples used in interpersonal communication studies published in communication journals in the past six years (2013–2018)?

Method

A set of criteria was used to narrow the population of journals to analyze. The first criterion was that the journal be affiliated with either the National Communication Association or the International Communication Association. That criterion ensured that the analysis included only journals that were under the full purview of communication scholars (e.g., in terms of editorships, editorial boards), and thus most representative of the research conducted by those in the discipline. While that criterion eliminated journals that often publish interpersonal communication research (e.g., *Journal of Social and Personal Research, Communication Research*), we felt that it was the appropriate decision for this initial analysis. The second criterion for journal selection was that they publish empirical pieces (e.g., eliminating *Quarterly Journal of Speech*). These criteria led to the inclusion of the following journals: *Communication Monographs* (CM), *Human Communication Research* (HCR), *Journal of Communication* (JOC), *Journal of Applied Communication Research* (JACR), the *Journal of International and Intercultural Research* (JIIR), *Communication and Cultural Studies* (CCS), and *Communication, Culture, and Critique* (CCC). Given our goal, we felt it important to be intentional in the inclusion of journals that might be especially attentive to cultural diversity. As a result, we added two journals: the *Howard Journal of Communication* (Howard) and the *Asian Journal of Communication* (AJC), resulting in a total of nine journals. All manuscripts published in these journals between 2013 and 2018, inclusive of online-first manuscripts appearing by June 2018, were coded. *Communication and Cultural Studies* did not publish any empirical interpersonal communication manuscripts during the time period in question and was dropped from the analyses, leaving us with eight journals in the analyses. Only articles including new empirical data (either qualitative or quantitative) were included (i.e., meta-analyses were excluded). It is worth noting that we did not identify cases in which the same sample was used across multiple articles (e.g., when authors publish multiple articles off the same data set). As a result, the likelihood is that a small number of studies that were coded represent such cases, and that some double-counting of samples are included in these data and result in a small amount of data skew, although it is probably less than 2–3% of all coded cases.

Seven undergraduate research assistants (RAs) were trained to be able to identify "interpersonal communication" articles from those in other areas and to find and code the following descriptive information about the sample (if reported): sample size, ethnic distribution, sex distribution, sexual orientation distribution, average age, average income, geographic location of data collection, and whether the sample was a college sample (a sample of college students) or not. Training around the identification of what is considered "interpersonal communication" began with a discussion of two manuscripts conceptualizing the field (Braithwaite & Baxter, 2008; Floyd, 2014) then proceeded to untangle how to operationalize that domain of studies. We took a broad approach: if the study had direct relevance to understanding processes or outcomes tied to dyadic communication, it was included. During the training process, the RAs coded randomly selected sample articles within the journals, decided if they fit the definition of interpersonal communication, and if so, coded for the required sample information. Results were then discussed as a group and disagreements resolved. Once we were confident that the coders were able to consistently identify articles according to this conceptualization and operationalization of interpersonal communication and were able to accurately identify characteristics of the sample, we gave each coder five articles to code on their own, reviewed and gave feedback, then repeated that task three times. Each coder was then assigned a particular journal for coding. We continued to check (and when relevant, correct) each RA's work until they successfully coded seven consecutive articles without error; they then continued to code the remainder of their journal without being checked. In cases when RAs were unsure of how to code an article, they were encouraged to contact us for guidance. RAs did so on less than 5% of the cases. After coding was completed for all journals, we assigned a randomly selected 20% of each coder's work to another RA for accuracy checks. If they believed any part of the code was in error, the RA highlighted the portion of the code in red, added the corrected code, and contacted us for a final decision. Finally, we checked all the data to ensure accuracy in the final conclusions reached. In the end, between the coder accuracy checks and our checks as authors, 100 errors were found and corrected across the many categories coded for each of the studies identified as interpersonal and empirical (total data cells = 5,148; error rate = 1.94%).

Results

One thousand four hundred and thirty ($N = 1,430$) articles were coded, of which 19% met the criteria as interpersonal and empirical ($n = 269$). The frequency of articles that were coded as "interpersonal communication" ranged from 3% to 49% of published articles across journals (see Table 13.1). Within those articles, 332 studies (accounting for multiple studies within some articles) formed the sample for this descriptive analysis, which were combined to represent the voices of 71,076 individuals (see Tables 13.1 and 13.2 for complete summary of the data). Data were separated by journal, then combined.

Reporting of Sample Characteristics

An important finding from these analyses is that authors often do not report basic characteristics of their samples, with that propensity varying across journals (see Table 13.1). Specifically, the percentage of participants whose ethnicity was reported ranged from 28% in JOC to 91% in CM. Overall,

Table 13.1 Summary of sample characteristics

	CM	HCR	JACR	JOC	JIIC	Howard	Asia	CCC	Total
Total number of IP articles	70	50	48	31	24	28	11	7	269
Percentage of total articles	49%	33%	34%	10%	20%	18%	5%	3%	19%
Total sample size of IP studies	19695	19315	5261	11108	4951	4496	6189	61	71076
White %	72%	62%	65%	62%	27%	64%	0%	29%	57%
Non-white %	1%	0%	1%	12%	0%	0%	0%	0%	1%
Black %	6%	6%	14%	3%	7%	14%	0%	10%	6%
Latinx %	12%	14%	7%	2%	9%	12%	0%	0%	10%
Asian %	6%	13%	4%	19%	55%	5%	92%	61%	20%
Other %	4%	5%	9%	1%	2%	5%	8%	0%	5%
Female %	62%	60%	77%	57%	57%	64%	72%	98%	63%
Of US	96%	77%	90%	34%	63%	77%	3%	66%	69%
Of ethnicity reported	91%	50%	65%	28%	59%	68%	76%	51%	63%
Of sex reported	97%	76%	80%	33%	68%	80%	64%	84%	74%
Of age reported	92%	77%	77%	33%	62%	32%	42%	31%	67%
Of college students	37%	61%	6%	32%	65%	53%	31%	31%	43%

Notes: See key for journal abbreviations in manuscript; "IP" = Interpersonal; "Non-white" represent cases in which authors only reported the percentage of white participants; "other" represents cases where either authors reported a category of "other" or listed identities that were not captured by the categories listed in this table; "Of US" reflect the percent of participants from samples collected in the United States; "Of [characteristic] reported" reflect the percent of participants whose (sample characteristic) was reported; "Of college students" reflect the percent of participant from samples that were collected in colleges or universities.

Table 13.2 Representation by continent

Continent	% of Samples	% of World Population	Under/Over- Representation Ratio
Africa	6.6%	16.0%	0.41
Asia	11.6%	60.0%	0.19
Australia/New Zealand	0.9%	0.4%	2.17
Europe	7.6%	11.0%	0.69
North America	69.2%	7.5%	9.23
South America	0.9%	8.6%	0.11
White	79.0%	19.0%	4.16
Black/Brown	7.6%	30.1%	0.25

Notes: The data reflect percentages from countries in which data were collected in the coded samples. The "% of world population" reflect the percent of world population represented by the combined population of those countries represented in the coded samples; "under/over representation ratio" was calculated by dividing data from "% of sample" by data from "% of world population." Within Africa, data were collected in Ethiopia ($n = 156$), Kenya ($n = 12$), Malawi ($n = 76$), Senegal ($n = 76$), South Africa ($n = 24$), Uganda ($n = 231$), and a sample which broadly referenced data collection in "Africa" ($n = 360$); within Asia, data were collected in China ($n = 2,727$), Israel ($n = 925$), Japan ($n = 629$), Lebanon ($n = 80$), South Korea ($n = 16$), Singapore ($n = 849$), and Taiwan ($n = 2,857$); within Europe, data were collected in Belgium ($n = 1,597$), Bulgaria ($n = 50$), England ($n = 40$), Germany ($n = 433$), the Netherlands ($n = 1,897$), Norway ($n = 27$), Portugal ($n = 252$), Slovakia ($n = 225$), Spain ($n = 44$), and a sample which broadly referenced data collection in "Europe" ($n = 14$); within North America, data were collected in Canada ($n = 120$), and the United States ($n = 49,081$); within South America, data were collected in Chile ($n = 512$), the Dominican Republic ($n = 22$), and Ecuador ($n = 132$); within Australia ($n = 159$) and New Zealand ($n = 458$). "White" combined data across continents and countries that include primary Caucasian/white populations (i.e., Australia//New Zealand, Europe, Canada, United States, Israel); "Black/Brown" combine data from countries in Africa, South America, and the Middle East (exclusive of Israel).

ethnic identity information was reported for only 63% of all participants. Participant sex was more frequently reported (74%), although also varying dramatically in report frequency across journals, with a range of 33% in JOC to 97% in CM. Finally, 67% of all participants were parts of samples in which their average age was reported, with a low of 31% in CCC and a high of 92% in CM. Authors reported the sexual orientation of only 7% of the over 71,000 participants, and approximately 5% of the studies included average income of participants in the sample. It is important to keep in mind that the analyses that follow only relate to the studies in which related information was provided.

Diversity in Terms of Ethnicity

Approximately 57% of participants whose ethnic identity was reported identified as white/Caucasian, with Asian at 20%, Latinx at 10% and black or African-American at 6%. All other ethnicities or multi-racial identities made up 6% of the samples. It may be worth noting that removing the *Howard Journal of Communication* (the aim of which is to "(publish) original and current research papers focusing on ethnicity and culture as they interact with communication," https://www.tandfonline.com/action/journalInformation? show=aimsScope&journalCode=uhjc20), the *Asian Journal of Communication* (the aim of which is to "highlight research on the systems and processes of communication in the Asia-Pacific region and among Asian communities around the world," https://www.tandfonline.com/action/journalInformation? show=aimsScope&journalCode=rajc20), and the *Journal of International and Intercultural Communication* (JIIC; the aim of which is to "(expand) understanding of international, intercultural, and cross-cultural communication"; https://www.tandfonline.com/action/journalInformation?show=aims Scope&journalCode=rjii20) from these analyses produces an increase in the percentage of white participants (to 71% of the sample) and a decrease in the number of Asian participants (to 12% of the sample), while maintaining similar levels of representation for Latinx and black communities in the United States.

If we go back to including all journals in our analysis, but restrict the analysis to data collected in the United States, the over-representation of white participants increases, with 66% of the sample identifying as white (vs. 61% across the entire sample), with 12% Latinx, 10% Asian, and 7% black. When compared to US census data on distribution of ethnicities (61% white, 18% Latinx; 13% black, 6% Asian; see https://www.census. gov/quickfacts/fact/table/US/PST045217), that translates to an 8% over-representation of the white community and an 80% over-representation of the Asian-American community, compared to a 53% and 90% under-representation of the Latinx population and black community in the United States, respectively.

The seeming over-representation of Asian ethnicities in US-based samples (10% of the sample vs. 6% of the census) is worth additional scrutiny. First, that over-representation in part reflects the fact that Asian-Americans are disproportionately likely to continue toward higher education ("The Rise of Asian Americans," 2013) and thus more likely to be included in convenience sampling (i.e., college samples) than other ethnic groups. Second, given the large number of students from Asia who come to the United States for education (https://www.iie.org/Research-and-Insights/Open-Doors/ Data/International-Students/Places-of-Origin) and their likely under-representation in US census figures, the 6% census figure of Asian Americans likely under-estimates the number of individuals of Asian ethnicity living in the United States at any one time. Finally, the Asian community is the only one for which a Communication journal exists to provide exclusive focus on their experiences. As a result, they are more likely to be represented in these data than ethnic groups without such a focused outlet for related scholarship. To be clear, though, the overall knowledge base in interpersonal communication, as reflected by these data, still dramatically under-represents the Asian experience. The population of the continent of Asia makes up 60% of the world's population. Only 11.6% of participants in this analysis were part of samples collected in Asia.

Diversity in Terms of Sex and Age

Sixty-three percent of the 52,485 participants whose sex was reported were female, ranging from 57% in JOC and JIIC to 98% in CCC (although the studies in CCC that fit our criteria only involved 61 participants). The weighted average (mean) age of participants was 27.08, ranging from an average of 21.66 (Howard) to 38.25 (JACR). The average (median) age of the population in the United States is 37.8 (https://factfinder.census.gov/faces/nav/jsf/pages/community_facts.xhtml?src=bkmk).

Representativeness for Universal Claims

Forty-three percent (43%) of participants were college students and 69% of participants were in the United States when the data were collected, with a wide range across journals on both of those fronts (see Table 13.1). That vast over-representation of the United States increases (to 76%) if journals with an explicit international focus (JIIC, AJC, CCC) are removed from the analysis. Given that most social scientific scholars generalize from their data to make knowledge claims that imply universality, an analysis that sheds light on the geographic spread of samples is important. Indeed, of note is that the population of participants who were included in this analysis represented 6 continents and 29 countries. Unfortunately, that masks the vast under-representation of lived experiences that these data reflect (see Table 13.2). For example, North America makes up 7.5% of the world's population, but 69% of the population of participants in this analysis, making North Americans (99% of the sample of North Americans are from the United States) over-represented in interpersonal communication knowledge claims by a magnitude of over 900% higher than their actual frequency. In contrast, for example, South Americans represent 8.6% of the world population but less than 1% of this population of participants, making them the most under-represented continent of people in knowledge claims made in interpersonal communication literature (i.e., 900% less represented than they should be were our samples a geographically accurate representation of world populations). If we separate the Arab world from the continents of Asia and Africa, the Arab population becomes even less represented than South America. In fact, only one study ($n = 80$) included participants from the Arab world.

So, while data were collected from samples across 29 different countries, the distribution across them was certainly not equal. Specifically, the United States (making up 69% of the sample and only 4.5% of the world population (country-specific population data retrieved from: https://www.census.gov/popclock/world; 16 times larger than its actual population representation) and Israel (making up 0.1% of the world population, but 1.3% of the sample population, 13 times larger than its actual population representation) were, by far, the two most over-represented populations in this six-year sample of participants. At the country level, given the absence of several large-population countries from the sample, ranking of under-representation is impossible, but it *is* striking that not one study during this period (and in these journals) was collected in either Mexico, the United States' neighbor to the south, or India, a country with over 1 billion people (over four times the population of the United States). In that sense, large-population countries that do not show up at all in these analyses are obviously those that are least represented.

As follow-up, we combined data in this sample from countries the population of which is mostly characterized black or brown people (i.e., African continent, South American continent, the Arab Middle East) and those of which the population is primarily composed of white people (i.e., Europe, United States, Canada, Israel). We then examined the data two ways: First, in terms of raw frequency, the voices of samples from Western, white-centric countries ($n = 56{,}149$) were more than ten times more frequent than those from non-Western, black- or brown-centric countries ($n = 5{,}414$). This despite the fact that the actual population of those same Western countries is 50% *smaller* than those non-Western countries. As a final follow-up, we analyzed the degree of over-representation of the white American college students (27% of the samples), compared to their actual worldwide representation (0.13% of the world population). White American college students are 213 times more represented in these samples than they should be, based on actual frequency of population representation.

Discussion

Interpersonal communication scholars have long argued for greater diversity in the samples being studied. The purpose of this analysis was to provide an empirical snapshot of the characteristics of samples that interpersonal communication scholars use to create supposedly generalizable, scientific knowledge. Our coding of empirical interpersonal communication articles across eight journals, including three with missions explicitly tied to culture, during a six-year window (2013–2018), resulted in data that represented 71,076 participants. The analysis revealed some hopeful trends, but, overall, dramatic skewness of sample characteristics on several fronts. The data also show that journals vary significantly in the degree of sample representativeness to the broader population. Key findings will be highlighted and suggestions made for structural change to address inequalities in the representativeness of the samples we use to create knowledge in interpersonal communication.

The Problem of Non-Reporting

The first data point that stands out is 63%—the percentage of the sampled population for which ethnic identities were reported. Moreover, one of the leading journals in our field, JOC, had ethnic distribution information for only 28% of the samples in the studies it published. In other words, 72% of participants in interpersonal communication studies published in JOC are of an ethnic background that is entirely unknown. This analysis is not unique in finding that social scientists often fail to report something as basic as the ethnic identity distribution of their samples. For example, Rad et al. (2018) found that "the vast majority of papers [in leading social psychology journals] give no information about their sample apart from gender" (p. 11402). What explains the fact that so many authors failed to report something as basic about their sample as its ethnic distribution, and that the related reviewers and, ultimately, editors failed to demand the reporting of such information? One explanation is that social science paradigms are premised on a goal of universal claims and generalizable knowledge. A risk of such a framework is that human behavior is sometimes seen as "culture free." Failure to consider a sample's ethnic distribution as a relevant piece of information, let alone as a critical litmus test of sample representativeness (and, therefore, results generalizability), as it should be, is a likely consequence.

Similar problems of non-reporting were revealed for both participant sex (74% reported, on average) and age (67% reported, on average), suggesting a larger problem with an assumption with key identifying characteristics of the sample are irrelevant to judgments of sample representativeness, or conversely that sample representativeness is not a relevant criterion for generalizability. Finally, participants' distribution on average income and sexual orientation was reported for only 5% and 7% of samples, respectively.

Diversity and Representativeness

There are many ways to examine sample representativeness in these data. Given that the vast majority of scholars never restrict their conclusions to any particular geographic boundaries (i.e., they make general claims about human behavior from their data), we might begin with a question of the extent to which the 71,076 participants were a fair representation of the world population's geographic distribution. Consistent with past analyses (e.g., Henrich et al., 2010), this sample of interpersonal communication studies failed on that front. Details to support that conclusion litter these results, but we start with the fact that 69% of the participants were from studies collected in the United States, despite the fact that only 4.5% of the world's population is there. In other words, the experiences of individuals in the United States are 16 times more represented in knowledge claims within the interpersonal communication literature than they should be, were those representations to actually reflect worldwide experiences. In contrast, for example, not a *single* voice came from data collected in India, which has a population of more than four times that of the United States, making up 17% of the world's population. Only 80 participants of the over 71,076 (0.1%) came from the Arab world, the population of which combines to exceed that of the United States by approximately 100 million people.

If we look across continents, Latin America is ten times *under*-represented in this sample of participants, compared to its representation in the worldwide population, while North America is nearly ten times *over*-represented. Asia is over five times *under*-represented, and Africa over two times (ballooning to 12 times if we remove one study with data from 3,843 participants in Malawi). An analysis that combines data in the sample from countries that have majority brown or black populations from those with majority white populations shows that participants from the former group of countries were represented ten times less than those from the latter, despite that they represented 1.5 times larger populations.

Another approach to this question is to examine data reported for ethnicity. That analysis is best done when data are restricted to those collected in the United States, since worldwide ethnicity distribution data are unreliable. With those parameters, we found that the sample over-represented white (by 8–16%, depending on journal inclusion) and Asian (by 40–80%) voices and substantially under-represented black (by 90%) and Latinx (by 53%) voices in the United States. Finally, data tied to age (mean = 27.08, with a standard deviation of approximately 13) showed that knowledge about interpersonal communication processes comes primarily from participants in their middle adolescence until early adulthood. Interpersonal experiences of individuals in their pre-adolescent or middle to late adulthood are nearly absent from our knowledge bank, yet, again, the claims of generalizability are almost never bounded by age categories.

While we assume that our broad-based frustration about the lack of representativeness for large segments of society (and over-representation for others) is clear, it is important to note this: Although we have chosen to highlight gaps in ethnic and geographic inclusivity in this chapter, the near absence of knowledge about other identity categories (e.g., those 40 and above) and the abject failure to even report sexual orientation (93% of participants in this sample did not include sexual orientation identities), let alone examine the experiences of the LGBTQ population, is highly problematic for what we can claim to know about interpersonal communication processes. Indeed, separate manuscripts focused on the implications for knowledge tied to each of these vast gaps is warranted.

Journal Variance

The analyses of these data showed vast differences on nearly every aspect of sample characteristics across journals (see Table 13.1). In some ways, this is not surprising. For example, "applied research" in the interpersonal communication discipline has been generally tied to the collection of samples outside college student populations. As such, it is not surprising that interpersonal communication studies published in the *Journal of Applied Communication Research* have by far the lowest percentage of college student samples (6% of participants, compared to the average of 43% overall) and the oldest average age of participants ($M = 38.25$ vs. average of 27.08 overall). It is also not surprising that the *Asian Journal of Communication* had, by far, the largest percentage of

Asian participants (92% vs. 20% overall) or that *Howard Journal of Communication* has the largest percentage of black participants (tied with JACR at 14% vs. 6% overall). In fact, the fact that the percentage representation of black voices in a journal titled after one of the leading historically black colleges and universities, and that emerged to give greater representation to the experience of people of color is not much higher is surprising and likely speaks to the very small number of interpersonal communication scholars who intentionally sample from the black community.

Of course, it is not surprising that culture- and/or community-focused "specialty journals" have samples that represent those missions. However, it is also worth noting that those journals often attract a smaller subset of readers with particular interest in those missions. As such, they have smaller journal impact factor scores (Howard is not indexed in the web of science; JACR = 1.0; AJC = 0.57) than the "generalist" journals (JOC = 6.95; HCR = 2.36; CM = 2.51; data based on Web of Science 2017 Journal Citation Report). The result is that this work is ghettoized as both different than mainstream and less important.

Given that the "specialty" journals fared on these dimensions in the ways we would expect, let us turn to the patterns found across the three "general" journals, each with relatively similar, broad-based missions to publish the best communication scholarship (HCR, CM, JOC). Here, we find some curiosities: Why, for example, is it that samples testing interpersonal communication published in JOC rarely included basic demographic information (ethnicity, sex, and age of participants; 28%, 33%, and 33%, respectively), while the samples in a journal with a mostly similar mission, CM, almost rarely did not include such information (91%, 97%, and 92%, respectively)? Or why is it that those same two journals differed in the opposite direction when it comes to the internationalization of knowledge claims, with only 34% of participants appearing in JOC-published samples coming from the United States, while that percentage is 96% in CM. The explanation may be tied to sub-areas of interpersonal communication research and the relative reputations of the various journals for publishing that work. JOC tends to be more tied to media research than interpersonal research, for example. Indeed, only 10% of the studies published in JOC were coded as interpersonal, and some of those may have reflected an intersection between interpersonal communication and media; perhaps media scholars are less likely to report basic demographic information and are more internationally inclined than are relational scholars, for example, who might be more likely to submit their work to CM. We did not code for media studies and, thus, could not perform that analysis, but that may be an analysis worth pursuing to test whether the problem of non-reporting is more acute in certain sub-areas of communication scholarship than others. Another possible explanation is that JOC belongs to the International Communication Association while CM is a journal of the National Communication Association, perhaps reflecting the degree of internationalization. But the internationalization of a discipline should not affect the need for scholars to submit research that is global in its generalization, in part through being global in its samples.

Ultimately, a definite difference among otherwise relatively similar journals are editors, and there is undoubtedly a difference in the degree to which each enforces particular reporting expectations or practices and/or pursues a mission that is focused on ensuring inclusivity and diversity of participant voices. Had our analysis spanned a longer time frame, we would have data to speak to the relative impacts of editor and journal. Undoubtedly, both play a role here. Another structural difference is in the number of editors reviewing manuscripts for each journal: Some journals (e.g., CM) have a historic pattern of relying on only one editor to make all final decisions, while others (e.g., JOC) rely on a system of multiple associate editors, making application of reporting expectations less consistent across manuscript submissions (based on the assigned associated editor). Of course, journals develop reputations over decades that undoubtedly exceed the impact of any particular editor, but the role of the editor is impossible to ignore here, especially when the enforcement of basic reporting practices is in question.

Another possibility that might explain differences across journals in reporting frequency tied to ethnic categories is the relative internationalization of that journal. The ethnic categories used for coding were US-specific; as such, they may not have much meaning (and thereby not used) for samples collected in other countries. Still, in that case, we would have expected that the authors use some other categorization scheme to reflect the demographic identity of their participants, and they too often did not.

Implications

In conversations with fellow social scientists about this project, the following challenges have been raised: (1) regardless of samples, studies that use sound scientific and statistical methods can give us confidence about claims of generalizability, (2) research based on theory would be expected to generalize across populations, so it is unfair to damn entire bodies of knowledge because of representational inadequacies of the samples, (3) it is unrealistic to expect samples that perfectly represent every possible population characteristic, (4) where is the evidence that bodies of knowledge do not generalize across identity categories? and (5) what do you propose we do? We will address each of these briefly, although we acknowledge that full treatment of these important issues and questions deserve more than the attention that we provide here.

First, the notion that a "sound study design" can overcome problems of sample representativeness reflects a misunderstanding of the basic distinction between internal and external validity. The study design (which helps give us confidence in causal claims) and related statistical procedures offer only as much power to generalize as the representativeness of the sample permits. Strong scientific methods used on a large randomly selected sample of participants that vastly over-represent white American college students can speak with confidence about the white American college student experience; that's it. That does not mean that the same pattern of results might not be found in other populations (indeed, replication should be an essential part of the scientific process; Open Science Collaboration, 2015), and, yes, the likelihood of such generalizability is stronger when the predictions are based on sound and culturally reflective theoretical foundations. Ultimately, though, if a sample primarily includes white American college students, then scholars *must* acknowledge and reflect on the ways in which that population's experience might shape any broader knowledge claims that can be made (see also Soliz & Phillips, 2018). So, why is it that authors speak in general terms about findings, as if they apply universally? Because somewhere along the line, we have eschewed sample representativeness as a necessary condition for making broad claims, in favor of comfort with white American college samples. Why? The explanation is a lengthy one, and not the purview of this essay. It undoubtedly starts with the lenses with which scholars see the world in front of them. With a discipline that is made primarily of white American students and scholars, most researchers have mostly white lenses, and implicit comfort with samples that reflect that experience. It continues with a system that encourages reliance on easily accessible, convenient, samples. The research universities responsible for the bulk of knowledge produced in the communication discipline are located in the United States and primarily enroll white students (for a range of socio-historical reasons). A sub-discipline like interpersonal communication that relies heavily on frequent publication for judgments of achievement in promotion and tenure reviews and has evaluation structures that generally discourages community impact as a criterion in those reviews, leads to pressures to rely on convenience sampling for the bulk of studies and resultant encouragement to ignore sample representativeness as a central part of the scientific process.

Second, the call is not for samples that perfectly represent all possible population characteristics. The call is for authors to take seriously the fact that their samples are representative of a very small sample of the population and that reliance on those samples comes with real consequences for the generalizability of knowledge claims. The call is also for greater replication of findings across a diverse range of samples. We demand (and will work toward) a discipline that takes seriously the need to be intentional in recruiting samples that are more diverse and inclusive than the ones that currently dominate the field. This will require intentional efforts toward international partnerships, toward collaborations with universities and colleges that are located in diverse geographical settings, and toward a commitment to collect data in populations that are under-represented (or, in some cases, potentially non-existent) in university settings.

Finally, evidence of the impact of culture on norms and behavioral practices is vast and not the purview of this essay (e.g., see Baldwin, Faulkner, Hecht, & Lindsley, 2006, Berry, Berry, Poortinga, Segall, & Dasen, 2002; Hyde, Tompson, Creswell, & Falk, 2015). At the broadest level, the failure to take a cultural approach to knowledge and the flawed embedded assumptions that the white American college perspective is universal lead to difficulty in asking questions beyond these frames. For example, why is it that there is almost no relational communication literature (for exception, see Minniear & Soliz, 2018) about family dynamics that have been shown in other disciplines to be critical to the mental health of children in communities of color (e.g., ethnic-racial socialization, for review, see Priest et al., 2014)? Or why is it, as Soliz and Phillips (2018) point out, that conversation orientation, openness, and directness, within families are framed in the communication literature as the productive orientations, when most communities outside of white, Western ones productively engage in a more conformity-oriented, relatively closed, and indirect style of communication? Of course, this problem goes far beyond theories or questions set within relational or family contexts. Many of our theories of disclosure, uncertainty management, conflict, identity management, negotiation, avoidance, and so on, are implicitly centered within Western assumptions of individualism and independence (among others) and have been generally tested only within those populations. Indeed, it is difficult for us (e.g., our students, our faculty, our journal reviewers) to think of communication questions or realities outside of these narrow frames, since they are the ones from which we learn the ostensibly universal core communication processes.

We could go on, but the point is that students within the discipline learn about communication questions and outcomes from a particular perspective (white and Western, mostly American) that then limits the ways in which they think about productive and unproductive patterns of communication, and frame questions to ask in culture-centric ways, yet they are generally blind to those frames. As such, as others have noted, the production of knowledge remain white, American centric, and potentially irrelevant to large swaths of the world's populations. The task is for communication scholars to become intentionally aware of the ways in which these restricted frames shape theories, questions, and knowledge claims. Of course, as we have noted, we are far from the first authors to argue for such cultural humility.

Proposed Changes

Indeed, despite decades of calls for diversifying the communication discipline, recent data from a variety of perspectives have shown that change has been slow. Knobloch-Westerwick, Glynn, and Huge's (2013) analysis of over 1,000 articles published in *Communication Research* and *Journal of Communication* between 1991 and 2005 found a wide gap in the citation frequency of female, as compared to male, authored articles. Mayer, Press, Verhoeven, and Sterne (2017) found a similar discrepancy in *The International Encyclopedia of Communication Theory and Philosophy* (2016), which, as the authors note, claims itself to be the "definitive reference work on communication theory and philosophy." In another analysis, Chakravartty, Kuo, Grubbs, and McIlwain (2018) coded the racial identities of journal article authors across 12 communication journals published between 1990 and 2016. They found that only 14% of the 5,262 manuscripts in the corpus they examined were first-authored by non-white scholars. They also examined citation patterns and, like the analysis by author sex, found a significant discrepancy in citation frequency, and their analysis of editorial boards showed those to also be primarily filled by white scholars. And now we add the data about sample characteristics that we reveal here. So, whether the question is about representativeness of authors, the distribution of knowledge claims through citation frequency, or the representativeness of participants in our samples, there is no challenging the fact that the knowledge that the interpersonal communication subfield has produced is based disproportionately on the experience of white American college students.

Appropriately, after decades of calls for change with little in the way of results, patience among some in the discipline has waned. For example, Mayer et al. (2017) argued that "to fix the white CIS man problem, we need to apply pressure everywhere the field reproduces itself." In response, they propose being purposeful in the inclusion of diverse authors in class syllabi, ensuring research from diverse authors as essential parts of doctoral exams, both in terms of the writing prompts and the related reading lists, and diversifying panels at conferences, as well as author lists in special journal issues, handbooks, and encyclopedias. Chakravartty et al. (2018) echoed those same calls for change, then added the need to diversify the roster of scholarly gatekeepers through increasing the number of scholars of color as journal editors and editorial board members, the possibility of collecting information about author characteristics (e.g., to allow for data collection and analysis tied to equity in editorial decisions across author identities), and the recommendation that reviewers offer feedback that "center issues of racial inequality" (p. 262). Soliz and Phillips (2018), in making a case for ethnic-racial and global diversity in the study of family communication, argued for an ideal which involves more diverse samples, but also recommend several other steps that can be taken to advance the goal of diversity of knowledge including (a) intentionality in the cultural framing of findings, regardless of the culture in question, (b) inclusion of culture throughout textbooks and edited books, as opposed to being the domain of a particular chapter or two, (c) including more research that speaks to the experience of a wide range of families in course syllabi, (d) remove the siloed approach to the study of culture throughout the discipline's academic spaces, and (e) change merit, promotion, and tenure evaluation processes in ways that reward the difficult work of ensuring wider sample representativeness or pursuing knowledge about under-represented populations.

Outside of the communication discipline, Stanley (2007) turned the lens to the role of editors in the efforts toward creating more inclusivity in the sciences. She called for the creation of improved mentorship systems for female faculty and faculty of color, and for the development of protocols that make reviewers aware of implicit biases that often disempower culturally grounded approaches, among other proposals. Rad et al. (2018) put the onus on both authors and editors. They called for authors to be required to report sample characteristics, to justify the sample population, to explicitly tie findings to populations and discuss the extent to which the results are or are not broadly generalizable, and to use whatever diversity exists within the sample to examine the potential moderating roles of culture. They also proposed that editors and reviewers should explicitly recognize and reward "non-WEIRD" samples as novel and important and set "diversity targets" (e.g., a goal of 50% of "non-WEIRD" samples). Finally, Hruschka, Medin, Rogoff, and Henrich (2018) identified several "necessary shifts" to combat limitations in diversity and inclusivity across several domains, ranging from sampling practices to institutional structures to the role of cultural reflections in theory development and testing, among others.

Together, these authors provide several recommendations with potential to make knowledge claims more representative of the experience of a population beyond white American college students. Given the overwhelming evidence of the need for more inclusive knowledge practices, it is time that the leaders of the National Communication Association and the International Communication Association work together to form a Task Force with a mission to develop a proposal for structural changes that addresses how the discipline will become more inclusive, diverse, and relevant in its knowledge generation practices. The task force should include a diverse representation of scholars who reflect the type of diversity being sought, and set goals, assessment methods, and timelines for change. We have already joined others in conversations with our association's leaders in hopes of encouraging action. In addition to the above-noted proposals for change that such a task force should consider, we add the following based on the particulars of our analyses and findings:

1   When not in conflict with ethical principles and when reviewing studies that include data collected at the individual level, require all authors to report information about basic sample characteristics (e.g., geographic location of data collection, participant sex, participant sexual orientation, ethnic distribution of the sample, average age, and socio-economic status).

2   Make intentional efforts to diversify editorial boards and ad hoc reviewer rosters.

3   Require as part of the selection criteria for editors a statement from nominees that addresses their plans for intentional efforts toward greater inclusivity and diversity of authors and samples, and intentional awareness of the role played by cultural factors in empirical findings.

4   End the practice of requiring that authors of studies that collect non-white or non-American samples add a comparison sample. We have heard of too many cases where authors of studies that include data from samples that exclusively or primarily involve communities of color or international samples receive feedback from reviewers, editors, or both that they collect a comparison sample of white participants or face rejection of the manuscript. Not once have we heard of authors who have received similar feedback tied to a mostly white American sample (that they must

collect additional data that reflect diversity, or face manuscript rejection). The fact that a population (white, American, college students) that represents 0.13% of the world population is somehow considered the baseline against which all other populations must be compared speaks to the deep structural and historical problem that the discipline faces on this front. This practice *must* stop.

In sum, this analysis is the latest one of many (for decades) that have taken the discipline to task for failing on the metric of diversity and inclusion. We offer new data that can serve as a baseline for future analyses that assess progress on the degree of sample representativeness in the area of interpersonal communication. Undoubtedly other sub-areas of the discipline vary in the acuteness of the problem, and it is likely that an analysis that went further back in history would show progress on this front over the 2–3 decades. Still, the fact that the population of the United States reflects 4.5% of the world population, yet 69% of the samples, or that the population of white students enrolled in universities in the United States represents 0.13% of the world population, yet 27% of the samples, is highly problematic. Moreover, the fact that these data are as they are despite the inclusion of communication journals with internalization and diversity within their mission statement, speaks to the work ahead of the discipline if it hopes to consider the knowledge it generates to be reflective of communication practices and outcomes outside of a very small part of the world.

As it stands, the general state of science within the area of interpersonal communication reflects a convenient science and knowledge generated from research in that area largely reflects knowledge about white American college student lives. By eschewing the critical scientific criterion of sample representativeness, we have created a sub-discipline that is founded on knowledge about white American elites and in which the experiences of entire identity groups within the United States, of entire continents of people, even, are almost entirely absent. By simultaneously holding tightly to the scientific promise of generalizability and universality, we implicitly treat those vast absent voices as collateral damage to pursuit of truth about interpersonal communication processes. As such, the experience of the white American college student is treated as representative of that of an African-American child growing up in inner city Chicago, the undocumented farm worker in California, the elderly disabled Palestinian in Gaza, and the parent struggling to provide for her family in the slums of Calcutta. We must do better.

References

Allen, B. J. (1995). "Diversity" and organizational communication. *Journal of Applied Communication Research, 23*, 143–155. doi:10.1080/00909889509365420

Arnett, J. J. (2008). The neglected 95%: Why American psychology needs to become less American. *American Psychologist, 63*(7), 602–614. doi:10.1037/0003-066X.63.7.602

Baldwin, J. R., Faulkner, S. L., Hecht, M. L., & Lindsley, S. L. (Eds.). (2006). *Redefining culture: Perspectives across the disciplines*. New York, NY: Routledge.

Berry, J. W., Berry, J. W., Poortinga, Y. H., Segall, M. H., & Dasen, P. R. (2002). *Cross-cultural psychology: Research and applications*. Cambridge, UK: Cambridge University Press.

Braithwaite, D. O., & Baxter, L. A. (2008). Introduction: Meta-theory and theory in interpersonal communication research. In D. O. Braithwaite, & L. A. Baxter (Eds.), *Engaging theories in interpersonal communication: Multiple perspectives* (pp. 1–18). Thousand Oaks, CA: Sage.

Chakravartty, P., Kuo, R., Grubbs, V., & McIlwain, C. (2018). #CommunicationSoWhite. *Journal of Communication, 68*(2), 254–266. doi:10.1093/joc/jqy003

Chevrette, R. (2013). Outing heteronormativity in interpersonal and family communication: Feminist applications of queer theory "beyond the sexy streets." *Communication Theory, 23*, 170–180. doi:10.1111/comt.12009

Cohen, M. R., & Nagel, E. (1934). *An introduction to logic and scientific method*. London: Routledge & Kegan Paul.

Davern, M. E. (2008). Representative sample. In P. J. Lavrakas (Ed.), *Encyclopedia of survey research methods* (pp. 720–722). Thousand Oaks, CA: Sage Publications.

Davis, J. L. (1995). *Changing the players and the game: A personal account of the Speech Communication Association Black Caucus origins*. Annandale, VA: Speech Communication Association. doi:10.1080/00909889509365420

Davis, S. M. (in press). Evoking issues of race and ethnicity in discussions about physiology and interpersonal communication. In J. Crowley, A. Denes, & L. Aloia (Eds.), *The physiology of interpersonal communication handbook*. New York, NY: Oxford University Press.

Floyd, K. (2014). Interpersonal communication's peculiar identity crisis. *Communication Studies, 65*(4), 429–431. doi:10.1080/10510974.2014.927291

Hecht, M. L., & Ribeau, S. (1984). Ethnic communication: A comparative analysis of satisfying communication. *International Journal of Intercultural Relations, 8*(2), 135–151. doi:10.1016/0147-1767(84)90036-1

Hecht, M. L., Ribeau, S., & Sedano, M. V. (1990). A Mexican American perspective on interethnic communication. *International Journal of Intercultural Relations, 14*(1), 31–55. doi:10.1016/0147-1767(90)90046-Y

Hendrix, K. (2005). An invitation to dialogue: Do communication journal reviewers mute the race-related research of scholars of color? *Southern Communication Journal, 70*, 329–345. doi:10.1080/10417940509373338

Hendrix, K. G., & Wilson, C. (2014). Virtual invisibility: Race and communication education. *Communication Education, 63*(4), 405–428. doi:10.1080/0363452 3.2014.934852

Henrich, J., Heine, S. J., & Norenzayan, A. (2010). The weirdest people in the world? *Behavioral and Brain Sciences, 33*(2–3), 61–83. doi:10.1017/S0140525 X0999152X

Houston, M. (2002). Seeking difference: African Americans in interpersonal communication research, 1975–2000. *Howard Journal of Communications, 13*(1), 25–41. doi:10.1080/106461702753555021

Hruschka, D. J., Medin, D. L., Rogoff, B., & Henrich, J. (2018). Pressing questions in the study of psychological and behavioral diversity. *Proceedings of the National Academy of Sciences, 115*(45), 11366–11368. doi:10.1073/pnas. 1814733115

Hyde, L. W., Tompson, S., Creswell, J. D., & Falk, E. B. (2015). Cultural neu-roscience: New directions as the field matures. *Culture and Brain, 3*(2), 75–92. doi:10.1007/s40167-014-0024-6

Knobloch-Westerwick, S., Glynn, C. J., & Huge, M. (2013). The Matilda effect in science communication: An experiment on gender bias in publication quality perceptions and collaboration interest. *Science Communication, 35*(5), 603–625. doi:10.1177/1075547012472684

Lannamann, J. (1991). Interpersonal communication as ideological practice. *Communication Theory, 1,* 179–203. doi:10.1111/j.1468-2885.1991.tb00014.x

Mayer, V., Press, A., Verhoeven, D., & Sterne, J. (2017). How do we intervene in the stubborn persistence of patriarchy in communication research? In D. T. Scott, & A. Shaw (Eds.), *Interventions: Communication theory and practice* (pp. 53–65). New York, NY: Peter Lang.

Minniear, M., & Soliz, J. E. (May, 2018). *Socialization in multiethnic-racial families: Examining the associations between parental communication about prejudice and discrimination and psychological well-being.* Presented at the Family Communication Pre-Conference at the International Communication Association 68th Annual Convention, Prague, Czech Republic.

Open Science Collaboration. (2015). Estimating the reproducibility of psycholog-ical science. *Science, 349*(6251), aac4716. doi:10.1126/science.aac4716

Orbe, M. P., & Allen, B. J. (2008). "Race matters" in the journal of applied com-munication research. *The Howard Journal of Communications, 19*(3), 201–220. doi:10.1080/10646170802218115

Parker, P. S. (2001). African American women executives' leadership communi-cation within dominant-culture organizations: (Re) conceptualizing notions of collaboration and instrumentality. *Management Communication Quarterly, 15*(1), 42–82. doi:10.1177/0893318901151002

Parker, P. S., & ogilvie, d. t. (1996). Gender, culture, and leadership: To-ward a culturally distinct model of African-American women executives' leadership strategies. *The Leadership Quarterly, 7*(2), 189–214. doi:10.1016/S1048-9843(96)90040-5

Priest, N., Walton, J., White, F., Kowal, E., Baker, A., & Paradies, Y. (2014). Un-derstanding the complexities of ethnic-racial socialization processes for both minority and majority groups: A 30-year systematic review. *International Journal of Intercultural Relations, 43,* 139–155. doi:10.1016/j.ijintrel.2014.08.003

Putnam, L. (1982). In search of gender: A critique of communication and sex-roles research. *Women's Studies in Communication, 5,* 1–9. doi:10.1080/07491409.1982.11089636

Rad, M. S., Martingano, A. J., & Ginges, J. (2018). Toward a psychology of Homo sapiens: Making psychological science more representative of the human population. *Proceedings of the National Academy of Sciences, 115*(45), 11401–11405. doi:10.1073/pnas.1721165115

"The Rise of Asian Americans." Pew Research Center, Washington, D.C. (April 4, 2013). Retrieved from https://www.pewsocialtrends.org/wp-content/uploads/sites/3/2013/04/Asian-Americans-new-full-report-04-2013.pdf

Shuter, R. (1976). The promise of participant observation research. *Journal of Applied Communication Research, 4,* 1–8. doi:10.1080/00909887609360219

Soliz, J., & Phillips, K. E. (2018). Toward a more expansive understanding of family communication: Considerations for inclusion of ethnic-racial and global diversity. *Journal of Family Communication, 18*(1), 5–12. doi:10.1080/15267431.20 17.1399890

Stanley, C. A. (2007). When counter narratives meet master narratives in the journal editorial-review process. *Educational Researcher, 36*(1), 14–24. doi:10.3102/0013189X06298008

Velasco, E. (2010). Inclusion criteria. In N. J. Salkind (Ed.), *Encyclopedia of research design, volume 1* (pp. 581–591). Thousand Oaks, CA: SAGE Publications. doi:10.4135/9781412961288

14 Organizing as a Tension between Tradition and Innovation

Promoting Inclusion in Academia

*Bernadette M. Gailliard, Shardé M. Davis,
Jennifer L. Gibbs, and Marya L. Doerfel*

Academic institutions often develop a policy that supports inclusion and diversity. Yet the policy, itself, cannot be used as evidence that an organization is inclusive, even if some people in such an organization say they feel seen or heard (Ahmed, 2012). This tension between policy and action was clearly observed within the communication discipline when, in June 2019, a discipline-wide debate occurred as the Executive Committee (EC) of the National Communication Association (NCA) challenged the efficacy of the Distinguished Scholars (DS) to diversify. The DS recognition by the NCA includes a very select group of scholars, with a maximum of five new inductees in any year, though some years have had fewer. The public controversy began with the existing DS members' response to a new and unexpected policy that takes the decision-making out of their hands in an effort to improve the diversity of these recognized distinguished scholars. The EC proposed that a new committee made up of elected and outstanding members from across the NCA would be formed as a way to improve the current relatively homogeneous makeup of the NCA DS. What ensued was a public debate including an emotional response by all but one of the DS who expressed their "intense reactions of anger and alienation toward NCA that have prompted [them] to write" (https://www. natcom.org/sites/default/files/NCADistinguishedScholars-Letter_from_ Zarefsky4.2.19.pdf). NCA president Star Muir defended the EC's decision to make such change because, among other reasons, "For the current members of the Executive Committee, 12 years of effort to make the Distinguished Scholar award process more inclusive has resulted in a less than 1% change in the composition of the awardees" (https://www.natcom.org/sites/default/files/ NCADistinguishedScholars-Letter_from_Muir-EC5.8.19.pdf). Muir and the EC (which is made up of the most diverse members in the history of the association) thus called for systemic change rather than the "tweaks" that found no purchase for the breadth of scholars who might be recognized for their work.

In an editorial that has since been withdrawn, an additional DS member who did not sign the general DS letter expressed his particular concerns over the changes. He pitted merit against diversity, setting up a false dichotomy that represents systemic racism at its core: he suggested that considering diversity candidates means sacrificing substance. His dichotomy suggests that an entire group, based on their identities, is incapable of doing what those holding the current title of DS can do. The communication discipline, along with many others, has the knowledge and empirical evidence to identify such claims for what they are: racist. Many scholars lamented the claims of this letter and responded with the evidence that demonstrated how institutional systems have used traditions nested in histories written by an elite few to marginalize whole groups of people and keep them from feeling included in the discipline. For example, a statement coauthored by the executive committees of the NCA Women's Caucus and Feminist & Women Studies Division stated:

> Indeed, there is copious existing research on the persistence of inequities experienced by scholars from marginalized identities at all levels and various intersections from undergraduate training to who is admitted to our profession, who is hired, published, promoted, tenured, awarded, and selected into leadership. Scholars of color especially, even across inflections of class, gender, sexuality, and ability, have not only been overlooked in and excluded from traditional academic pathways of recognition and reward, but have also faced questions about the worth of their scholarship, their citational practices, and their voice each time a challenge is presented to the usual order of business. The Feminist and Women Studies Division of NCA was formed in response to this very sort of bias against methodology, objects/subjects of study, interventionist orientations, and recognition that what and how we engage in scholarship is, at its core, political.
> (see http://bernadettemariecalafellphd.com/?page_id=892)

As days passed, more voices clarified the optics and elitist structures being manifested by these statements. Statements were issued by additional NCA divisions and various blog posts emerged. As a result of the public discussion, many signatories of the DS letter stepped forward to retract their names, make their own statements of clarity, and many apologized with humility by expressing their own short-sightedness about policy versus systemic change. The author of the letter that pitted diversity against merit also apologized and identified action items to repair and improve systemic processes over which he has control. To that end, the DS members from Pennsylvania State wrote: "Distinguished Scholars called out a technical or procedural error in what is instead a moral issue" (see http://bernadettemariecalafellphd.com/?page_id=858).

The individual responses signaled their own interests in advancing inclusion and how particular actions could be adopted to move the discipline forward. Yet, as Doerfel's narrative about her role in the NCA OCD top paper walkout presented in the preface of this book also illustrates, seemingly progressive individuals can often block progress. As noted in the preface, in her role as division chair, her top paper response to the division revealed a clash between policy and practice. Because she views herself as a diversity and in-clusion ally, she was blind to the very ways her actions perpetuated racism until some of the audience members stood up and walked out in protest. In both cases, institutional practices such as making policies and giving official speeches create "a sense of ease and familiarity, an ease [such that, when chal-lenged,] can also take the form of incredulity at the naivete or ignorance of the newly arrived outsiders" (Ahmed, 2012, p. 25).

Both the DS and OCD cases underscore the fact that by design, organi-zations are systems that perpetuate control, power, and influence. Moreover, even the most well-intentioned and moral may unwittingly perpetuate com-munication practices that organize exclusion. But the seeds of understanding how organizations work began with different goals in mind. Organizational studies began a century ago, initiated with research by the likes of engineers such as Frederick Winslow Taylor and industrial psychologists such as George Elton Mayo. This initial research aimed to understand why organizations were not as efficient as they should be. Early studies set the stage for orga-nizational studies as a discipline to adopt an underlying assumption that ra-tionality, efficiency, and systems of control constituted ideal organizational functioning. Myriad evidence has shown that organizations and individuals pursue these goals. Yet their attempts to be rational fall short, often relying on tradition, heuristics, and gut instincts (March, 1994).

Human action perpetuates the traditions that make organizations not so rational. Decisions are made that are predicated on tradition, and tradition is difficult to change (March & Simon, 1993). Regardless of people's actual reliance on traditions, gut instincts, and heuristics, rationality continues to be the discourse used to describe the ideal way to design organizational systems. Reflecting an interpretive shift in organization studies in the 1980s (Eisenberg, 1984; Pacanowsky & O'Donnell-Trujillo, 1983), Mumby and Putnam (1992) challenged the apparent preference by practitioners and scholars alike for ra-tional decision-making. They argued that rationality and emotionality should not be pitted against each other. Rather, Mumby and Putnam defined bounded emotionality as "an alternative mode of organizing in which nurturance, car-ing, community, supportiveness, and interrelatedness are fused with individual responsibility to shape organizational experiences" (p. 474). Like this shift from efficiency and rationality to emotionality and organizing, this chapter exam-ines the organizational positions we privilege as scholars (both in general and in the communication discipline specifically) and argues for the need to shift our positions given the associated implications for diversity and inclusion.

As scholars, we play an important role in shaping the communication disci-pline as an organization. As members of that organization, professors socialize the next generations of scholars that follow. Yet an ironic twist underlies the statement Sir Isaac Newton made famous – "standing on the shoulders of gi-ants" has been viewed as the ideal form of progress. Although this is a maxim built into the model of knowledge production across academic disciplines, the creators of such knowledge were homogeneous with their particular values, assumptions, and access. As the academy in general aims to be diverse, it is built on a history of homogeneity. The giant shoulders represent a particular type of knowledge with a particular point of view that modeled what distinguished scholarship is. With respect to the NCA DS controversy described at the beginning of this chapter, the particular model of scholarship that warranted the title NCA Distinguished Scholar was therefore assessed with criteria that made sense for the set of traditions and values established in 1991 when the honor was first instituted. As such, when it comes to generating knowledge, standing on the shoulder of giants – even when the discoveries are purportedly empirical and quantitative – is still systemically a function of the current value systems of those generating that knowledge. In other words, what questions to ask, hypotheses to test, concepts to use represent a certain set of values and assumptions (e.g., Doerfel's questions about white supremacy and her concerns with the tone white supremacy as a construct evoked), or ways to evaluate success (e.g., erroneously pitting diversity against quality) are nested in a set of larger cultural assumptions. Thus, it is important to understand how our legacy is defined by the organizations and systems that support and impact our work.

Relatedly, we must acknowledge that in our work, we take discursive positions, both consciously and unconsciously. These positions are consequential and have material impacts on the way scholarship is created in the field. These positions also have biases that need to be examined. Decades of organizational studies scholarship have demonstrated the ways in which both formal and informal positions inside and among organizations that make up larger communities are powerful and influential. Positions privilege and lend power to the people who occupy them. Powerful people become brokers of information, and likewise, brokers can become powerful people. As such, power in the form of brokering information between groups, across organizations, and through communities facilitates greater access to resources for those brokers (Brass & Krackhardt, 2012; Castells, 2013; Smith et al., 2014). As a result of such positions, these brokers, therefore, control the system's resources. Resources come in many forms – financial, material, social support, expertise, knowledge, and control of discourses. Like in corporations and nonprofits, these resources are highly valued and sought after by academics. As such, "discourses construct phenomena and phenomena do not exist independent of discourse (which is itself a phenomenon)" (Grant & Marshak, 2011, p. 205). Put another way, discourses normalize views of which resources are valuable or not valuable, and who has earned them. In turn, discourses are a resource to be controlled (van Dijk, 2008). In her capacity as chair giving a speech, Doerfel controlled the discourse in the division. As a leader, she brokered what "counts" for the division's attention.

By critically examining higher education as the organizing backbone of academic life, we are able to attend to the blind spots the very academics who produce knowledge about privilege and access (and therefore inclusion and exclusion) have, yet may not even be aware of. These power-laden blind spots limit academic scholarship and practices through privileging certain discourses over others. The DS letter shows that 66 people were upset about the process. Their concern about the process revealed their own blind spot about the system they were a part of, perhaps because that system supported their own rise and legitimacy in the communication discipline. Likewise, although she was working on this very book about inclusion at the time of her speech, Doerfel took up the top paper speech as something the person in power (the chair of the division) does without attending to the impacts of her speech on the progression of the organizational communication field or the experiences of her colleagues in the room. As detailed in the preface of this book, her speech and aspects of her performance reproduced white values.

The DS response suggests those individuals equated a change in criteria with a challenge to their own identities. Similarly, Doerfel's concerns with the use of 'white supremacy' ended up revealing her underlying assumptions about treating racism as a binary. Together, both examples demonstrate how academic institutions (and the individuals that comprise them) are sustained by a system constructed through ambiguous language and decision-making processes. Such ambiguity in language and process serves to "preserve their privileged positions" (Eisenberg, 1984, p. 234). On a larger level, organization theory about power and influence points to some of the general positions that are privileged in academia and how they impact academic practices of inclusion. It also offers some alternative positions that we might consider, which would move us toward a legacy that increases the impact of our work. In the following sections, we consider positions that are privileged in academia in general, and communication specifically, including (a) diversity over inclusion and (b) tradition over innovation. We draw on scholarship about the experiences of underrepresented groups in academia to illustrate ways in which these members are marginalized yet exhibit agency as they navigate these tensions as well as suggest structural solutions that privilege inclusion and innovation.

What Positions Do We Privilege?

Organizations are defined by positions of power and influence. Universities are no different. In varying degrees, there are powerful positions, such as chairs, deans, provosts, and presidents. There are variably powerful and powerless groups, as well. Universities have hiring committees, promotion and tenure committees, university senates, curriculum committees, and diversity committees. But what makes one position or committee more influential and therefore more powerful than another? Management theory views power as associated with resource control (Cook, 1977; Pfeffer & Salancik, 1978) while social network theory regards it as a function of one's structural position (Astley & Sachdeva, 1984) because brokers in networks are facilitators or gatekeepers of information flows.

Communication scholars have largely focused on power as being produced or enacted through discursive practices (Foucault, 1979; Hall, 1997). In this sense, power is routinized and institutionalized in everyday organizational discursive practices (Mumby & Stohl, 1991). Through discursive practices, certain rules of organizing are taken up, and in the process of enacting those rules and articulating their meaning, those rules come to reproduce themselves (Raffnsøe, Mennicken, & Miller, 2017). Indeed, the way we think and act has come to be recognized as both transformed and constrained by what we communicate and how we communicate at work and in organizations.

Whether the discourses are formal or informal, the processes reify existing structures and norms through sensemaking. Sensemaking involves the meaning-making process of interacting with others through organizational systems and practices which are enacted and understood (Weick, 1995). When it comes to the transformation of historically white and male institutions like colleges and universities, how this transformation is talked about, framed, and socially constructed, and how policy gets (re)formed and debated, therefore, shapes the sensemaking of organizational members. As such, sensemaking has the potential to reproduce or transform the values of the system, though, as Ahmed (2012) has shown, sometimes diversity policies can be window dressing that "perform" the university's diversity without enacting systemic change.

Discourses about social phenomena like diversity and inclusion construct reality and how we understand and live that reality (Gergen, 2000). As scholars have argued for decades, the academy must transform its discourses and practices in order to move beyond the status quo and support inclusion and equity at all levels. At the most basic level, research demonstrates that discourses around diversity traditionally privilege the experiences and ideals of white, male, heterosexual, Judeo-Christian, able-bodied, western identities. This position discounts the experiences of other identity groups and their intersections (Crenshaw, 1989) and renders those individuals invisible or, at best, marginalized. This is evidenced in academia in myriad ways, particularly in the composition of faculty and the focus of research studies. Put simply, the canon of most disciplines is written by and about white, male, heterosexual experiences and perspectives. Questioning these traditions necessarily opens up important conversations about what "counts" as meaningful scholarship, particularly in cases when the work is to be evaluated for promotion, tenure, and merit. Likewise, at the individual level, questioning tradition fosters interrogation of such decisions as who is invited to speak at colloquia and what is discussed. As these examples demonstrate, communicative experiences that are guided by both formal (a speaker is invited to campus; a paper accepted and presented at a conference) and informal (the speaker presents and socializes about her topic before and after the event, at meals, and/or cocktail hours) discourses and systems privilege certain positions and identities.

Inclusion as a communicative process aims to redesign the status quo into an evolving process of opportunity rather than a static state that denies access. We posit a move from diversity as a way to identify access to a focus on inclusion as a set of discursive practices that shape meaning and constitute the challenges and opportunities academia is facing. By differentiating diversity and inclusion in this way, we assert that a cosmetic focus on diversity may undermine more substantial inclusion efforts. Diversity is the noun; the count of how many are represented. Inclusion is the verb; the communicative actions that support and/or undermine the ability for systems to be diverse. We contend that the communication discipline (and academia more broadly) can become more inclusive by challenging traditional positions of diversity and tradition and engaging in new discourses that support inclusion and innovation.

Diversity Over Inclusion

Discourses around diversity are not new and seem to be everywhere. Use the keywords "diversity" and "academia" and over 500,000 articles will be identified in Google Scholar. Limit that search to 2019 and almost 20,000 articles come up. However, diversity and inclusion are often vaguely intertwined and the underlying emphasis tends to be on representation (diversity) over processes (inclusion) (see also Ahmed, 2012). For example, diversity statements communicate the desire to increase numbers of underrepresented faculty and students on campus. Administrators, however, do little to address current issues like student protests and faculty grievances about the treatment of minoritized people on campus. Social justice movements such as Black Lives Matter in the United States and Rhodes/Fees Must Fall in South Africa have not only revived questions about representation within the academy, but also "exposed ongoing inequities, including the prohibitive cost of higher education, insufficient attention to race and racial inequality in curricula, and racially hostile campus climates" (Chakravartty, Kuo, Grubbs, & McIlwain, 2018, p. 257).

A focus on representation is not bad; it is just incomplete. Studies have shown how a lack of diversity in various academic disciplines creates challenges for members of underrepresented groups and also for larger social systems. For instance, Maranto and Griffin (2011) asserted that women faculty members, as compared to men, face a "chilly climate" where they are excluded, devalued, and marginalized in their departments. More specifically, scholarship on women in STEM disciplines is replete with examples of how women face a multitude of disadvantages due to a lack of representation in these professions. They inhabit male-dominated occupations and organizations where they often feel isolated and disenfranchised (Ko, Kachchaf, Hodari, & Ong, 2014; Rios & Stewart, 2015). They lack both instrumental and social support to help facilitate their retention and advancement in the discipline (Armstrong & Jovanovic, 2015; Griffin, Gibbs, Bennett, Staples, & Robinson, 2015). They also have to deal with issues of work-life balance more actively and overtly than their male counterparts (Rigg, Coller, Reynolds, Levin, & McCord, 2015). Being the only woman (or one of few) means that women also tend to carry "token" status where they feel they have to represent all women and often work that much harder to prove their worth (Stewart, Malley, & Herzog, 2016). Such systemic inequities make it that much more challenging to professionally distinguish oneself, especially if part of being distinguished is to be a prolific publisher while time is taken up by other institutional service needs like serving on committees, reviewing, and mentoring.

On a larger scale, researchers from multiple disciplines have found evidence of unconscious biases present in a variety of organizational contexts. At the most fundamental level in STEM, people do not associate women with science. Results from implicit association tests demonstrate that both men and women more readily associate "male" with science and "female" with arts than the reverse (Nossek, Banaji, & Greenwald, 2002). This cultural bias is evident in home life, too. A recent Pew Research poll reported that although men are more active in housekeeping and parenting than they were in the 1980s, taking care of the home and children continue to be viewed as women's work (Livingston & Parker, 2019). The Pew study's findings help explain the particularly gendered burden women faculty with children have: although men are now more active as parents, they are disproportionately pressured to be the breadwinners. So, even if a woman faculty member is part of a dual-career family whose husband is more involved at home and with the kids, when over 75% of those polled believe the man's main responsibility is to serve as breadwinner, his work takes precedence. The United States' culture still expects the working mother to shoulder the parenting so the man can do his job.

Unfortunately, this emphasis on diversity often precludes or overshadows discussions of inclusion. While representation matters and increasing the numbers of individuals from underrepresented groups is important, so too are the lived experiences of those who are marginalized. Underrepresentation is important *because* it fosters feelings of social isolation, increased self-doubt, and decreased job satisfaction among members of these groups (Allen, 2007; Jackson, 2000; Rigg et al., 2015; Rockquemore & Laszloffy, 2008). Women faculty, faculty of color, LGBTQI+ faculty, differently-abled faculty, international faculty, and others talk about feelings of being "outsiders within" (Collins, 1991). People from such groups exist in liminal spaces and borderlands (Anzaldúa, 2012) where they straddle multiple worlds and social systems. It is important to attend to these experiences as opportunities for identifying how to move toward more inclusive practices.

In communication, scholars have critiqued the discipline's lack of inclusion through discussion of their own experiences as well as larger systemic issues. A prime example of how individuals navigate this space in the discipline is found in Allen, Orbe, and Olivas' (1999) discussion of their simultaneous enchantment and disenchantment with the field. Through autoethnography and dialogic analysis, these scholars explore how the experience of difference manifests in tears, pain, and isolation that requires additional emotional labor that is both taxing and liberating. Similarly, Shenoy-Packer (2016) recounts her experience of double-consciousness as she manages the emotional burden of being a South Asian Indian woman in the role of professor in an American classroom. She says:

I admit that when I take on my professorial role in front of my students, I am careful to include only as much information about India and

Indians as is essential to the context under discussion in case I get accused of pushing India on disinterested students...I have a heightened awareness of this concern and try to be mindful of everything I say in mixed (Indian/non-Indian) company. I, of course, realize that even in mundane everyday professional communication, I might be shouldering the responsibility of representing my country of origin, and although this can be a fulfilling and empowering experience, there are times when I just want to be me. Even if it is just for a day, I want to shed my otherness, blend in, and move around in the multiple spaces I simultaneously inhabit with no cultural expectations and no stereotypes to live up to or shatter.

(p. 153)

At the organizational level, scholars have published critiques about the lack of thorough and intentional consideration of diverse experiences in communication theory and pedagogy. Jackson (2000) explores the "invisibility, dismissal, and devaluation of Black intellectualism [he has] observed in the academy" (p. 48). He argues that although there has been a strong history of African American communication theories since at least the 1980s, few, if any, of them have been valued by the mainstream such that they are widely distributed, discussed in textbooks, tested and refined by empirical studies, and/or cited consistently in research. More broadly, Brenda J. Allen and her colleagues demonstrate how mainstream communication scholarship and pedagogy tend to treat race as an ahistorical, essential, and depoliticized aspect of identity (Ashcraft and Allen, 2003; Orbe & Allen, 2006). According to Allen (2007), "this scholarship rarely refers to the racial paradox, which characterizes the "both/and" nature of race as an artificial, dynamic, political construction based on white supremacy, with material consequences such as privilege and discrimination" (p. 260). Moreover, in their analysis of communication articles published between 1990 and 2016, Chakravartty et al. (2018) found that women and nonwhite scholars have been and continue to be marginalized when it comes to who is publishing, being cited, and editing mainstream communication journals.

While the above examples focus primarily on issues of gender and race, texts such as *Presumed Incompetent: The Intersections of Race and Class for Women in Academia* (Gutierrez y Muhs, Niemann, Gonzalez, & Harris, 2012), *Our Voices: Essays in Culture, Ethnicity, and Communication* (Gonzalez & Chen, 2016), and *Queer Intercultural Communication: The Intersectional Politics of Belonging In and Across Differences* (Eguchi & Callafel, 2019) demonstrate that the experiences of being marginalized and/or erased in both micro and macro discourses are common for communication scholars (and others) who identify as and/ or research LGBTQI+, differently-abled, working class, international, and other populations (also, see Braithwaite & Thompson, 1999; Chevrette, 2013; Cruz, McDonald, Broadfoot, Chung, & Ganesh, 2018; Munshi, Broadfoot, & Smith, 2011; Pal & Dutta, 2008). For scholars who live at the intersections (Crenshaw, 1989) of these identities to be successful in the field, they often feel pressured to codeswitch, roleflex, and enact other adaptive behaviors that reflect the privileged identities. Institutional discourses that are enacted at all levels of the field communicate a necessity to adapt in order to facilitate one's matriculation up the professional ladder – an endeavor that is only sometimes successful, often uncomfortable, and always risky.

Thus, a focus on inclusion matters in order to create environments in which diverse groups are supported, celebrated, and empowered to be themselves and still feel valued. When diversity is emphasized, it becomes a numbers game. A focus on representation means hiring more women, people of color, LGBTQI+, and so forth. This makes departments look more diverse, but without an additional focus on inclusion, this change is cosmetic and unsustainable (Ahmed, 2012). This problem is evident in the NCA DS controversy, too. As President Muir's response letter noted, incremental changes in the system such as encouraging more nominations from scholars of color did not produce any real change. Rather than a focus on getting more diverse scholars to apply, the proposed changes in policy have resulted in a new structure for decision-making that reflects a change in the makeup of the executive council. Dismantling exclusionary structures is critical to transformation. Although members of privileged groups may feel alienated and angry due to the perceived changes in status or control, changing structures to be more inclusive is about opening up opportunities for new voices to be heard and provides a catalyst for more enduring growth as the discipline engages in future sensemaking and organizing processes.

Just as decision-making in a professional association like NCA has evolved, inclusion efforts in universities extend beyond decision-making in hiring and admissions. They include efforts to mentor, retain, and promote underrepresented groups so that members of these groups rise up through the ranks. This means creating inclusive climates that are affirming and empowering for those who are isolated, or one of few. It means greater incorporation of scholarship from underrepresented groups on course syllabi into lessons and teaching techniques – beyond talking about "diversity" only one week of the semester. It means including standard language for why teaching evaluations of women faculty, faculty of color, or international faculty are lower than others (white males) and seeking more equitable ways to evaluate teaching overall. It means transforming structures rather than putting the burden of change on individuals. Finally, it means accounting for and normalizing different group experiences rather than seeing them only as individual differences that are anomalies or exceptions to the norm, or requiring those from underrepresented groups to constantly reinvent the wheel to show that their experience is valid.

These issues bring to bear evolving values and systems that generate or block opportunities. Framing diversity as a numbers game undermines efforts to design more inclusive systems, setting up false dichotomies like merit versus diversity, and otherwise limiting the number of individuals who can be meritorious. The original NCA DS process, for example, was unnecessarily restrictive by requiring that DS have been in the field for 20 years and only allowing a maximum of five per year. As such, if there are more than five nominees in a given year, decision-making may end up being a numbers game rather than a holistic decision about the potential candidates. Diversity is only an indicator of inclusion. Transforming such long-standing systems substantially, not incrementally, is necessary to create meaningful change and a move toward more actual inclusive practices. This also generates tensions between tradition and innovation, discussed next.

Tradition Over Innovation

A second tension is evident in the emphasis on tradition over innovation. Tradition means doing things the way they have always been done, and it is often used as a justification to maintain the status quo. As a result, despite the recognition that problems exist in academia, academic entities have a tendency to perpetuate themselves over time. Students learn implicit norms and practices from their advisors, and in turn, they teach their own students to do the same. DS perpetuate their own distinguishing qualities for future generations. Divisions perpetuate traditions such as the top paper response format that may work to stifle voices for change. While many traditions have value and are worth continuing, an emphasis on tradition may also work to impede innovation, in terms of trying out new ways of being or doing academic life. Tradition works to bolster the resilience of organizations but also makes them less responsive to change.

This emphasis on tradition over innovation shapes what is valued in much of academia: research over teaching and community engagement, as well as work over life. Scholarship in peer-reviewed journals and books is prioritized over other forms of impact, including mentoring, public scholarship, and engagement in communities. The tenure and promotion process (especially at R1 institutions) tends to be standardized in ways that do not reflect flexible ways of working or alternate models of impact. It tends to undervalue work that is not published scholarship and privileges flagship journals and scholarly books published by a university press. Inflexible models such as this serve to further marginalize many people from diverse groups because their scholarship appears to be "non-standard." For example, tenure and promotion files for faculty of color (especially women of color and those with multiple intersectional identities) typically include more service and community engagement than grant awards and publications. Also, some faculty employ methodological creativity and digress from the theoretical canon. Yet the canon, as noted above, is based on the shoulders of (white) giants. Being methodologically creative and not emphasizing the canon extends ripe opportunities to discover ideas that would not have been realized otherwise. The standard canon and methodologies, after all, often do not adequately encapsulate the experiences of underrepresented populations. Despite the extra labor involved in conducting such non-conformist research and getting it published, these faculty are penalized for having fewer publications or scholarship published in lower-tier journals. Preserving such rigid norms and expectations for scholarship can mean that a field becomes an ideological echo chamber that stymies work "at the margins" and precludes itself from the transformative possibilities of effecting change beyond academia. Relatedly, faculty members do not expose the next generation of scholars (i.e., graduate students) to non-academic careers, despite the fact that academia is changing and tenure-track jobs are not as readily available as they once were. It does a disservice to graduate students not to train them for non-academic work in similar ways to how we train them to do research. They need to understand how to apply research outside of the ivory tower, especially in a field like communication where people and communities can take advantage of and benefit from our work.

Another issue that affects (particularly) women's experiences in the academy is the relationship between work and family priorities. Scholars have found that family formation and academic success are closely related for women in higher education. According to Mason and Goulden (2004), women may be more successful in obtaining tenure if they forgo or delay marriage and childbirth. Additionally, the study found that, in general, women who pursued tenure-track careers were different from women who dropped out of the academic pipeline. Women climbing the ladder-rank in academia were more likely to get divorced and less likely to marry or have children than those who drop out of the academic pipeline (Mason & Goulden, 2004; Wolfinger, Mason, & Goulden, 2008). Even when women stay married, research shows that they are at a disadvantage compared to married men in relation to tenure and promotion decisions when they have children (Xie & Shauman, 2003). This is likely related to decreased productivity in the form of publications as the women are responsible for the majority of the childcare responsibilities at home and caregiving obligations for (grand)parents, yet receive limited institutional support (like funding) and even less administrative support in the workplace than their male counterparts (Carr et al., 1998; Stack, 2004). While many women across the US face these challenges, it should come as no surprise that the issues compound for faculty situated at the intersection of multiple identity frames. Women of color faculty, for example, must navigate gendered, racial, and likely other types of covert discrimination – colleagues might be less willing to cover one's class when a family emergency arises or share best practices for transitioning back to work from maternity leave. Implicit bias can disproportionately reduce the level of flexibility in the workplace or one's willingness to leverage that flexibility out of fear that their commitment to the job will be negatively judged. Not to mention, implicit bias (along with other barriers) can create "cold academic climates" that stymie their research productivity and engagement in department and university affairs. Finally, the emotional tax levied on many women faculty of color as a result of unfair treatment can compound income inequality that is pervasive in the academy. An annual report on faculty compensation salaries by the American Association of University Professors (AAUP) shows that 93% of all participating institutions pay men more than women at the same rank (https://www.aaup.org/report/annual-report-economic-status-profession-2017-18). Though the report did not calculate compensation by gender and race, some AAUP chapters are calling for improvements in equity for women faculty *and* faculty of color. Some faculty salaries are below the market rate and, consequently, those persons cannot afford certain privileges that increase their quality of life (i.e., childcare and/or living near the school). As noted above, Livingston and Parker (2019) and the Pew poll confirm that this array of pressures on women has yet to substantially change.

This tenuous work-life relationship for women in higher education is an important organizational consideration across all fields (including communication) because women discuss work-life balance as one of the primary reasons for leaving the academy (Ward, 2013). For faculty, support and mentoring were found to be key solutions for motivating women to remain (Rockquemore & Laszloffy, 2008; Wolfinger et al., 2008). Shollen, Bland, Finstad, and Taylor (2009) propose that in order to retain women as faculty members, departments will have to implement mentoring programs that help women think through their career goals and create active strategies for achieving these goals. We argue that Shollen et al.'s recommendations, while progressive, still put the burden on women and what they need to do, leaving their male counterparts to business as usual. Developing training and mentoring for men in such programs (and particularly those in leadership positions) to understand and enact more inclusive communication and organizing practices is a reasonable complement in supporting women (Tracy & Rivera, 2010).

When we shift from a focus on tradition to a focus on innovation, this opens up new possibilities and paradigms. It means changing our current academic practices and structures. This includes providing implicit bias training for faculty, administrators, and students. It means decolonizing syllabi by carefully considering which scholars are included in syllabi and increasing the diversity of voices, perspectives, and epistemologies that are studied. It means training chairs and deans on the unique challenges that underrepresented groups face as faculty (see, for example, www.effectivefaculty.org). It means creating groups that help support and connect people with similar experiences to help overcome isolation; hearing from others like them can help those from underrepresented groups feel validated and supported knowing they are not the only ones. It means encouraging people in high-level positions to use their power and privilege on behalf of those who lack it (in both big and small situations). Most importantly, in terms of execution, these initiatives need to be supported with institutional dollars and other tangible resources. Faculty should have dedicated space on campus where the support groups can convene privately and without interference from others. Universities should also conduct periodic salary reviews to acutely address gender and race pay inequity. Offering faculty who are underrepresented in the academy pre- and post-tenure teaching releases is another resource that can account for the emotional labor they shoulder to simply carry out their professional duties. Knowing that there are inconsistencies in how the university workplace is structured and the familial needs of the current workforce, universities should also dedicate monies to build child care centers on campus and low-rent faculty housing in nearby neighborhoods, low-interest home loans, and university-hired social workers to help employees learn about caring for aging relatives (Luna, Medina, & Gorman, 2010). Decision-making committees across academia, like the NCA executive committee discussed earlier, are making substantial changes that may not be comfortable for those who traditionally have been in positions of power, authority, and by association, viewed as elite. But innovation is necessary to transform academic institutions into more equitable spaces that allow individuals from *all* groups to thrive. Diversity efforts are not enough; reframing the discussion to address questions of inclusion, equity, and justice while also backing those decisions with institutional dollars are vital steps to effecting structural change (see https://www.insidehighered.com/views/2017/03/30/colleges-need-language-shift-not-one-you-think-essay).

What Should We Do About It?

The organizing structures discussed in this chapter center on issues of power and its multifaceted nature in academia. Power is embedded in organizations like universities and professional associations through positions and committees as well as in resources and the discursive practices of their members. Change is thus necessarily multipronged. It is systemic. It requires meting out material and informational resources. It is discursive. It involves understanding how traditions become reified through (inter)actions and are therefore difficult and painful to alter. It is about identity. It causes individuals to interrogate how our multiple intersectional identities impact our decision-making processes and to evaluate our subject positions within a particular historical and situational context. Consider the resistance to change in the cases of the NCA DS and the OCD top paper panel – as many of the NCA DS have demonstrated in their work, change comes when we deconstruct the systems, discourses, identities, and assumptions that undergird the status quo. Subverting broken structures is inherently messy and puts people outside of their comfort zones. But, doing so is a critical next step for centering the voices, experiences, and needs of faculty from historically underserved, underrepresented, and oppressed groups.

Deconstruct Knowledge Production Structures

Academia is (inherently) a political space, such that power is yielded, exerted, and resisted by its members. Systems of privilege and oppression are built into the fabric of academic and scholarly practices, such that certain paradigms, theories, methods are organized into a hierarchy that disproportionately penalizes scholarship that deviates from (arbitrary) standards of merit. Those interested in making lasting, structural changes must make a personal commitment to upending the legacy of systemic oppression by changing the way "good" and "rigorous" knowledge and knowledge production are defined, approached, and evaluated. First, decolonize the dominant intellectual traditions to address westernization, and more specifically, biases toward American scholars(hip) (Munshi et al., 2011). While the field of communication was cemented by the US American-based scholars, its reach far surpasses the global North in the present day. The deconstruction of Eurocentric/Western knowledge structures and the de-marginalization of global scholarship are critical first steps. In addition, digress from the theoretical canon. Most mainstream communication theories were developed by white (male) scholars who examined communication behavior through a white (male) lens and tested the theories on predominantly white samples, which yielded findings that should only apply to white people (Allen, 2007; see also Afifi & Cornejo in this volume). We must place greater value on cultural frameworks and models that more aptly describe communication behaviors of under-researched groups (Jackson, 2000). Relatedly, amplify diverse voices by citing more scholars of color (especially women of color), LGBTQI+ scholars, trans* scholars, and international scholars. There is a ritualistic practice of citing certain intellectual camps in the field, much of which is comprised of white/male/cisgender/heterosexual people. Relying upon a biased "canon" of scholarship reinforces barriers to inclusion; thus it is crucial that communication scholars divest from this citations-based power structure. Finally, decenter the methodological and paradigmatic traditions that are privileged in the field. It is widely recognized that (post)positivism is considered the dominant paradigm in communication and its research and theories typically constitute the "mainstream." A bias toward this kind of work means that standards for "good science" privilege (post)positivist research designs, methods, samples (including sample size), and analyses, which can discourage work "at the margins." To wit, at the OCD Top Paper panel, Doerfel noted her epistemological roots in post-positivism. As such, she was deferential to the quality of the work but was ultimately ill-equipped to assess a paper grounded in critical theory. Changing traditions, like the division chair being the de facto reviewer, opens up the discussion of a whole audience rather than the gatekeeper (division chair) controlling the discourse. Decentering the dominant thought traditions extends opportunities for researchers to discover a wider variety and more representative experiences of people throughout the world. While the aforementioned suggestions might seem overtly political, we (the authors) contend that a critical revaluation of communication scholarship is crucial to effecting long-lasting change.

Re-Think Promotion, Tenure, and Merit-Based Pathways

In line with deconstructing the field's discourses around knowledge production, academics must also re-think the procedures for promotion and tenure and expand notions of what is considered meritorious scholarship. Universities have begun to create more inclusionary structures as part of their promotion pathways. For example, some institutions have recognized the value of their professional teachers through instituting non-tenure track (NTT) promotion ladders (we see such systems at our respective universities of Rutgers, the University of California, and the University of Connecticut). Universities also have found ways to value engaged scholarship as part of the tenure package (e.g., the University of North Carolina at Chapel Hill) and recognize the public scholar, whose work resonates outside of academe including OpEds in highly-regarded American periodicals (i.e., *New York Times, The Chronicle of Higher Education*) or books that land on best seller lists (e.g., Robin DiAngelo, author of *White Fragility*, has been on the *New York Times* Best Seller list for 48 weeks at the time of this writing). Some, more senior faculty, have taken substantial steps to bridge the gap between research in the academy and the local community by opening centers for social justice. For example, Patricia Parker, Organizational Communication scholar at the University of North Carolina at Chapel Hill, founded the Ella Baker Women's Center for Leadership and Community Activism. Its mission includes serving disenfranchised communities by providing community organizing training for residents to build social capital and work for social justice in their own communities and beyond (for more information, visit https://www.ellabakerwomenscenter.org). As such, an important action to take would be to recognize the public work that is already being done by many scholars. This may be done by valuing public scholarship more explicitly in the tenure and promotion process and consideration of merit reviews, and by incorporating it into graduate coursework as is sometimes done in undergraduate courses.

Similar opportunities exist for rethinking the ways we value various forms of service in the academy. Research demonstrates that faculty from traditionally underrepresented groups (e.g., women, people of color, and LGBTQI+) are disproportionately involved in service roles such as mentoring (Rockquemore & Laszloffy, 2008). Faculty mentor students through formal channels such as being the research advisor for students in undergraduate research programs or faculty supervisor for undergraduate student organizations. Mentorship also takes place in less formal venues, whereby students regularly meet with faculty to seek advice on personal struggles, professional aspirations, and even course material for which that person is not the instructor. They are sought out by students (and other faculty) both because of their identity characteristics and research expertise to provide academic, emotional, social, and instrumental support. While this work contributes to advancing the field and its impact, this invisible labor is often undervalued and overlooked during evaluation. Some universities, like Rutgers, have added faculty mentoring as a separate criterion in their promotion and tenure review to highlight the contributions of faculty in this area; other universities should follow suit.

Additionally, faculty should be encouraged and recognized when they are more innovative in the ways to think about and support faculty and graduate students. This broadens a field's reach in terms of external impact. For example, having communication scholars in the research arms of Facebook, Microsoft, and other high tech or media organizations that are on the cutting edge of communication work with mass audiences can work to improve such companies' communication practices and their societal impacts. In this way, we can extend notions of impact beyond scholarly publications to include more direct impacts on external communities.

Train Doctoral Students for Non-Academic Roles

Although applied research needs trained professionals who are similar to doctoral students who become academics in that they understand and are able to carry out the same research skills as research faculty, there is still room for better training for those who want to work outside of academia. Current attempts at this by organizations like Beyond the Tenure Track, Versatile PhD, and Beyond the Professoriate cater to the "alt-ac" career track. Academic norms and discourses should be reframed to widen the scope of acceptable careers beyond tenure-track positions at R1 universities. While this is often what faculty mentors know best due to their own experience, such positions may not cater to the professional goals and needs of all students. Rather than encouraging students to conform to a single-career model, we need to change our discourses to be more inclusive in valuing careers in teaching, policy, industry, or other fields. Even more, we can create institutional structures that support students pursuing these careers and provide greater transparency about the fact that R1 universities are not the only viable places for placement. This professional development should be institutionalized and done over time (e.g., Rutgers iJOBS program which is part of NIH BEST, http://www.nihbest. org/). Such programs aim to work alongside advisors to enhance training opportunities for graduate students by exposing them to and preparing them for a variety of career options in the dynamic workforce landscape outside of academia. This takes away the secrecy and guilt students sometimes feel for not wanting to pursue R1 positions, thus fostering more inclusion for nontraditional paths in the profession. Of course, our mentoring should also include supporting students who do want to be successful in R1 careers and creating more inviting and inclusive structures to attract them to the discipline.

Be Unafraid and Don't Take Change Personally

If the cases of the NCA DS and OCD top paper walkout teach us anything, it is that changing systems of control has implications for everyone. The individuals involved in these cases had to and did recognize their own part (rather than being fragile) and relinquish control. History and tradition define who scholars are, but academic systems evolve, much like the individuals who embody those systems. Criteria change and past precedent becomes a flawed approach in assessing what is valuable, meaningful, and warrants recognition today. Indeed, it is not new to say that decision-making and organizations are rife with emotions, which may be valuable in systems flawed by presumptions of rationality (March, 1994; March & Simon, 1993; Mumby & Putnam, 1992). By making such change feel personal, the ensuing fragility shifts attention to helping people feel better about themselves instead of keeping the attention on the system that needs changing. Thus, taking change efforts personally ends up blocking change (Ahmed, 2012; Diangelo, 2018). Relatedly, since changing systems has implications for everyone, we all must take part in the process.

And in doing so, individuals must take responsibility to seek out information about what has been accomplished in the past and must be pursued in the future. It is not the responsibility of the oppressed to educate the oppressors. Faculty from underrepresented groups often play a central role in changing systems within and beyond the academic sector, putting their livelihood on the front line in pursuit of justice and equity. When moments (such as the DS controversy or the OCD top paper walkout) occur, faculty from underrepresented groups need their colleagues to step up, realize how that one moment coheres to the larger movement, and boldly serve (in solidarity with others) as allies.

Conclusion

The tendencies to value diversity over inclusion and tradition over innovation are just two examples of the positions we privilege in academia and how they have become institutionalized within our discipline with material consequences for the way we do work. By instead privileging inclusion and innovation, we can expand the potential impact of our discipline in a number of ways. First, our research is more reliable and has greater ecological validity when it includes more diverse perspectives and theories that are generated from consideration of more diverse samples (see the chapter by Afifi & Cornejo). Second, our faculty, disciplines, and professional associations are stronger when more identities are represented, supported, and deemed meritorious, and in which underrepresented individuals feel able to fully express themselves and know that their contributions are valued. Finally, our work has farther reach and impact when our academic boundaries are considered permeable and we freely interact and exchange information and resources with other professions and sectors. As the organizational milieu is changing in all sectors, we also need to re-examine the fundamental practices and beliefs that guide our work as they may be having unintended consequences such as marginalizing groups of people or inadequately preparing our graduates for the opportunities that abound in the 21st-century workplace.

References

Ahmed, S. (2012). *On being included: Racism and diversity in institutional life*. Durham, NC: Duke University Press.

Allen, B. J. (2007). Theorizing communication and race. *Communication Monographs, 74*(2), 259–264. doi:10.1080/03637750701393055

Allen, B. J., Orbe, M., & Olivas, M. O. (1999). The complexity of our tears: Dis/enchantment and (in)difference in the academy. *Communication Theory, 9,* 402–430.

Anzaldúa, G. (2012). *Borderlands/La Frontera – The New Mestiza*. San Francisco, CA: Aunt Lute Books.

Ashcraft, K. L., & Allen, B. J. (2003). The racial foundation of organizational communication. *Communication Theory, 13,* 538.

Armstrong, M. A., & Jovanovic, J. (2015). Starting at the crossroads: Intersectional approaches to institutionally supporting underrepresented minority women STEM faculty. *Journal of Women and Minorities in Science and Engineering*, *21*, 141–157. doi:10.1615/JWomenMinorScienEng.2015011275

Astley, W. G., & Sachdeva, P. S. (1984). Structural sources of interorganizational power: A theoretical synthesis. *Academy of Management Review*, *9*(1), 104–113. doi:10.2307/258237

Braithwaite, D. O., & Thompson, T. L. (1999). *Handbook of communication and people with disabilities: Research and application*. New York: Routledge.

Brass, D. J., & Krackhardt, D. M. (2012). Power, politics, and social networks in organizations. In G. R. Ferris & D. C. Treadway (Eds.), *Politics in organizations: Theory and research considerations* (pp. 355–375). New York: Routledge.

Carr, P. L., Ash, A. S., Friedman, R. H., Scaramucci, A., Barnett, R. C., Szalacha, L. E., … Moskowitz, M. A. (1998). Relation of family responsibilities and gender to the productivity and career satisfaction of medical faculty. *Annals of Internal Medicine*, *129*, 532–538. doi:10.7326/0003-4819-129-7-199810010-00004

Castells, M. (2013). *Communication power*. Oxford: Oxford University Press.

Chakravartty, P., Kuo, R., Grubbs, V., & McIlwain, C. (2018). #CommunicationSoWhite. *Journal of Communication*, *68*, 254–266. doi:10.1093/joc/jqy003

Chevrette, R. (2013). Outing heteronormativity in interpersonal and family communication: Feminist applications of queer theory "beyond the sexy streets". *Communication Theory*, *23*(2), 170–190.

Collins, P. H. (1991). *Black feminist thought: Knowledge, consciousness, and the politics of empowerment*. New York: Routledge.

Cook, K. S. (1977). Exchange and power in networks of interorganizational relations. *Sociological Quarterly*, *18*, 62–82. Retrieved from http://www.jstor.org/stable/4105564

Crenshaw, K. (1989). Demarginalizing the intersection of race and sex: A black feminist critique of antidiscrimination doctrine, feminist theory, and antiracist politics. *University of Chicago Legal Forum*, 139–167. Retrieved from https://chicagounbound.uchicago.edu/cgi/viewcontent.cgi?article=1052&context=uclf

Cruz, J., McDonald, J., Broadfoot, K., Chung, A. K-C., & Ganesh, S. (2018, online). "Aliens" in the United States: A collaborative autoethnography of foreign-born faculty. *Journal of Management Inquiry*. doi:10.1177/1056492618796561

Diangelo, R. (2018). *White fragility: Why it's so hard for white people to talk about racism*. Boston, MA: Beacon Press.

Eguchi, S., & Callafel, B. M. (2019). *Queer intercultural communication: The intersectional politics of belonging in and across differences*. Lanham, MD: Rowman & Littlefield.

Eisenberg, E. M. (1984). Ambiguity as strategy in organizational communication. *Communication Monographs*, *51*, 227–242. doi:10.1080/03637758409390197

Foucault, M. (1979). *Discipline and punish: The birth of the prison* (trans. Alan Sheridan). New York: Vintage.

Gergen, K. (2000). *The saturated self: Dilemmas of identity in contemporary life* (2nd ed.). New York: Basic Books.

Gonzalez, A., & Chen, Y. (2016). *Our voices: Essays in culture, ethnicity, and communication* (6th ed.). New York: Oxford University Press.

Grant, D., & Marshak, R. J. (2011). Toward a discourse-centered understanding of organizational change. *The Journal of Applied Behavioral Science*, *47*, 204–235. doi:10.1177/0021886310397612

Griffin, K., Gibbs Jr., K. D., Bennett, J., Staples, C., & Robinson, T. (2015). Respect me for my science: A Bourdieuian analysis of women scientists' interactions with faculty and socialization into science. *Journal of Women and Minorities in Science and Engineering, 21,* 159–179. doi:10.1615/JWomenMinorScienEng.2015011143

Gutierrez y Muhs, G., Niemann, Y. F., Gonzalez, C. G., & Harris, A. P. (2012). *Presumed incompetent: The intersections of race and class for women in academia.* Logan: Utah State University Press.

Hall, S. (1997). The work of representation. In S. Hall (Ed.), *Representation: Cultural representations and signifying practices* (pp. 13–74). London: Sage.

Jackson, R. L. II. (2000). So real illusions of Black intellectualism: Exploring race, roles, and gender in the academy. *Communication Theory, 10,* 48–63.

Ko, L. T., Kachchaf, R. R., Hodari, A. K., & Ong, M. (2014). Agency of women of color in physics and astronomy: Strategies for persistence and success. *Journal of Women and Minorities in Science and Engineering, 20,* 171–195. doi:10.1615/JWomenMinorScienEng.2014008198

Livingston, G., & Parker, K. (2019, June 12). 8 facts about American dads [Webpage]. Retrieved June 12, 2019, from Pew Research Center website: https://www.pewresearch.org/fact-tank/2019/06/12/fathers-day-facts/

Luna, G., Medina, C., & Gorman, M. S. (2010). Academic reality "show": Presented by women faculty of color. *Advancing Women in Leadership, 30* (11), 1–18. Retrieved from http://advancingwomen.com/awl/awl_wordpress/

Maranto, C. L., & Griffin, A. E. (2011). The antecedents of a 'chilly climate' for women faculty in higher education. *Human Relations, 64,* 139–159. doi:doi:10.1177/0018726710377932

March, J. G. (1994). *A primer on decision making: How decisions happen.* New York: The Free Press.

March, J. G., & Simon, H. A. (1993). *Organizations* (2nd ed.). Cambridge, MA: Blackwell.

Mason, M. A., & Goulden, M. (2004). Marriage and baby blues: Redefining gender equity in the academy. *Annals of the American Academy of Political and Social Science, 596,* 86–103. doi:10.1177/000271620459600104

Mumby, D. K., & Putnam, L. L. (1992). The politics of emotion: A feminist reading of bounded rationality. *The Academy of Management Review, 17,* 465–486. doi:10.2307/258719

Mumby, D. K., & Stohl, C. (1991). Power and discourse in organizational studies: Absence and the dialectic of control. *Discourse & Society, 2*(3), 313–332. doi:10.1177/0957926591002003004

Munshi, D., Broadfoot, K. J., & Smith, L. T. (2011). Decolonizing communication ethics: A framework for communicating otherwise. In G. Cheney, S. May, D. Munshi (Eds.), *The handbook of communication ethics* (pp. 139–152). New York: Routledge.

Nossek, B. A., Banaji, M. R., & Greenwald, A. G. (2002). Harvesting implicit group attitudes and beliefs from a demonstration web site. *Group Dynamics: Theory, Research, and Practice, 6,* 101–115. doi:10.1037/1089-2699.6.1.101

Orbe, M., & Allen, B. J. (2006). 'Race matters' in applied communication research. Paper presented at the National Communication Association convention, San Antonio, TX.

Pacanowsky, M. E., & O'Donnell-Trujillo, N. (1983). Organizational communication as cultural performance. *Communication Monographs, 50,* 126–147. doi:10.1080/03637758309390158

Pal, M., & Dutta, M. J. (2008). Theorizing resistance in a global context processes, strategies, and tactics in communication scholarship. *Annals of the International Communication Association, 32*(1), 41–87.

Pfeffer, J., & Salancik, G. R. (1978). *The external control of organizations.* New York: Harper & Row.

Raffnsøe, S., Mennicken, A., & Miller, P. (2017). The Foucault effect in organization studies. *Organization Studies, 40*, 155–182. doi:10.1177/0170840617745110

Rigg, L., Coller, B., Reynolds, J., Levin, A., & McCord, C. (2015). Academic career satisfaction: The roles of gender and discipline. *Journal of Women and Minorities in Science and Engineering, 21*, 125–140. doi:10.1615/JWomenMinorScienEng.2015012713

Rios, D., & Stewart, A. J. (2015). Insider and outsider-within standpoints: The experiences of diverse faculty in science and engineering fields. *Journal of Women and Minorities in Science and Engineering, 21*, 295–322. doi:10.1615/JWomenMinorScienEng.2015010375

Rockquemore, K. A., & Laszloffy, T. (2008). *The Black academic's guide to winning tenure—Without losing your soul.* Boulder, CO: Lynne Rienner Publishers.

Shenoy-Packer, S. (2016). Navigating the third space with double-consciousness: South Asian Indian Women in the American Workplace. In A. Gonzalez & Y. Chen (Eds.), *Our voices: Essays in culture, ethnicity, and communication* (6th ed.) (pp. 148–155). New York: Oxford University Press.

Shollen, S. L., Bland, C. J., Finstad, D. A., & Taylor, A. L. (2009). Organizational climate and family life: How these factors affect the status of women faculty at one medical school. *Academic Medicine, 84*, 87–94. doi:10.1097/ACM.0b013e3181900edf

Smith, J., Halgin, D., Kidwell, V., Labianca, G., Brass, D. J., & Borgatti, S. P. (2014). Power in politically charged networks. *Social Networks, 36*, 162–176. doi:10.1016/j.socnet.2013.04.007

Stack, S. (2004). Gender, children and research productivity. *Research in Higher Education, 45*, 891–920. Retrieved from http://www.jstor.org/stable/40197370

Stewart, A. J., Malley, J. E., & Herzog, K. A. (2016). Increasing the representation of women faculty in STEM departments: What makes a difference? *Journal of Women and Minorities in Science and Engineering, 22*, 23–47. doi:10.1615/JWomenMinorScienEng.2016014785

Tracy, S. J., & Rivera, K. D. (2010). Endorsing equity and applauding stay-at-home-moms: How male voices on work-life reveal aversive sexism and flickers of transformation. *Management Communication Quarterly, 24*, 3–43. doi:10.1177/0893318909352248

van Dijk, T. A. (2008). Discourse, power and access. In T. van Dijk (Ed.), *Discourse and power* (pp. 65–84). New York: Palgrave Macmillan.

Ward, W. E. (2013). *Gender Summit 3 – North America.* Plenary presentation given at Gender Summit 2013, Washington, DC.

Weick, K. E. (1995). *Sensemaking in organizations.* Thousand Oaks, CA: Sage.

Wolfinger, N. H., Mason, M. A., & Goulden, M. (2008). Problems in the pipeline: Gender, marriage, and fertility in the Ivory Tower. *Journal of Higher Education, 79*, 388–405. doi:10.1080/00221546.2008.11772108

Xie, Y., & Shauman, K. A. (2003). *Women in science: Career processes and outcomes.* Cambridge, MA: Harvard University Press.

Index